DA
SHE
FANTASY
FOOTBALL
1993

DANNY SHERIDAN'S FANTASY FOOTBALL 1993

The Nation's Leading Handicapper
Presents the Game
For Football Fans Everywhere

BY

DANNY SHERIDAN

EDITED BY ROBERT E. KELLY

COLLIER BOOKS
MACMILLAN PUBLISHING COMPANY
NEW YORK

MAXWELL MACMILLAN CANADA
TORONTO

MAXWELL MACMILLAN INTERNATIONAL
NEW YORK   OXFORD   SINGAPORE   SYDNEY

Collier Books
Macmillan Publishing Company
866 Third Avenue
New York, NY 10022

Maxwell Macmillan Canada, Inc.
1200 Eglinton Avenue East
Suite 200
Don Mills, Ontario M3C 3N1

Macmillan Publishing Company is part of the Maxwell Communication
Group of Companies.

ISBN 0-02-025303-6

ISSN 1062-600X

Macmillan books are available at special discounts for bulk purchases for
sales promotions, premiums, fund-raising, or educational use.
For details, contact:

Special Sales Director
Macmillan Publishing Company
866 Third Avenue
New York, NY 10022

First Collier Books Edition 1993

10 9 8 7 6 5 4 3 2 1

Printed in the United States of America

CONTENTS

INTRODUCTION   ix

ONE ON ANY GIVEN GAME DAY   1

The Concept   1
The Rules of Play   3

    The Draft 3 • Scoring 6 • Bonus
    Points 8 • Scoring Examples 9 •
    Weekly Play 12 • The Supplemental
    Draft 15 • Bye, Bye: The New 18-Week
    NFL Schedule 16 • Summary 17

TWO JUST WIN, BABY   18

Fees   18
Prizes   19
Speaking of Awards   21
Quotable Quotes of 1992   23

THREE THE SECOND SEASON: THE PLAYOFFS   25

The Draft   25
Rules of Play   26
Fees and Prizes   26
No Supplemental Draft   27
No Other Changes   27
Advanced Version of Playoff Rules   27

FOUR VARIATIONS ON A THEME   29

The Point System   29
Prizes and Fees   31
Playoffs   31
What About Trades?   31
Taxi Squads   32
Roster Holdovers   32

FIVE DRAFTING STRATEGY   **34**

   Overview: Whom Should I Pick?   34

   1. Pay Attention to Your Rules   34
   2. Do Your Homework   34
   3. Prepare Player Lists and Model Rosters   35
   4. Aim for the Target Score   36
   5. Watch Those Scoring Trends   39
   6. At Home in the Dome   40
   7. The Double-Down Theory   40
   8. Playoff Strategy   41
   9. The "X" Factor   42
   10. Final Tips   42

SIX   TEAM SCOUTING REPORTS   **44**

   American Conference   45
   Buffalo Bills   45
   Cincinnati Bengals   50
   Cleveland Browns   54
   Denver Broncos   58
   Houston Oilers   62
   Indianapolis Colts   66
   Kansas City Chiefs   70
   Los Angeles Raiders   74
   Miami Dolphins   77
   New England Patriots   81
   New York Jets   84
   Pittsburgh Steelers   88
   San Diego Chargers   92
   Seattle Seahawks   96

   National Conference   99
   Atlanta Falcons   99
   Chicago Bears   103
   Dallas Cowboys   107
   Detroit Lions   111
   Green Bay Packers   114
   Los Angeles Rams   119
   Minnesota Vikings   122
   New Orleans Saints   125
   New York Giants   129
   Philadelphia Eagles   132
   Phoenix Cardinals   136

	San Francisco 49ers	139
	Tampa Bay Buccaneers	144
	Washington Redskins	147
SEVEN	PLAYER SCOUTING REPORTS	**153**
	Quarterbacks	153
	Running Backs	174
	Wide Receivers	202
	Tight Ends	235
	Kickers	250
EIGHT	NFL DRAFT 1993	**269**
	Draft Analysis	271
NINE	THE FINAL WORD	**280**
APPENDIX A	SAMPLE FORMS FOR REPORTING WEEKLY RESULTS	**283**
APPENDIX B	SUGGESTED WEEKLY SCHEDULE FOR EIGHT TEAMS	**285**
APPENDIX C	DANNY SHERIDAN'S OFFICIAL FANTASY STATISTICS FOR THE 1992 SEASON	**287**
	Players in Alphabetical Order	287
	Players Ranked in Order of Scoring	293
APPENDIX D	SAMPLE ROSTERS	**299**

INTRODUCTION

THE 1992 SEASON was a historic season for the National Football League, in many respects. For one thing, it seemed like every time you turned around, one of the league's greatest players had broken another of the NFL's all-time records. Of course, for every record broken there's a player who is no longer an answer to a sports trivia question. The big loser in 1992 was Steve Largent, former wide receiver for the Seattle Seahawks. He owned three of the NFL's greatest records for wide receivers going into the 1992 season, but owns them no more. First, in Week One, Buffalo's James Lofton broke Largent's record for most career yards for a receiver. Then, Washington's Art Monk surpassed his mark for career receptions in Week Six. Finally, the 49ers' redoubtable Jerry Rice passed Largent's mark for touchdown passes in Week Fourteen. Largent will still make the Hall of Fame someday, but probably won't look back on 1992 as one of his favorite years.

In other landmark performances, the Raiders' Eric Dickerson moved past the Cowboys' Tony Dorsett into second place on the all-time rushing list, with Chicago's Walter Payton, one of the new inductees to the Pro Football Hall of Fame, squarely, but distantly, in his sights. Miami's Dan Marino tied Colts legend Johnny Unitas's career total of 290 touchdown passes, second on the all-time list, and he now needs 53 more touchdowns to surpass Fran Tarkenton's record total of 342. Based on Marino's track record, look for that record to fall sometime in the last few weeks of the 1994 season, or the first few weeks of 1995.

Continuing with the quarterback position, one of the game's great players, Houston's Warren Moon, surpassed the mark of 50,000 passing yards for a career in 1992—21,228 of which were accumulated in the Canadian Football League—becoming the first NFL quarterback to reach that amazing total. Moon also became the all-time leading passer for total yardage in pro football history in 1992, breaking the record of 50,535 yards set by Ron Lancaster, who played from 1960 to 1978 in the Canadian Football League.

Among the placekickers, the Saints' Morten Andersen booted

three field goals of 50 yards or longer during the 1992 season and finished the season with an NFL record 21 field goals of 50 yards or more. He passed the Chiefs' Nick Lowery, who finished the 1992 season with 19 field goals of 50 or more yards in length. Andersen should add to his all-time record in this category in the seasons to come.

On the coaching side, Miami's Don Shula joined one of the game's legends, "Papa Bear" George Halas, as one of the only two NFL coaches to win 300 games. George Siefert won his 50th game as the 49ers' head coach in 1992 after taking over for Bill Walsh in 1989, reaching this total faster than any other coach in NFL history.

Several franchises passed notable milestones. The San Diego Chargers, under first-year coach Bobby Ross, reached the playoffs after losing their first four games, the first team in NFL history to achieve this feat. The Buffalo Bills became the second team in NFL history to reach the Super Bowl three straight times. Of course, they also became the first team to lose in the Super Bowl three straight times. The Dallas Cowboys returned to the Super Bowl for the sixth time in franchise history, setting the NFL record for most Super Bowl appearances by a team. They scored the most points ever by one team in the Super Bowl on their way to a smashing victory over Buffalo, bringing to mind one of the two most famous scores in football history, 73–0, the score of the Chicago Bears' romp over the Washington Redskins in the 1940 NFL Championship Game. (The other most famous score is 16–7, the score of the New York Jets' stunning victory over the Baltimore Colts in Super Bowl III.) The Cowboys won their third Super Bowl, becoming the fifth team to win three or more of the coveted crowns.

All of these achievements are remarkable in their own right. They reflect years of effort and achievement over the course of many seasons on the football field. Ironically, perhaps the most important occurrence affecting the NFL in 1992, which was also years in the making, happened off the field. In a development of monumental proportions, the players and the owners finally agreed to settle their differences and entered a historic labor agreement establishing, among other things, a program of free agency for NFL players. In the longest and perhaps most important competition in the history of the league, the players appear at first blush to have beaten the owners soundly. But, the truth is, there are no losers as a result of this momentous agreement.

The ball started rolling when Hall of Fame tight end John Mackey went to court in 1972, suing the NFL for free agency, and won the case, freeing himself and other NFL players like John Riggins to sign with other teams. The players union and the owners then entered into a series of labor agreements, punctuated by a strike in 1982, up until the crucial year of 1987. At that point, negotiations broke down, the players struck again, and legal war was declared in the courts. When, on September 10, 1992, the jury found in favor of the group of plaintiffs, led by Freeman McNeil, in the action brought by the players challenging the Plan B free agency procedure, the handwriting was written on the wall. When Judge David Doty declared Keith Jackson and fellow plaintiffs Webster Slaughter, Garin Veris, and D. J. Dozier (referred to by some as the Jackson Four) free agents on September 24, 1992, the handwriting was set in stone for all but the most obstinate to see.

Despite the clear warnings that the players would probably win free agency in the class action suit filed by Reggie White and many other players, it still took all of the considerable skills at the employ of Commissioner Paul Tagliabue, himself an antitrust lawyer, to convince the owners of the wisdom in settling their dispute with the players. Commissioner Tagliabue finally convinced the owners in December 1992 to settle with the players, dragging the owners kicking and screaming into the labor world's community of nations, and not a moment too soon.

While their initial reaction may not have been so charitable, the pro football owners will be thanking Commissioner Tagliabue for his persistent efforts to settle the NFL's labor problems for years to come. Peace on the labor front will allow the owners, under the steady hand of Tagliabue, to assure the economic stability and perhaps even the cultural dominance of the NFL as we move toward the 21st Century. The NFL can now negotiate television contracts secure in the knowledge that player strikes will not interfere with the schedule. The NFL can move forward with its plans for expansion, bringing the game live to even more cities across the country. It can move forward with its plans for the international development of professional football, resurrecting the World League of American Football and eventually marketing the NFL game to the rest of the world. With the players as friends, not foes (or, if not friends, at least business partners) the National Football League can get on with the business of becoming the dominant sport in America, if it isn't already, and the lingua franca of the sports world around the globe.

Of course, let us not forget another important product of the labor agreement for football fans—free agency, meaning real free agency, not Plan B-style free agency. By creating the possibility of real player movement between franchises, the labor agreement takes a bold step. It establishes the mechanism that will for the first time expose the NFL owners to their own weaknesses. Previously, the NFL owners had ingeniously set up the league's rules of operation to avoid the mistakes made by their brethren in the baseball owners' fraternity. The system was designed to protect themselves from themselves, to keep expenses in the form of players' salaries low and profits high. And this system worked remarkably well. On the one hand, the revenue-sharing arrangement between the owners, which was the economic cornerstone of the league, virtually eliminated the economic incentive to win—that is, the incentive to bid up players' salaries. A team with an 0–16 record took the same share of the league-wide revenues that a team with a 16–0 record received.

With that taken care of, the owners then established other rules designed to eliminate the ability of that handful of owners who still wanted to win anyway to put together winning teams consistently. These impediments were restrictions on free agency, such as the compensation due for the signing of a free agent in the form of first-round draft picks, that severely limited a so-called free agent's desirability to other owners. They also prevented owners from spending freely on star players. Then there were other rules to diminish competition, like the parity scheduling concept, which punishes teams with winning records.

Make no mistake about it: These impediments worked. In XXVII seasons, nine NFL teams have still not made it to the Super Bowl, only 14 teams have made it more than once, and only nine teams have made it three or more times. Five teams have made it just once. Only six AFC franchises have ever won the Super Bowl, and two of those teams, Baltimore and Pittsburgh, were originally NFL franchises, which switched over to the AFC when the AFL and NFL merged after the 1969 season. No AFC team, regardless of origin, has won the Super Bowl recently, as the AFC's nine-game losing streak in the Big Dance will attest. And NFL salaries remain relatively low. Or they did until owners started throwing multimillion-dollar contracts around like Frisbees after the official opening of the free-agent season last March (1993).

The football owners may have had a point in their protectionist stance. If you look at the baseball model, the owners do not share revenue either among themselves or in a formal agreement with the players, and free agent salaries are out of sight. The star players' salaries might be justified, but paying a million bucks a year for a utility infielder is ridiculous. (On the other hand, the National Basketball Association, with its revenue-sharing agreement and salary-cap provisions, is the model of economic prosperity and peaceful labor relations in professional sports.) So, human nature being what it is, maybe the football owners can't be blamed for trying to protect themselves from their human weaknesses.

But old habits die hard. The owners have still tried to protect themselves from themselves in the labor agreement. The labor agreement does contain several restrictions—such as the salary cap, the franchise player exemption, and the so-called Rooney Rules—which limit the ability of the teams with the best records to acquire an unlimited amount of free agent players. Player movement will be restricted somewhat as a result. But what is important is that for the first time in the modern history of the league, the owners who don't want to win will be flushed out of hiding and exposed for what they are. And the owners who want to win will keep on winning.

There has existed for many years now another group of football owners who make no bones about their desire to win each season. These are the owners of fantasy football teams all across the country. These owners organize leagues, draft teams, and play to win each year. These fans have participated in their own fantasy football leagues. And you can, too.

The following chapters will explain the methods and theories you can use to establish your own fantasy football league and create your own teams, year after year. The book will also provide statistical information and scouting reports that will assist you in analyzing an NFL player's performance from a fantasy owner's perspective and help you select the best players to draft for your fantasy team. It will provide help for those of you who participate in the growing number of computer leagues and newspaper contests as well. With the help of this book, you will find yourself, a fantasy owner, pacing back and forth in your own personal skybox every Sunday, rooting for NFL players like you never have before.

For those of you hearing about fantasy football for the first time, let me point out that participation in a fantasy football league is a fascinating experience, for many reasons. First, as a casual or even devoted fan of an NFL team, you might think you know a lot about the abilities of many NFL players even as you read this introduction, and any true football fan is certainly entitled to that opinion. Obviously, most football fans know a Barry Sanders from a backup linebacker whose major responsibility each week is to commit mayhem during kickoff returns. However, when you're nervously poring over NFL rosters two hours before your fantasy league draft, and you realize you're more familiar with the players in the Bud Bowl than you are with the NFL wide receivers who scored the highest number of fantasy points at that position last year, you will have learned a valuable lesson, even if too late: It takes a lot more than just being familiar with members of your favorite team or with the All-Pro players around the league to prepare for a 10- or 20-round fantasy draft. And, more importantly, to be a successful fantasy coach.

You will also be amazed at the change in the way you watch NFL games after starting a fantasy football league. That regional double-header game between the Indianapolis Colts and the Cleveland Browns, usually watched only by die-hard football fans killing time until the kickoff of the national game, now becomes a matter of great concern if, say, one of your running backs is Rodney Culver and your quarterback is Vinny Testaverde. You might also find that your season comes down to the last Monday Night Game, like it did for some of you last season. Down by a point, that point the only obstacle between you and the league title, you watch in agony as your wide receiver, Jerry Rice, reaches out and stretches the ball across the goal line while being tackled, only to be denied a touchdown by the referees. After eighteen weeks of NFL play, a single touchdown in the final game of the season now may ultimately prove the difference between the league title and runner-up status in your fantasy league.

NFL football, already enormously entertaining, acquires a totally new dimension when you create your own fantasy league. The steadily growing popularity of fantasy sports leagues all across the country is easy to understand. Not only is participating in such a league fun, it is also intellectually challenging—and emotionally challenging as well. You can begin to see, on a much smaller scale, what a real NFL coach must feel as he paces the sidelines on Sunday afternoon, his blood pressure soaring as kickoff approaches. You begin to understand a coach's agony as all the hours of careful thought and preparation for an entire season, all the championship dreams, go up in smoke because your most reliable and experienced running back coughs up the pigskin with two minutes to go in the game. You experience all the thrills of owning an NFL franchise, without the headaches. You also become the butt of an avalanche of locker-room humor when you and your fellow owners congregate at a local restaurant and needle one another about the past week's results during the Monday Night tilt. Of course, you don't share in the NFL's television revenue package, but that would probably spoil the purity of fantasy competition, anyway. (See Chapter Two, which discusses how much you can win playing this game. It's about equal to the Super Bowl loser's share, divided by the number of points scored against the Buffalo Bills by the Dallas Cowboys in Super Bowl XXVII. In other words, not a whole lot.) While a fantasy franchise is not quite the real thing, it truly is the next best thing to being there.

This book will make forming and participating in a fantasy league simple and easy for the uninitiated. If you are a veteran of the fantasy game, with an existing league, then you will probably want to proceed straight to Scouting Reports, which I hope you find useful, if not uncannily accurate. For those of you who unfortunately did not benefit from the wisdom and foresight contained in the first three editions of my book, welcome aboard, and it's about time.

But seriously, folks, in this book I have tried to remove some of the mystery involved in assembling a fantasy league and a good fantasy team by describing as many of the potential stumbling blocks as possible. As many of you readers already know, aside from the information found in this book, experience is the best teacher, especially when it comes to fantasy football. So, as the kickoff for the upcoming NFL season rapidly approaches, once again I encourage you to round up some friends, form a league, draft your teams, and, armed with copies of this book, have a memorable fantasy season. While the whole process may seem like a lot of effort at first, I can assure you that when you look back on the fun and excitement you and your friends experienced over the course of the season, you'll be glad you played fantasy football.

DANNY SHERIDAN'S FANTASY FOOTBALL 1993

ONE

ON ANY GIVEN GAME DAY

THE CONCEPT

BEFORE WE DIVE INTO the mechanics of the fantasy game, let's briefly discuss the concept of the sport for the rookies. Not surprisingly, the concept of fantasy football is simple. As you might have guessed from what you've already read, fantasy football closely parallels professional football itself. You organize a group of people to form your own league, with each person acting as owner/coach. The number of persons you will want to bring together in a league is completely at your discretion, but a standard range is from six to 12 owners (eight is the recommended number, for reasons that will be explained in more detail later in the book).

Once your league is formed, the next step is to designate a commissioner. This should be a person the owners can rely on to manage the affairs of the league, such as keeping track of roster changes, handling any fees that are paid into the league fund by the owners for the privilege of participating in the league, and, if possible, putting together some sort of newsletter announcing the weekly results.

As in real life, the commissioner's job is crucial to the continued life of your league, since he or she is the glue that holds the league together. So select someone responsible, someone with scruples, someone you can trust to handle money. I understand that a commissioner has absconded with league funds on more than one occasion, so choose your leaders wisely. Bank of Credit and Commerce International (BCCI) officers should probably be eliminated from consideration early in the contest. And lawyers are only to be considered as a last resort.

As an owner/coach of a fantasy football franchise, you are responsible for running the franchise, both in the front office and on the field. Basically, you acquire a roster of players through a draft, which is conducted just as the real NFL draft is. As the NFL players score on the real football field, so do they accumulate points for you in your league. For example, if you are fortunate enough to be able to draft Emmitt Smith as one of your running backs, and he takes a handoff and runs in for a touchdown, as his fantasy owner you get points for his touchdown as well. If your quarterback is Steve Young, and he drills a touchdown pass to Rice in the end zone, you get points for Young's scoring pass, too, even if Rice is some other owner's receiver. An owner's weekly roster is set by his league's preseason fantasy draft. This eliminates most of the real-world anxiety an NFL coach experiences as he decides starting lineups each week and makes substitutions during a game. However, if your league decides to adopt a slight variation of my rules (discussed later on), the owners may even act as real NFL coaches and set their "active" roster each week, making substitutions for the prior week's players if they so desire. The owners will have to designate those players on their expanded, permanent roster who will actually be eligible to score that particular week, while some other players "sit on the bench."

Like NFL franchises do, fantasy owners may pick up free agents and cut players during the season through a supplemental draft. If your league opts to play with the more advanced version of my rules, you engage in head-to-head competition each week, just like NFL teams, with wins and losses recorded in weekly standings compiled from the results of those fantasy games. You establish new rosters for postseason play, which culminates in the pomp and pageantry of the Super Bowl. If your team has posted a dismal record at the end of the season, you regroup over the summer, review game films, and then make a key decision for the franchise: You immediately purchase a copy of this book, commit it to memory, and select a winning team on Draft Day.

Like NFL football, fantasy football offers a form of instant gratification. You get a defined competitive result every week, with new results just a few days away. Indeed, the fact that the regular season is only 18 weeks long, not including playoffs, can be very disappointing. When the AFC has committed its final turnover and the Super Bowl game has finally ended, you will find there is a huge void in your life that cannot be filled by the annual office pool known as March Madness, or by the soporific effects of the (so-called) National Pastime.

Perhaps former commissioner Pete Rozelle had something when he articulated the NFL's version of manifest destiny by stating that the NFL should be a broader part of the sports calendar. In light of that expressed desire, and the additional television revenue involved, it's no wonder the NFL expanded the length of the season to 17 weeks in 1990, and expanded the season to 18 weeks for the 1993 season. With labor peace in effect, the NFL will also continue its plans to make NFL football an international phenomenon by resurrecting the World League of American Football (WLAF). Pretty soon there will be quality professional football year-round. The prospect of participating in fantasy football leagues while waiting for the NFL season to start should fill the void I described above for most fantasy fans.

Professional football in the spring is nothing new, of course. The United States Football League played spring football from 1983 through 1985, before the league suspended operations in 1986. The USFL nurtured some great players for the NFL who are still active, such as Jim Kelly, Herschel Walker, Anthony Carter, Bobby Hebert, Gary Clark, and Ricky Sanders. While barristers schooled in the arcane world of antitrust law ended the life of the USFL in a federal court-room in New York City several years ago, its spirit will live on in the form of the WLAF.

THE RULES OF PLAY

THE DRAFT

The specifics of fantasy football league play under my rules are simple to master. For play to begin, the league must generate player rosters for each owner. So, at some time before the start of the NFL season, the owners in the league you have created hold a draft, similar to the one used by professional leagues to draft collegiate players. (You may certainly hold your draft at some point after the season has started, if for some reason your league is unable to hold its draft until then. But a late start obviously penalizes those conscientious owners who do their homework before the draft, and who do not need a week or two of actual results to help them draft a good team.) Each owner/coach drafts a team of 12 players, as follows:

2 Quarterbacks (QB)
3 Running Backs (RB)
4 Receivers (WR)
2 Kickers (K)
1 Defensive Team (DT)

The player pool consists of all players currently on NFL rosters or those placed on injured reserve for the upcoming season. Unlike Rotis-serie baseball owners, a fantasy football owner may not retain the rights to any player who was on his fantasy roster in the prior year. As emotionally attached as an owner might become to a Steve Young or an Emmitt Smith—or even an Eric Dickerson, hard as that might be to imagine after his performance last season—a player and his owner must part company at the end of every season, creating a system of true free agency. (Like NFL owners do in the real world, the fantasy owners may also decide to change the rules with respect to holding over some players from year to year. I discuss some of these rule variations in Chapter Four.)

The fantasy draft is conducted along the same lines as the NFL draft. Once everyone has congregated in the chosen place and settled in, the fantasy owners draw numbers to determine who makes the first draft choice, the second, the third, and so on. A few minutes after the selection order has been established, the draft begins.

After the first round is completed, the second round is conducted in reverse order, so that the person with the last pick in the first round now has the first pick in the second round. In other words, the corner man gets two picks in a row. For this reason, an owner shouldn't panic if he pulls the final position in the draft. With back-to-back picks, that owner has two picks before anyone else gets a second pick at the start of the draft. Of course, that may not be any consolation if you had your heart set on Emmitt Smith for your first pick, because he should be long gone by the time it's your turn to employ pick number eight and select your first player. But that's life. Just be prepared for that contingency going into the draft, and have an alternative strategy ready to go.

The other advantage to having the last pick in the first round is that you get a sense of the direction the draft is taking prior to making your first two selections. This can pay off as well, as you have time to adapt your draft strategy to the exposed strategy of the other owners.

The second round of the draft continues in reverse order down to the owner with the first pick. He then also has two draft picks in a row (the last pick of the second round and the first pick of the third round), as the draft order turns the corner again. At that point, the selection order returns to its original first-through-last alignment. The draft proceeds in this way, back and forth, for 12 rounds, until all coaches have filled their team rosters at each position.

During each round of the draft a coach may fill any position on his team roster. For instance, an owner is not required to fill, let's say, the quarterback position on his roster in the first round of the draft. If one of your fellow owners has been sitting under a hole in the ozone layer all afternoon on Draft Day, for example, and firmly believes in his heart and soul that a defensive team should be his top priority, then he has every right to pluck the Seattle Seahawks' defense, the worst fantasy defense in the league in 1992, right away. Once the laughter dies down, the serious fantasy owner will try in the first few rounds to grab as many high-scoring players as possible in the most strategic positions. Defensive teams are the least valuable element of a successful fantasy team, so that selection should be the final entry on your shopping list. (See my more thorough discussion of Drafting Strategy in Chapter Five.)

As you might expect, the same player cannot be drafted by two coaches, as the underlying concept already discussed would logically dictate that no NFL player could play for two teams at once, not even Deion Sanders. Once a player has been drafted, his name is removed from the list of players eligible for the draft.

It is suggested that, just before the draft, the coaches agree on a time limit for owners to make each player selection. This precautionary measure will guarantee that the draft will be completed relatively quickly. A fantasy draft could last as long as the NFL's new, improved collegiate draft without some reasonable time restriction imposed by the owners. This is especially true for those of you who will be conducting a fantasy draft for the first time. A one-minute limit seems to work well, especially if the owners have done some preparation for the draft.

Let me offer some practical pointers to make the draft easier for all concerned. Because of the rather intense nature of the activity (believe it or not), and the need to concentrate carefully on what you are doing, the draft should be conducted in an environment where distractions can be kept to a minimum. You will have butterflies anyway, as your entire season's success hangs in the balance. So, it will make your life a lot easier if one of your fellow owners can offer the use of his rec room, set up a big table, and stock the fridge. Who knows: With any luck, a poker game, complete with that dying breed, that most detested of all tobacco products—big, fat stogies—will break out to help the owners relax after the big event.

If your group is too large for that type of setting, then one handy alternative is a neighborhood restaurant, with a cozy private room tucked away in the back somewhere. No matter where you end up conducting your draft, it definitely helps to have a disinterested observer waiting on your group, rather than having one of the league's coaches jumping up and down to get refreshments for people in the middle of the draft. Depending upon the number of people in your group, the draft can last two to three hours, even if you establish a one-minute limit between selections. That's a pretty long time, so you should make sure everyone is comfortable.

You should also have room enough to spread out your crib sheets, so that you can refer to your notes, and this book, without knocking someone else's Bud Light, er, papers off the table, or worse, being accused of trying to peek at someone's well-researched proprietary information. It also is a tremendous help, but not a requirement, to have a "recording secretary" present at the draft who is not one of the owners. This person can keep track of the draft order and record everyone's picks as they are made. Because of the difficulty in keeping track of all the players while the draft is being conducted, as sure as the officials will blow a call in each NFL game, there will be several times when an owner who hasn't been keeping track of things as carefully as he or she should tries to draft a player already taken by another owner in an earlier round of the draft. Even though it might be an honest mistake, such confusion can be eliminated by an ever-vigilant recording secretary. If one of the owners has to keep track of all the draft choices, the draft will become more complicated than it already is, at least for one person.

After the draft is completed, each coach should receive a complete roster of every other coach's 12-man team from the commissioner. This allows an owner to keep track of what each team is doing over the weekend. If you haven't already developed this reflex action, you will find that when the informative Greg Gumbel breaks into an NFL broadcast to announce a scoring update during an NFL game, every owner instinctively reaches for his league roster to see not only what player scored, but more important, what owner.

While you are preparing for your draft, it is very important to keep in mind that whatever scoring rules you eventually adopt for your league will dictate the type of player you want on your team. For example, many of you may already participate in an established fantasy football league. If you do, then you will probably have some rules different from the ones I describe here. If the rules emphasize only the scores put up on the board by the real NFL players, as these rules do, then the fact that a running back racked up close to 1,000 yards last year doesn't help you, especially if that back scored as few touchdowns as, let's say, Harold Green of the Cincinnati Bengals, who scored only 2 rushing touchdowns in 1992, despite accumulating 1,170 yards. If one of your backs was the obscure (at least on Draft Day 1992) rookie Rodney Culver of the Indianapolis Colts, you were very lucky, indeed. Even though there were literally dozens of NFL backs who rushed for more yardage, there were no backs in the NFL who rushed for as few yards (321) and scored as many touchdowns (7) as Culver did last season.

SCORING

Basically, the underlying principle of these scoring rules is that when one of the NFL players on your roster scores on the field, you score, too. Points are awarded if any of your players scores a touchdown, field goal, or point after touchdown. Points are awarded to each scoring player according to the following system, which is based upon the actual point system used by the NFL. For example, if the Tampa Bay Buccaneers' new designated scorer, Reggie Cobb, barrels over from the

1-yard line, as he did for 8 of his 9 scores last season, that's 6 fantasy points for Cobb's owner on each touchdown run. If the Dolphins' Pete Stoyanovich drills one through the uprights from the 20, that's 3 fantasy points for Stoyanovich's owner. Since a quarterback and a wide receiver theoretically share responsibility for a passing touchdown, they also share the points, with 3 points apiece for the respective owners. The following is the basic fantasy scoring table:

QB passes for touchdown	3 points
QB runs for touchdown	6 points
RB runs for touchdown	6 points
RB catches pass for touchdown	3 points
RB throws pass for touchdown	3 points
WR catches pass for touchdown	3 points
WR runs for touchdown	6 points
WR throws pass for touchdown	3 points
DT (Defensive Team) scores TD	6 points
DT (Defensive Team) scores safety	2 points
K kicks field goal	3 points
K kicks point after touchdown	1 point

Please note that in the scoring table, the term "wide receiver" (WR) also includes tight ends, and "defensive team" (DT) also includes special teams. (While there is no special treatment of tight ends under my system, I do realize that many leagues, and the burgeoning number of newspaper fantasy contests, place tight ends in a separate scoring category. For that reason, I have included a separate section for tight ends in the Scouting Reports in Chapter Seven.) The term "special teams" means both the kicking and receiving teams. Faked or botched punts or field goals that result in a touchdown for the kicking team are counted as scores for the defensive team (DT), as are kickoff and punt returns for touchdowns. The simple rule of thumb is that, except for a successful field goal or extra point, a fantasy owner's defensive team (DT) receives fantasy points anytime his or her special teams score on the field.

In the event that the player actually scoring the defensive (special) team's touchdown is also on the roster of a fantasy owner's team, then two full fantasy scores are awarded, one each to the defensive team and the individual player scoring the touchdown. In other words, if the Rams' Todd Kinchen runs a punt back for a touchdown, as he did *twice* in one game in Week Seventeen last year (tying the NFL record held by six other players, and becoming the first player to do so since the Cards' Vai Sikahema accomplished this feat against Tampa Bay on December

21, 1986), Owner X, who selected the Rams as his defensive team, and Owner Y, who chose Kinchen as one of his receivers, would each receive six points.

Finally, if one of your players does not score, for whatever reason, he gets zero points for the week. If your player doesn't suit up for a particular week, either due to injury or due to his NFL team's not playing that particular week, chalk up the dreaded goose egg for that player that week as well. But don't lose any sleep over it; that's just part of the game, like lost fumbles, television time-outs, and the NFC representative winning the Super Bowl.

BONUS POINTS

Bonus points for exceptional yardage are also awarded to players scoring on basic offensive plays. A touchdown pass of *50 yards or more from the line of scrimmage* results in double points for both the passer (usually the quarterback) and the receiver (usually a wide receiver or running back)—6 each, instead of the standard 3. Double points are also awarded to a player (usually a running back) who scores on a run of *50 yards or more from the line of scrimmage* (12 points instead of 6). If the running back scores on a pass reception of 50 yards or more, the back is awarded 6 points, as is the quarterback.

Field goals of *45 yards or more* receive 6 points rather than 3. So, if the Dolphins' Stoyanovich attempts a field goal from the opponent's 35-yard line, and successfully kicks the bonus boot through the uprights, Stoyo's fantasy owner is entitled to the bonus-point total, or 6 points, not just 3, since the kick was exactly a 45-yard field goal.

There is one exception to the general rule regarding bonus points: *Scores by a defensive team are never doubled.* This rule also applies to an individual player, like rookie receiver Todd Kinchen in the earlier example, who, while on the field as part of the special-teams unit, starts upfield with the first punt return of his NFL career and runs the punt back 61 yards for a touchdown, as he did for the first of his two touchdown returns in the same game against the Atlanta Falcons last season. He would simply receive 6 points, and not any bonus points, for that particular effort, even though the return was over 50 yards. The defensive team involved would also only receive 6 points for such a score. Again, regardless of the distance covered by the play, such a score is never doubled for the individual scoring on the special-teams unit or for the defensive team itself.

SCORING EXAMPLES

The following scoring examples are designed to demonstrate the various ways that fantasy owners score points through the actions of real NFL players. Obviously, I can't provide examples in this book that address every possible scoring contingency. If a situation comes up that your league has not experienced before and it raises doubt about the way to calculate the proper fantasy score, the owners should vote on it. A league can also choose to vest such decision-making authority in its commissioner, if that's easier.

Just so you new owners will have some reference points to help your decisions, the following are some scoring examples and the proper ruling with regard to points scored in each scenario:

1. One of your wide receivers comes from his split position, takes a handoff, and scores on an end-around play. The Vikings' Anthony Carter, the 49ers' Jerry Rice, and the Jets' Terance Mathis all scored on this type of play last season. If one of these players were on your roster last season, you received 6 points for his rushing touchdown just as if he were a running back scoring on a running play. You double the points if the run is 50 yards or more from the line of scrimmage.

2. One of your running backs throws a pass for a touchdown, as the Redskins' Earnest Byner did in Week Two last season, the third straight season he has thrown a touchdown pass. You would be credited with 3 points, just as if he were a quarterback. Double the points if the play covers 50 yards or more from the line of scrimmage.

3. Your quarterback scores on a sneak from the 1-yard line, as Mark Rypien did twice in Week Six against Denver in the Monday Night Game last season. You receive 6 points for each touchdown just as if he were a running back. Double the points if the run is 50 yards or more from the line of scrimmage. (Believe it or not, this is not an impossible scenario. Randall Cunningham bolted 54 yards for a score in Week Nine of the 1990 season. This remarkable bonus run was just one of the reasons why R.C.'s return in 1992 was heralded by fantasy football owners across the country. The 49ers' Steve Young almost matched this feat in 1992 when he rambled 39 yards for a score in San Francisco's win against the Los Angeles Rams in Week Five.)

4. Your defensive team scores a safety by sacking an opposing quarterback in his own end zone. The defensive team receives 2 points for a safety, *not* the 6 points that would be awarded if a member of the defensive team had picked up an opposing quarterback's fumble and run into the end zone and scored a touchdown. Eight of the 28 NFL teams were credited with safeties last season. (See Chapter Six, where I discuss each score by a defensive team. I also have a summary of each

defensive team's fantasy points in my Official Fantasy Statistics in Appendix C.)

5. Your kicker picks up a fumbled snap during a field goal attempt, and with visions of glory, or survival, flashing before his eyes, takes off downfield and, narrowly avoiding one tackler after another, miraculously stumbles into the end zone. The fact that the snap was fumbled by the holder transforms the situation from the basic field goal attempt, where the special teams receive no fantasy points for the successful field goal, to one where additional fantasy points may be scored. In such a situation, your kicker would receive 6 points for the running touchdown. A passing touchdown in that situation would net 3 points each for the passer and receiver. Remember that the defensive team itself is also entitled to a full score for this botched field goal. Please note that the same scenario for a botched extra point would result in only 1 point for the defensive team, since a touchdown cannot be scored during an extra point attempt, even if the ball is run into the end zone instead of kicked through the uprights. This ruling was called for as recently as 1989, when Steve Largent ran the bobbled snap on the extra point in for a Seahawks conversion against the Bills during the Monday Night Game in Week Thirteen.

6. Remember that while field goal units technically fall under the definition of "special teams," a defensive team does not receive points for successful field goals or extra points.

7. If a receiver catches a pass and laterals the ball to a teammate, the quarterback and the teammate who actually scores, not the initial receiver, each get 3 points (or 6, if this is a play from beyond the bonus distance). Since these types of plays are most often executed by design, it seems fair that the play be considered a passing touchdown, with points to the quarterback and the player who scores. However, if a receiver fumbles a ball and a teammate picks it up from the ground and takes it into the end zone (assuming this touchdown is permissible under the applicable NFL rules), this constitutes a running touchdown worth 6, or 12, points for someone on an active roster.

8. A running back, let's say Thurman Thomas, takes a handoff on the 2-yard line and hurdles into the air, over the top, on his way into the end zone. Just as he is about to cross the goal line, he is popped by a linebacker, and the ball squirts out of his hands into the end zone. The blocking back on the play, Carwell Gardner, alertly spots the fumble in the end zone and pounces on it. The referees actually make the first call and award a touchdown to Gardner. In this situation, Gardner receives 6 points for scoring the touchdown, even though he was not the initial ballcarrier. Since this happened while the offensive team was on the field, no points are awarded to the owner of the Bills' defensive team.

Had Gardner picked up a fumbled punt or kickoff in the end zone, the Bills' defensive team would have received a fantasy score as well.

9. Phoenix Cardinals linebacker Eric Hill picks up a San Francisco fumble, as he did in the Cards' shocking 24–14 victory over San Francisco in Week Nine last season, and starts to rumble upfield. Mike Sherrard, one of the 49ers' wide receivers on the field during that play, in turn strips the ball away from Hill, and heads the other way with the ball. Sherrard goes 39 yards for a score, his only touchdown of the season. Obviously, Sherrard gets 6 points for his touchdown. But if you are the owner of the 49ers' defense, do you get points, too? Yes, and it counts, as only Marv Albert could say. The San Francisco fumble turned its offensive team into a defensive team for fantasy purposes for as long as the Cardinals' Hill had the ball. Sherrard's strip of the ball and return for a touchdown was the equivalent of a defensive back's return of an intercepted pass for a TD at that point.

10. An NFL team lines up for a routine field goal. The ball is snapped to the holder. Instead of placing the ball down for the kicker, the holder jumps up and passes the ball to a receiver, who has been masquerading as a blocker, in the end zone for a touchdown. What is the proper point distribution in this situation? You make the call. If you said that the receiver gets 3 points and the defense (special teams) receives 6, you are correct. The fake field goal turns the ordinary field goal attempt into a special play, for which fantasy points are awarded if there is a score. And if the holder turns out to be a player on someone's active roster, like a backup quarterback, then he receives 3 points for the touchdown pass. Of course, if the fake field goal fails, then no points are awarded.

This brings up an important point. Fantasy owners who rely upon newspapers for their scoring summaries should be aware that such sources are not always as descriptive or accurate as one might hope. Last year, the scoring summary in one newspaper described a touchdown in Denver's game against Dallas in Week Fourteen as "Tillman 81-yard pass from Marshall." An unobservant fantasy owner might skip over the reference to Marshall, forgetting for the moment that the Broncos have no quarterback named Marshall but that they do have a wide receiver by that name. Obviously, this was the old flea flicker play, run to perfection. While it was not a play involving the Broncos' special teams, it was a play that called for special attention.

The same goes in the scoring example involving Mike Sherrard that I just described. The notation "Sherrard 39-yard fumble return" in the scoring summary does not clearly indicate that there might be some points in that play for the fantasy owner of the 49ers' defense. You should bring any unclear item like this, plus any other discrepancies you might find in the newspaper, to the commissioner's attention, so that he can award the right score. Do the right thing, and be as fair to each other as possible.

WEEKLY PLAY

All right, the draft is over, and rosters are set. Now what do you do? Generally, you sit back and root for your players to score as many points as possible, more than anyone else in your league on a consistent basis. But, specifically, what form will your league's weekly competition take? I am going to suggest three sets of rules for you to choose from. These rules will determine the exact nature of your league's competition. All three versions are simple and easy to follow. The difference is that each successive version calls for more direct involvement by the league owners. So, take your pick, depending upon how much effort your buddies are willing to put into maintaining the league.

Basic Version: Total Points   In the simplest version of my rules of competition, the league owners determine the weekly standings by adding each owner's total points for the week to the total points already accumulated for the season. The owner with the most points at the end of the season wins, the owner with the next-highest total finishes second, the next-highest third, and so on down the line. The person with the highest point total for the week would win a bonus to be determined as part of the package of prizes adopted by your league. (See Chapter Two for some suggestions.) You might also want to award some type of booby prize to the lamentable owner who scores the fewest points each week. (That would be one trophy you definitely do not want to retire.)

Each owner's major responsibility is to monitor the scores for each of his players over the weekend, compile the results, and report them to the commissioner on Monday morning. This helps the commissioner compile the scores and ensure they are correct. (See Appendix A for a sample of forms to use for reporting weekly standings and results.)

This basic method may have the most appeal to those of you organizing a fantasy football league for the first time, since it requires the least amount of organizational effort.

Intermediate Version: Basic Head-to-Head Competition   This method employs direct competition between the team owners each week, just like in the NFL. The team with the highest total score in each game for a particular weekend wins its respective game. For example, using some of the teams in Appendix A, if Team One, the Coach's Road Holes, is matched against Team Two, the Markie de Sades, in a particular week, and the Road Holes score 39 points while the de Sades only score 26, the Road Holes receive a win and the de Sades are entered in the loss column. The owner with the highest winning score each week wins a cash bonus as well (discussed in the next chapter). The theory underlying the distribution of weekly prizes is that even owners with poor won-lost records, who might otherwise be out of the running for the end-of-the-season prizes, can retain some incentive, and dignity, during each of the games in the latter part of the season.

Your opponent for any particular week is determined by a rotational schedule, based on the order of draft. The first week Team One plays Team Two, Team Three plays Team Four, and so on. Each subsequent week the order changes, so that every team plays every other team before the schedule repeats itself. (See my proposed schedule for an eight-team league in Appendix B.)

This version requires increased participation by the league owners, since you also need to keep track of your opponent's score so you can report the scores for both teams to the commissioner. While this method might require a little more involvement by the owners, the benefit is that it more closely parallels real NFL competition. It also places less of a premium on a team's total points and more emphasis on a team's ability to score points consistently from week to week. For example, a team might lead its league in total points early in the season but have a record below .500 because the team had two very high-scoring weeks, followed by four mediocre weeks against high-scoring competition. Now, part of your destiny rests not only on your own scoring ability, but also on the number of points your opponent puts on the board in a particular week.

Advanced Version: Expanded Rosters   The third version of the rules, one that might be more appealing to the experienced fantasy owner, is the concept of expanded rosters, which allows an owner to employ additional coaching skills. Under this method, each owner drafts *twice* the number of players that will be needed each week. The standard roster for this version of the rules includes 20 players, distributed as follows:

2 Quarterbacks (QB)
6 Running Backs (RB)
8 Receivers (WR)
2 Kickers (K)
2 Defensive Teams (DT)

Then, before the NFL games for that particular week take place, the owner must designate *10* of those 20 players (50 percent of the players in each roster category) as the players who are eligible to score points for him that week. You can picture the 10-player list as your "active" roster for that week. The 10 players are designated each week as follows:

> 1 Quarterback (QB)
> 3 Running Backs (RB)
> 4 Receivers (WR)
> 1 Kicker (K)
> 1 Defensive Team (DT)

Please note that points scored by the 10 members of your roster not designated to play in any particular week *are not counted in league play.* In other words, let's say I have drafted the Cleveland Browns' Terry Metcalf as one of my six running backs, and we're going into the third weekend of play in the 1992 season. I'm looking over the numbers from the first two weeks, to figure out which three running backs of mine to play this week. I look at Metcalf's numbers. Hmm, let's see. After two weeks of play, he's caught 5 passes for 70 yards, and rushed only 3 times for 15 yards. He hasn't scored a touchdown yet, either. Terry, you're riding the pines this week. So, I leave him out of the starting lineup in Week Three, and what happens? Metcalf scores 1 rushing touchdown and catches 3 touchdown passes, 2 of them from bonus territory. How many fantasy points do I get from this fabulous performance? Zero, since Metcalf, for the purpose of scoring fantasy points for my team, is on my mythical bench for that week. And if I lose to my opponent by fewer than the 21 points Metcalf scored that week, I put myself on probation and don't allow myself to sit in the owner's box for the rest of the season.

Under these rules, each owner must call in his weekly roster to the commissioner each week, by close of business on Friday (Wednesday, if there is a Thursday game). After you turn in your weekly roster, you *CANNOT make substitutions,* even in the event of an injury to a player before the game. It is not unheard of for a player listed as questionable in Friday's NFL injury report in the newspaper to aggravate an injury on Saturday or on Sunday warming up for the game, resulting in his sitting out the afternoon. Because that player was listed as questionable, not doubtful, you might have included him in your weekly roster. That's the way the old cookie crumbles. Give that player a goose egg for the week, and be more careful in the future.

Because of the excess number of players on the roster to begin with, a supplemental draft (a procedure I will explain in a moment) is not nearly as critical under these rules as it is for those using the standard rules. However, the fact remains that there will still be talented players, primarily rookies, who will be overlooked in the initial draft and who would be valuable additions to a fantasy team. Rather than holding supplemental drafts, you might employ a drop/add system under which an owner can drop one player and add another who is not on anyone else's roster. This system is only recommended if you have a reliable commissioner who is willing to keep track of the various transactions over the course of the season. It is also recommended that the commissioner charge a small fee for each drop/add, to lower the incentive to change players willy-nilly, and to increase the postseason banquet fund.

This expanded-roster method requires the most involvement by fantasy owners, as you can see. However, the payoff is that you now begin to feel like a real coach, making substitutions that will, you hope, spur your team on to victory. On the other hand, there are few worse feelings than watching several of your benchwarming players dominate the video highlights while your starters are doing their best Seattle Seahawks imitation.

Whichever method your league adopts, its success depends in large measure upon each owner's calling in the scores every week. It's unfair to require your commissioner to spend the time to tote up everyone else's scores as well as his own, especially if he has a newsletter to write. If you fail to call in your score, the commissioner, unfairly burdened with additional work, has the power to declare your score for that week void.

THE SUPPLEMENTAL DRAFT

What happens when one of your players becomes a human highlight film for the monster hits of the week, cartwheeling through the air on his way to a headfirst crash landing on the artificial turf? If any of your players are hurt and must go on injured reserve for a month during the season, what do you do? What if one of your dark-horse draftees turns out to be a candidate for the glue factory, while a player who sat out his first year, like Ricky Watters of the San Francisco 49ers, whom nobody drafted, has burst on the NFL scene like Halley's Comet and is scoring touchdowns at a blinding clip? If you are using the basic or intermediate rules of competition just described, you now have a roster space that you need to fill, in order to keep your roster at full strength. Don't despair. Under these proposed rules it is possible to have a second bite of the apple and make roster changes once the NFL season is under way. Here's what to do:

Every four weeks during the season, the owners come together to hold a supplemental draft. An owner may discard as many players as he wants. If you want to get rid of the whole bunch and start from scratch, go right ahead, but it will cost you. (See discussion below about replacement fees.) When an owner discards his players, they go into the supplemental pool and that owner forfeits all rights to them. If someone else wants to draft those discarded players now, he or she is free to do so. The supplemental pool consists of all players discarded by the owners, plus those players who had not previously been on anyone's roster.

The supplemental draft is conducted just like the preseason draft. However, the basis for the order of the draft changes. Now, the owners' won-lost records up to that point determine the draft order. The owner with the worst record drafts first, the owner with the next-worse record drafts second, and so forth. Ties are broken by total points scored by the tied teams. The draft then reverses order in the second round, as in the preseason draft, and continues back and forth by round until all the owners have refilled their rosters with the proper quantity of players. Some owners may need to draft more players than others because they are dropping more players back into the supplemental pool. Once an owner has filled his roster back to the proper number of players, he may no longer make supplemental selections in that quarter's draft. The new rosters will be official until the next supplemental draft.

An owner is not required to participate in any of the supplemental drafts. If he likes the way things are going with his team up to that point in the season, he can sit it out. This procedure is designed to allow dissatisfied owners to improve their teams and stay competitive for the rest of the season.

I would also again suggest that the league establish a replacement fee for each player dropped and added to an owner's roster. As I have said, these drop/add fees will help keep the number of transactions down, and more important, will also serve to defray the cost of your league's banquet at the end of the season.

BYE, BYE: THE NEW 18-WEEK NFL SCHEDULE

In 1990, the NFL implemented its plans to expand the 16-game season over 17 weeks. That having proved a success, the NFL announced during the offseason that it was implementing a new 18-week schedule for the 1993 season. As a result, the very simple rules discussed above creating balanced rosters for weekly play instantly have become even more complicated than they were before. For example, with the various byes for each team built into the 1993 schedule, there will be only 8 weeks in 1993 when all 28 teams play. What happens in the upcoming season when it's one of your players' turn to take a mandated week off, while a reduced number of NFL teams hit the field? My rule is simple: If a player doesn't play in the real NFL game, for whatever reason (byes, injury), he doesn't score any points for his fantasy owner.

There are several reasons for this approach. First, I have included more than one player in each roster category except for defensive team, and defensive teams rarely score for a fantasy owner anyway. The proposed rosters are specially designed to alleviate scoring problems when one of your players has a bye. In addition, each owner can pick up an NFL schedule as part of his draft preparation and find out which teams are scheduled to sit out which weekends, and can draft accordingly. The same strategy is applicable to the supplemental drafts.

Like nature, the fantasy owner abhors a vacuum—a roster spot occupied by an injured or vacationing player, who has no chance of scoring that particular week. But remember, everyone is in the same boat. The season will be the same length for each owner, and the byes should balance out over the long run. Besides, the supplemental draft and the expanded-roster rules provide plenty of flexibility for those owners who want to avoid as many byes for their roster players as possible.

SUMMARY

The rules of the fantasy football game are simple to remember. Every team owner selects 12 players broken down into the five roster categories discussed above, unless you use the expanded-roster method of competition. My fantasy scoring system parallels the real NFL scoring system, except that the quarterback and receiver split the 6 points for a touchdown. If a player doesn't score on the field, he receives no fantasy points. The teams either compete on the basis of total points scored over the entire season or rotate opponents on a weekly basis. Owners may participate in a supplemental draft every four weeks to change rosters and (they hope) upgrade the quality of their respective teams. The most points or the best record wins, depending upon which system you employ. The owners have more fun than the law allows. And that's just the story for the regular season.

TWO

JUST WIN, BABY

WHILE THE SPIRIT OF COMPETITION should be inspiration enough for most red-blooded sports fans to participate in a fantasy football league, there might be some readers who feel that some sort of economic incentive is called for. The recession looks like it's over, and the forces of capitalism that have been pent up for three years have cabin fever and are chomping at the bit to be free. So, in the spirit of helping the economy back on its way to health, I will suggest the following fees as a simple guideline for those owners inclined to vie for cash prizes at the end of the season.

These fees and prizes are merely suggestions. Obviously, each league can pass its own set of rules tailored to its own definition of risk and to individual budgets.

Please note that the following fees and prizes are based on an eight-team league. You will probably want to adjust the contributions and percentages of the awards based upon the actual number of owners in your league. You might also want to increase the number of persons who qualify for cash awards at the end of the season, to reduce the number of disgruntled losers.

FEES

The following are model fees for the basic, intermediate, and expanded-roster versions of my rules. The basic concept is the same for all three versions; that is, you have to pay to play. However, the amount of the fees involved varies, depending upon the rules your league uses and how much you want the weekly and final payouts to be. But whatever the amount of money involved, the underlying principle remains constant: Score the most points.

Basic Method The model fee to participate in a league using my basic rules is $200 an owner for the season. Once the season starts, each owner must make payments in advance for each quarter of the season.

Consequently, each owner must cough up $50 before the start of the season and before Weeks Five, Nine, and Thirteen. The commissioner can collect checks from every owner at each of the four drafts—the one preseason and the three supplementals—since these events coincide with the first three quarters of the season.

Intermediate and Expanded-Roster Method   The model fee for owners in a league using my intermediate or advanced-rule versions is $500 an owner for the season. Payments are made quarterly, as in the basic version. Each payment is $125 in this case. The fees are higher because the payouts are different, as you will see in a moment.

Transaction Fees   Your league should also charge a transaction fee for each player dropped or added by an owner in each of the supplemental drafts, and in the drop/add procedure used in the expanded-roster rules. I would suggest that a league charge $5 per roster spot changed by an owner using the supplemental draft, and $10 for each drop/add under expanded-roster rules. This money should be kept in a separate pool, to reimburse the commissioner for postage and copying charges, if any, and to defray the costs of a league gathering at the end of the season.

PRIZES

The quarterly contributions create a pool of money for the payment of cash prizes for weekly and season winners, regardless of which rules are involved.

Basic Method   For the weekly prize, the owner with the highest score over the weekend receives $25. All other prizes are deferred to the end of the season.

At the end of the seaason, the four teams with the highest number of total points receive prizes based on the following scheme:

Most points	50% of remaining pool
Second-most points	25% of remaining pool
Third-most points	15% of remaining pool
Fourth-most points	10% of remaining pool

These percentages translate into the following amounts, if you use my suggested contribution of $200:

First place	$535
Second place	$270
Third place	$160
Fourth place	$110

In the interest of fairness, as well as the important bonding ritual of public humiliation, your league should also award a $75 booby prize to the owner who scores the fewest points during the season. This prize is more than equitable compensation for the unsuspecting owner who drafted Mark Rypien or Brad Baxter in the first round of the draft last season.

Intermediate and Expanded-Roster Method   For the weekly prize under these versions, the four winners each week receive $30 for their victories. The owner with the highest score over the weekend will win an additional $10, for a total of $40 for that owner. As a result, if your team plays around .500 ball during the season, and even if you never rack up high points for any given week, you will still recoup at least $240 of your original $500 investment.

At the end of the season, the team with the highest number of total points, accumulated over the course of the season, receives a prize of $150 (this amount is subtracted right off the top of the pool of fees remaining at the end of the season). This award usually goes to the owner with the best record, but it does not necessarily have to, as you will find out. The remaining fees are distributed according to the same percentages used in the basic rules, and translate into the following amounts, if you use my suggested contributions:

First place	$755
Second place	$380
Third place	$225
Fourth place	$150

If your group really gets into the fun of fantasy football during the season, I would recommend a season-ending banquet for the awarding of prizes, with a good roast reserved for the big winners—and, depending upon how close a group you all are, for the big losers, too. Your banquet can be funded in part by the transaction fees accumulated over the course of the season from the supplemental drafts. This war chest should be significant, especially if a lot of owners goofed in the original draft. Whatever the size of the pot, make sure that the league winner puts some of his winnings back into circulation and springs for the balance of the awards banquet check.

SPEAKING OF AWARDS

Speaking of awards, it's time for my annual awards to the players who have made the most positive, and negative, contributions to the fantasy game in 1992.

	Biggest Surprises	Biggest Disappointments
QB	Stan Humphries	Mark Rypien
	Brett Favre	John Elway

San Diego's Stan Humphries and Green Bay's Brett Favre were both freed from their backup situations by trades, and posted great numbers while leading their new teams to their best seasons in years. Washington's Mark Rypien had a disastrous season, falling from 28 touchdown passes in 1991 to 13 in 1992. Denver's John Elway was injured for most of the second half of the season, and as a result posted his lowest number of touchdown passes since his rookie year in 1983.

	Biggest Surprises	Biggest Disappointments
RB	Barry Foster	Eric Dickerson
	Ricky Watters	Christian Okoye

Both of these Biggest Surprises at running back came out of nowhere in NFL terms and had outrageously good seasons. Pittsburgh's Barry Foster rushed for 1,690 yards and 11 touchdowns, while San Francisco's Ricky Watters rushed for 1,013 yards and scored 11 touchdowns overall. On the other hand, the Chiefs' Christian Okoye fell from 1,031 yards and 9 rushing touchdowns in 1991 to only 448 yards and 6 rushing touchdowns in 1992. Dickerson had a miserable scoring year in his first season with the Raiders, his second low-scoring season in a row. Much more was expected from both of these players in 1992.

	Biggest Surprises	Biggest Disappointments
WR	Sterling Sharpe	Andre Reed
	Anthony Miller	Anthony Carter

It's no coincidence that the biggest surprises at wide receiver were hooked up with the biggest surprises at the quarterback opposition in 1992. Green Bay's Sterling Sharpe, after two subpar seasons, had one of the greatest seasons by a receiver in NFL history. San Diego's

Anthony Miller finished among the fantasy scoring leaders, as he had done earlier in his career. On the other hand, Buffalo's Andre Reed had the lowest-scoring year of his distinguished eight-year NFL career. And Minnesota's Anthony Carter scored the lowest number of touchdowns in his entire professional career (three years USFL, eight years NFL) in 1992.

	Biggest Surprises	Biggest Disappointments
K	Steve Christie	Jeff Jaeger
	John Carney	Roger Ruzek

Steve Christie moved from Tampa to Buffalo on the Plan B program, and demonstrated his kicking skills all the way through the regular season to the Super Bowl. John Carney helped spark the Chargers to their first playoff appearance since 1982 by kicking 16 of his 26 field goals in the last six games of the 1992 season. The Raiders' Jeff Jaeger dropped from 116 points in 1991 to 73 points in 1992, and the Eagles' Roger Ruzek dropped from 111 points in 1991 to 88 points in 1992.

	Biggest Surprises	Biggest Disappointments
DT	Kansas City Chiefs	New York Giants
	New England Patriots	Seattle Seahawks

The Kansas City defense scored 9 touchdowns, and the special teams returned a couple of punts for touchdowns, as the Chiefs were the highest-scoring defense in the league. The Patriots jumped from zero interception returns for touchdowns during the prior two seasons to 3 in 1992, and added 3 more defensive touchdowns on fumble returns, for a total of 6 touchdowns overall. The Giants and the Seahawks, two of the tougher defenses in the real world of the NFL, recorded only 3 fantasy scores between them in 1992.

Comebackers of the Year

QB	Jim Everett
RB	Cleveland Gary
WR	Sterling Sharpe
K	Norm Johnson
DT	Vikings

The Rams rebounded in 1992 under new head coach Chuck Knox, and Everett and Gary led the way. Sterling Sharpe, after two seasons lost in the frozen tundra of Green Bay, reclaimed his spot as one of the preeminent receivers in the game with a season for the record books. Atlanta's Norm Johnson kicked 4 field goals from beyond the 50-yard line in 1992, tops in the league, after kicking only 1 from beyond the 50-yard line during the prior three seasons. The Vikings returned to the top ranks of fantasy defenses with a great season in 1992. They scored 6 touchdowns in a four-week period in mid-season, on their way to scoring 8 touchdowns and 1 safety overall.

Rookies of the Year

RB	Rodney Culver
K	Lin Elliott

Ricky Watters was not a true rookie under NFL rules, so Rodney Culver, with his 7 rushing touchdowns for the Colts, wins the prize. The Cowboys' Elliott was one of the highest-scoring fantasy kickers in the NFL, rookie or no.

QUOTABLE QUOTES OF 1992

Department of Redundancy Department:

Steelers Coach Bill Cowher, after Pittsburgh's first loss of the 1992 season in Week 4, said that during its bye week the team would undergo what Cowher called a "self-analysis of ourselves."

Take a Memo to the Commissioner of the WLAF:

DT Mike Golic, after the Eagles' first loss of the 1992 season, in Week 6 to the Chiefs, regarding the upcoming game against Washington and overconfidence: "I think that after the way we played we'd take a new Alaskan expansion team seriously, let alone the Washington Redkins."

But He's Got to Work on His Horizontal Game:

Al Saunders, the Chiefs' assistant coach for receivers, on the emergence of rookie Willie Davis as a deep threat: "He's an explosive player with great vertical speed."

Who's That Guy With the Beard and the Long Hair:

Cards Coach Joe Bugel, who vowed to let the players shave the heads of all the coaches should they make the playoffs for the first time in 11 seasons: "Mohawks, baldos, whatever they want. I'd shave my whole body if it meant making the playoffs."

It Must Be the Altitude Department:

Denver safety Steve Atwater on the Broncos' uncanny ability to win at home: "It's tough for the fat lady to sing here."

I Thought It Was Reginald Dwight the Whole Time:

Saints Coach Jim Mora enjoyed the bye week during Week Eight last season and had his eyes opened when he attended a concert by Elton John. "I didn't realize he sang all those songs."

Way to Change People's Minds About Stereotypes Department:

"It's not voodoo. Strange things will happen. I believe in that." Protest leader Dennis Banks's comments about a religious curse put on the Chiefs and the Redskins by Native Americans protesting outside Arrowhead Stadium.

At Least You're Still in the League, Kevin:

"He's the coach. He can feel any way he wants." Kevin Butler responding to reporters after Mike Ditka called him "gutless," "mentally weak," and "the worst kickoff man in the league."

THREE

THE SECOND SEASON:
THE PLAYOFFS

THERE'S NO REASON for the fun of your fantasy football season to end after the final game of the NFL's regular season. All your league has to do is extend the fantasy rules to the playoffs, creating a brand-new season, just as the NFL does. The rules are similar to those used during the regular season, with a few minor changes.

THE DRAFT

In the week between the wild-card playoff games and the divisional playoff games, a draft is held using the same rules as the preseason draft. There are two basic differences between the playoff draft and the draft used to select regular-season rosters. First, as in the supplemental draft, the order of the playoff draft is determined by the standings, in this instance by the order of finish during regular-season play. The person who finishes last in the standings picks first in the playoff draft, the person who finishes next to last picks second in the playoff draft, and so on. The playoff draft is conducted round by round in the same manner as the regular-season draft described in Chapter One. Once again, owners may not retain the rights to any player on their regular-season roster. Everybody starts with a clean slate in the playoffs, just like in the NFL. You can look at the advantage given to the fantasy owners with the worst regular-season performances as the equivalent of the NFL's home-field advantage, flipped over on its head.

The second difference between regular-season and postseason play is that because the player pool is limited to the eight NFL teams that have made it past the first round of the NFL playoffs, the number of players available for the playoff draft is much smaller than the number available for the regular draft. For that reason, there are only eight rounds in the postseason draft, broken down into the following number of positions:

1 Quarterback (QB)
2 Running Backs (RB)
3 Receivers (WR)
1 Kicker (K)
1 Defensive Team (DT)

Using this format, each owner will have a shot at drafting a starting quarterback, kicker, and defensive team from each of the remaining NFL playoff teams.

RULES OF PLAY

As in my basic method of play during the regular season, the owners compete for prize money in the playoffs based only on *total points* accumulated during the playoffs, points being awarded in the same fashion as during the regular season. The owner with the greatest number of total points at the end of the Super Bowl is the winner, with the rest of the standings calculated in descending order of points scored.

As NFL teams are eliminated from the playoffs, the players on those teams may no longer score points for their fantasy owners. As a result, in determining your picks in the playoff draft, your handicapping skills in picking which teams are going to the Super Bowl are as valuable as predicting which players will do the most scoring. The fewer players left on your roster going into the Super Bowl, the more likely it is that you will not be going to Disney World with the game's MVP after the game. Obviously, in last season's NFL playoffs, if you had loaded up on the Bills or the Cowboys, and drafted a team that included Messrs. Christie and Elliott, you were a big winner. If, on the other hand, you liked the Redskins and the Chargers to go all the way, drafting Rypien and Humphries, Carney and Lohmiller at every turn, you didn't have much fun during the playoffs, did you?

FEES AND PRIZES

There is only one payment to be made in postseason play. The recommended fee to compete in the postseason is $100 per owner, for a total pool of $800, again assuming an eight-team league. The prize money is distributed as follows:

First place	$500
Second place	$200
Third place	$100

These figures can be adjusted to accommodate the number of owners in your league.

NO SUPPLEMENTAL DRAFT

The playoff season isn't long enough to hold a supplemental draft. However, I would recommend as a general rule that you permit each owner to drop *one* of the players on his roster from a team eliminated from the playoffs, and to substitute a player on a playoff team still alive for the big prize. The deadlines for this player transaction should be Wednesday of the weeks before the conference championships and the Super Bowl.

NO OTHER CHANGES

All other rules regarding league play remain the same in the postseason session. Of course, participation in the postseason by the regular-season coaches is purely optional. However, even if your ego and pocketbook have taken a beating during the regular season, the postseason offers a splendid opportunity to recoup some of your initial investment. This is especially true since the worse your regular-season record was, the better your draft position for the playoffs will be.

ADVANCED VERSION OF PLAYOFF RULES

If your league has eight teams, as my rules suggest, your league has another option for playoff activity. This option offers more intriguing strategic considerations than the basic version of the playoff rules I just described. Under this advanced version of the playoff rules, your league would draft players *before* the playoffs start, with NFL players from *12* playoff teams available to stock the eight fantasy teams in your league.

This option changes the playoff strategy completely. Under the basic playoff rules, every owner theoretically starts the playoffs on the same level playing field as the other owners. All the NFL players drafted will play in NFL games in the first round of the fantasy playoffs, since the wild-card games have been played the week before. However, under the advanced version, the players drafted from the wild-card teams, and on two of the division winners, have the possibility of playing *one more NFL playoff game* than the remaining four division champions, who sit out the first week of playoff action. (Admittedly, this doesn't happen very often, since only four wild-card teams have ever reached the Super Bowl, and only one wild-card team has ever won the Super Bowl. But don't forget that the Buffalo Bills were a wild-card entry in the NFL playoffs last season. They may not have won the Super Bowl, but fantasy owners using the advanced-playoff format who drafted Steve Christie, after an initial scare, laughed all the way to the bank.)

This advanced format gives fantasy owners who consider themselves serious handicappers and who like taking risks the chance to draft players on the wild-card teams they think will last deep into the playoffs. That way, these fantasy owners can get out in front of the pack early, with players on the wild-card teams piling up points a full week before the players from the remaining playoff teams play their first game. The trick is trying to hang on to that early lead when the players from the remaining NFL playoff teams begin to accumulate points. The old fable of the tortoise and the hare comes to mind in this situation. Regardless of which playoff option you choose, however, you will have loads of fun.

Needless to say, if there are more than 12 owners in your league, you will have to make some serious adjustments to tailor your league's size to the number of NFL players available in the playoffs.

FOUR

VARIATIONS ON A THEME

THE RULES I HAVE SUGGESTED in this book present three versions of rules for your league to play fantasy football. These rules should work well for any league. But I also know that, like snowflakes, each set of rules adopted by fantasy leagues around the country have their own wrinkles that make them different and distinct. The rules I have proposed are certainly not the tablets brought down by Moses from the Mount, and you may want to tinker with them to create your own individualized version. Here are a few thoughts on some of the more common variations found in other leagues.

THE POINT SYSTEM

The scoring system proposed in this book uses the actual numerical value of the NFL scores themselves. This makes it easy for a fantasy owner to watch a game and calculate his score as the action on the field progresses. Now, why the NFL has seen fit to make the value of a touchdown 6 points, as opposed to 5 or 7 or 10, and a field goal only worth 3 points is another question, the ins and outs of which are too lengthy to discuss here. But these point values did not materialize out of thin air. At the turn of the century, a field goal was equal in worth to a touchdown. As offensive prowess and the nature of the game evolved, the value of a field goal was lowered to 3 points (in 1909) and a touchdown's worth was increased to 6 (in 1912).

However, it may be time for the NFL to change its scoring rules again. Because, as I am sure you noticed, scoring in the NFL was down for the third straight year in 1992, sinking to the lowest level for the NFL since 1978. This is a direct result of measures taken by the NFL prior to the 1990 season to shorten the length of games. The game clock is no longer stopped when the player with the ball goes out of bounds, except in the last two minutes of the first half and the last five of the second half. As a result, published reports indicate that the NFL is toying with the idea of changing its scoring rules. Certainly the use of the 2-point conversion, an exciting element of the college game, would be a welcome addition.

You and your fellow owners need not be so cautious on this issue. Feel free to adopt changes in my point system. One system that seems to work for other leagues is awarding 10 points for a running touchdown, 5 for passing touchdowns (5 each to the passer and receiver), and 5 for field goals. Extra points are 2, and all scores by defensive teams are 10 points, regardless of their nature. (Under this scenario, a safety's as good as a 100-yard kickoff return.) Bonus rules for long-distance scoring plays are the same as those described in Chapter One. A system like this results in higher scores per game. However, the fantasy results remain the same, since the number of touchdowns scored on the playing field remains constant and the relative value of the scores remains approximately the same.

This brings up a good point: If you change the relative value of scores, remember that this will affect the outcome of your fantasy games. For instance, if your league decides that field goals will remain 3 points and extra points 1, but that rushing and passing touchdowns will be increased to 10 and 5 points, respectively, you have shifted the ratio of scores. The result is that your league has devalued the kicking game severely and that, conversely, touchdowns have become much more valuable. Again, it doesn't matter what scoring system your league adopts, as long as you realize where the emphasis in the scoring scheme lies and draft accordingly.

Another variation of the scoring system that some leagues use is to add scoring categories for other statistical areas of the game, such as yards gained in a game by running backs and wide receivers and yards passed for by quarterbacks. For instance, some leagues award additional points for 300-yard passing games by quarterbacks, 100-yard rushing games by backs, and 100-yard receiving games by pass catchers. Some leagues require each team to select one rookie, or one tight end, as an additional roster category. Some leagues even go so far as to award points to a team's offensive line for blocking on rushing touchdown plays, or to select coaches who get fantasy points for covering the spread each week. Some leagues also have moved the bonus territory for field goals back from 45 to 50 yards.

You can certainly make your rules as complicated as you want. I would advise caution, however, because adding statistical categories such as the ones just described really complicates what is a fairly simple system.

PRIZES AND FEES

Another obvious element that can be changed is the amount of money the members of the league are willing to contribute during the season. Coaches could vote to eliminate them altogether, and just contribute enough funds to cover expenses. Or the funds could be increased if the coaches have deeper pockets and want to raise the ante. It seems to me that the percentages presented earlier are essentially fair and that the distribution enables half the owners to get something back. However, this is a free country, so exercise your voting privilege if you think a change is warranted. The same principle would obviously also apply to the playoffs.

PLAYOFFS

Speaking of the playoffs, some leagues may not want to go through the process of reconvening all the owners for a second draft at the end of the season and basically starting all over again for such a short period of time. One alternative is to use the last two or three weeks of the regular season as the league's fantasy playoffs. The top finishers in the standings square off against each other in a single-elimination tournament, just like the NFL playoffs. The playoff teams are weighted according to their season records. The rosters are kept the same, and the scoring rules don't change. In this case, the final standings are determined by the results of the fantasy playoffs, and the end of the fantasy season coincides with the end of the regular NFL season. This is basically the no-muss, no-fuss approach to the fantasy season. It is also the nothing-to-do-during-the-NFL-playoffs approach.

WHAT ABOUT TRADES?

I know, I haven't said a word about what could be a most fascinating aspect of the fantasy game. Well, I hate to disappoint you, but you should not allow trades. First of all, trades are an administrative nightmare, because of the short time between games. Notifying everyone in the league during the week, which would be only fair, is too heavy a burden for a commissioner, even one with lots of time on his hands. Second, trades offer too tempting an opportunity for late-season hanky-panky—you know, the old gag where a team vying for the league lead trades Marcus Allen, who has 3 touchdowns, to Basement Bertha in return for Terry Allen, who has 14 touchdowns, in the next-to-last week of the season. Of course, future considerations will be rumored to be part of the deal, to be consummated sometime after the owner who has just landed the high-scoring running back wins his last two games, collects the winner's prize, and has a little extra cash to throw into the deal. There is no need to ruin friendships over a game like fantasy football, so don't even provide the temptation.

The Rotisserie league rules for fantasy baseball permit trading, which is understandable, given the length of the baseball season and the tradition of trading players in Major League Baseball, a practice that has been largely abandoned in pro football. However, the Rotisserians do recognize the potential for abuse, and as a result place restrictions on trades after the All-Star Game and prohibit trades altogether after August 31. And, that makes sense.

TAXI SQUADS

Every fantasy league is now faced with the problem of the new NFL schedule. The byes in the NFL schedule create an imbalance in the fantasy rosters several times during the season. One week, an owner may not have a quarterback, or a kicker, while his opponent is benching his fourth receiver. I have said elsewhere in the book that it will all balance out over the course of the season, so take your byes like the steadfast fantasy owner that you are. For those of you who may feel differently, here is a proposed solution. At the draft, and at each supplemental draft, create a "taxi squad," composed of one player for each roster category. Each taxi squad would consist of four players and a backup defensive team, and each owner could then substitute these backups during those weeks when the starter's NFL team is scheduled for a bye. If more than one player from a roster category is scheduled for a bye, too bad. Otherwise, if you create a taxi squad with 10 players, you might as well adopt the expanded-roster concept, with all the additional logistics that accompany it, and be done with it.

ROSTER HOLDOVERS

Once your fantasy league attains veteran status, the issue of holding players over from one year to the next, as is done in Rotisserie baseball, might be added to your league's agenda. As you know by now, the standard roster under my basic and intermediate rules includes just 12 slots, with 20 spots for my expanded-roster rules. This is not a huge number of players, compared to the entire NFL player pool available to fantasy owners each year. So I wouldn't suggest holding players over from year to year, since this lessens the amount of preparation required for Draft Day, the most exciting day of the year for fantasy football players. It would also lessen competition, since there are only so many great players, from a fantasy perspective, in the NFL. Finally, this variation would also prevent more than one owner from experiencing the thrill of having a star like Jerry Rice or Emmitt Smith on his team, a thrill everyone should experience at least once. But if your league is composed of fantasy sports nuts who have grown accustomed to the long-term contract concept used in baseball's Rotisserie leagues, then I don't see great harm in allowing each team to hold over one player per year, as long as that player can only be kept for two years in a row. (The life expectancy of an NFL career is so short that there should be some time limit on the amount of years an owner can retain a star player before he goes back in circulation.) Your league should determine the appropriate "holdover fee" if you decide to adopt such a rule. It is definitely worth something to have Jerry Rice or Emmitt Smith suit up for you two years running.

FIVE

DRAFTING STRATEGY

OVERVIEW: WHOM SHOULD I PICK?

OBVIOUSLY, THE POINT OF THIS GAME is to assemble the team that scores the most points each week. The difficult question is, How does one assemble a team that *has the best chance* to score the most points, week in and week out, during the season? While certainly not as funny as David Letterman's nightly Top Ten lists, at least not intentionally, here are my Top Ten Tips for putting together a winning fantasy football team.

1. PAY ATTENTION TO YOUR RULES

First and foremost, understand your rules. Your draft strategy should flow directly from your rules. If you follow my rules religiously, fine. If you add your own variations, great. Whatever rules your league uses, analyze them carefully and rely on them to dictate what players are valuable and what players aren't. For instance, if the rules adopted by your league favor rushing touchdowns, as mine do, then, all else being equal, an Emmitt Smith or Barry Sanders is more valuable than a Sterling Sharpe or an Anthony Miller. If your rules put equal emphasis on passing and rushing touchdowns, let's say, then quarterbacks such as Young and Marino are the kind of players you are looking for early in the draft, and running backs move down sharply on your wish list. Just be familiar with your rules, and use common sense to tailor your draft strategy accordingly.

2. DO YOUR HOMEWORK

To get the edge in selecting a high-scoring roster, the first thing a fantasy owner needs to assess is an NFL player's real statistical value, and not what I call his "marquee" value. A player may strap on a hat for a team in one of the country's media centers and have his picture plastered on posters in kids' bedrooms across the country. But a player's popularity may have no correlation to his value to fantasy owners.

The fantasy value of a player, at least as far as my rules go, relates directly to a player's ability to get into the end zone. Forget yardage, forget headlines, forget personal feelings toward a player. Strictly remember performance, because those who forget the past are doomed to repeat it, especially in fantasy football. Statistics are a critical consideration to any fantasy owner who is serious about drafting a good team. And the most important feature of an NFL player's statistics from last year and years past is their use as tools to predict this year's great performances.

That's why I include my Official Fantasy Statistics, based on the stats from the 1992 season, in Appendix C of this book. These numbers are calculated by converting each NFL score by each offensive player and defensive team during the 1992 season to my rules for fantasy scoring.

One reminder: Prepare for your fantasy draft. I can guarantee you that 18 weeks will become an eternity right before your very eyes if your season starts with a string of low-scoring weeks, burying you behind the rest of the pack. And you *will* get buried if you go into the draft cold—that is, without doing some serious reading and thinking about the players necessary to assemble a competitive fantasy team. Those owners who do prepare have an enormous competitive edge over those owners who don't put in the little time and effort necessary to get ready for the draft. Only a fool doesn't look for that edge, especially when it's so easy to come by. So, do your homework; it will pay big dividends by the end of the season. Remember my motto: If you fail to prepare, you're preparing to fail.

3. PREPARE PLAYER LISTS AND MODEL ROSTERS

Not only am I going to tell you to do your homework, I'm even going to give you a specific assignment: Use this book, and other sports publications once you have purchased this book, to put together player lists and model rosters. Believe me, there is nothing worse than entering the middle rounds of a draft, with your adrenaline wearing off and your focus beginning to blur, and not having a clue as to who to select next. Draw up lists of the most desirable players by roster position and you won't have to worry about being caught in a daze.

As you make up your lists before the draft, you can divide players into three fantasy categories. The first group is that core of players who have established a substantial scoring level that does not vary much from year to year. You should identify those players, and use them to form the foundation of your fantasy roster. Star players like Emmitt Smith and Barry Sanders are going to score a substantial amount of touchdowns every year. What may be even more important on Draft Day, though, is to recognize that you can depend on players like Washington's Earnest Byner, San Francisco's Tom Rathman, and Cleveland's Kevin Mack to score a lesser, but just as consistent, amount of touchdowns every year.

The next category are those players who will be able to improve their scoring totals in the upcoming season. For instance, did a player's injury result in far fewer touchdowns than the same player would have scored if healthy, and, if so, is that player 100 percent healthy going into this season? What rookie or perennial benchwarmer who did little or no scoring last year is going to move into the starting lineup this year and increase his touchdown total by leaps and bounds? In other words, who is going to be the Barry Foster or Ricky Watters of the 1993 season?

The third category are those players who will not repeat, or come close to repeating, their scoring totals from last season. For instance, did a player have a "career year" in 1992, scoring points at a level never before reached in his career? Since the player has scaled new heights, does that mean he is not likely to post such a high fantasy score again this year? This is a particular problem with kickers, whose scoring totals are really at the mercy of the success of a team's entire offense during the season. Take, for example, the Raiders' Jeff Jaeger or the Eagles' Roger Ruzek, who had great scoring years in 1991, only to dip down to their usual scoring levels in 1992.

It also helps to try to imagine how the first few rounds of the draft will go. This will assist you in recognizing the direction of the draft as it begins to actually unfold, and make it easier to adjust accordingly when it is your turn to pick a player. But, hey, it's your team. You can select it wisely and have lots of fun during the 1993 NFL season, or you can follow the action from your position at the back of the pack all season.

4. AIM FOR THE TARGET SCORE

If what I've suggested so far isn't clear, perhaps a different approach will help illustrate the point. When you are making up your draft lists, use the individual player's scoring totals for last year and, using those totals, aim for what I call the "target score." I have analyzed a typical league's scoring from years past, with a special focus on last season, and have found that an average of 38 points per week is enough for a team to contend for the league title under any of the versions of my rules. Now, 38 points in one week may or may not seem like a lot of points at first glance. So, let's take a look at what kind of fantasy performance, over the course of a season, will give a fantasy team an average of 38 points per week, using my basic 12-player roster. First, we need a season total to conduct our analysis. Thirty-eight points a week translates into a total of 646 points for the entire 17-week season. (Next year, the model will be based on the new 18-week schedule.) Let's take a look at some representative rosters, based on last year's fantasy scoring, which should demonstrate that assembling the type of team just discussed is far from an impossible task. Here's one example of a roster that might have been put together by the person with the first pick in the 1992 draft. (Players in each category are listed in their order of probable selection.):

Warren Moon	63
Jim Everett	69
Barry Sanders	63
Earnest Byner	42
Tom Rathman	42
Michael Haynes	36
Mark Duper	24
Tim Brown	27
Jay Novacek	18
Chip Lohmiller	135
Chris Jacke	111
Houston Oilers	26
TOTAL	**656**

Sanders, Moon, and Lohmiller would have been the first three picks, with Haynes taken in the fourth round. The rest of this roster would have fallen into place with little or no problem. As you can see, once you put together the high-scoring core of Sanders, Moon, and Lohmiller with your picks in the early rounds, the fantasy scoring by the remainder of these players surpasses the target score.

The person with the second pick in the draft might have put together a roster that looked like this:

Steve Young	105
Dave Krieg	69
Emmitt Smith	117
Herschel Walker	54

Kenneth Davis	42
John Taylor	12
Ernest Givins	30
Fred Barnett	21
Willie Anderson	21
Gary Anderson	119
David Treadwell	94
Buffalo Bills	20
TOTAL	**704**

Smith would have been the first pick on this roster, with Young going in the second round and Walker in the third. Taylor would have gone fourth, to complete the double-down move. After these four picks, none of the remaining players are likely to have been in great demand too early in most drafts before the 1992 season, including Steve Young, who had not yet demonstrated over the course of a full season how talented he is. In 1992, he fully demonstrated his value, and he might go in the first round this year. In any case, once again the target score is bettered with ease.

Try one more roster, that of the owner with the third pick in our imaginary draft:

Randall Cunningham	93
Neil O'Donnell	45
Thurman Thomas	63
Lorenzo White	48
Terry Allen	84
Andre Rison	36
Sterling Sharpe	45
Irving Fryar	15
Ricky Sanders	12
Norm Johnson	114
Jim Breech	91
Detroit	30
TOTAL	**676**

The core group here would have been Thomas, Cunningham, White, and Rison. Allen and Sharpe would have slipped down to the fifth and sixth round in most drafts, since Allen merely offered potential prior to the 1992 season, and Sharpe had not posted high fantasy numbers in two seasons. As with our other sample rosters, the remaining players would have been available in the subsequent rounds of a normal draft prior to the 1992 season.

In Appendix D, I've put together some additional rosters that demonstrate how an owner did not have to be a genius to draft a team in 1992 that would have put at least 646 points on the board.

SUMMARY

As I stated at the beginning of this chapter, my own statistical research shows that 38 points per week should be sufficient to finish in the top half of the league, and in the money, in a typical fantasy football league. I hope I have demonstrated that 38 points is not an impossible dream, and that it is actually a quite realistic goal with a good drafting strategy and knowledge of the players available. Under my rules, a core group of two to four high-scoring players goes a long way toward ensuring fantasy football success.

One last comment about the target score: It is helpful to keep track of the point totals of your players during the draft. (Pen and paper are almost as essential on Draft Day as a copy of this book.) As you select a player, put him in the proper roster category on your scratch sheet and add his points from the prior season to the total you have already accumulated. This will provide you with a barometer regarding the strengths of the players you have already drafted, and the areas you need to pursue with your next picks. When you make your final, "most wanted" list for Draft Day 1993, remember to include the players' point totals from the prior season next to their names. This extra effort will enable you to keep track of your accumulated total during the draft more easily.

5. WATCH THOSE SCORING TRENDS

Overall, NFL scoring was down again in 1992, for the third straight year. For instance, in 1989, the last year under the old rules governing the game clock, four teams scored more than 400 points during the season. The 400-point level has been reached only six times in the three seasons since then. The NFL scoring average has declined each of the last three years under the new rules. The team average was 330 points in 1989, 322 points in 1990, and only 304 points in 1991. In 1992, the team average fell again, to just below 300 points (299.6 points per team, to be precise). Nine of 12 AFC teams, and 14 NFL teams overall, failed to score 300 points during the 1992 season. NFL scoring totals in 1992 were the lowest since the 1978 season, the first year the league used the 16-game schedule. As you might expect, there were some parallel trends in fantasy scoring as well. For instance, running-back scoring dipped in 1992. In 1991, 13 backs scored more than 50 fantasy points; in 1992, only 10 backs surpassed that figure. Quarterback scoring was also down. In 1989, there were 11 quarterbacks with fantasy totals above 70 points; in 1990, there were eight; in 1991, only seven; and in 1992, six. Wide-receiver scoring was down as well. There were nine receivers with 30 or more points in 1991, but only six with that many in 1992. (There were 14 receivers with 30 or more points in 1989.)

It's clear after three years of statistical evidence that the NFL's new rules affecting the game clock, which were designed to shorten the length of the NFL games, have resulted in less scoring. Unless the NFL goes back to the old rules, the same trend should hold true in 1993. What does that mean in fantasy terms? The high-scoring fantasy players needed to form your core roster group become increasingly valuable, since there are fewer points being scored overall.

6. AT HOME IN THE DOME

Here is another of my cardinal rules regarding draft strategy: All things being equal (read "Once Chip Lohmiller and Pete Stoyanovich have been drafted"), *favor kickers who kick indoors.* Indoor kickers have a significant advantage over their booting brethren who labor alfresco. The elements, which can wreak havoc late in the season in cities with colder climates, like Buffalo, Chicago, Cleveland, and New York, will not come into play for at least half of a dome kicker's games. This fact lends greater consistency to a kicker's season-long performance. Coaches are much more likely to let a kicker bomb away indoors, where the environment is dry and wind-free and the turf is nice and artificial for clean placement and sure footing. The great season enjoyed in 1992 by Morten Andersen, resident placekicker at the Superdome, in leading all NFL kickers in fantasy scoring, is a perfect illustration of this principle.

7. THE DOUBLE-DOWN THEORY

There's a strategy I have dubbed my "Double-Down Theory" that is designed to maximize your fantasy scoring: Try to match at least one of your quarterbacks with his favorite receiver. If you can draft a high-scoring quarterback as well as his favorite receiver, you get *double the points* on a regular basis whenever these two team up for a touchdown. Why not try to match Steve Young with Jerry Rice, Chris Miller with either Andre Rison or Michael Haynes, Warren Moon with either Ernest Givins or Haywood Jeffires? Dan Marino to Mark Duper or Brett Favre to Sterling Sharpe wouldn't be a bad exacta either. Just don't get too carried away with the Double-Down Theory. Don't select a quarterback, two wide receivers, and a kicker from the same team. All the Saints' "D" has to do is throw a shutout at the NFL team you've loaded up on, and your fantasy totals for the week will resemble a customary 1992 performance by the Seattle Seahawks' offense.

8. PLAYOFF STRATEGY

Drafting strategy for postseason play requires a different approach. At this stage of the season, a fantasy owner must be not only a shrewd judge of talent, but also a peerless prognosticator. Generally, the owner with the most players going into the Super Bowl wins. But that's easier said than done.

Let me offer a few helpful hints. As a general rule, kickers are the most valuable players on a playoff roster. This might not come as a surprise. As you can see from the fantasy statistics in Appendix C, kickers represent the highest-scoring fantasy category. No other fantasy player scored as many points as each of the top six kickers did last season. The general advantage offered by kickers increases as your opponents' kickers get eliminated from the playoffs. So, if you can draft one of the two kickers going to the Super Bowl, you will, in all likelihood, finish in the playoff money. For example, if you drafted Steve Christie or Lin Elliott last year, you probably won, or came close to winning, your fantasy playoff pool. Troy Aikman of the Cowboys might have been the Super Bowl MVP, but Christie or Elliott was the tournament MVP for fantasy owners. After kickers, quarterbacks make up the next most valuable player category in the playoffs, followed by running backs, wide receivers, and defensive teams. Quarterbacks seem to take over in the big games (10 of the last 15 Super Bowl MVPs have been quarterbacks). A running back who is a designated scorer for a team favored to make the Super Bowl is a good player to have during the playoffs as well.

9. THE "X" FACTOR

Let me bring up one other important factor in your overall drafting strategy. This is what might be called the human element, or "X factor." First, you will be amazed how team-oriented a regular fan's appreciation of pro football is once you have lived through a fantasy football season. While you still root for your favorite team, you will find that scoring plays by your fantasy players become equally important. You may also find that your dislike of other teams may be tempered by the fact that one of your prime fantasy players is on that previously hated NFL roster. Admittedly, it is tough to go through the season rooting for players on teams you personally despise. Consequently, there is a fantasy football corollary to the "best available athlete" theory recited over and over by NFL general managers before the annual pro football draft. All things being equal, you should take the player you personally feel most comfortable rooting for, fantasy football rosters aside. For example, if you think Mike Ditka got a raw deal from Bears management (and I do), then don't draft the Bears as your defensive team. The whole idea is to enjoy the game as much as possible. Sometimes a real NFL owner gets stuck with a talented player whose on-and-off-the-field antics render him virtually untradable. You can avoid that whole problem in your fantasy league by drafting players you like.

Another part of the "X factor" is the temptation to draft players only from your favorite team. On the one hand, it probably is not such a good idea to put all of one's emotional eggs in the same competitive basket. On the other hand, if your favorite team is the 49ers, Cowboys, or Bills, be my guest and load up.

10. FINAL TIPS

Even if you employ my Top Ten Tips, the success of your team will be affected by many other factors. Obviously, a great deal depends on how shrewd your fellow owners are. If they have all participated in fantasy leagues before, they have a big advantage over newcomers. You will be amazed at how much easier it is to prepare for a draft once you have been through it before. There is no teacher like experience when it comes to selecting a fantasy football team. So, if you've never been in a league before, and you are going into your league with veterans of other fantasy football leagues, you will have to work a little harder to assemble a decent team. But if you have done your homework and put together a strategy, and a few other owners make some poor selections in the first few rounds, you will have more good players to select and should do fine.

As far as good lineups go, you should have read enough by now to know that if your first three picks are Emmitt Smith, Pete Stoyanovich, and Sterling Sharpe, you're on the way toward assembling a pretty good team. (If your fellow owners let you get away with that maneuver, do everything in your power to keep them together for a few more years while you siphon their money into your bank account.) Check out some more of my sample rosters in Appendix D, though, for more realistic, yet potentially successful, fantasy rosters for the 1993 season.

Patience is a precious commodity at the draft. So go for the safe picks in the first few rounds, putting together that core group I talked about earlier, and then gamble on those long shots you've been dying to draft. Do not—repeat, *do not*—waste your first or second pick on a long shot. Long shots will invariably drop down to the later rounds if your fellow owners have any kind of sense of how to play this game. Once you draft your core group of scorers from several roster categories, *then* play your hunches and take your chances.

The last and perhaps most important, yet most fickle, ingredient is luck. Of course, under my rules the luck of the draw determines the order of the draft. The number you pull from the deck of cards or out of the hat can mean the difference between your taking Emmitt Smith with the first pick or maybe implementing the Double-Down Theory with your eighth and ninth picks. Luck in the form of injuries can determine the success of a season, decimating a fantasy squad as quickly and efficiently as they can a real NFL squad. A sprained ankle here, a torn anterior cruciate ligament there, and the wheels can fly off your carefully crafted fantasy juggernaut faster than you can say, in Chris Berman's inimitable style, "He could go all the way!" As you can see, there are innumerable variables to forging a successful season, which is what makes fantasy football the exasperating, but extremely enjoyable, game that it is.

SIX

TEAM SCOUTING REPORTS

FANTASY FOOTBALL is a game based largely on the performances of individual players. But it is still worthwhile to examine a player's performance in the context of team performance, which is what this chapter is all about. The analysis in this chapter breaks down each NFL team into offensive and defensive squads. I will discuss the offensive players who had a significant impact upon their NFL squad's performance in 1992. The reports on the offensive players will focus on their performances in the real world of NFL football in 1992. For instance, when I refer to the points scored by the kickers on each team, I am talking about the real points scored in the NFL by them, not their fantasy scoring totals. I will discuss a player's fantasy football performance in the detailed scouting reports on the individual players that follow in the next chapter.

I have included in my analysis of the offensive players a breakdown of the yardage for scoring plays. At the end of each section discussing a team's offense I will point out to you the yardage of each score by that team's prominent scorers for the last three years. The charts will show the length of each touchdown pass thrown by quarterbacks, the length of each scoring run by running backs, the length of each touchdown catch by receivers, and the length of each field goal by kickers. This information should help you decide which players are the most valuable under almost any scoring system, not only mine.

This chapter also contains my analysis of each defensive team. But unlike my discussion of each team's offense, this analysis is from the fantasy point of view. (Those of you who have used my book in the past should be familiar with the information found here.) This breakdown will allow you to see how each NFL defensive team scored its fantasy points last season. I will also show you the fantasy scoring totals for each defense during the past four years. With any luck, these defenses will continue their scoring patterns in the upcoming year, and you will be ready to select the high-scoring defensive teams on Draft Day.

For those of you whose rules reward defensive teams based on the amount of points surrendered each week, I have included a breakdown of the scoring given up by each team on a weekly basis last season. While my rules do not award points on that basis, this analysis might come in handy for some of you readers in leagues with more complicated scoring rules.

Speaking of defensive teams, I noted earlier in the book that drafting your defensive team should not occupy a great deal of your predraft research. On the other hand, you obviously don't want to draft a defensive team that has little or no chance of putting some fantasy points on the board for you. For instance, without reading this section some uninformed fantasy owners might think that the Giants' defense is more valuable to have on their fantasy squad than, say, the Phoenix Cardinals' defense. Wrong, Meadowlands breath. Since the Giants' defense and special teams scored 12 points last season, while the Cards' scored 20, (one Phoenix player alone, defensive back Robert Massey, returned 3 interceptions for touchdowns in 1992), just the opposite is true. That's why I have compiled the following information for you smart owners who prepare for your fantasy draft with all this information at your fingertips.

AMERICAN CONFERENCE

BUFFALO BILLS

OFFENSE

Okay, everyone knows the Buffalo Bills turn into the Buffalo Bobs by the end of each of their Super Bowl performances. But, while they are now the only team to lose three straight Super Bowls, they are also only the second team in history to *appear* in three straight Super Bowls. They didn't get to the NFL's big Roman Numeral game for no reason. The main reason is that the Buffalo Bills have been an offensive juggernaut in recent years. They have gained over 5,000 yards in total offense each of the last three years, one of only four NFL teams to do so during that period. Those other teams are:

Houston
Miami
San Francisco

Buffalo entered 1992 seeking to gain 6,000 yards or more for the second consecutive year. The Bills fell short of that mark by a mere 107 yards. With a few more yards gained, they would have joined some very select company:

NFL Teams with Consecutive 6,000-Yard Seasons:

Three Years	1983–85 Chargers
Two Years	1988–89 Bengals
	1983–84 49ers
	1980–81 Chargers

The Chargers are the only NFL team to manage this feat three years in a row, 1983–85, and five in a row if you ignore 1982, a strike-shortened season. That's a remarkable achievement by Don Coryell's Chargers, also known as "Air Coryell," who, like Buffalo, didn't have a bad running game.

In addition to moving the ball up and down the field, Buffalo also puts it in the end zone. The Bills have finished first, second, and third in the league in scoring the last three years, scoring 428 points in 1990 and 458 in 1991, before dipping to a mere 381 points in 1992. Buffalo's secret of success may lie in the fact that they have been ranked third, seventh, first, and first in rushing yards per game over the last four years in the NFL. The NFL's equivalent of the fundamental, philosophical chicken-or-egg question is, Does the run set up the pass, or vice versa? There are strong opinions pro and con on this issue. Buffalo answers the question by doing both equally well. Now if they could just translate this offense into Super Bowl success.

Buffalo also was the classic quick starter in 1992, but then unfortunately faded fast. In 1992, after four games, the Bills had outscored opponents 153–45. Their average of 38 points per game in the first four weeks was the most since 1968, when three NFL teams averaged more than that total during the first month. But then Buffalo averaged only 13 points during the next four games, and 19 points per game the last 12 games of the 1992 season. They certainly could have used some of those early-season points during their showdown against the Cowboys.

Quarterback

While there are some grumblings about his being overrated after his disappointing performance in Super Bowl XXVII, the fact of the matter is that Jim Kelly has become one of the two or three best quarterbacks in the game during the last three NFL seasons. Even without the guidance of quarterback coach Ted Marchibroda, who assumed the head coaching job for the Indianapolis Colts, Kelly rolled on in 1992. He is a particularly potent fantasy weapon early in the season. Kelly threw 10 touchdown passes in the first six games of the 1990 season, 10 touchdown passes in the first three games of the 1991 season, and 10 touchdown passes in the first four games of the 1992 season. (The flip side of a hot start, of course, is a not-so-hot finish. Kelly threw only 14 touchdown passes in the last 10 games of the 1990 season, 23 touchdown passes in the last 13 games of the 1991 season, and 13 touchdown passes in the last 12 games of the 1992 season.) If he ever maintains his early-season pace for an entire year, every single-season passing mark is in jeopardy.

Running Back

Overall, Thurman Thomas continued to perform as one of the elite stars in the NFL in 1992. But upon closer inspection, 1992 was really an up-and-down season for this Pro Bowler. Thomas had an absolutely torrid start in 1992. He scored 4 touchdowns in the first week against the Rams, and 6 in the first two games. Thomas led all NFL players, including kickers, in scoring after three weeks of the season, and all touchdown scorers for the first six weeks of the season. But after that hot start, he cooled off dramatically, scoring only 2 touchdowns during Weeks Five through Fourteen. Thomas ended up with 12 touchdowns, 9 rushing and 3 receiving, first in the AFC and fifth in the NFL overall. He still piled up yardage as only Thurman Thomas can do, and he led the NFL in combined rushing and receiving for the fourth year in a row, breaking Jim Brown's record of three years. But he still disappointed somewhat in the all-important scoring category, especially after getting out of the scoring blocks so quickly.

Kenneth Davis played his supporting role to the hilt for the second straight season. In 1991, Marv Levy used Davis to spell Thomas in the second half of the season, allowing Thomas to be fresh for the playoffs. Levy had that luxury because the Bills won 8 of their first 9 games, opening a 3-game cushion over their closest opponents in the AFC East during that time. Buffalo could coast to the division title in the second half, with only the home-field advantage in question, so Davis played more. He had 39 carries for 223 yards and 1 touchdown in the first nine games of 1991, compared with 90 carries for 401 yards and 3 touchdowns in the last seven. (Thomas had only 112 carries for 545 yards and 2 touchdowns in the last seven games in 1991.) In 1992, Davis had only 71 carries for 286 yards and 1 touchdown in the first nine games. But starting with the critical Monday Night showdown in Miami in Week Eleven, in which he scored 2 touchdowns, Davis had 68 carries for 327 yards and 5 touchdowns in the last seven games. (Thomas had 142 carries for 726 yards during the last seven games, but scored only 3 touchdowns during that time.) Carwell Gardn ·, a 235-pound fullback type, played a supporting role, mostly in goal line situations, rushing for 166 yards and 2 touchdowns.

Receiver

Andre Reed is one of the best receivers in the NFL, and a First Echelon receiver in my Scouting Reports in the 1991 and 1992 editions of this book. He mirrored Thurman Thomas in 1992, piling up yardage (913 yards in 1992) but disappointing in the scoring column. In fact, Reed put up the lowest scoring total of his eight-year career, with only 3 touchdown receptions. And like Thomas, Reed also fell out of the First Echelon in this year's Scouting Reports.

James Lofton passed significant milestones in his great NFL career in 1992, touching up his Hall of Fame resume in the process. He became the all-time yardage leader for receivers in Week One, surpassing Steve Largent's record of 13,089 yards. He also tied Charley Joiner for third place on the all-time list for number of receptions, ending the season with 650 on the nose. He tied for the lead among the Bills' receivers in touchdown passes with Pete Metzelaars as well.

At tight end, Pete Metzelaars had an outstanding season. Filling in for the injured Keith McKeller, Metzelaars had 30 receptions for 298 yards, but most important, 6 touchdowns. This 11-year pro filled in so well at tight end, he passed his totals for receptions, yardage, and touchdowns from each of the prior two seasons after Week Three of 1992.

Kicker

Former Tampa Bay kicker Steve Christie adjusted to his new environment in the frigid climes of upstate New York very nicely in 1992, kicking 24 field goals. His 115 points were the most in his career. He kicked 4 field goals in Week Eleven's Monday Night showdown in Miami, one of them a 54-yarder, which tied him with three other kickers for the longest field goal in the NFL in 1992. He also proved his postseason mettle by booting 8 field goals during the Bills' trip through the playoffs to the Super Bowl, including the field goal to win the game in Buffalo's historic 32-point comeback against Houston in the playoffs. While the ghost of Scott Norwood's Super Bowl XXV miss against the Giants still haunts the franchise, you can't blame Christie.

Yardage Breakdown on Scoring Plays—1990

Touchdowns	1–10	11–20	21–30	31–40	41–50	+50	Total
Kelly	8	10	1	1	1	3	24
T. Thomas	7	2	1			1	11
K. Davis	3	1					4
Reed	2	4		1		1	8
Lofton	1				1	2	4

Field Goals	11–20	21–30	31–40	41–50	+50	Total
Norwood		9	5	6		20

Yardage Breakdown on Scoring Plays—1991

Touchdowns	1–10	11–20	21–30	31–40	41–50	+50	Total
Kelly	10	9	5	2	2	5	33
T. Thomas	4	3					7
K. Davis	3					1	4
Reed	4	2	3			1	10
Lofton	1	2	1		1	3	8

Field Goals	11–20	21–30	31–40	41–50	+50	Total
Norwood	1	7	3	6	1	18

Yardage Breakdown on Scoring Plays—1992

Touchdowns	1–10	11–20	21–30	31–40	41–50	+50	Total
Kelly	8	6	4		2	3	23
T. Thomas	7	2					9
K. Davis	5					1	6
Reed		2			1		3
Lofton		2	3		1		6
Metzelaars	4		1			1	6

Field Goals	11–20	21–30	31–40	41–50	+50	Total
Christie	2	10	4	5	3	24

DEFENSE

The Bills' defense has been a consistent fantasy scoring unit over the last three years, ranking as high as third but never ranking lower than 13th during this stretch. This NFL defense doesn't dominate (its shutout in Week Three against the Colts was the Bills' first regular-season shutout since Week Eleven of the 1990 season against another AFC powerhouse, the New England Patriots), but it gets the job done. You can do a lot worse on Draft Day 1993. DT scores for 1992:

23-yard interception return
82-yard interception return
18-yard fumble return
Safety—running back tackled in end zone

Fantasy Rankings: 1992—20 points (Tied for 13th)
1991—24 points (Tied for 7th)
1990—30 points (3rd)
1989—12 points (Tied for 21st)

Past Performance Key: Buffalo scored 18 of its 20 defensive fantasy points in the first four weeks of the 1992 season.

1992 DT Game Summaries:

Shutouts	One
0–7 Points	Three
8–14 Points	One
15–21 Points	Seven
Over 21 Points	Four

CINCINNATI BENGALS

OFFENSE

The Bengals, under new head coach David Shula, got off to a good start, with victories in their first two games of the season. But then they went into a tailspin, as the adrenaline boost of a new system wore off and the reality of their lack of talent, amply demonstrated by their sorry 1991 performance, hit the team. It may be hard to believe, but as recently as 1988, the Bengals were the AFC champions, with an offense second to none. Cincinnati scored a whopping 448 points in 1988, and led the NFL in total yards, with 6,057. As noted above, the 1988–89 Bengals were one of three teams in NFL history to post consecutive seasons of 6,000 or more total yards. But then, the deluge. Cincinnati has declined offensively each year since 1989, to the point where the team could muster just 3,919 yards of total offense, third-lowest total in the NFL, and just 274 points in 1992. The Bengals have a long way to go to recapture the glory days of the franchise offensively, but don't have to look deep into the past to remember.

Quarterback

Boomer Esiason may not have realized it, but he was living on borrowed time as the starting quarterback for the Bengals in 1992. He should have seen it coming when the Bengals shocked most NFL draftniks by selecting Houston's David Klingler with their first-round pick in the 1992 draft. After Boomer's disappointing performance for the first part of the season, he was benched in Week Thirteen for David Klingler. Head coach David Shula, eager to institute his own regime in Cincinnati, may really have had no choice. Boomer had his lowest completion total (144), yardage total (1,407), and touchdown total (11) since 1984, his first year in the league. Perhaps even more tellingly, his yardage average per attempt had dropped from 9.21 in 1988 to 7.75 in 1989, 7.54 in 1990, and 6.98 in 1991. In 1992, it hit rock bottom, having fallen to 5.08 yards per attempt by the time he was benched for Klingler. The last straw came in Week Twelve, when Boomer completed 12 passes for only 64 yards in a 19–13 loss against Detroit. The Bengals were going nowhere as far as any playoff considerations were concerned, anyway, so they figured, why not see what the highly touted rookie can do. Klingler completed 47 of 98 passes for 530 yards and 3 touchdowns in his five-week stint at the end of the season. Even without Boomer's trade to the Jets in the offseason, the fans have witnessed the future at the quarterback position in Cincinnati, and his name is David Klingler.

Running Back

Harold Green emerged as a fine NFL back in his third year in the league, from a yardage-production point of view. He rushed 265 times for 1,170 yards, the most for a Bengal since 1989. But Green did not score much, posting only 2 rushing touchdowns for his efforts. Derrick Fenner was the scoring leader in the Bengals' backfield, rushing for 500 yards and 7 touchdowns in 1992. Fenner scored 2 touchdowns in the last game of the season against the Colts, perhaps cementing his role as the designated scorer for the Bengals at the goal line in 1993.

Receiver

The leader of the Bengals' receiving corps, Eddie Brown, went down in the preseason with a neck injury and missed all of 1992 on injured reserve. His presence was sorely missed, as no Bengal receiver had more than 35 receptions or accumulated more than 408 yards. This ranks with the league's worst performance of the year for a group of wide receivers:

Team Name	Number of Receptions by Leading Wide Receiver
Seattle	27 (Tommy Kane)
Cincinnati	35 (Tim McGee)
Kansas City	42 (J. J. Birden)

Team Name	Number of Yards by Leading Wide Receiver
Seattle	369 (Tommy Kane)
Cincinnati	408 (Tim McGee)
NY Giants	610 (Ed McCaffrey)

Tim McGee recovered from a slow start to lead Bengals receivers in receptions and yards, as dubious as that distinction might be, given the chart you've just read. He tied with Jeff Query for the team lead in touchdown receptions, with only 3. Query came on strong in the second half of the 1992 season after David Klingler was promoted to the starting job at quarterback. He scored all 3 of his touchdowns in the last four weeks of the season, hooking up with Klingler on 2 of his 3 scoring passes, one of them an 83-yard bonus bomb against the Chargers in Week Fifteen. At tight end, Rodney Holman had his worst season since 1984, with only 26 receptions for 266 yards, and 2 touchdowns, very un-Holmanlike numbers. Overall, Cincinnati passed for only 1,943 yards, its fewest number of net passing yards since the 1970 season. This group will suffer further in the absence of free agents McGee, who signed with the Washington Redskins, and Holman, who signed with Detroit in the offseason.

Kicker
Jim Breech, like Ol' Man River, just keeps rolling along, albeit in not very spectacular fashion. He has been the Bengals' kicker almost without interruption since he signed with the team as a free agent on November 25, 1980. (He did not play with the team in the 1987 replacement games.) He has scored 100 or more points in a season just four times in his 14-year career, and has not reached the 100-point mark since 1986. Still, he became the NFL's 11th player to reach 1,200 career points in 1992, and ended the season with 1,246 points, 10th best on the NFL's all-time list. Breech kicked 19 field goals in 1992, and scored 88 points total. Breech doesn't have the real strong leg like the new breed of NFL kickers, players like Chip Lohmiller and Pete Stoyanovich, and their ancestors, like Morten Andersen and Nick Lowery. He belongs to the old school of NFL kicker, like Gary Anderson of the Steelers and Matt Bahr of the Giants, who embody NFL longevity and remain highly effective NFL performers.

Yardage Breakdown on Scoring Plays—1990

Touchdowns	1–10	11–20	21–30	31–40	41–50	+50	Total
Esiason	10	4	6		3	1	24
E. Brown	3	1	3		2		9

Field Goals	11–20	21–30	31–40	41–50	+50	Total
Breech	1	6	5	5		17

Yardage Breakdown on Scoring Plays—1991

Touchdowns	1–10	11–20	21–30	31–40	41–50	+50	Total
Esiason	1	5	2	2	2	1	13
E. Brown		2		1			3
McGee		1	1		1	1	4

Field Goals	11–20	21–30	31–40	41–50	+50	Total
Breech	1	8	8	6		23

Yardage Breakdown on Scoring Plays—1992

Touchdowns	1–10	11–20	21–30	31–40	41–50	+50	Total
Esiason	4	2	4	1			11
Klingler	1		1			1	3
Fenner	4	2		1			7
McGee			3				3

Field Goals	11–20	21–30	31–40	41–50	+50	Total
Breech	2	6	8	3		19

DEFENSE

The Bengals made great strides defensively under new head coach David Shula from a fantasy perspective in 1992. The Bengals' defense posted more fantasy points in the first three weeks of the 1992 season that it did in all of 1991. Then, like the offense, reality set in and the defense only posted a single fantasy score the rest of the way. Carl

Pickens, the Bengals' second-round pick in the 1992 NFL draft, may prove to be an exceptional punt returner, based on his performance last season. But by any measure this fantasy defense should not be selected early in the draft. DT scores in 1992:

75-yard fumble return

22-yard fumble return

95-yard punt return

66-yard interception return

Fantasy Rankings: 1992—24 points (Tied for 11th)

1991—14 points (Tied for 15th)

1990—28 points (Tied for 4th)

1989—18 points (Tied for 15th)

Past Performance Key: The Cincinnati defense has not posted a shutout since the 13th game of the 1989 season, against the Cleveland Browns.

1992 DT Game Summaries:

Shutouts	None
0–7 Points	One
8–14 Points	Two
15–21 Points	Six
Over 21 Points	Seven

CLEVELAND BROWNS

OFFENSE

The Browns' offense was a major disappointment once again in 1992. But Browns fans might be used to that by now. The Browns have not scored 400 points or more in a season since 1966, when Leroy Kelly and Paul Warfield were tearing up the NFL. More recently, the Browns have not scored 300 points in a season since 1989. Injuries decimated the Browns' quarterbacks in 1992, and what little potential firepower the team's offense had went down with those injuries. Only a tremendous performance by the Browns' defense kept Cleveland competitive on the field.

Quarterback

The Cleveland quarterback situation epitomized what was a rough year all around for quarterbacks in the NFL in 1992. ("Quarterbacks and Their Injuries" could definitely have been a show on "Oprah Winfrey" or "Donahue" last year). First Kosar went down in the Browns' Monday Night loss to the Dolphins in Week Two. Then his replacement, Todd Philcox, promptly broke his thumb (but threw 3 touchdowns—2 of them *after* breaking his thumb) in Cleveland's win against the Raiders in Week Three. The broken thumb sidelined Philcox, so journeyman Mike Tomczak, who had been welcomed into the Browns' fold after Kosar's injury, held the fort capably until Philcox, then Kosar, returned. But a healthy Kosar (or Philcox, for that matter) is still not the answer to the Browns' lack of scoring, as the team's poor scoring totals in recent years demonstrate.

Running Back

Kevin Mack missed the first four weeks of the 1992 season due to injury. After that, he returned to form as the Browns' designated scorer, and scored 6 touchdowns, all of them on the ground and from close in (Mack's longest touchdown run in 1992 was 7 yards). "Touchdown" Tommy Vardell, much ballyhooed as the Browns' first pick in the 1992 NFL draft, became Sit-Down Tommy in goal line situations after a lackluster early-season start in place of the injured Mack. All was not lost, as he ended up rushing for 369 yards, but he scored zero touchdowns. James Brooks was an expensive ($850,000) disappointment as a Plan B pickup, and was released during the fifth week of the season. Eric Metcalf had a fabulous game in Week Three, scoring 4 touchdowns, 3 of them on passes, and 2 of those from 69 and 63 yards. Metcalf ended the season with 7 touchdowns, reclaiming his title as one of the best all-purpose backs in the NFL.

Receiver

Not surprisingly, Cleveland's receivers generally had an off year. The Browns' crew (Eric Metcalf doesn't count—he's a running back) only scored 10 touchdowns the entire season, the fourth-lowest mark for receivers in the league. Michael Jackson, in the absence of free agent Webster Slaughter, who signed with Houston, emerged as a budding NFL star, scoring 7 touchdowns, which tied Metcalf for the team lead. (He must be sick of the "Gloved One" references by now, don't you think?) Now if he could just work on getting a capable quarterback, or a healthy one, to throw the ball to him.

Kicker

Matt "Smoky" Stover had a chance to grab the ring of NFL immortality last season. He made 4 field goals in Week Eight, but missed 3 others in the same contest. He could have tied the NFL record for most field goals in one game with a perfect performance. Too bad he blew it, because that might have been the only way the otherwise mediocre Stover could ever get into the Pro Football Hall of Fame. Stover scored only 92 points in 1992, reminding no one in Cleveland of Lou "The Toe" Groza in the process.

Yardage Breakdown on Scoring Plays—1990

Touchdowns	1–10	11–20	21–30	31–40	41–50	+50	Total
Kosar	3	4	1	1	1		10
Mack	5						5
Slaughter		3			1		4

Field Goals	11–20	21–30	31–40	41–50	+50	Total
Kauric		6	4	4		14

Yardage Breakdown on Scoring Plays—1991

Touchdowns	1–10	11–20	21–30	31–40	41–50	+50	Total
Kosar	8	3	2	1		4	18
Mack	7					1	8
Slaughter		2				1	3

Field Goals	11–20	21–30	31–40	41–50	+50	Total
Stover	1	6	4	4	1	16

Yardage Breakdown on Scoring Plays—1992

Touchdowns	1–10	11–20	21–30	31–40	41–50	+50	Total
Kosar	5		1	1		1	8
Mack	6						6
Jackson	1		2	1	2	1	7

Field Goals	11–20	21–30	31–40	41–50	+50	Total
Stover	2	12	4	2	1	21

DEFENSE

Most teams throughout NFL history are better either on offense or on defense. Rarely is an NFL team great, or even very good, on both sides of the ball. For example, since the AFL and NFL merged in 1970, only five teams have led their conferences in both points scored and fewest points allowed, and only one team, the 1972 Miami Dolphins, led the whole NFL in both categories. (And they went undefeated.) It could be argued that one reason for this situation is the background of the respective head coaches, who were either offensive or defensive specialists on their way up the coaching ladder. A team's outlook usually is a reflection of its head coach's orientation or philosophy. Cleveland is no exception to this theory. Coach Bill Belichick, and two of his three predecessors, Bud Carson and Marty Schottenheimer, were all defensive coordinators prior to assuming the head coaching spot in Cleveland. It is no accident that the Browns' defense has carried their offense through difficult times over the last four years. The Cleveland defense held its opponents under 300 points each season from 1987 to 89 and in 1991 and 92. (The 1990 season admittedly was a disaster, with the defense giving up 462 points. But that's why Belichick is the head coach, and not the aforementioned Carson or his replacement, Jim Shofner, a former offensive coordinator.) On the other hand, the offense has averaged only 282 points per season during the last four years, so the defense had to be good.

Cleveland had another solid fantasy season in 1992. In the first edition of my book, the Browns were ranked in the First Echelon, having come off a 42-point effort in 1989. With defensive guru Bill Belichick's system solidly entrenched, the Browns' defense is back as a consistent fantasy scorer. Forget about Cleveland's won-lost record when contemplating your fantasy draft. Look for the Junkyard Dawgs to howl once again in 1993. DT scores for 1992:

> 32-yard fumble return
> 73-yard fumble return
> 92-yard interception return
> 75-yard punt return
> Fumble recovered in end zone for touchdown

Fantasy Rankings: 1992—30 points (Tied for 7th)
1991—32 points (Tied for 4th)
1990—24 points (Tied for 8th)
1989—42 points (2nd)

Past Performance Key: Cleveland's four-year fantasy average of 32 points per season is second in the league during that time.

1992 DT Game Summaries:

Shutouts	None
1–7 Points	One
8–14 Points	Six
15–21 Points	Five
Over 21 Points	Four

DENVER BRONCOS

OFFENSE

The Broncos offense is deceptively effective, as a look at the numbers over the years show. Denver is certainly not a great scoring machine. Its offense has ranked no higher than 12th in the league in any of the last three seasons. Looking back further, Denver has not led the NFL, or even its own division, in scoring since 1973. Denver has never posted 400 points in any season in franchise history, dating back to 1960, a mark in futility matched by only five other NFL franchises. (Then again, until this season, Denver had never been shut out twice in one season.) Never an offensive force, Denver seems to score just enough to win.

On the other hand, the Denver offense is one of the most consistent from a yardage point of view. Going into the 1992 season, Denver had accumulated at least 5,000 yards of offense every year since 1985, a seven-year streak that was the fourth longest in the NFL. The other streaks, not counting strike-shortened 1982, were:

San Francisco	1979–present
Washington	1981–present
Miami	1981–present

(Since these respective streaks began, the four teams listed had made 12 Super Bowl appearances among them prior to 1992, so there must be something to racking up the yardage consistently each season.) Unfortunately, the Broncos' 5,000-yard streak came to an end in 1992 (as did Washington's). It ended primarily because of the shoulder injury to John Elway that forced him to miss five of the last six games of the season. Elway usually contributed at least 3,000 yards to the Broncos' offense each year, but his seven-year streak of consecutive-3,000-yard seasons, second-best in NFL history (tying him with Joe Montana for that honor), came to an end in 1992. The offense could lag with defensive coach Wade Phillips replacing Dan Reeves as head coach. Elway may not have cared for Reeves, but Danny was an offensive wizard.

Quarterback

Bill Clinton may have dubbed himself "The Comeback Kid" after his performance in the New Hampshire primary in 1992 on his way to the White House, but the NFL's version of the Comeback Kid, John Elway, locked up that title a long time ago. Elway has brought the Broncos from behind in the fourth quarter 31 times in his 10-year career, 30 times to victory and once to a tie. And, when healthy, he continued to work his last-minute magic in 1992, leading the Broncos to victory in the fourth quarter three times in 1992, against the Raiders in Week One, the Chiefs in Week Five, and the Oilers in Week Seven, before a bum shoulder virtually ended his season. In his abbreviated season, Elway threw for 2,242 yards and 10 touchdowns. He also managed to score 2 rushing touchdowns, to extend his streak to seven years in which he has scored at least 1 rushing touchdown and giving him a career total of 22. Reserve quarterback Tommy Maddox, the Broncos' first-round pick and the 25th pick overall in the 1992 draft, became the youngest quarterback to throw a pass in the NFL since 1946. In doing so he demonstrated why he may be the quarterback of the future, but not of the present. During his short stint as Elway's replacement in the latter stages of the 1992 season, he led the Broncos to consecutive losses to the Raiders and the Seahawks, two of the worst teams in football in 1992.

Running Back

The Broncos running game continued to lag behind the passing game in 1992. Denver's backs rushed for 94 yards per game during the 1992 season, fourth-lowest in the league, and the Broncos' record was 8–8. This continued a trend established by the team's offense in prior years:

1992	94 yards per game	8–8 record	no playoffs
1991	126 yards per game	12–4 record	conference finals
1990	117 yards per game	5–11 record	no playoffs
1989	131 yards per game	11–5 record	Super Bowl
1988	113 yards per game	8–8 record	no playoffs
1987	131 yards per game	10–4–1 record	Super Bowl
1986	104 yards per game	11–5 record	Super Bowl

With the exception of the 1986 season, the recent pattern is clear. If the Broncos average 125 to 130 yards rushing per game, they produce a superior record. But, how does this compare to the rushing average per game for the Super Bowl champions during the same period of time?

1992	Dallas	132.5 yards per game
1991	Washington	128 yards per game
1990	NY Giants	128 yards per game
1989	San Francisco	122 yards per game
1988	San Francisco	157 yards per game
1987	Washington	140 yards per game
1986	NY Giants	140 yards per game

With the exception of the 1989 San Francisco team, every Super Bowl winner since 1986 has averaged at least 128 yards per game rushing during the regular season. There's one vote for the importance of the running game.

On an individual level, no Denver back has stepped up to fill Bobby Humphrey's shoes consistantly since the end of the 1990 season. Gaston Green rushed for 1,037 yards in 1991, the third straight year a Denver back had rushed for more than 1,000 yards. However, Green dropped to only 648 yards in 1992, and just 2 touchdowns. Greg Lewis rushed for only 268 yards, and Reggie Rivers chipped in with only 282. One of new head coach Wade Phillips's most urgent responsibilities will be to find a consistent rushing game for the Broncos. Signing free agent running back Rod Bernstine from division-rival San Diego is a strong step in the right direction.

Receivers

The Three Amigos are a thing of the past. In fact, the group is down to just one Amigo due to free agency movement. Mark Jackson had his best year since 1990 in terms of receptions and yardage, and had the most touchdown passes of his career. He caught 48 passes for 745 yards and posted 8 touchdown receptions in 1992. This was the highest touchdown total for a Bronco receiver since Steve Watson scored on 13 receptions in 1981. Only seven NFL teams did not have a player with 7 or more touchdown passes in a season from 1989 to 1992. But Jackson, a free agent, followed his former coach Dan Reeves to New York, signing with the Giants. Vance Johnson caught only 24 passes, his second year in a row with fewer than thirty receptions after averaging more than 53 receptions during the 1985–90 seasons. His 2 touchdowns in 1992 was his lowest total since 1986. Shannon Sharpe submitted his application for Amigohood with one of the best seasons for a tight end in the league. He had a career year in 1992, with career highs in receptions (53), yards (640), and touchdowns (2). Arthur Marshall had a solid rookie year, with 26 receptions for 493 yards, a 19-yard average, and one touchdown, an 80-yarder.

Kicker

David Treadwell was a steady kicker during the regular season, but still had his lowest point total in his four seasons in the league. He kicked 20 of 24 field goals and scored a total of 88 points in 1992. His accuracy is no problem, (an 83 percent field goal percentage, and no missed extra points), but he also had the lowest number of field goal attempts and extra points of his career.

Yardage Breakdown on Scoring Plays—1990

Touchdowns	1–10	11–20	21–30	31–40	41–50	+50	Total
Elway	7	3	4	0	0	1	15

Field Goals	11–20	21–30	31–40	41–50	+50	Total
Treadwell	1	13	3	8	0	25

Yardage Breakdown on Scoring Plays—1991

Touchdowns	1–10	11–20	21–30	31–40	41–50	+50	Total
Elway	6		4			3	13
G. Green	1	1				2	4
V. Johnson	2		1				3

Field Goals	11–20	21–30	31–40	41–50	+50	Total
Treadwell	6	10	8	3		27

Yardage Breakdown on Scoring Plays—1992

Touchdowns	1–10	11–20	21–30	31–40	41–50	+50	Total
Elway		2	2	3	1	2	10
G. Green	1					1	2
Lewis	4						4
M. Jackson	1	1	2	2	1	1	8

Field Goals	11–20	21–30	31–40	41–50	+50	Total
Treadwell	2	9	5	4		20

DEFENSE

This defense did a great job in the real world of the NFL in 1991, but slipped in 1992. John Elway led the Broncos to 12 regular-season victories with only the 12th-highest point total in the league in 1991. This was largely because the Denver defense gave up only 235 points, the third-lowest total in the league that season. In 1992, the defense gave up 329 points, and not surprisingly, the Broncos only posted an

8–8 record. The Broncos, without a talented return man, are a middle-of-the-road fantasy defense, not having achieved a higher ranking than 10th over the last three seasons. Don't saddle the Broncos too early on Draft Day. DT scores for 1992:

> 54-yard fumble return
> 46-yard interception return

Fantasy Rankings: 1992—12 points (Tied for 24th)
1991—18 points (Tied for 10th)
1990—18 points (Tied for 12th)
1989—26 points (Tied for 8th)

Past Performance Key: Denver's fantasy total of 12 points in 1992 was its lowest in four years.

1992 DT Game Summaries:

Shutouts	One
1–7 Points	One
8–14 Points	Three
15–21 Points	Four
Over 21 Points	Seven

HOUSTON OILERS

OFFENSE

In the final analysis, Houston had a disappointing year in 1992. Questions abound. Did opponents finally figure out how to defense the Houston version of the run-and-shoot? Is the run-and-shoot offense just a gimmick, an offense incapable of winning championships in the NFL? Or is Coach Jack Pardee, he of the lifetime 44–46 regular-season coaching record in the NFL prior to assuming the reins at Houston, another example of the Peter Principle, a person who has risen to his level of incompetence? Certainly, he has been at least a modest success at Houston. Prior to his arrival in 1990, Houston had never been the AFC Central Division champ, as it was in 1991. In fact, Houston had not been a division winner since 1967, before the NFL-AFL merger in 1970. But the Oilers were expected to move to a higher level in 1992 and instead took a step back. Their failure to repeat as division champs and to move up in the NFL ranks to the level of a genuine Super Bowl contender raises concerns about their ability to reach that level in 1993—or at all, for that matter—under Pardee. Houston's historic collapse in the playoffs against Buffalo may have been the last straw. As the Moon begins to set in Houston, you wonder how clearly Coach

Pardee hears the wolves howling, especially with new defensive coach Buddy Ryan looking over his shoulder.

Quarterback

Warren Moon became professional football's all-time leader in passing yardage in Week Seven, breaking the record of 50,535 yards set by Ron Lancaster, who played from 1960 to 1978 in the Canadian Football League. He also became one of the all-time great NFL punching bags, as he courageously tried to lead the Oilers to success in 1992 behind the skimpy "protection" afforded a quarterback in the run-and-shoot offense. (Run-and-shoot quarterbacks might as well wear targets instead of numbers on their jerseys, for all the protection they receive in that offensive scheme.) Moon was knocked out of games three weeks in a row in mid-season, the last time with a broken shoulder, suffered in Week Eleven against the Vikings and sidelining him until the last week of the season. These injuries resulted in Moon's throwing only 18 touchdown passes in 1992, his lowest total since 1988. "Commander" Cody Carlson proved an able backup for him, but to paraphrase Treasury Secretary Lloyd Bentsen, himself a Texan, Carlson is no Warren Moon—as, indeed, few quarterbacks in football history have been.

Running Back

Houston's version of the run-and-shoot offense uses the running game as a supplement to its passing game, which is its main weapon in moving the ball up and down the field. In addition, the Oilers' offense uses its receivers almost as running backs when it moves toward the goal line. (Of the Oilers' touchdown passes, 43 have been from 10 yards or under during the past three years, the most in the league.) Under these circumstances, you would expect the Houston running backs to play second fiddle to the passing game, especially at the goal line. This was not true in Lorenzo White's case in 1992. White had an excellent year, rushing for 1,226 yards and scoring 7 rushing touchdowns. His rushing-yardage total in 1992 was the highest in his five-year career, and the most by an Oiler since Earl Campbell rushed for 1,301 yards in 1983. He also caught 57 passes for 641 yards and 1 touchdown. White's total of combined yards from scrimmage was 1,867, third-highest in the AFC behind Barry Foster and Thurman Thomas.

Receiver

It almost seemed like bringing the proverbial coals to Newcastle when the Oilers signed talented wide receiver Webster Slaughter from Cleveland as one of the "Jackson Four" free agents prior to Week Four of the 1992 season. The Oilers already had Haywood Jeffires, Ernest Givins, and Curtis Duncan. But you can never have enough talented players in the NFL. Slaughter almost instantly fit into the fine receiving corps in Houston, scoring 4 touchdowns on only 39 receptions and piling up 486 yards. His 12.5 yards per catch led the team in 1992. Ernest Givins caught 67 passes for 787 yards, and led the team with 10 touchdown passes. Haywood Jeffires did not become the first NFL receiver to record 100 receptions in a season twice, but did come close, leading the team with 90 receptions, for a total of 913 yards. Curtis Duncan caught 82 passes for 954 yards, the leading yardage total on the team in 1992, but caught only 1 touchdown pass.

Kicker

Al Del Greco made a clutch field goal to beat Kansas City in overtime in Week Three. But things changed for him later in the season. He missed the winning kick, a 39-yard attempt, with six seconds left against Pittsburgh in Week Nine, and missed a 41-yarder with 1:49 left against the Dolphins in Week Twelve, which would have put the Oilers ahead by 3 points. (The Oilers lost the game when Pete Stoyanovich made a 52-yard field goal with two seconds remaining in the game.) These performances were reminiscent of his clutch pooch against Denver in the 1991 playoffs, and may have been a portent of things to come for the Oilers in the playoffs. Overall, Del Greco proved a major disappointment in the scoring department in 1992. Despite Houston's high-powered offense and the fact that he kicks at home indoors, Del Greco still managed to finish with only 104 points, sixth-best among AFC kickers and 10th-best in the league overall.

Yardage Breakdown on Scoring Plays—1990

Touchdowns	1–10	11–20	21–30	31–40	41–50	+ 50	Total
Moon	14	6	4	5	2	2	33
L. White	8						8
Givins	5	2	1	0	0	1	9
Jeffires	2	2	0	1	1	2	8

Field Goals	11–20	21–30	31–40	41–50	+ 50	Total
Zendejas		3	2	2		7

Yardage Breakdown on Scoring Plays—1991

Touchdowns	1–10	11–20	21–30	31–40	41–50	+50	Total
Moon	13	2	3	4		1	23
White	4						4
Givins	3	1	1				5
Jeffires	5	1	1				7

Field Goals	11–20	21–30	31–40	41–50	+50	Total
Del Greco	1	4	2	2	1	10

Yardage Breakdown on Scoring Plays—1992

Touchdowns	1–10	11–20	21–30	31–40	41–50	+50	Total
Moon	11	3	3			1	18
White	7						7
Givins	6	2	2				10
Jeffires	7	2					9

Field Goals	11–20	21–30	31–40	41–50	+50	Total
Del Greco	4	9	3	4	1	21

DEFENSE

Many people would argue that fantasy stats don't relate to the results of the real NFL game. But look at the results. The top six fantasy scorers in 1992 were, in descending order, Kansas City, Minnesota, New England, New Orleans, Dallas, and Philadelphia. The only ringer in that bunch is New England. The rest were all playoff teams in 1992, with Dallas the NFL champ. The bottom six teams were the Raiders, Chicago, Denver, Giants, San Diego, and, last and certainly least, Seattle. Their combined record in 1992 was 39–57, even with San Diego's 11–5 record included. Houston's fantasy scores dipped in 1992, from 36 points, good for third place among fantasy defensive teams in 1991, to 26 points, good for only 10th place. Not surprisingly, its record dipped, too, from 11–5 in 1991 to 10–6 in 1992. Despite this dip in scoring, the Houston defense should continue to be a solid fantasy defense in 1993. DT scores for 1992:

15-yard fumble return
Safety—quarterback ran out of end zone
8-yard fumble return
10-yard fumble return
26-yard interception return

Fantasy Rankings: 1992—26 points (10th)
1991—36 points (3rd)
1990—14 points (Tied for 18th)
1989—16 points (18th)

Past Performance Key: Houston's defense had not given up more than 29 points in a game during the 1992 season before its crushing 41–38 loss to Buffalo in the playoffs.

1992 DT Game Summaries:

Shutouts	One
1–7 Points	Two
8–14 Points	Four
15–21 Points	Five
Over 21 Points	Four

INDIANAPOLIS COLTS

OFFENSE

Sophomore head coach (and offensive guru) Ted Marchibroda made some progress in improving the Colts offense in 1992. The Colts went from the worst offense in 1991 to the fifth-worst in the league in 1992. In fact, the Colts' total of 143 points in 1991 was not only the lowest in the league, but the lowest since the NFL began a 16-game schedule in 1978. Even more interesting was the fact that there were three NFL teams with fewer than 200 points in 1991. Aside from the Patriots' total of 181 points in 1990, *no* NFL team prior to 1991 had scored fewer than 200 points in a season since the NFL began its 16-game schedule. Why this sudden dip in production in the last three seasons? Not being a great believer in coincidences, I think there were other factors at work.

Going into the 1991 season, some NFL observers predicted that many NFL teams would copy the success of the Giants against the Bills in Super Bowl XXV, by gearing their offenses to the running game. Well, that prediction just didn't fly, because a close look at the statistics shows that the coaches didn't let the air out of the ball. Thirteen of the 28 NFL teams had more rushing attempts than passing attempts in 1990. Even though the Giants beat the Bills in the Super Bowl, the members of the coaching fraternity must have been more impressed with the losers' passing attack, because only seven teams rushed more times than they passed in 1991. In 1992, the pendulum swung back, with 11 teams running more often than they passed.

But maybe the Giants were on to something. The three teams mentioned above who scored fewer than 200 points in 1991 were Indianapolis, Tampa Bay, and Phoenix. All three teams had 100 more passes than rushing attempts in 1991. The combined records of NFL teams with 100 more passes than rushes in 1991 was 40–88. On the other hand, teams that rushed more than they passed all posted winning records. In 1992, Seattle passed 74 more times than it ran on its way to a 2–14 record. The combined records of NFL teams with 100 more passes than rushes in 1992 was 55–57. Only three of the 11 teams with more rushes than passes posted losing records in 1992. So it would seem that there is more than a kernel of truth in the old saying that a good running game goes a long way toward ensuring success in the NFL.

Indianapolis maintained its pass/rush ratio at the level of at least 100 more passes than rushes in 1992, but, with the benefit of a generous schedule, won eight more games in 1992 than in 1991. This eight-game swing ties the best jump in NFL history. Interestingly enough, the other team to accomplish this swing was the 1975 Baltimore Colts, coached by none other than the same Ted Marchibroda. The Baltimore version of the Colts posted a combined 21–7 record in the two seasons after its big improvement, so don't be surprised if the Indianapolis version continues to do well under Marchibroda.

Quarterback
When you look up the term "hard luck" in the dictionary, you may find Jeff George's picture there illustrating the definition. Since being selected with the first pick in the NFL draft in 1990, George has been frequently injured and has missed games in two of his three NFL campaigns. After missing the first four weeks in 1992 with a strained ligament in his right thumb, injured during preseason, George went down with a broken wrist in Week Eleven. George continues to display flashes of brilliance when healthy. Overall in 1992, George completed 167 of 306 passes for 1,963 yards and 7 touchdowns. But the jury of NFL fans still awaits a full season's performance.

Running Back
This area became a black hole that you don't need the Hubble telescope to spot in the wake of the departure of Eric Dickerson. The Colts' 1,169

yards rushing in 1991 was the league low, and the lowest since the Falcons rushed for only 1,155 yards in 1989. The Colts' total of 1,102 yards in 1992 was even worse, and again the league low. On an individual level, the Colts' leading rusher was Anthony Johnson, with only 592 yards. He had the fifth-lowest total for a rushing leader of any team in the NFL in 1992:

Team Name	Number of Yards by Leading Running Back
Atlanta	363 (Steve Broussard)
New England	451 (Jon Vaughn)
Cleveland	543 (Kevin Mack)
New Orleans	565 (Vaughn Dunbar)
Indianapolis	592 (Anthony Johnson)

Johnson also caught 49 passes for 517 yards, and scored 3 touchdown passes, but no touchdowns on the ground. On the other hand, Johnson's rookie running mate, Rodney Culver, had an impressive scoring year for the Colts, racking up 7 rushing touchdowns and 9 touchdowns overall, while rushing for only 321 yards. This touchdown total was the best for a Colts back since Dickerson's 14 in 1988.

Receiver

Since the Colts have reached the legal limit of black holes allowed by NFL rules on any given team, let's just say that this bunch could have all the talent in the world and you'd never know it. Reggie Langhorne ended up as the Colts' leading receiver in 1992, posting career-high numbers in receptions (65) and yardage (811), but scoring only 1 touchdown, Bill Brooks caught 44 passes for 468 yards but only 1 touchdown, the lowest total of his seven-year career. Clarence Verdin returned 2 punts for touchdowns in 1992, to tie for the league lead, but was used sparingly as a receiver. Tight end Kerry Cash jumped from 1 reception in his rookie season of 1991 to 43 receptions for 521 yards and 3 touchdown passes in 1992.

Kicker

Dean Biasucci continued his career decline in 1992. After missing 11 field goals in 1991, he botched 13 of them in 1992. His total of 72 points in 1992 barely surpassed his total of 59 in 1991. Once one of the premier kickers in the game, Biasucci seems to have lost his touch.

Yardage Breakdown on Scoring Plays—1990

Touchdowns	1–10	11–20	21–30	31–40	41–50	+50	Total
George	5	4	3	0	2	2	16

Field Goals	11–20	21–30	31–40	41–50	+50	Total
Biasucci	2	4	7	2	2	17

Yardage Breakdown on Scoring Plays—1991

Touchdowns	1–10	11–20	21–30	31–40	41–50	+50	Total
George	6	2	1		1		10
Brooks	3		1				4

Field Goals	11–20	21–30	31–40	41–50	+50	Total
Biasucci	2	4	4	3	2	15

Yardage Breakdown on Scoring Plays—1992

Touchdowns	1–10	11–20	21–30	31–40	41–50	+50	Total
George	3	1	1	1		1	7
Culver	6			1			7

Field Goals	11–20	21–30	31–40	41–50	+50	Total
Biasucci		4	6	5	1	16

DEFENSE

The Colts' defense improved only marginally in 1992, despite the team's emphasis on defensive players in the 1992 draft. The top two picks in the draft, Steve Emtman and Quentin Coryatt, moved right into the lineup and bolstered the defense, at least until they got hurt in mid-season. Emtman went down in Week Ten with a torn knee ligament, but not before galloping 90 yards with an interception for a score in Week Eight against Miami. Coryatt fractured his wrist in the same game. While the defense improved on the field, it did not score enough fantasy points in 1992 to justify selecting it on Draft Day 1993. DT scores in 1992:

> 84-yard punt return
> 90-yard interception return
> 53-yard punt return

Past Performance Key: The Colts' 6–0 shutout of New England in Week Fourteen was the team's first shutout since it shut out San Diego in the eighth game of the 1988 season.

Fantasy Rankings: 1992—18 points (Tied for 17th)
1991—6 points (Tied for 24th)
1990—12 points (Tied for 22nd)
1989—30 points (6th)

1992 DT Game Summaries:

Shutouts	One
1–7 Points	Three
8–14 Points	Three
15–21 Points	Three
Over 21 Points	Six

KANSAS CITY CHIEFS

OFFENSE

Critics love to affix a descriptive name to an era, and in pop culture, many of these tag lines stick. For example, the 1960s were lionized in story and song as the Age of Aquarius. Some people have dubbed recent times the Information Age. The 1990s are the Age of the Statistician in professional sports. The statistician has been elevated to venerated status in the sports industry. As a result, sports fans cannot watch an event without being flooded with the most arcane of statistical trivia, most of it unwanted and certainly unnecessary, at every opportunity. At the end of a typical Monday Night Game, for example, you will have been informed not only of the number of sacks, pressures, deflections, hurries, anxiety attacks, and general feelings of malaise—plus or minus 3 percentage points to compensate for sampling error—caused by the defense, but also the number of completions thrown on the third Sunday of the month when the defense is in the "loose change" or "two bits" or "buddy, can you spare a dime" configuration.

Having said all that, there appears to be a stat that is almost infallible in determining the success of an NFL team.

Aside from the 1982 strike year, no—repeat, *no*—NFL team prior to the 1992 season had ever won the Super Bowl without averaging at least 4 yards per carry or at least 6 yards per passing attempt during the regular season. Only two teams had won the Super Bowl while failing to average at least 6 yards per pass attempt during the season, and both of those teams averaged at least 4 yards per carry. In fact, 19 of the 26 Super Bowl winners prior to the 1992 season had averaged *both* 6 yards a passing attempt and 4 yards a carry. This trend continued in 1992. The Super Bowl winners, the Dallas Cowboys, averaged 7.33 yards per pass attempt and 4.2 yards per carry during the regular season. The team they defeated, the Buffalo Bills, had comparable numbers of 7.23 per attempt and 4.4 yards per carry.

Is this benchmark totally arbitrary? Based on the exit polls, I don't think so. In 1990, seven teams reached the 4/6 mark, and they combined for a 68–44 record, a winning percentage of .607. In 1991, six teams hit the mark and combined for a 62–34 record, a winning percentage of .645. In 1992, a whopping 12 teams hit the mark and combined for an 86–74 record, a winning percentage of .538. So it seems clear that the 4/6 mark is a sure ingredient for winning games in the NFL.

By the way, the Chiefs, the first losers of the Super Bowl, still hold the mark for the highest rushing average, 5.2 yards per carry, of any team ever to make the Super Bowl. They averaged 8.3 yards per pass attempt as well. Maybe if they hadn't been playing Green Bay at the height of the Packs' NFL hegemony, the Chiefs might have fared better. It also didn't hurt that the Packers averaged *8.9* yards per pass attempt during that 1966 season, while their defense gave up only 163 points, best in both the NFL and AFL.

Quarterback

The Chiefs didn't need to get much more production from their quarterback position to improve the overall effectiveness of their offense, since that position was woeful for them in 1991. Sure enough, Plan B free agent Dave Krieg didn't add much. With his best years behind him in Seattle, Krieg threw for 3,115 yards, but only 15 touchdowns. He did lead the team to the playoffs, but it was one-and-out at the hands of the up-and-coming San Diego Chargers. While perhaps a cut above his predecessor, Steve DeBerg, Krieg may not be capable of leading the Chiefs to the next level at this point in his career, which is why the Chiefs traded for Joe Montana.

Running Back

Talk about being loaded at one position. The Chiefs have three excellent backs—Christian Okoye, Barry Word, and Harvey Williams. Word started the season with three 100-yard games, and led the team with 607 yards rushing for the year. But Word gave way to Okoye in the middle of the season, as the Nigerian Nightmares returned from a preseason holdout and early-season injuries. Okoye ran for 448 yards and 6 touchdowns, leading the team in the latter category. Williams added 262 yards rushing and 1 touchdown.

Receiver

Kansas City has one talented crew at wide receiver. Willie Davis emerged in his first year as a legitimate deep threat. He averaged 21 yards per catch, the best in the league, and led the team in passing yards, with 756. Tim Barnett, cousin of the Eagles' Fred Barnett, came back from early-season injuries and had an impressive second half, scoring 4 touchdowns in the last seven weeks of the season. J. J. Birden, always a deep threat as well, disappointed in 1992, scoring only 3 touchdowns, although they included a 72-yard bomb against the Seattle Seahawks in Week Two.

Kicker

Nick Lowery, one of the NFL's best kickers, picked up where he left off in 1991. He kicked 14 field goals in the last seven weeks of the 1991 season, then kicked 12 more in the first six weeks of 1992. He finished the season strong again, making 22 of 24 field goals on his way to a total of 105 points, fifth-best among kickers in the AFC. Lowery has now scored 100 points in 10 separate seasons, adding to his NFL record. Lowery has reached the century mark in five consecutive seasons and in nine of the last 10.

Yardage Breakdown on Scoring Plays—1990

Touchdowns	1–10	11–20	21–30	31–40	41–50	+50	Total
DeBerg	7	5	3	2	2	4	23
Okoye	7						7
Word	2	1				1	4

Field Goals	11–20	21–30	31–40	41–50	+50	Total
Lowery	3	6	19	6		34

Yardage Breakdown on Scoring Plays—1991

Touchdowns	1–10	11–20	21–30	31–40	41–50	+50	Total
DeBerg	9	5			1	2	17
Okoye	8					1	9
Word	3	1					4

Field Goals	11–20	21–30	31–40	41–50	+50	Total
Lowery	4	9	9	3		25

Yardage Breakdown on Scoring Plays—1992

Touchdowns	1–10	11–20	21–30	31–40	41–50	+50	Total
Krieg	5	1	1	1	4	3	15
Okoye	6						6
Word	3				1		4
Barnett	1		1		1	1	4

Field Goals	11–20	21–30	31–40	41–50	+50	Total
Lowery	3	7	8	3	1	22

DEFENSE

Kansas City has been on the fantasy roller coaster the last three years. The Chiefs' defense fell from First Echelon status in 1990 to the middle of the pack with a disappointing fantasy performance in 1991. But they bounced back big time in 1992 leading all NFL teams in fantasy scoring for the season with an amazing 66 points. (Only four NFL running backs exceeded that fantasy total in 1992.) Kansas City's aggressive and talented defense should remain in the upper fantasy ranks in 1993. DT scores for 1992:

46-yard punt return
99-yard interception return
36-yard interception return
25-yard interception return
86-yard punt return
22-yard interception return
30-yard fumble return
Blocked punt recovered in end zone

32-yard interception return
36-yard interception return
Fumble recovered in end zone

Past Performance Key: The Chiefs' total of 66 fantasy points is the highest total in the four editions of this book.

Fantasy Rankings: 1992—66 points (1st)
1991—14 points (Tied for 15th)
1990—26 points (Tied for 6th)
1989—20 points (Tied for 13th)

1992 DT Game Summaries:

Shutouts	None
1–7 Points	Three
8–14 Points	Two
15–21 Points	Seven
Over 21 Points	Four

LOS ANGELES RAIDERS

OFFENSE

Has Al Davis lost his magic touch? The Raiders started 0–4, their worst record starting the season in 28 years. They finished at 7–9, missing the playoffs for the fifth time in seven years. These are hard times for the franchise, indeed. Since the Raiders capped off the 1983 season with a victory over Washington in the Super Bowl, the team has won exactly one playoff game, a 20–10 victory over Cincinnati in the 1990 divisional playoffs. But better days are ahead. If a talent judge like Al Davis can't take advantage of genuine free agency in the NFL, no one can. As most football fans know, the Raiders' team motto is "Commitment to Excellence." As long as the commitment remains, the excellence should return for the Silver and Black.

Quarterback

The term "Hobson's choice" provides a great allegory. This phrase originally comes from the practice of an Englishman named Thomas Hobson who rented horses about 400 years ago. The customer was offered a "choice" of horses by Mr. Hobson, but could only have the one that happened to be nearest the stable door. It was that horse or nothing—in other words, no real choice at all. Putting aside the equine aspects of the comparison, the term "Hobson's choice" fittingly describes the quarterback situation on the Raiders. In 1992, Jay Schroeder completed 123 of 253 passes, a 48.6 percent completion rate, for

1,476 yards and 11 touchdowns. Todd Marinovich wasn't much better, completing 81 of 165 passes, a 49.1 percent completion rate, for 1,102 yards and only 5 touchdowns. Vince Evans, who has played quarterback in the NFL in three different decades, was the only Raiders quarterback with a completion rate over 50 percent in 1992, as he completed 29 of 53 passes for 372 yards and 4 touchdowns. Maybe if Marinovich had a "vich-ectomy" and dropped the last four letters of his name the Raiders might have something. Even with the signing of free agent Jeff Hostetler from the Giants, the quarterback situation in Lotus Land festers.

Running Back

This was another sore spot for the proud franchise in 1992. Eric Dickerson was brought in from the Colts for fourth- and eighth-round draft picks in the 1992 draft, which speaks volumes about the decline of this great player's career. The whole was less than the sum of its parts in the Raiders' backfield, as Dickerson and Co. (Marcus Allen and Nick Bell) combined for 1,794 rushing yards and only 7 rushing touchdowns. Only three teams scored fewer rushing touchdowns than the Raiders in the NFL in 1992 (Atlanta, Seattle, and New England). Dickerson did not have a 100-yard game rushing until Week Twelve (at which point he became the first Raider running back in 29 regular-season games to reach that mark), and finished with only a pair of 100-yard rushing games. Nick Bell led the team with 3 rushing touchdowns, among them a 66-yard run, the third-longest TD gallop in the NFL in 1992. Marcus Allen feuded with owner Al Davis and rushed for only 301 yards while seeing limited playing time. Allen is now with Kansas City.

Receiver

Tim Brown was a paragon of excellence in an otherwise disappointing year for the Raiders team. Brown led the team in receptions with 49, in yards with 693, and in touchdown catches with 7. The rest of the Raiders' receivers had disappointing years. Willie Gault had only 27 receptions for 508 yards and 4 touchdowns. "Swervin' " Mervyn Fernandez performed one of the great disappearing acts in the league, catching only 9 balls for 121 yards and zero touchdowns. After a great season in 1991, tight end Ethan Horton also disappointed. In 1991, Horton led the team with 53 receptions, for 650 yards and 5 touchdowns; in 1992, he caught only 33 passes, for 409 yards and 2 touchdowns. Alexander Wright came over from the Cowboys in a midseason deal and impressed, with 12 catches for 175 yards and 2 touchdowns.

Kicker

Jeff Jeager mirrored the overall club performance and was a major disappointment after what appeared to be his breakthrough year in 1991. He missed only 5 field goals in 1991, making 29 of 34. He missed 8 in just the first five weeks of the season in 1992, and missed 11 overall. He kicked 29 field goals and scored 116 points in 1991. But in 1992, Jaeger kicked only 15 field goals and scored just 73 points.

Yardage Breakdown on Scoring Plays—1990

Touchdowns	1–10	11–20	21–30	31–40	41–50	+50	Total
Schroeder	10	5	0	0	2	2	19

Field Goals	11–20	21–30	31–40	41–50	+50	Total
Jaeger	1	5	3	6	0	15

Yardage Breakdown on Scoring Plays—1991

Touchdowns	1–10	11–20	21–30	31–40	41–50	+50	Total
Schroeder	6	4	1	1		3	15
Bell	2	1					3
T. Brown		1	3			1	5

Field Goals	11–20	21–30	31–40	41–50	+50	Total
Jaeger	5	5	10	7	2	29

Yardage Breakdown on Scoring Plays—1992

Touchdowns	1–10	11–20	21–30	31–40	41–50	+50	Total
Schroeder	6	3		2			11
Bell	2					1	3
T. Brown	3	1		1		2	7

Field Goals	11–20	21–30	31–40	41–50	+50	Total
Jaeger		4	3	5	3	15

DEFENSE

The Raiders' defense continued an encouraging trend in 1992. It surrendered 268 points in 1990, 297 in 1991 and 281 points in 1992. Kansas City, New Orleans, Philadelphia, and San Francisco were the only teams who surrendered less then 300 points in each season during the same period. But 1992 was a disappointing year in the defensive fantasy category. The Raiders' defense posted a very low number of fantasy points for the third straight year. This defense is better than it looks for fantasy purposes, but not good enough to waste an early draft selection on. DT scores in 1992:

Safety—punter tackled in end zone

Blocked punt recovered in end zone

102-yard interception return

Past Performance Key: The Raiders were the only team in the NFL to record 2 shutouts in 1992.

Fantasy Rankings: 1992—14 points (23rd)

1991—14 points (Tied for 15th)

1990—18 points (Tied for 12th)

1989—32 points (Tied for 4th)

1992 DT Game Summaries:

Shutouts	Two
1–7 Points	Three
8–14 Points	One
15–21 Points	Three
Over 21 Points	Seven

MIAMI DOLPHINS

OFFENSE

I'm not going out on a limb when I say that Don Shula is one of the two or three great coaches in NFL history. He is also one of the luckiest, in the sense that he has been able to coach three of the greatest players ever to play the game at one position, quarterback. In his first stint as a head coach at Baltimore, he had Johnny Unitas, maybe the best quarterback who ever passed the pigskin. Then he was fortunate enough to coach Bob Griese, a Hall of Fame quarterback, at Miami. But the only quarterback of the three he didn't inherit and selected on his own may turn out to be the best one of all, Dan Marino. Few coaches are fortunate to have one player during their reigns with the talent of a Unitas, Griese, or Marino, never mind three. (Look what former Redskins coach Joe Gibbs accomplished in Washington offen-sively without what most would call a great quarterback, with apolo-gies to Joe Theismann, Doug Williams, and Mark Rypien.) Perhaps it is the true measure of Shula's greatness that this former defensive back who started as a defensive coach was able to mold his philosophy to match the offensive talent he was given.

Quarterback

In a game where injuries come with the territory and performances vary from year to year, Dan Marino's consistency speaks for itself. Marino played in all of the Dolphins' games in 1992, something he has accom-plished in eight of his 10 years in the NFL. In 1992, he completed 330 of 554 passes for 4,116 yards, an NFL-record ninth consecutive year with 3,000 yards. With his 330 completions, Marino has now reached at least 300 completions five seasons in a row and eight of the last nine. He threw for 24 touchdowns in 1992, the 10th consecutive year he has thrown 20 or more. The flip side of Marino's consistency is that he has settled into a level of play that does not rise to the personal standards he set early in his career. Since Marino threw 44 touchdown passes in 1986, he has not thrown more than 28 in one season. Ralph Waldo Emerson observed that a foolish consistency is the hobgoblin of little minds. There isn't a coach in the NFL who wouldn't love to be haunted by a quarterback with Marino's consistent talents.

Running Back

The diminutive Mark Higgs had a fine season for the Dolphins, rushing for 915 yards and 7 touchdowns. Bobby Humphrey, picked up in a trade with Denver for Sammie Smith in May of 1992, was used primar-ily as a pass receiver last season. Humphrey caught 54 passes, the most on the team, for 507 yards and 1 touchdown. He also rushed for 471 yards and 1 touchdown. Humphrey's personal difficulties during the off-season received national attention, and may hamper him during the 1993 season.

Receiver

Mark Duper continued his impressive career comeback in 1992, snaring 44 passes for 762 yards and 7 touchdowns, his highest total since 1987. Mark Clayton, the other half of the Marks Brothers, caught only 43 passes for 619 yards and 3 touchdowns in 1992, due to his subpar health. Despite missing the first three games of 1992 waiting for his historic bid for free agency to be resolved, Keith Jackson led Miami receivers with 48 receptions, and his 5 touchdown passes were second to Mark Duper's 7 on the team. With a whole preseason to acclimate himself further to Marino and the Dolphins' offense in 1993, look for Jackson along with new Marks Brother free agent Mark Ingram and former Patriot Irving Fryar to make a fine receiving corps even better.

Kicker

Pete Stoyanovich had another terrific year kicking for Miami, cementing his position as one of the premier kickers in the game. Stoyo booted 30 field goals in 1992, 4 of them from 45 yards or longer. He scored 124 points, the highest total in the league in 1992. If Chip Lohmiller isn't The Man when it comes to NFL kickers, then Stoyo is.

Yardage Breakdown on Scoring Plays—1990

Touchdowns	1–10	11–20	21–30	31–40	41–50	+50	Total
Marino	7	6	3	3		2	21
Clayton	1	1		1			3
Duper	2	1	1			1	5

Field Goals	11–20	21–30	31–40	41–50	+50	Total
Stoyanovich	2	7	7	3	2	21

Yardage Breakdown on Scoring Plays—1991

Touchdowns	1–10	11–20	21–30	31–40	41–50	+50	Total
Marino	13	5	3	2	2		25
Higgs	3	1					4
Clayton	4	4	1	2	1		12
Duper	2	1	1		1		5

Field Goals	11–20	21–30	31–40	41–50	+50	Total
Stoyanovich	2	9	10	8	2	31

Yardage Breakdown on Scoring Plays—1992

Touchdowns	1–10	11–20	21–30	31–40	41–50	+50	Total
Marino	9	4	2	4	3	2	24
Higgs	6	1					7
Jackson	3	1	1				5
Duper	1		1	2	2	1	7

Field Goals	11–20	21–30	31–40	41–50	+50	Total
Stoyanovich	1	9	14	4	2	30

DEFENSE

The Dolphins rebounded from a horrible fantasy scoring effort in 1991 with a decent output in 1992. Louis Oliver tied the NFL record with a 103-yard interception return for a touchdown in Week Five against the Buffalo Bills. As Don Shula continues to add young talent on the defensive side of the ball, look for the Dolphins to improve their fantasy scoring again in 1993. DT scores in 1992:

> 103-yard interception return
> 30-yard interception return
> 35-yard interception return

Past Performance Key: The Miami defense has not posted a shutout since the fourth game of the 1987 season, against the Kansas City Chiefs.

Fantasy Rankings: 1992—18 points (Tied for 17th)
1991—6 points (Tied for 24th)
1990—32 points (Tied for 2nd)
1989—20 points (Tied for 13th)

1992 DT Game Summaries:

Shutouts	One
1–7 Points	One
8–14 Points	Three
15–21 Points	Five
Over 21 Points	Six

NEW ENGLAND PATRIOTS

OFFENSE

The Pats are a disaster. It is almost impossible to believe that this franchise represented the AFC in Super Bowl XX only seven years ago. In a true example of trickle-down economics, the unsettled financial situation of ownership seems to have percolated through the entire organization. The Patsies had employed three head coaches over the four seasons prior to 1992, and after losing Coach MacPherson for a stretch of games last season while he recovered from his bout with diverticulitis, management fired him two weeks after the 1992 season ended. New head coach Bill Parcells is no stranger to the rebuilding process. The Giants had suffered through nine losing seasons in the 10 years prior to his taking over the team in 1983. Parcells, who started his pro coaching career as a linebacker coach for the Patriots in 1980, clearly has his work cut out for him here. If any coach can turn things around in a hurry, though, it's Parcells. Keep in mind that he won two Super Bowls with the Giants, to cap off the 1986 and 1990 seasons.

Quarterback

Quick, which college had the most former quarterbacks on NFL rosters in 1992? Notre Dame? Not. Northeast Louisiana? Don't laugh—two NFL quarterbacks, Stan Humphries and Bubby Brister, hail from that school. Miami, known as Quarterback U? Close. (It had five—Craig Erickson, Bernie Kosar, Jim Kelly, Vinny Testaverde, and Steve Walsh.) The correct answer is that football factory located in College Park, Maryland, the University of Maryland. That's right. The Terrapins boasted more former quarterbacks playing for NFL teams in 1992—six—than any other school. The Pats' version was Scott Zolak. (The other former Terps playing quarterback in the NFL in 1992 were Boomer Esiason, Stan Gelbaugh, Neil O'Donnell, and Frank Reich, he of the greatest pro and college comebacks in football history fame. The sixth Terp is Mike Tice, who is a tight end in the pros, but was a quarterback at Maryland.) When Hugh Millen went down, Zolak took over and led the Pats to a pair of consecutive wins in Weeks Eleven and Twelve, their only victories in 1992. The Pats played four quarterbacks over the course of 1992, so who will be the starter in 1993 is anyone's guess. First pick in the NFL draft drew Bledsoe, as the early favorite for the job. Bonus question time: What's a terrapin?

Running Back

The Pats have talent at this position, and still had virtually no running game in 1992. Leonard Russell, the Pats' first pick in the 1991 draft, has talent, but no support. Russell rushed for 959 yards and 4 touchdowns in 1991, but fell to only 390 yards and 2 touchdowns in 1992. Russell's NFL classmate Jon Vaughn obviously has talent as well. In his second season Vaughn rushed for 451 yards to lead the Pats in 1992, with 1 touchdown. He also posted a 28.2-yard average on kickoff returns, including a 100-yard return for a score in Week Sixteen against the Bengals. John Stephens remains a mystery. He rushed for 2,001 yards in his first two years in the league (1988–89), but has rushed for only 1,248 yards in the three seasons since then. (Stephens' trade to the rejuvenated Green Bay Packer franchise could revive his career as well.) As a group, the Pats' backs did not score a rushing touchdown until Week Ten of the 1992 season.

Receivers

The talent at this position is another of the few bright spots for the Pats. Or, I should say, was, until Irving Fryar was traded to Miami in the offseason. Fryar caught 55 passes, the second-highest total of his career, for 791 yards, third-best of his career, in 1992. Fryar also scored 4 touchdowns last season. "Marvelous" Marv Cook led all tight ends with 82 receptions in 1991, the fourth-highest reception total in the NFL that season, but dropped to 52 receptions in 1992, with only 2 touchdowns. Greg McMurtry added 35 receptions for 424 yards and 1 touchdown.

Kicker

Charlie Baumann is an undistinguished NFL kicker. He kicked just 11 field goals in 1992, the longest of which was 44 yards, and scored a total of 55 points overall. Not surprisingly, he was the lowest-scoring kicker of those who played all 16 games in the NFL in 1992.

Yardage Breakdown on Scoring Plays—1990

Touchdowns	1–10	11–20	21–30	31–40	41–50	+50	Total
Fryar			2	2			4
Cook	2	1	1	1			5

Field Goals	11–20	21–30	31–40	41–50	+50	Total
Staurovsky		1	3	4	7	1	16

Yardage Breakdown on Scoring Plays—1991

Touchdowns	1–10	11–20	21–30	31–40	41–50	+50	Total
Millen	2	1		2	2	2	9
Russell	4						4
Fryar				1	1	1	3
Cook	1	1	1				3

Field Goals	11–20	21–30	31–40	41–50	+50	Total
Baumann		2	1	4		7

Yardage Breakdown on Scoring Plays—1992

Touchdowns	1–10	11–20	21–30	31–40	41–50	+50	Total
Millen	2	3	1	2			8
Russell	2						2
Fryar		1		2		1	4
Cook	2						2

Field Goals	11–20	21–30	31–40	41–50	+50	Total
Baumann	2	5	2	2		11

DEFENSE

The Patsies snuck up on everyone in 1992 with their defensive fantasy performance. They racked up 36 fantasy points, tied for third-best in the NFL. This significant jump in performance could be an illusion, based on the Pats' prior fantasy record. But the team's schedule is relatively favorable in 1993, and Bill Parcells is nothing if not a great defensive coach. All in all, I would wait before selecting this defense on Draft Day, because believe me, it'll be waiting for you at the end of the draft. DT scores in 1992:

25-yard fumble return
49-yard interception return
41-yard interception return
82-yard interception return
19-yard fumble return
30-yard fumble return

Fantasy Rankings: 1992—36 points (Tied for 3rd)
1991—12 points (Tied for 21st)
1990—6 points (Tied for 26th)
1989—6 points (28th)

Past Performance Key: The Pats exceeded their combined total of fantasy points from the prior three years with their 36-point effort in 1992.

1992 DT Game Summaries:

Shutouts	None
1–7 Points	Two
8–14 Points	Two
15–21 Points	Four
Over 21 Points	Eight

NEW YORK JETS

OFFENSE

The Jets are rivals with their fellow residents of the Meadowlands (and landlord) in many areas, including the attention of the New York media and football fans. The "new" franchise in town never has captured the affection of the Big Apple like the Giants, except perhaps during the Namath era. But the Jets share a dubious distinction with their older rivals. As the following shows, it's been a long time since either team's offense lit up the scoreboard for a whole season:

Longest Time Since Team Led Conference in Scoring

AFC		NFC	
NY Jets	1960	Phoenix	1948
Houston	1961	Detroit	1954
Kansas City	1966	Giants	1963
Denver	1973	Atlanta	1981
Indianapolis	1976		

Never Led Conference in Scoring

New Orleans	Born 1967
Seattle	Born 1976
Tampa Bay	Born 1976

It's amazing when you realize that the Jets franchise is still defined by Joe Namath and the team that slew the dragon in the Super Bowl 24 years ago. Maybe if the Jets had drafted Dan Marino instead of Ken O'Brien in 1983, or Joe Montana instead of Marty Lyons and Mark Gastineau in 1979, their image might not be rooted in ancient history. The fact remains that since the Jets were born as the New York Titans in 1960, the franchise has had only *eight* winning seasons in 33 years. (The Jets have never won more than 11 games during a regular season; the 49ers have won 10 or more games 10 seasons in a row.) GM Dick Steinberg and Coach Bruce Coslet have a heavy dose of past history to overcome as they continue to rebuild this traditionally mediocre franchise.

Quarterback

As the refrain of the rock-and-roll classic from the 1950s goes, the quarterback situation for the Jets is all shook up. Second-year pro Browning Nagle took over the reins of the offense from Ken O'Brien in 1992 and made progress toward becoming a polished pro quarterback. He completed 192 of 387 passes for 2,280 yards and 7 touchdowns. But he didn't make enough progress, so management brought in Boomer Esiason from Cincinnati in an offseason trade. Ken O'Brien, who filled in capably at midseason for the Jets, completing 55 of 98 passes for 642 yards and 5 touchdowns, will now fill in for Brett Favre in Green Bay in 1993. Nagle will get some more NFL seasoning as he backs up Boomer in the coming season.

Running Back

The Jets' running backs were a big disappointment in 1992. Brad Baxter appeared after 1991 to be poised on the brink of NFL stardom. Despite rushing for only 666 yards, his 11 rushing touchdowns in 1991 led the AFC, and tied him for third in the entire league. Baxter fell to 6 touchdowns in 1992, the same total he scored in 1990. He did post a career high 698 yards rushing, and averaged 4.6 yards per carry, a personal best as well, in 1992. Blair Thomas continued to disappoint as well. Thomas rushed for only 440 yards on 97 carries and scored zero touchdowns. The newly-acquired Johnny Johnson will probably derail the under-achieving B. T. Express and relegate him to backup status in the upcoming season. Freeman McNeil, one of the heroes of the players' campaign for free agency, rushed for only 170 yards in his NFL swan song.

Receiver

This fine group of receivers was decimated by the premature retirement of Al Toon on November 27, 1992, after suffering his ninth concussion in eight professional seasons. Toon had compiled impressive career numbers, finishing with 517 receptions for 6,605 yards and 31 touchdowns. Toon ranks third in the number of receptions compiled by a player in his first five years in the league, behind new leader Sterling

Sharpe and Roger Craig. Rob Moore is a star in waiting. He had 50 receptions in 1992, and led the team in receiving yardage with 726 yards. He also scored 4 touchdowns to lead the Jets' receivers in that category. Terance Mathis is a deep threat as well as a return specialist. Rookie Johnny Mitchell showed promise in 1992 of becoming one of the best tight ends in the league. Chris Burkett, who led the Jets with 57 receptions in 1992, chose to forego free agency and re-signed with the team, solidifying their fine receiving corps.

Kicker

The NFL kickers' version of musical chairs was in full swing with the Jets in 1992. With a good preseason, Jason Staurovsky beat out Raul Allegre for the starting job left open by the retirement of Pat Leahy. Staurovsky then proceeded to lose the job with a lousy first four games of the regular season, missing 5 of 8 field goals. His replacement, Cary Blanchard, came on as a solid kicker, making 16 of 22 field goals on his way to scoring 65 points.

Yardage Breakdown on Scoring Plays—1990

Touchdowns	1–10	11–20	21–30	31–40	41–50	+50	Total
O'Brien	7	1	1		2	2	13
Baxter	5		1				6
Toon	2	1	1		2		6
R. Moore	4					2	6

Field Goals	11–20	21–30	31–40	41–50	+50	Total
Leahy	2	13	6	2		23

Yardage Breakdown on Scoring Plays—1991

Touchdowns	1–10	11–20	21–30	31–40	41–50	+50	Total
O'Brien	4	3		1	2		10
Baxter	11						11
B. Thomas	2	1					3
R. Moore	2	2			1		5

Field Goals	11–20	21–30	31–40	41–50	+50	Total
Leahy	3	16	7			26

Yardage Breakdown on Scoring Plays—1992

Touchdowns	1–10	11–20	21–30	31–40	41–50	+ 50	Total
Nagle	2	2	1	1	1		7
Baxter	6					6	
R. Moore		2	1		1	4	

Field Goals	11–20	21–30	31–40	41–50	+ 50	Total
Blanchard	2	2	7	5		16

DEFENSE

While we're on the subject of factors that define the Jets' franchise, defense isn't one of them. The Jets have never had what you would call a killer defense, a defense like that of the Eagles today, or of the Lawrence Taylor-led Giants of a few years ago, or of the Super Bowl Bears of 1985. Sure, their Super Bowl team had a solid defense, but only Jets fans could name a player on it. Sure, the Sack Exchange with Joe Klecko, Gastineau, and company made headlines in the early 1980s, but that was more light than heat. From the days of the New York Titans to the Weeb Ewbank era to Bruce Coslet's teams today, the emphasis has always been placed squarely on the offense to lead the franchise, and more important, to put fannies in the seats. The structural weakness of the Jets' defense is illustrated by the following chart:

Last Season Defense Recorded a Shutout (Prior to 1992)

AFC		NFC	
NY Jets	1982	Phoenix	1981
Seattle	1986	Detroit	1983
Miami	1987	Tampa Bay	1985
New England	1987	Atlanta	1988
Indianapolis	1988	LA Rams	1988

(The Jets had a shutout going against the Bengals in Week Eleven of the 1992 season, but lost it in the fourth quarter. They now have sole possession of the longest streak without a shutout since the Cardinals shut out the Giants in Week Fifteen of the 1992 season. Indianapolis, Miami, Atlanta, and the Rams also broke their shutout skid in 1992, three of those shutouts coming at the expense of the hapless Patriots, while Miami earned its whitewash against the Colts.) Only two players who spent the bulk of their careers with the Jets are in the Pro Football Hall of Fame, Don Maynard and Joe Namath, and neither was a defensive player. John Riggins, who was a Jet for his first four years in the league, is in the Hall, but he made his real mark in NFL history with the Washington Redskins. Weeb Ewbank, the coach of the Super Bowl Jets, has also been inducted.) Unless the Jets change the emphasis of their franchise philosophy, the history of their uninspired defense fact won't change anytime soon, although signing free agents Ronnie Lott, Leonard Marshall, and Eric Thomas is a step in the right direction. From a fantasy perspective, the Jets posted fabulous numbers in 1989, and have been mediocre since. Despite the addition of the new players on defense, that may not change in the immediate future either.

DT scores in 1992:

> 77-yard interception return
> Safety—quarterback sacked in end zone
> 23-yard interception return
> 20-yard interception return

Fantasy Rankings:　1992—20 points (Tied for 13th)
　　　　　　　　　　　1991—18 points (Tied for 10th)
　　　　　　　　　　　1990—14 points (Tied for 18th)
　　　　　　　　　　　1989—38 points (3rd)

Past Performance Key:　The last Jets shutout was a 25–0 victory over the Baltimore Colts in the thirteenth week of the 1981 season.

1992 DT Game Summaries:

Shutouts	None
1–7 Points	One
8–14 Points	Three
15–21 Points	Six
Over 21 Points	Six

PITTSBURGH STEELERS

OFFENSE

The Steelers have had some great running backs; the names John Henry Johnson and Franco Harris jump immediately to mind. Old-timers (and lawyers) may remember Byron "Whizzer" White and Bill Dudley, who in 1946 led the league not only in rushing, but in punt returns and interceptions as well. Barry Foster tried to join this elite group last season, leading the AFC in rushing and falling just 23 yards short of leading the NFL as well. At the same time, he also put to an end a drought of truly biblical proportions:

Last Time Team Had Conference Rushing Leader (Prior to 1992)

AFC		NFC	
Pittsburgh	1946	Philadelphia	1949
New England	1967	NY Giants	1951
Cleveland	1968	San Francisco	1954
Denver	1974	Washington	1972
Houston	1981	Green Bay	1973
NY Jets	1982	Phoenix	1975

Never Had Conference Rushing Leader

Tampa Bay	Born 1976
Minnesota	Born 1961
Miami	Born 1966

Pittsburgh is no longer the answer to the trivia question about which NFL team has gone the longest without a conference rushing leader, thanks to Barry Foster's great year in 1992.

Quarterback
Neil O'Donnell was leading the Steelers to the best record in the AFC, and the home-field advantage, and everything was coming up roses, when he broke his right leg in Week 14 against the Seahawks. Bubby Brister took over and led the Steelers into the playoffs, but, with a rusty O'Donnell at the helm, Pittsburgh lost to Buffalo in its first playoff game since 1989. O'Donnell did not post the best stats in the world, completing 185 of 313 passes for 2,283 yards and only 13 touchdowns in 1992. But with Barry Foster running wild, and the Steelers defense controlling most games, he didn't need to excel.

Running Back
Barry Foster had an almost unparalleled season for a running back. He rushed for 1,690 yards and 11 touchdowns in 1992. His total of 1,690 yards in 1992 has been exceeded by only eight running backs in the history of the NFL, including Emmitt Smith in 1992. He added 344 yards on 36 receptions to finish with a combined yardage total from scrimmage of 2,034 yards, third-best total in the league. All this from

a man who had rushed for 691 yards total in his two years in the league prior to 1992 (488 of them in 1991). His quantum leap of 1,202 rushing yards from one season to the next ranks with the best season-to-season leaps by a running back. Here are some comparable quantum leaps in recent memory (for backs who rushed for some yardage in the first year and totaled at least 1,000 yards in the second year).While some of these players leaped back to mediocrity almost as fast as they jumped up, look for Foster to keep posting excellent numbers in the years to come.

Player Name	Leap From (Year)	Leap to (Year)
Earnest Jackson	39 yards—1983	1179 yards—1984
Curt Warner	40 yards—1984	1094 yards—1985
John Settle	72 yards—1987	1024 yards—1988
Greg Bell	86 yards—1987	1212 yards—1988
Charles White	126 yards—1986	1374 yards—1987
Barry Word	133 yards—1987	1015 yards—1990
(Word did not play in 1988, and sat out the 1989 season)		
O. J. Anderson	208 yards—1988	1023 yards—1989
Gary Anderson	260 yards—1987	1119 yards—1988
Gaston Green	261 yards—1990	1037 yards—1991
Gerald Riggs	437 yards—1983	1486 yards—1984
Christian Okoye	473 yards—1988	1480 yards—1989
Joe Morris	510 yards—1984	1336 yards—1985
James Wilder	640 yards—1983	1544 yards—1984

Receiver

Veteran Steeler Louis Lipps departed, but Dwight Stone continued his development as a solid NFL receiver. He caught 34 passes for 501 yards and 3 touchdowns. Jeff Graham led the Steelers in 1992 with 49 receptions and 711 yards, and added 1 touchdown. Ernie Mills had a solid sophomore season, with 30 receptions for 383 yards and 3 touchdowns. Tight end Eric Green ran afoul of the NFL's drug policy, and may not meet the expectations held for him since he was drafted with the Steelers' first pick in 1990. After scoring 13 touchdowns in his first two seasons in the league, Green caught only 14 passes in 1992, and scored only 2 touchdowns.

Kicker

Gary Anderson quietly put together another spectacular season as he quietly tries to kick his way to Canton. He booted 28 of 36 field goals, and scored 113 points overall. His 113 points in 1992 puts him 14th on the all-time scoring list with 1,123 points. His 257 career field goals place him 9th.

Yardage Breakdown on Scoring Plays—1990

Touchdowns	1–10	11–20	21–30	31–40	41–50	+50	Total
Brister	13	7					20
Hoge	6				1		7
Foster	1						1
E. Green	5	2					7

Field Goals	11–20	21–30	31–40	41–50	+50	Total
Anderson	1	4	7	8		20

Yardage Breakdown on Scoring Plays—1991

Touchdowns	1–10	11–20	21–30	31–40	41–50	+50	Total
O'Donnell	2	2	2	2	1	2	11
Foster						1	1
E. Green	2		3	1			6
Stone				1	1	3	5

Field Goals	11–20	21–30	31–40	41–50	+50	Total
Anderson	1	7	9	5	1	23

Yardage Breakdown on Scoring Plays—1992

Touchdowns	1–10	11–20	21–30	31–40	41–50	+50	Total
O'Donnell	7	4	2				13
Foster	7	2	1			1	11
Stone	2		1				3

Field Goals	11–20	21–30	31–40	41–50	+50	Total
Anderson	2	12	11	3		28

DEFENSE

The Steel Curtain may be a relic of the past, but the Steelers' defense evoked memories of days gone by in 1992, surrendering 225 points, the fewest in the AFC and second-best in the league. Still, Pittsburgh's defense remains a perennial fantasy disappointment. The Steelers obviously have the talent to move up in scoring in 1993, but there is no reason to risk an early draft pick on that possibility in 1993. DT scores in 1992:

65-yard interception return

80-yard punt return

34-yard fumble return

Fantasy Rankings:	1992—18 points (Tied for 17th)
	1991—24 points (Tied for 7th)
	1990—14 points (Tied for 18th)
	1989—12 points (Tied for 21st)

1992 DT Game Summaries:

Shutouts	One
1–7 Points	Three
8–14 Points	Six
15–21 Points	Three
Over 21 Points	Three

SAN DIEGO CHARGERS

OFFENSE

Where have you gone, Don Coryell, a stadiumful of Charger fans turn their lonely eyes to you. Or at least they used to, until GM extraordinaire Bobby Beathard moved west from Washington and NBC Sports and rebuilt the team. The icing on the cake was Beathard's trade with his old team. "Trade" is probably not the right word; "fleece" is more like it. Beathard fleeced the Redskins of Stan Humphries after starting quarterback John Friesz went down in preseason. Humphries moved into the starting position after the first game of the season, and once he learned the system, led the Chargers to their record-breaking season (first NFL team to start 0–4 and still reach the playoffs). It was the Chargers' best season since, well, Don Coryell was the coach.

Humphries and Co. brought back memories of the early 1980s, when the Chargers had the best offense in the NFL, maybe in NFL history. In the five full seasons from 1980 to 1985 (strike-shortened 1982 was a nine-game season), the Chargers led the NFL in total yards gained in four out of the five years, and in points scored two of the five. The Chargers amassed over 6,000 total yards in all five of those years, and became one of only two teams in NFL history to throw for more than 4,000 yards and rush for more than 2,000 yards in one season, in 1981. (The only other team to perform this feat was, believe it or not, the St. Louis Cardinals, in 1984.) Those glory days are long gone, but things have turned the corner for the Chargers' offense and there is a place called hope in Jack Murphy Stadium after 1992's encouraging performance.

Quarterback

Stan Humphries, freed from former head coach Joe Gibbs's doghouse in the nation's capital by his former GM, Beathard, put up dazzling numbers after a slow start to lead the Chargers to their best season since 1980. Humphries completed 263 of 454 passes for 3,356 yards and 16 touchdowns, the best numbers by a Lightning Bolts quarterback since Dan Fouts completed 254 of 430 passes for 3,638 yards and 27 touchdowns in 1985. John Friesz, the starter before his preseason injury, may turn out to be the Wally Pipp of the quarterback department in the AFC West.

Running Back

Injuries dogged the Killer Bs, Marion Butts and Rod Bernstine, in 1992. They combined for 1,600 yards rushing and 14 touchdowns on the ground in 1991, but injuries limited the pair to only 1,308 yards and 8 touchdowns between them in 1992. The Chargers were one of the most improved teams in the AFC in 1992. With free agent Bernstine departed to division rival Denver, a healthy Butts for a whole season becomes critical to ensure greater improvement for the Lightning Bolts in 1993. In addition, Ronnie Harmon proved a capable back in his fill-in role and as a receiver out of the backfield. He led all NFL running backs in receptions with 79, third-best total in the AFC overall. He also rushed for 235 yards and 3 touchdowns (4 touchdowns overall). Eric Bieniemy, in a backup role, rushed for 264 yards and 3 touchdowns as well.

Receiver

With an improved passing game in San Diego, Anthony Miller had a big year and returned to the ranks of the premier receivers in the NFL. He had 72 receptions for 1,060 yards and 7 touchdowns, adding another on a fumble return. Nate Lewis caught 34 passes in 1992, and he posted career highs in receiving yardage, with 580 yards, and touchdown receptions, with 4. Shawn Jefferson had a solid season in his second year in the league, catching 29 passes for 377 yards and 2 touchdowns. Tight end Derrick Walker had the best season of his three-year career in 1992, catching 34 passes for 393 yards and 2 touchdowns.

Kicker

Since taking over for Fuad Reveiz in Week Five of the 1990 season, John Carney has improved in each of his three years with the Chargers, capping his development with his best season in 1992. Carney jumped from 19 field goals in each of his first two years as a Lightning Bolt to 26 in 1992, and leaped from 84 points in 1990 and 88 points in 1991 to 113 points in 1992. As the Chargers' offense continues to mature, so should Carney's point totals.

Yardage Breakdown on Scoring Plays—1990

Touchdowns	1–10	11–20	21–30	31–40	41–50	+50	Total
Tolliver	4	4	5	2	1		16
Butts	8						8
Bernstine	2	1		1			4
A. Miller	1	1	4	1			7

Field Goals	11–20	21–30	31–40	41–50	+50	Total
Carney	5	6	5	3		19

Yardage Breakdown on Scoring Plays—1991

Touchdowns	1–10	11–20	21–30	31–40	41–50	+50	Total
Friesz	7	2	2		1		12
Bernstine	7					1	8
Butts	4	1	1				6
A. Miller	1	1	1				3

Field Goals	11–20	21–30	31–40	41–50	+50	Total
Carney	1	6	6	4	2	19

Yardage Breakdown on Scoring Plays—1992

Touchdowns	1–10	11–20	21–30	31–40	41–50	+50	Total
Humphries	4	5	3	1	2	1	16
Bernstine	3	1					4
Butts	4						4
A. Miller	1	2	1	1	1	1	7

Field Goals	11–20	21–30	31–40	41–50	+50	Total
Carney	1	12	5	8		26

DEFENSE

I discussed above the offensive legacy the Chargers established in the early 1980s. Unfortunately, their defensive history is just the opposite. While the offense was averaging 400 points a full season played from 1979 through 1985, the defense was averaging the same point total, never allowing fewer than 390 points in any full season from 1981 through 1986. But the San Diego defense ignored past history and showed marked improvement in 1992. This can be directly attributed to another shrewd personnel move by GM Beathard, this time on the coaching side. Beathard lured defensive genius Bill Arnsbarger back to the sidelines after he resigned from his position as athletic director at the University of Florida in January of 1992. Arnsbarger has coached in five Super Bowls, mainly as Don Shula's defensive coach with Baltimore and Miami.

Back on the sidelines with the Chargers in 1992 after being out of the NFL since 1984, it was as if Coach Arnsbarger had never left. Ranked 19th overall in the NFL in 1991, the Lightning Bolts' defense moved up to 4th in 1992. Junior Seau emerged as one of the NFL's impact players on defense. The Chargers were only the third team in NFL history to lose their first four games and then win their next four, on their way to 11 victories during the 1992 season that were due in large part to their maturing defense. The positive defensive results on the field were not reflected in fantasy football, however, as the Chargers scored only 12 fantasy points, the same number as they scored in 1991. That number should improve in 1993. DT Scores in 1992:

> 26-yard interception return
> Safety—quarterback sacked in end zone
> Safety—quarterback sacked in end zone
> Safety—quarterback sacked in end zone

Past Performance Key: The Lightning Bolts led all NFL teams with 3 safeties in 1992. No other team recorded more than 1 safety last season.

Fantasy Rankings: 1992—12 points (Tied for 24th)
1991—12 points (Tied for 21st)
1990—26 points (Tied for 6th)
1989—18 points (Tied for 15th)

1992 DT Game Summaries:

Shutouts	None
1–7 Points	None
8–14 Points	Five
15–21 Points	Four
Over 21 Points	Seven

SEATTLE SEAHAWKS

OFFENSE

Seattle's team records on offense are dominated by three players—Curt Warner, Dave Krieg, and Steve Largent—who were the heart of the franchise in the Seahawks' salad days from 1983 to 1989. Only Marino, Kelly, and Moon have surpassed Krieg's 32 touchdown passes in 1984 since that time; Warner is Seahawk's career rushing leader; and Largent's stellar career record was discussed earlier. Unfortunately, the offense has fallen apart since their departure. This was clear in 1992, as the Seahawks put together the worst offensive performance in the NFL in 15 years. The Seahawks scored 140 points, the lowest total since the Bucs set the modern NFL mark for scoring futility in 1977, when they notched a measly 53 points in their second year of existence and their first year in the NFC. After 10 games, the Seahawks had scored only 59 points; the 49ers scored 56 points in one game against Atlanta in Week Seven last season. In addition to their scoring futility, the Seahawks compiled just 3,374 total yards, the lowest mark in the NFL in 1992.

Quarterback

The Seahawks finished the season with Kelly Stouffer and Stan Gelbaugh sharing duties at quarterback. "Slingin' Sammy" Gelbaugh is perhaps the most-traveled pro quarterback this side of Babe Laufenberg, having played in Canada in the CFL, in Europe in the WLAF, and for three teams in the NFL. One of five former University of Maryland signal-callers who played quarterback in the NFL in 1992, Gelbaugh may not be a member of that fraternity in 1993, if Dan

McGwire, the Seahawks' first-round pick in 1991, returns from injury to cement a roster spot. Gelbaugh completed only 121 of 255 passes for 1,307 yards and 6 touchdowns in 1992. These numbers just won't do in the NFL. That's why the Seahawks took quarterback Rick Mirer with their first pick in the draft.

Running Back

This area might not be as bad as you might think for Seattle. The leading rusher last year was Chris Warren, with 1,017 yards, the most for a Seattle back since Curt Warner rushed for 1,025 yards in 1988. John L. Williams continued to toil in the obscurity of the Kingdome, leading the team in receptions with 74 and tying for the team lead in touchdown scoring with 3 TDs.

Receiver

Name the Seahawks receiver who caught the most passes in 1992 and win a prize. In fact, name any Seattle receiver and win a prize. If you said Steve Largent, you were close enough. Brian Blades is a fine receiver who missed the first 12 weeks of the season due to injury. He returned with a splash in Week Thirteen, catching a Gelbaugh pass at the gun to send the Monday Night Game against Denver into overtime. Seattle eventually won on a John Kasay field goal, which may have been the highlight of its otherwise dreary season. Blades finished the season with 19 receptions for 256 yards and 1 touchdown. But the Seattle receiver with the most receptions in 1992 was Tom Kane, with only 27 receptions for 369 yards and 3 touchdowns. Free agents Kelvin Martin and Ferrell Edmunds will bolster this crew in 1993.

Kicker

John Kasay contributed to the overall ineffectiveness of the team by suffering through a sophomore slump following a fine rookie season. After making 25 of 31 field goals in 1991, he booted only 14 of 22 in 1992, the longest from 43 yards, and dropped from 102 points to only 56.

Yardage Breakdown on Scoring Plays—1990

Touchdowns	1–10	11–20	21–30	31–40	41–50	+50	Total
Krieg	7	3	1	1	1	2	15
Fenner	13	1					14

Field Goals	11–20	21–30	31–40	41–50	+50	Total
N. Johnson	2	7	9	4	1	23

Yardage Breakdown on Scoring Plays—1991

Touchdowns	1–10	11–20	21–30	31–40	41–50	+50	Total
Krieg	7	2	2				11
Fenner	4						4

Field Goals	11–20	21–30	31–40	41–50	+50	Total
Kasay	1	5	11	6	2	25

Yardage Breakdown on Scoring Plays—1992

Touchdowns	1–10	11–20	21–30	31–40	41–50	+50	Total
Gelbaugh	3	2	1				6
Warren	2		1				3
Kane		1	2				3

Field Goals	11–20	21–30	31–40	41–50	+50	Total
Kasay		4	9	1		14

DEFENSE

This is another example of the difference between the real world of the NFL and the fantasy football realm. The Seattle defense, led by All-Pro defensive tackle Cortez Kennedy, is one of the better defenses in the AFC. It tied Miami for the fifth-ranked defense in the AFC in yards allowed in 1992. But the 'Hawks had the lowest-scoring fantasy defense in the league in 1992. Enough said. Since the only way to go is up, the Seahawks should score more often in 1993, but not enough for fantasy owners to waste a pick on them.

DT scores in 1992:
52-yard fumble return

Fantasy Rankings: 1992—6 points (28th)
1991—18 points (Tied for 10th)
1990—6 points (Tied for 26th)
1989—6 points (28th)

Past Performance Key: Seattle has the lowest total of fantasy points over the past four years.

1992 DT Game Summaries:

Shutouts	None
1–7 Points	One
8–14 Points	Two
15–21 Points	Eight
Over 21 Points	Five

NATIONAL CONFERENCE

ATLANTA FALCONS

OFFENSE

In case you haven't noticed, the South is definitely on the rise again. In the world of politics, a Razorback and a Volunteer combined to win a huge victory for the Democrats while bagging the biggest prize in the land in the 1992 presidential election. In the sports world, Atlanta carries the banner leading the charge to the front of the pack of prominent sports cities in America. The Braves have been baseball's Senior Circuit entry in the last two World Series. The 1996 Summer Olympics are just around the corner, and the centennial of the Modern Games will focus the eyes of the world on Atlanta like no city has ever been watched before. The Falcons christened a new home for the 1992 season, the Georgia Dome, one of the newest and nicest sports facilities in the country. And Super Bowl XXVIII will be held there on January 30, 1994. But the Falcons will only be there as spectators if they maintain their present course on the playing field and fail to keep up with the parade. The Falcons had their lowest point total since Jerry Glanville arrived in 1990. The Red Gun offense is very exciting, which will keep the customers in the new, expensive seats satisfied in the short term. But the Falcons better get back on the winning track in 1993, or the rebel yells could get mighty loud, for all the wrong reasons, in the Dome next season.

Quarterback

It was the same old story in 1992 for Chris Miller, and it's safe to say that he must be real tired of this plot line by now. For the third year in a row, Miller was having an excellent season that was either interrupted or cut short due to injury. Miller threw for 1,739 yards and 15 touchdowns in eight games before ripping up his knee in Week Nine. Miller will be back in 1993, but playing his eight home games on the hard carpet of the new Dome in a run-and-shoot offense, which provides little or no protection to a quarterback, doesn't bode well for the injury-prone Miller. Wade Wilson, the Vikings' reject, played very well in Miller's absence, throwing 10 touchdown passes in the Falcons' last three games and 13 overall in 1992. This performance proved Wilson's ticket to free agent success in the offseason, when he signed with New Orleans for big bucks.

Running Back

It wasn't so long ago that running backs were the trademark of the Falcons. William Andrews had consecutive 1,000-yard rushing seasons from 1979 through 1983 (not counting the 1982 strike year), then Gerald Riggs ripped off years of 1,486, 1,719, and 1,327 yards from 1984 through 1986. (Only Eric Dickerson and Walter Payton, the NFL's two all-time leading rushers, accumulated more rushing yards during that time.) John Settle emerged from free agent obscurity to rush for 1,024 yards in 1988. But the running-back tradition in Atlanta has been put in mothballs recently. Since Glanville arrived with his Red Gun offensive scheme in 1990, no Falcons back has rushed for more than 717 yards in a season. In fact, the Falcons' leading rusher in 1992 had fewer rushing yards than any other team leader in the NFL:

Team Rushing Leader	Number of Yards
Broussard (Falcons)	363
Vaughn (Patriots)	451
Mack (Browns)	543
Dunbar (Saints)	565
Johnson (Colts)	592
Word (Chiefs)	607

Rookie Tony Smith, the first-round pick for the Falcons in the 1992 draft, rushed for 329 yards, and he may be Atlanta's back of the future. But Steve Broussard put in a bid for his old job by rushing for 363 yards to lead the team in 1992 (not such a great distinction, as the chart above reveals). Everyone knows the Red Gun offense is designed to feature the passing, not the running, game. But Atlanta's tradition, and the stats discussed elsewhere in this section, clamor for a return to a stronger running game in the Georgia Dome.

Receiver

This may be the best receiving corps this side of the 49ers, and has been for two years running. Michael Haynes and Andre Rison combined for 131 catches, 2,098 yards, and 23 touchdowns in 1991. No pair of receivers save for Jerry Rice and John Taylor matched Rison and

Haynes in all three categories that season. Even with the injury to Miller, the Atlanta duo combined for 141 catches, 1,929 yards, and 21 touchdowns last year. No pair of receivers in the NFL, not even Rice and Taylor, matched Rison and Haynes in all three categories in 1992. The very capable supporting cast of Drew Hill, Tony Jones, and Mike Pritchard added 151 catches, 1,588 yards, and 9 touchdowns last season.

Kicker

The resurgent Norm Johnson is enjoying his tenure in Atlanta. After being cut by Seattle in 1991, he caught on with Atlanta and enjoyed his second fine season in a row in 1992, kicking 18 of 22 field goals, 4 of them from 50 or more yards, for a total of 93 points.

Yardage Breakdown on Scoring Plays—1990

Touchdowns	1–10	11–20	21–30	31–40	41–50	+50	Total
Miller	9	3	2			3	17
Rison	2	5	1			2	10

Field Goals	11–20	21–30	31–40	41–50	+50	Total
Davis		7	7	6	2	22

Yardage Breakdown on Scoring Plays—1991

Touchdowns	1–10	11–20	21–30	31–40	41–50	+50	Total
Miller	6	8	6	1	2	3	26
Broussard	4						4
Rison	4	6	1	1			12
Haynes	1	1	2		3	4	11

Field Goals	11–20	21–30	31–40	41–50	+50	Total
Johnson		10	3	6		19

Yardage Breakdown on Scoring Plays—1992

Touchdowns	1–10	11–20	21–30	31–40	41–50	+50	Total
Miller	4	4	3	1	1	2	15
Rison	5	1	3		1	1	11
Haynes	1	4	1	1	1	2	10
Pritchard	1	3		1			5

Field Goals	11–20	21–30	31–40	41–50	+50	Total
Johnson		6	4	4	4	18

DEFENSE

Consistent with the overall fortunes of the Falcons in 1992, the leading fantasy defense by far in the 1990 and 1991 seasons collapsed last year. In the real world of the NFL, the Falcons were the most porous defense in the league last season, giving up a league-high 346.8 yards per game. By the time Neon Deion figured out which sport he wanted to play, the Falcons' defense was already in the back of the pack from a fantasy perspective. Jerry Glanville, football's corollary to Billy Martin, took over a losing team and immediately pumped the Falcons up for a couple of years with an aggressive, exciting, if limited, brand of ball. But as has happened before, Glanville appears to have run out of gas after his initial success. If Sanders should choose baseball over football, taking his superior ability to return kicks and interceptions with him, the value of the Falcons' defense, even with their agent acquisitions, drops through the floor. DT scores for 1992:

> 99-yard kickoff return
> 73-yard kickoff return
> 69-yard fumble return

Past Performance Key: Atlanta had been first in fantasy points the two seasons prior to 1992.

Fantasy Rankings: 1992—18 points (Tied for 17th)
1991—42 points (1st)
1990—50 points (1st)
1989—12 points (Tied for 21st)

1992 DT Game Summaries:

Shutouts	One
1–7 Points	One
8–14 Points	Two
15–21 Points	Three
Over 21 Points	Nine

CHICAGO BEARS

OFFENSE

The Bears and the Giants are two of the oldest continuous NFL franchises, dating back to 1920 and 1925, respectively. I don't know if there is a connection, but they are also two of the most conservative NFL franchises. This philosophy is reflected not only in the management of each team (neither franchise has ever been particularly active in the Plan B market, for example), but also, and especially, on the field. The Bears franchise, at least in modern times, has never been—and as long as the direct philosophical descendant of George Halas, Mike Ditka, paced the sidelines, probably never would have been—what you would consider a passing team. For example, the team record for passing yardage in a season was set by none other than Bill Wade in 1962, thirty-one long years ago. The amount of that record yardage is 3,172. That's right. As you will read elsewhere, nine NFL quarterbacks passed that figure in 1992 alone. In fact, Wade's record is the lowest for season yardage of any team in the NFL.

Another team record is even more amazing. Sid Luckman set the team record for touchdown passes in a season in 1943 with 28. Yes, 1943. And Luckman threw 7 of those touchdown passes in one game that season, in a 56–7 rout of the New York Giants. No Bear quarterback has thrown 28 or more touchdown passes in a season in 50 years! The following reveals another drought of biblical proportions for the Bears and Giants in the touchdown-pass department:

Last Year Team Had Conference Touchdown Pass Leader

AFC		NFC	
Kansas City	1966	Chicago	1949
Indianapolis	1968	NY Giants	1963
NY Jets	1972	Dallas	1979
Denver	1973	Atlanta	1981
New England	1979	Green Bay	1983
		Phoenix	1984

Never Had Conference Touchdown Pass Leader

Seattle	Born 1976
Tampa Bay	Born 1976
New Orleans	Born 1967

Yes, it has been 30 years since the Giants' Y. A. Tittle set the then-NFL record for touchdown passes in a season with 36. And it could be another 30 years before a Giants quarterback throws 36 touchdowns in a season, if the present approach of the team is any indication, even with new head coach Dan Reeves on board. In fact, with the possible exception of Dallas, none of the teams listed above seem likely to end their drought any season soon, based on franchise philosophies and talent currently on hand. As the old expression says, "The more things change, the more they stay the same." And the Bears' new head coach, Dave Wannstedt, is a defensive coordinator. So, even though he's not an old Bear, he will probably embrace the franchise's traditional offensive philosophy like one.

Quarterback

The 1992 season started innocently enough for Bears quarterbacks. Jim Harbaugh was having a good season statistically, at least as Bears quarterbacks go, early in the year. But the disastrous interception of a pass he threw on an audible against the Vikings in Week Five precipitated the Bears' descent into oblivion in the 1992 season, and the eventual firing of Mike Ditka. Harbaugh ended up the 1992 season with 202 completions in 358 attempts for 2,486 yards and 13 touchdown passes. Peter Tom Willis took over in the latter stages of the season and reminded Bears fans more of Bobby Douglass than of Bill Wade, completing 54 of 92 passes for 716 yards and 4 touchdowns. More to the point, Willis also threw 8 interceptions during his brief stint as the Bears' starter.

Running Back

As I pointed out in last year's edition of this book, 1992 was a critical year for Neal Anderson. It proved to be a disappointing one. Anderson rushed only 156 times for 582 yards, his lowest total since 1987, when he shared the billing on the Sweetness Farewell Tour. Brad Muster chimed in with his worst year in three, rushing for 414 yards, adding 389 yards on 34 pass receptions, and scoring only 5 touchdowns overall. Darren Lewis got the starting nod over Anderson for a few games later in the season, and, while he quickly returned to the backup role, did show promise for the Bears at the goal line, and rushed for 4 touchdowns on only 90 carriers.

Receiver

Two wide receivers led the Bears in pass catching for the second consecutive year, after a Bear running back had been either the leading or second-leading receiver on the team every season since 1972. Tom

Waddle had a solid season considering the team's overall offensive ineffectiveness. He led the Bears' receivers with 4 touchdown receptions, hauling in 46 receptions for 674 yards overall. Wendell Davis had a solid year, leading the Bears with 54 receptions for 734 yards, and contributing 2 touchdowns. The production from the tight ends was virtually nonexistent, with Keith Jennings catching only 23 passes for 264 yards and 1 touchdown.

Kicker

Kevin Butler earned his red badge of courage during the Bears' game against Tampa Bay in Week Eleven, when Ditka called him "gutless," "mentally weak" (a slight improvement over "gutless"), and the "worst kickoff man in the league" (a major improvement over "gutless"). Brimming with confidence after this inspiring pep talk, Butler missed a 44-yard field goal with one second to go against the Bucs that would have tied the game and sent it into overtime. Butler missed 7 of 26 field goals during the 1992 season, 4 of which came in two of the three Chicago losses of 3 points or less in 1992. He finished the season with 91 points, the fifth year out of the last six that he has not exceeded the century mark in points. Chicago, known as "The City of Big Shoulders," may not be strong enough to carry Butler around for another season, unless he improves.

Yardage Breakdown on Scoring Plays—1990

Touchdowns	1–10	11–20	21–30	31–40	41–50	+50	Total
Harbaugh	2	4		1		3	1
N. Anderson	7	2			1		10
Muster	3	3					6

Field Goals	11–20	21–30	31–40	41–50	+50	Total
Butler	1	9	4	9	3	26

Yardage Breakdown on Scoring Plays—1991

Touchdowns	1–10	11–20	21–30	31–40	41–50	+50	Total
Harbaugh	5	3	2	2	1	2	10
N. Anderson	2	1	2		1		6
Muster	6						6
W. Davis	1	1	1	1	1	1	6

Field Goals	11–20	21–30	31–40	41–50	+50	Total
Butler	2	8	3	6		19

Yardage Breakdown on Scoring Plays—1992

Touchdowns	1–10	11–20	21–30	31–40	41–50	+50	Total
Harbaugh	4	4	1		3	1	13
N. Anderson	2	2			1		5
Muster	2	1					3
Waddle	1		1		1	1	4

Field Goals	11–20	21–30	31–40	41–50	+50	Total
Butler	2	9	7	1		19

DEFENSE

The Monsters of the Midway were featured on the cover of *Sports Illustrated* after the first game of the season, and, in the hallowed tradition of the *Sports Illustrated* cover jinx, it was all downhill from there. The Bears posted their worst record since 1975, largely due to an inadequate defense. The 1992 season marked their worst performance in years. The defense, which had surrendered 300 points or more only once from 1983 to 1992, proceeded to give up 361 points last season. From a fantasy perspective, Da Bears had their fourth low-scoring year in a row. With his background as a defensive coordinator, new head coach Dave Wannstedt should help turn this group around. But until he does, even die-hard fans don't need this defense on their fantasy squad. DT Scores in 1992:

Fantasy Rankings: 1992—12 points (Tied for 24th)
1991—6 points (Tied for 24th)
1990—18 points (Tied for 12th)

1989—12 points (Tied for 21st)

Past Performance Key: Chicago failed to post a shutout for the first time since 1987.

1992 DT Game Summaries:

Shutouts	None
1–7 Points	One
8–14 Points	Two
15–21 Points	Four
Over 21 Points	Nine

DALLAS COWBOYS

OFFENSE

The 'Boys are back in town, and they're Bad, with one of the most fearsome offenses in the game. Their championship season, culminating in a 59–17 thrashing of the Buffalo Bobs, er, Bills, was no fluke. In four short years Jimmy Johnson, who dominated college football during his head coaching tenure at Miami, has created a latter-day version of the vintage Cowboys of the late 1970s in Dallas. The troika of Aikman, Smith, and Irvin compares favorably to Staubach, Dorsett, and either of the Pearsons, take your pick. And that comparison speaks volumes. But before the sports world goes overboard with all this dynasty talk, let's remember that the NFL is entering the era of true free agency. The Cowboys' competitors in the NFC East, for example, could open up their franchise checkbooks and pick up a few key players, and the balance of power would shift overnight. With the flash of a checkbook, the Cowboys' dynasty could turn into just another victim of a bloodless coup, NFL style, before you could say "Welcome to Super Bowl XXVIII."

Quarterback

Troy Aikman finally began to justify the Cowboys drafting him with the first pick overall in 1989, first by staying healthy and second by leading the 'Boys to Super Bowl victory. He threw 4 touchdown passes against the Bills, winning the game's MVP Award while punching his ticket to Disney World. Aikman completed 302 of 473 passes for 3,445 yards and 23 touchdowns in 1992, all career highs for the young quarterback. The bad news for the rest of the NFL is that the young Aikman should only get better, starting in the 1993 season.

Running Back

Emmitt Smith emerged in 1992 as perhaps the best running back in the game. In training camp, Smith talked about rushing for 2,000 yards, and he passed the laugh test. While he didn't reach that lofty level (only Eric Dickerson and O. J. Simpson have rushed for 2,000 yards in one season), his overall numbers for 1992 compare favorably with those of the best season of any running back in NFL history. He finished the 1992 season as the NFL's leading rusher for the second straight year, only the ninth player in NFL history to achieve that feat. Smith rushed for 1,713 yards on an NFC-leading 371 carries, and scored 18 touchdowns. His yardage total broke Tony Dorsett's team record of 1,646 yards, set in 1981. He added 59 pass receptions for 335 yards and 1 touchdown. Smith is the key to Dallas's success. Including the 1992 postseason, the Cowboys are 30–1 when Smith carries 20 or more times and 21–1 when he gains at least 100 yards.

If he stays healthy, and if the spoils of free agency don't lure him to another team, Smith will break all of Tony Dorsett's career records in the Big D as he gallops his way to Canton.

Receiver

After a sensational year in 1991, Michael Irvin held out in the preseason of 1992, seeking new terms (read: more money) for his old contract. His brinksmanship paid off, literally, as he inked a new deal on the eve of the first regular-season game against the Redskins, after having missed the entire training camp. He played in the Cowboys' 23–10 victory against the Redskins in the first Monday Night Game of the season anyway, and picked up right where he'd left off the prior season. He led the Cowboys in receiving in that first game, and went on to lead the team for the entire season, with spectacular numbers. In 1992, Irvin had 78 receptions for 1,396 yards and 7 touchdowns, with 1 bonus bomb. His 6 catches for 114 yards and 2 touchdowns sparked the 'Boys to their Super Bowl XXVII victory. Alvin Harper continued to develop in his second year in the league. He caught 4 touchdown passes on only 35 receptions in 1992, averaging 16.1 yards per catch. In addition to catching 3 touchdown passes, Kelvin Martin also returned 2 punts for touchdowns in 1992. Jay Novacek, a Plan B pickup before the 1991 season, had another solid year at tight end, catching 68 balls for 630 yards and 6 scores, second-best among Dallas receivers after Irvin. Only one other pair of receivers in the NFL, Sterling Sharpe and Jackie Harris, combined for more yards than Irvin and Novacek in 1992.

Kicker

Lin Elliott had a shaky start in his rookie year, but came on like gangbusters as the season progressed. In one stretch in the middle of the season Elliott kicked 8 field goals in three games, and ended with 24 field goals and 119 points, fourth-best total in the league. This is an impressive scoring total in light of the fact that he missed 11 field goals during the season.

Yardage Breakdown on Scoring Plays—1990

Touchdowns	1–10	11–20	21–30	31–40	41–50	+50	Total
Aikman	5	2	3			1	11
E. Smith	8	2			1		11
Irvin	2	1	1			1	5

Field Goals	11–20	21–30	31–40	41–50	+50	Total
Willis		4	7	7		18

Yardage Breakdown on Scoring Plays—1991

Touchdowns	1–10	11–20	21–30	31–40	41–50	+50	Total
Aikman	7	1	2	1			11
E. Smith	8	1		1		2	12
Irvin	4		2			2	8

Field Goals	11–20	21–30	31–40	41–50	+50	Total
Willis	3	5	10	7	2	27

Yardage Breakdown on Scoring Plays—1992

Touchdowns	1–10	11–20	21–30	31–40	41–50	+50	Total
Aikman	11	4	5	1	1	1	23
E. Smith	13		3	1		1	18
Irvin	3	1	1		1	1	7

Field Goals	11–20	21–30	31–40	41–50	+50	Total
Elliott		7	9	5	3	24

DEFENSE

The Cowboys had a high-scoring fantasy defense for the second year in a row. Under the guiding hand of Dave Wannstedt, now the head coach of the Chicago Bears, the defense reflected the aggressive philosophy of head coach Jimmy Johnson. It was the number one defense in the league in the regular season, and showed its mettle in the off-season, causing 9 turnovers and scoring 2 touchdowns in the Super Bowl while leading the Cowboys to the world championship. Like the whole franchise, Dallas's defense has arrived as a league power, and should post solid fantasy numbers again in 1993. DT scores for 1992:

79-yard punt return
Safety—punt blocked in end zone
3-yard blocked punt returned for touchdown
15-yard interception return
74-yard punt return
26-yard fumble return

Fantasy Rankings: 1992—32 points (Tied for 5th)
1991—38 points (2nd)
1990—14 points (Tied for 18th)
1989—24 points (Tied for 10th)

Past Performance Key: Dallas's 27–0 shutout of Seattle in Week Six of the 1992 season was its first shutout since the first game of the 1978 season (38–0 against Baltimore).

1992 DT Game Summaries:

Shutouts	One
1–7 Points	Two
8–14 Points	Six
15–21 Points	Three
Over 21 Points	Four

DETROIT LIONS

OFFENSE

The Lions are another of the older NFL franchises, like the Giants and the Bears. They were born as the Portsmouth, Ohio, Spartans in 1930, moving to Detroit in 1934. Like their "elderly" counterparts in the NFL, the Lions have not established a great legacy of offensive scoring prowess in the past. Prior to the arrival of Barry Sanders and the Silver Stretch, the Lions were known mainly for their defense, if anything. Most of the Lions' team records in passing belong to Bobby Layne, who left the team in 1958. They have not led their conference in scoring since 1954, and are one of six teams in history never to score 400 points in a season. This is a truly impressive achievement when you consider how many chances they've had over the years to reach this mark; no NFL team has been trying longer to score 400 points. And while Barry Sanders certainly is a key to an explosive offense, the run-and-shoot offense may not be the right vehicle for this particular pride of Lions to make franchise scoring history.

Quarterback

The Lions' offense presents another situation where you find run-and-shoot quarterbacks getting pounded and injured and missing portions of the season. Rodney Peete was injured all year, and ended up with only 123 completions on 213 attempts, for 1,702 yards and just 9 touchdown passes. Erik Kramer started a few games in mid-season, was largely ineffective, and then was demoted to third string in Week Thirteen of the season. The disappointing Andre Ware, the seventh pick overall in the 1990 draft, started the last three games of the season and was adequate. The Lions' quarterbacks combined for an NFC-low 231 completions, with 21 interceptions, third-highest in the NFC.

Running Back

Barry Sanders had a very un-Sanders-like year in 1992. If anything, his performance underscored the importance of a solid, and healthy, offensive line to an offensive scheme. (See also Washington Redskins, 1992 version.) Most of you are familiar with the personal tragedies that struck members of the Lions' offensive line in the latter part of the 1991 season and prior to the 1992 campaign: the paralysis of Mike Utley and the untimely death of Eric Andolsek. These unfortunate events, and the effect they had on the team's offense in 1992, demonstrated that even a superstar like Barry Sanders needs good blockers in front of him to open holes and get the ground game going. As a result, Sanders rushed for 1,352 yards and only 9 touchdowns in 1992, the lowest TD total of his four-year career. The next-leading rusher on the team after Sanders was Andre Ware, with 124 yards.

Receiver

Willie Green emerged as a presence among NFL receivers in 1992. He caught 5 TD passes on only 33 receptions, to lead the team in the touchdown-pass category. Herman Moore made a significant splash in his second year in the league, snaring 51 passes for 966 yards, most on the team. He averaged 18.9 yards per reception, tying New Orleans's Quinn Early for the NFC lead among receivers with more than 17 receptions. Brett Perriman posted career highs in receptions, with a team-leading 69, and yards, with 810.

Kicker

Jason Hanson had a fine rookie season as he replaced Ed Murray as the Lions' kicker. He scored 93 points, missing just 5 of 26 field goals, for a field goal percentage of 80%. He should do better in 1993 with a year in the league under his belt, especially since he kicks in a dome.

Yardage Breakdown on Scoring Plays—1990

Touchdowns	1–10	11–20	21–30	31–40	41–50	+50	Total
Peete	5	2	3	1	1	1	13
B. Sanders	8	3		1	1		13

Field Goals	11–20	21–30	31–40	41–50	+50	Total
Murray		6	4	3		13

Yardage Breakdown on Scoring Plays—1991

Touchdowns	1–10	11–20	21–30	31–40	41–50	+50	Total
Kramer	4	4	1	1		1	11
Sanders	9	3	1		1	2	16
Green		3	3			1	7

Field Goals	11–20	21–30	31–40	41–50	+50	Total
Murray	1	3	8	7		19

Yardage Breakdown on Scoring Plays—1992

Touchdowns	1–10	11–20	21–30	31–40	41–50	+50	Total
Peete	2	1	1	2		3	9
Sanders	5	2			1	1	9
Green		1	1	1		2	5
Moore		1			1	2	4

Field Goals	11–20	21–30	31–40	41–50	+50	Total
Hanson	1	5	9	5	1	21

DEFENSE

Neon Deion gets the publicity, but pound for pound, the Lions may have the best return man in the game in Mel Gray. (Gray became the first player in NFL history to lead the league in both kickoff and punt returns in 1991.) He's the key to the Lions' high-scoring fantasy defense, which had its second strong season in a row. While not that impressive from a real-world, NFL perspective (they were the ninth-ranked defense in the NFC in 1992), the Lions have demonstrated for two years running that they are a solid fantasy defense, and with All-Pro linebacker Pat Swilling in the fold, they are a solid selection on Draft Day 1993. DT scores for 1992:

58-yard punt return
56-yard blocked field goal return
21-yard fumble return
89-yard kickoff return
7-yard blocked punt return

Past Performance Key: The Lions' defense has not recorded a shutout since the first game of the 1983 season (11–0 against Tampa Bay.)

Fantasy Rankings: 1992—30 points (Tied for 7th)
1991—32 points (Tied for 4th)
1990—18 points (Tied for 12th)
1989—12 points (Tied for 21st)

1992 DT Game Summaries:

Shutouts	None
1–7 Points	Two
8–14 Points	Four
15–21 Points	Two
Over 21 Points	Eight

GREEN BAY PACKERS

OFFENSE

The Packers turned the corner in only one season under offensive guru Mike Holmgren. Once they adapted to the new system around mid-season Green Bay hit stride. The Packers won four games in a row in the latter half of the 1992 season, the first time they had achieved this feat in eight years. They did this on their way to a 9–7 record, the Packers' best since 1989, while making a serious run at the playoffs. Their offense, not surprisingly, was geared toward the passing game. I say not surprisingly for two reasons. Mike Holmgren, as the former offensive coordinator for the San Francisco 49ers, obviously likes a strong passing game. The other reason is that the Packers have not been known to have a strong running game for quite some time. In fact, the Pack and the Dolphins currently lead the league in the dubious distinction of having gone the longest period of time without a 1,000-yard rusher. The last season either the Pack or the Fish had a 1,000-yard rusher was 1978. If you can name either or both of those players, you probably ought to get out of the house more often (answer below).

Last Time Team Had 1,000-Yard Rusher (Prior to 1992):

Green Bay	1978
Miami	1978
Minnesota	1981
Pittsburgh	1983
NY Jets	1984
Raiders	1985
Cleveland	1985
Tampa Bay	1985
Philadelphia	1985
Phoenix	1985

After the 1992 season, the list now looks like this, with Green Bay and Miami still at the top:

Green Bay	1978
Miami	1978
NY Jets	1984
Raiders	1985
Cleveland	1985
Phoenix	1985

What's the big deal about a 1,000-yard rusher? First, despite a comeback in 1992, they are slowly becoming an endangered species:

Year	Number of 1,000-Yard Rushers
1981	15
1982	0 (strike season)
1983	16
1984	13
1985	16
1986	8
1987	2 (strike season)
1988	12
1989	11
1990	8
1991	7
1992	13

Second, while not a guarantee of winning, having a 1,000-yard rusher in your backfield sure helps. The combined record of teams with 1,000-yard rushers over the last four years is as follows:

1989	103–72	58.8%
1990	71–57	55.4%
1991	80–32	71.4%
1992	110–98	52.8%

That's not to say that a bad team can't produce a running back with a 1,000-yard season. Seattle, at 2–14, and Cincinnati, at 5–11, for example, had 1,000-yard rushers in Chris Warren and Harold Green, respectively, and Rodney Hampton rushed for 1,000 yards for the 6–10 Giants. But the won-lost record of teams without a 1,000-yard rusher in 1992 was 114–126, a won-lost percentage of .475. Throw out Seattle's record and the won-lost record for the teams with 1,000-yard rushers rises to .560, the equivalent of a 9–7 record, which was good enough for the Washington Redskins to qualify for the playoffs in 1992. (Speaking of Washington, the Redskins' Earnest Byner missed his third consecutive 1,000-yard season by only two yards.)

If you are still not convinced that a 1,000-yard rusher is important, you should know that of the 19 Super Bowl winners since Super Bowl VI who played a full schedule of games (excluding 1982 and 1987), 16 have had 1,000-yard rushers. (Interestingly, Emmitt Smith was the first league rushing champ to play in a Super Bowl.) This is all a long-winded way of saying that the Pack won't really be Back until it gets more yards from its running backs. After trading for running back John Stephens, they're on the right track. Answer to the above question: The last players for the Packers and Dolphins with 1,000-yard seasons were Terdell Middleton, Green Bay, and Delvin Williams, Miami.

Quarterback

Brett Favre was one of the big surprises to burst on the NFL scene in 1992. Acquired (I think the word is more appropriately "stolen") from Atlanta in a trade for a No. 1 pick prior to the 1992 draft, Favre demonstrated he was for real by throwing a winning touchdown with only 13 seconds left in a game against the Bengals in Week Three. Needless to say, Favre was the starting quarterback the rest of the season. He completed 302 of 471 passes for 3,227 yards and 18 touchdowns, the best numbers from a Packer QB since Don Majkowski in 1989. The Pack was 1–2 before Favre became the starter and 8–5 after he did, for a 9–7 record, only the second winning season for the storied Green Bay franchise since 1979 (not counting the strike year of 1982). The Packers just missed making the playoffs for the first time since 1972 (again not counting 1982). Favre was a big part of Green Bay's success in 1992, and the young player could become an NFL star in Coach Holmgren's sophisticated passing offense. Ken O'Brien, acquired from the Jets in an off-season trade, supplies solid backup.

Running Back

Vince Workman had another, well, workmanlike season for the Pack. He led the Packers in rushing (for the second straight year) with 631 yards. When it came to scoring, though, Workman failed to live up to the standard he set for himself in 1991, as the rushing game suffered at the hands of the explosive passing game in Green Bay in 1992. Workman was one of three Green Bay backs to rush for a pair of touchdowns, Darrell Thompson and Harry Sydney being the other two. The Falcons and the Patriots were the only other teams without a running back who scored 3 or more rushing touchdowns. In fact, the Pack had the third-worst rushing offense in the NFC. John Stephens will help change those numbers.

Receiver

Sterling Sharpe returned to prominence as one of the best receivers in the game. In 1989, Sharpe had a Hall of Fame season, catching 90 passes for 1,423 yards and 12 touchdowns. He did not come close to matching those totals until 1992, when new head coach Mike Holmgren installed Sharpe as the Jerry Rice in the Packers' new offensive scheme. Sharpe responded with another Hall of Fame season, catching an NFL record 108 passes for 1,461 yards and 13 touchdowns. His performance eclipsed those of the other receivers on the Packers. The next-leading receiver was tight end Jackie Harris, with 55 receptions. Sharpe and Harris combined for 2,056 yards, the most by a receiving duo in the NFL in 1992.

Kicker

Chris Jacke had another steady season for the Pack. He started slowly, with only 6 field goals in the team's first five games. But Jacke kicked 11 field goals from Weeks Eleven to Fifteen. Overall, he scored 96 points, with 22 field goals. This total is impressive, considering the miserable weather conditions in Green Bay and Milwaukee later in the season.

Yardage Breakdown on Scoring Plays—1990

Touchdowns	1–10	11–20	21–30	31–40	41–50	+50	Total
Majkowski	5	2	2			1	10
Sharpe	2	2				2	6

Field Goals	11–20	21–30	31–40	41–50	+50	Total
Jacke	1	9	10	1	2	23

Yardage Breakdown on Scoring Plays—1991

Touchdowns	1–10	11–20	21–30	31–40	41–50	+50	Total
Majkowski	2	1					3
Workman	6	1					7
Sharpe	1	2				1	4

Field Goals	11–20	21–30	31–40	41–50	+50	Total
Jacke		9	4	4	1	18

Yardage Breakdown on Scoring Plays—1992

Touchdowns	1–10	11–20	21–30	31–40	41–50	+50	Total
Favre	9	4	1	1	1	2	18
Workman	2						2
Sharpe	5	4	1		1	2	13

Field Goals	11–20	21–30	31–40	41–50	+50	Total
Jacke	1	4	9	6	2	22

DEFENSE

The big news here is the signing of free agency's biggest prize, perennial All-Pro defensive end Reggie White. All of a sudden, the Packer defense is respectable. Still, prior to Reggie's arrival, the Pack was a consistently low-scoring fantasy defense. Even with White anchoring the defensive line, I wouldn't expect a big jump in fantasy scoring by this defense in 1993. In addition to the signing of White, another promising sign is the development of the Pack's first-round pick in the 1992 draft, and fifth pick overall, Terrell Buckley, who is a real threat as a punt returner (he returned 58 yards for a touchdown in Week Three) as a well as a superior coverage man.

58-yard punt return
18-yard fumble return
33-yard interception return

Fantasy Rankings: 1992—18 points (Tied for 17th)
1991—14 points (Tied for 15th)
1990—18 points (Tied for 12th)
1989—14 points (Tied for 19th)

Past Performance Key: Buckley's punt return for a touchdown was the first by a Packer since Ron Pitts returned one during the 1988 season.

1992 DT Game Summaries:

Shutouts	None
1–7 Points	Two
8–14 Points	Five
15–21 Points	One
Over 21 Points	Eight

LOS ANGELES RAMS

OFFENSE

George Bernard Shaw once remarked, "He who can does. He who can't, teaches." All NFL players reach the point where they can't "do" anymore, and some then join the coaching ranks, where their performance is judged on another level. Historically, there's a lot to be said for having been an NFL player before joining the coaching ranks. For instance, the three most successful coaches in NFL history—at least if winning games is the criterion—are George Halas, Don Shula, and Tom Landry, all former players. Of course, there are many fine coaches, like the current coach of the Rams, Chuck Knox, who never played on the pro level. Does it make a difference today whether you are a former NFL player or not? Let's look at how the records of the 14 former NFL players coaching in the NFL in the 1992 season stack up against those of the non-NFL players. (Coach Dennis Green is counted as a nonplayer, since his professional experience came in the Canadian Football League, not the NFL. Likewise Mike Holmgren, who was drafted by the St. Louis Cardinals in 1970, but was released without accumulating any NFL playing experience.)

1992 record of coaches who played in NFL:	103–121
1992 record of coaches who did not play in NFL:	121–103

(For what it's worth, nonplayers also led former players in master's degrees in 1992, by a 7–2 margin.) With the hirings, firings, and retirements of NFL head coaches after the 1992 season, the number of head coaches with playing experience in the NFL remains at 14. We'll see who can do and who can't do next season.

Quarterback

Jim Everett improved somewhat after a disastrous year in 1991 (277 completions, 3,438 yards, only 11 touchdowns), completing 281 of 475 passes for 3,323 yards and 22 touchdowns. While he did not return to the Olympian heights of 1988 and 1989, when he led the league in touchdown passes two years running (no quarterback had done that since Y. A. Tittle for the 1962–63 Giants), he did make a substantial comeback from his abysmal 1991. In fact, Everett is a strong candidate for Comeback Player of the Year.

Running Back

Cleveland Gary is another favorite for Comeback Player of the Year. He had a spectacular year in 1990, rushing for 808 yards and 14 touchdowns. Early-season fumbles in 1991 led to permanent residence in John Robinson's doghouse. Let out by the former Rams coach only on occasion, Gary rushed for just 245 yards and 1 touchdown in 1991. Fast forward to 1992, where Gary had a career-high 1,125 yards, plus 7 rushing touchdowns, under the patient hand of Chuck Knox. And patience was necessary, because Gary continued to lose the ball in 1992, tying Minnesota's Terry Allen and Pittsburgh's Barry Foster for the league lead in fumbles among running backs, with 9.

Receiver

Henry Ellard and Willie "Flipper" Anderson, as recently as four years ago, were one of the premier receiving tandems in the league. In 1989, they combined for 114 catches for 2,528 yards and 13 touchdowns. But in 1992, neither player was even the leading receiver on the team. (Cleveland Gary led the team in receptions, with 52.) To add insult to injury, Ellard's streak of four consecutive years with 1,000 yards receiving, the second-longest mark in the league behind Jerry Rice, was snapped in 1992. Anderson, continuing to put his move on Ellard's old spot as the top receiver on the team, caught 38 passes for 657 yards for a 17.3 yardage average, highest on the team. He also led the team in touchdown catches, with 7. Tight end Jim Price proved a picture of consistency with his second solid season in a row. He caught 35 passes and scored 2 touchdowns in 1991, and caught 34 passes and scored 2 touchdowns in 1992.

Kicker

Tony Zendejas is as accurate as they come. He did not miss a field goal in 1991. Carrying over his streak from prior seasons, Zendejas had made 23 straight field goals, challenging Kevin Butler's record of 24, before he missed a 47-yard attempt in Week Two. Zendejas wound up missing only 5 field goals in 1992. The downside is his low point totals. He scored only 83 points in 1992, the 11th-lowest total in the NFC and 20th overall in the league among kickers.

Yardage Breakdown on Scoring Plays—1990

Touchdowns	1–10	11–20	21–30	31–40	41–50	+50	Total
Everett	11	3	1	3	3	2	23
Gary	12	1	1				14
Ellard		1		1	1	1	4
Anderson				2	1	1	4

Field Goals	11–20	21–30	31–40	41–50	+50	Total
Lansford	3	5	5	2		15

Yardage Breakdown on Scoring Plays—1991

Touchdowns	1–10	11–20	21–30	31–40	41–50	+50	Total
Everett	4	7					11
Delpino	9						9
Ellard	1	2					3
Anderson		1					1

Field Goals	11–20	21–30	31–40	41–50	+50	Total
Zendejas		5	7	5		17

Yardage Breakdown on Scoring Plays—1992

Touchdowns	1–10	11–20	21–30	31–40	41–50	+50	Total
Everett	8	6	2	5		1	22
Gary	7						7
Ellard				3			3
Anderson	1	3	1	2			7

Field Goals	11–20	21–30	31–40	41–50	+50	Total
Zendejas	3	4	5	3		15

DEFENSE

The Rams tightened up their defense somewhat in 1992, but the improvement was negligible. They gave up the most points in the NFL in 1991, and forced the lowest number of turnovers in the league as well. In 1992, they allowed the second-highest number of points, plus the second-highest number of yards. As I'm sure Coach Knox knows, there is lots of room for improvement here. The Rams have never been a high-scoring fantasy defense, and I'd pass on them unless you're an Aries. DT scores in 1992:

Safety—quarterback sacked in end zone
24-yard interception return
61-yard punt return
35-yard punt return

Fantasy Rankings: 1992—20 points (Tied for 13th)
1991—14 points (Tied for 15th)
1990—12 points (Tied for 22nd)
1989—18 points (Tied for 15th)

Past Performance Key: The Rams' defense posted a shutout in 1992 for the first time since the sixth game of the 1988 season.

1992 DT Game Summaries:

Shutouts	One
1–7 Points	None
8–14 Points	Two
15–21 Points	Two
Over 21 Points	Eleven

MINNESOTA VIKINGS

OFFENSE

If you look back at the 1988 San Francisco 49ers coaching staff, you will see three names that now have a common denominator: George Siefert, Mike Holmgren, and Dennis Green. All of them were head coaches in the NFL in 1992, and newcomers Green and Holmgren look like they will be part of the NFL landscape, along with Siefert, for a long time. Green became the first rookie coach to win a division title since Bud Carson did it with Cleveland and fellow former assistant George Siefert did it with San Francisco in 1989. The Vikings made the playoffs for the first time since 1989, although their appearance there was brief. Green has been a success at every coaching job he's had, and should continue to excel in Minnesota.

Quarterback

Green decided early on that Rich Gannon was his quarterback, and the Vikes waived Wade Wilson as a sign of their confidence in him. With this vote of confidence in hand, Gannon threw for 1,905 yards and 12 touchdown passes in the Vikes' first 6 games, but was benched in Week Thirteen of the season after a few ineffective starts. His replacement, Sean Salisbury, threw only 3 touchdown passes in the last 6 games for the Vikings in 1992. The quarterback position, which has always been a traditional strong suit for this team, was a disappointment in 1992. This may be why the Vikings acquired veteran quarterback Jim McMahon in the offseason. How effective the 34-year old McMahon, who attempted only 43 passes in 1992, will be in running the Vikings' offense remains to be seen.

Running Back

Terry Allen emerged as an NFL star in 1992. He rushed for 1,201 yards and 13 touchdowns, and caught 49 passes for 478 yards and 2 more TDs. Allen's was the first 1,000-yard season for a Viking since Ted Brown rushed for 1,063 in 1981. His total also broke Chuck Foreman's team rushing record of 1,155 yards, set in 1976. The veteran Roger Craig chipped in with 416 yards and 4 touchdowns in 1992.

Receiver

Sometimes it's tough to keep the Carters straight. That's understandable, since they both are tremendous receivers. Cris Carter caught 53 passes for 681 yards and 6 touchdowns before he went down with a bad shoulder in Week Twelve. Anthony Carter caught 41 passes for 580 yards and 2 touchdowns. In Week Five, Anthony Carter became the eighth player in NFL history to have a 100-game reception streak. Unfortunately, seven weeks later Carter failed to catch a pass, ending his consecutive game streak at 105, sixth-longest in NFL history. Hassan Jones caught 4 touchdown passes on only 22 receptions. Tight end Steve Jordan caught 2 touchdowns in 1992, including the Vikings' longest scoring play from scrimmage, 60 yards.

Kicker

Fuad Reveiz had an excellent season kicking in the Dome in 1992, posting the best numbers of his career since his rookie year of 1985. Reveiz kicked 19 field goals and scored a total of 102 points, the fifth-highest total for kickers in the NFC.

Yardage Breakdown on Scoring Plays—1990

Touchdowns	1–10	11–20	21–30	31–40	41–50	+50	Total
Gannon	6	3	1		3	3	16
Walker	4					1	5
A. Carter	2	2	1		1	2	8
C. Carter			1		1	1	3

Field Goals	11–20	21–30	31–40	41–50	+50	Total
Reveiz		5	3	3		11

Yardage Breakdown on Scoring Plays—1991

Touchdowns	1–10	11–20	21–30	31–40	41–50	+50	Total
Gannon	8	1	2		1		12
Walker	8	1				1	10
A. Carter	2		2		1		5
C. Carter		1	2	1	1		5

Field Goals	11–20	21–30	31–40	41–50	+50	Total
Reveiz	2	7	4	4		17

Yardage Breakdown on Scoring Plays—1992

Touchdowns	1–10	11–20	21–30	31–40	41–50	+50	Total
Gannon	1	5	2	1	2	1	12
Allen	12	1					13
A. Carter		1			1		2
C. Carter		2	4				6

Field Goals	11–20	21–30	31–40	41–50	+50	Total
Reveiz	1	3	8	5	2	19

DEFENSE

The Vikes seriously regrouped in 1992 to climb back to near the top of the fantasy heap, the best showing for the Purple People Eaters since they held the top spot in 1989. With the exception of the 1991 season, the Vikings have had one of the best fantasy defenses in the NFL in each of the last four years. In one four-week stretch in 1992, the Vikings scored a total of 6 touchdowns—outscoring the vaunted offense of the Washington Redskins during that time! The Vikes have the talent and coaching to return to their position in the upper ranks of defensive teams in 1993. DT scores for 1992:

Safety—quarterback chased out of end zone
35-yard interception return
84-yard interception return
19-yard interception return
22-yard fumble return
27-yard interception return
58-yard fumble return
25-yard interception return
51-yard interception return

Fantasy Rankings: 1992—50 points (2nd)
1991—12 points (Tied for 21st)
1990—28 points (Tied for 4th)
1989—46 points (1st)

Past Performance Key: The Vikings have averaged more fantasy points per season (34) than any other NFL defense over the past four years.

1992 DT Game Summaries:

Shutouts	None
1–7 Points	Four
8–14 Points	Three
15–21 Points	Seven
Over 21 Points	Two

NEW ORLEANS SAINTS

OFFENSE

It's hard to believe that the Saints impersonated an offensive power-house as recently as the 1987 season, when they scored 422 points, the only time in franchise history the Saints have broken the 400-point barrier. As the old saying goes, "Even a blind squirrel finds an acorn every once in a while." But to be fair, there are two things you can count on as surely as the sun coming up tomorrow morning from Jim Mora's teams: They win, and they don't score. (The franchise has never led its division in scoring.) For instance, in 1992, New Orleans compiled a 12–4 regular-season record, while scoring 13 points or fewer in five of its 16 games. This should not be a surprise. The Saints scored 13 or fewer points in 11 of 32 games in the 1990–91 seasons while compiling an impressive 19–13 record. In fact, the Saints are 21–5 in those games in which they scored 20 or more points over the last three years. So, if the Saints ever put together a high-scoring offense, look out.

Quarterback
Bobby Hebert made no one forget franchise hero Archie Manning, but he still posted solid numbers in 1992, completing 249 passes for 3,287 yards, the highest single-season yardage total of his career. He threw 19 touchdown passes, 3 of those bombs of 50 yards or more. Thirteen of Hebert's 19 TD passes came in the first nine games of the Saints' season. New Saints quarterback Wade Wilson can do better.

Running Back
This area has been a perennial problem area since the departure of Rueben Mayes. In a conference known for its collective ability to run the football, New Orleans had only the 11th-ranked rushing game in the NFC in 1992. The Saints' 1992 first-round pick, Vaughn Dunbar, was the leading rusher for the Saints last season, with 565 yards, plus 3 touchdowns. (Dunbar's 565 yards was the most by an NFL rookie in 1992, since San Francisco's Ricky Watters was technically not a rookie.) Dalton Hilliard was the top scorer for the Saints during the 1992 season with 7 touchdowns, 4 of them pass receptions. Craig Heyward rushed for 416 yards and 3 touchdowns. Heyward's rushing total in 1992 was the second-highest of his five-year career.

Receiver
Eric Martin is one of the NFL's best receivers, quietly. The Saints' leading receiver for the past six seasons, he had 68 receptions in 1992, for 1,041 yards and 5 touchdowns. These were the most receptions and yards for Martin in a season since 1989. Quinn Early also impressed in 1992, filling in capably for the injured Floyd Turner, who spent the season on injured reserve. Early caught 30 passes for 566 yards (a career high) and 5 touchdowns, averaging 18.9 yards a catch, the best mark in the NFC. Rookie Torrance Small added 23 receptions for 278 yards and 3 touchdowns.

Kicker
Morten Andersen is one of the best kickers in the game. He made 29 of 34 field goals in 1992, and totaled 120 points, tying Washington's

Chip Lohmiller for second place in scoring. Andersen was one of only three NFL kickers with 5 field goals in one game in 1992. He had 7 field goals from 45 yards or longer in 1992, tying him with Norm Johnson for the league lead. Andersen ended the season with 21 field goals of 50 yards or more in his 11-year NFL career, an NFL record.

Yardage Breakdown on Scoring Plays—1990

Touchdowns	1–10	11–20	21–30	31–40	41–50	+50	Total
Walsh	6	2	2	1	1		12
Heyward	3				1		4

Field Goals	11–20	21–30	31–40	41–50	+50	Total
Andersen	2	4	5	9	1	21

Yardage Breakdown on Scoring Plays—1991

Touchdowns	1–10	11–20	21–30	31–40	41–50	+50	Total
Walsh	7	1	1	2			11
Hebert	2	3			3	1	9
Hilliard	3					1	4
Heyward	4						4
E. Martin	3	1					4
Turner	4	2			1	1	8

Field Goals	11–20	21–30	31–40	41–50	+50	Total
Andersen		7	11	5	2	25

Yardage Breakdown on Scoring Plays—1992

Touchdowns	1–10	11–20	21–30	31–40	41–50	+50	Total
Hebert	5	9	1	1		3	19
Hilliard	1	2					3
Heyward	3						3
Dunbar	3						3
E. Martin	1	3				1	5
Early	2	1		1		1	5

Field Goals	11–20	21–30	31–40	41–50	+50	Total
Andersen	2	9	7	10	1	29

DEFENSE

This is a fabulous defense in both the real world of the NFL and for fantasy purposes. With all the talent on this defense, plus its ball-hawking ability (its 38 takeaways in 1992 tied for fourth in the league, while its 20 fumble recoveries tied for second), the Saints should stay in the upper ranks of fantasy defenses in 1993, and several years beyond that. DT scores for 1992:

19-yard fumble return
71-yard interception return
28-yard fumble return
34-yard interception return
48-yard interception return
76-yard fumble return

Past Performance Key: The Saints were the only team in the NFL that did not give up more than 21 points in one game in 1992.

Fantasy Rankings: 1992—36 points (Tied for 3rd)
1991—18 points (Tied for 10th)
1990—8 points (Tied for 25th)
1989—26 points (Tied for 8th)

1992 DT Game Summaries:

Shutouts	One
1–7 Points	Four
8–14 Points	Five
15–21 Points	Six
Over 21 Points	None

NEW YORK GIANTS

OFFENSE

The Giants continued their conservative, smash-mouth style of play on offense in 1992 under departed head coach Ray Handley. Bill Parcells's successor played the game just like Parcells, only with much less successful results. It's like the Giants, located on the opposite end of the continent, are the mirror image of the 49ers when it comes to offensive philosophy: No matter who is coaching, or who is at quarterback, the Giants are going to run a conservative offense. The Giants haven't scored 400 points since 1963, when Y. A. Tittle threw 36 touchdown passes in a 14-game season. That was also the last time the Giants led the NFL in scoring. While it is questionable that defense wins games without a solid offense to support it (see the New Orleans Saints' won-lost record in the playoffs, for example), there is no question that such an offensive style, when not effective, is deadly boring to watch. Despite the lack of offensive excitement in the Meadowlands, the availability of Giants season tickets remains as rare as a courteous driver behind the wheel of a New York City taxi. Giants fans hope new head coach Dan Reeves will return the franchise to the glory years of the Parcells era. If he doesn't, those season-ticket holders will let him know, loud and clear, how unhappy they are.

Quarterback

The quarterback controversy may not have been invented in New York, but it has been raised to the level of an art form there. The trio of Phil Simms, Jeff Hostetler, and former coach Ray Handley proved an incendiary mix, the flames of which were fanned 24 hours a day by the local all-sports radio station. Coach Reeves will be spared this problem, as the Giants have signed Phil Simms to a new contract while allowing free agent Jeff Hostetler to seek greener pastures with the Raiders. Simms completed 83 of 137 passes for 912 yards and 5 touchdown passes in 1992, while Hostetler completed 103 of 192 passes for 1,225 yards and 8 touchdown passes. Simms isn't getting any younger, so look for 1992 rookies Kent Graham and Dave Brown to become part of the Giants' plans soon. The passing offense, which produced a longest touchdown pass of 25 yards in 1992, will have to be revamped.

Running Back

Rodney Hampton solidified his credentials as one of the NFL's premier backs in 1992. He rushed for 1,141 yards, his second consecutive 1,000-yard year, making him the first Giant back to accomplish this feat since

Joe Morris did it in the 1985–86 seasons. He rushed for 14 touchdowns, the second-highest total in the league and the most for a Giant since O. J. Anderson rushed for 14 in 1989. Hampton is a bona fide star, and Reeves should be glad to have the talent at running back that he lacked in Denver as he begins his tenure as the Giants' head coach. Jarrod Bunch rushed for 501 yards and 3 TDs in a backup role, averaging an impressive 4.8 yards per carry.

Receiver

The way the Giants' offense has been designed in the past, a receiver as talented as Jerry Rice might be lining up on the wing and you would never know it. Stephen Baker and Mark Ingram, the Giants' first-round pick in the 1987 draft, certainly have talent, which is why the Dolphins signed Ingram as a free agent. Their reception totals might be a bit low (Ingram caught 27 passes in 1992, Baker only 17), but Ingram averaged 15.1 yards per catch in 1992 and Baker a whopping 19.6, the best mark in the NFC for a player with 17 or more receptions. But they just aren't going to be given a chance to display this talent fully as long as the Giants' offense stresses the running game. Look for Coach Reeves to find a way to use his receivers, including old friend Mark Jackson.

Kicker

Matt Bahr gave his usual solid, dependable, but not spectacular performance for the first three-quarters of the 1992 season, kicking 16 field goals and scoring 77 points. Ken Willis was picked up after he was waived by the Bucs in mid-season to fill in for the injured Bahr, and he finished the season as the placekicker for the Giants. Look for a serious competition between the two in training camp.

Yardage Breakdown on Scoring Plays—1990

Touchdowns	1–10	11–20	21–30	31–40	41–50	+50	Total
Simms	6	4	1	1	1	2	15
O. J. Anderson	11						11
Hampton	1	1					2
Ingram		2			2	1	5

Field Goals	11–20	21–30	31–40	41–50	+50	Total
Bahr	3	6	4	4	0	17

Yardage Breakdown on Scoring Plays—1991

Touchdowns	1–10	11–20	21–30	31–40	41–50	+50	Total
Simms	1	6	1				8
Hostetler	2	2		1			5
Hampton	8	1	1				10
Baker		3	1				2

Field Goals	11–20	21–30	31–40	41–50	+50	Total
Bahr		6	8	7	1	22

Yardage Breakdown on Scoring Plays—1992

Touchdowns	1–10	11–20	21–30	31–40	41–50	+50	Total
Simms	3	2					5
Hostetler	2	4	2				8
Hampton	11	2				1	14
McCaffrey	1	3	1				5

Field Goals	11–20	21–30	31–40	41–50	+50	Total
Bahr	2	3	8	3		16

DEFENSE

Going into the 1992 season, the Big Blue special teams had not returned a kickoff for a touchdown in 20 years. That's right, 20 years. In another NFL drought of biblical proportions, the immortal Rocky Thompson had a kickoff return for the Giants in 1971 and again in 1972, and no Giant had done it since. But then Dave Meggett stunned the Giants' faithful by returning a kickoff 92 yards for a touchdown against the Eagles in Week Twelve. The Giants are no longer the coleaders in the "Last Time a Team Returned a Kickoff for a Touchdown" department:

1. Denver   1972
2. Tampa   Never in Franchise History (Born 1976)
3. Phoenix/St. Louis   1979
4. Philadelphia   1984
5. NY Jets   1986

While Giants fans may have grown used to the absence of a fleet return specialist streaking into the end zone with a kickoff until Meggett's magnificent runback, they certainly are not familiar with the disappointing defense they watched in 1992. Old age continued to set in, as L.T. conducted his 1992 farewell tour (there'll be a 1993 version as well) around the league before blowing out his Achilles tendon in Week Ten. The Giants allowed more than 300 points to opponents for the first time since 1988. Their defense, second to last in fantasy scoring in 1991, tied with three other teams for the 24th spot in fantasy scoring in 1992. O. J. Anderson said it best after the Giants lost to the Redskins at home in the Meadowlands in Week Fourteen. "It used to be that we walked on the field and people shook in their pants. . . . Nobody fears us anymore. That's the sad part." Sad, indeed. If the new Giants braintrust does not shore up the defense with talented youth in the off-season, look for less fear and more sadness in the Meadowlands in 1992. DT scores for 1992:

> 69-yard interception return
> 92-yard kickoff return

Fantasy Rankings: 1992—12 points (Tied for 24th)
1991—6 points (Tied for 24th)
1990—24 points (Tied for 8th)
1989—28 points (7th)

Past Performance Key: The 47 points New York gave up against the Eagles in Week Twelve is the most points surrendered by a Giants defense since the team's 49–13 loss to Washington in the second week of the 1975 season.

1992 DT Game Summaries:

Shutouts	None
1–7 Points	Two
8–14 Points	Three
15–21 Points	Four
Over 21 Points	Seven

PHILADELPHIA EAGLES

OFFENSE

The Eagles dominated the league in one offensive category in 1992: most controversial personnel moves at most offensive positions. They had what was probably the most publicized quarterback controversy in many years, benching perhaps the most talented quarterback in the league, Randall Cunningham, for a veteran backup, Jim McMahon, more widely known for his attitude than his ability to throw a spiral.

The Eagles then added a controversy at the running-back position for good measure. In the process, they had careened downhill from their position as the Beast of (NFC) East to another one-and-out playoff disappointment by the end of the season. Rich Kotite, a former NFL player at tight end, certainly demonstrated courage with some of these moves, but whether they demonstrated wisdom is another story.

Quarterback

This was one of the stranger personnel situations in the NFL in 1992, and it shouldn't have been. Randall Cunningham appeared to be completely healed from the knee injury that caused him to miss the entire 1991 season. One of the premier quarterbacks in the league prior to his injury, Cunningham returned in 1992 and threw 8 touchdown passes in the first three games of the season, and 12 in the first seven. But after a shaky start against Phoenix in Week Eight, and a poor half against Dallas in Week Nine, Coach Kotite benched Cunningham in favor of McMahon. McMahon almost rallied the Eagles to victory against the Cowboys, and then led them to a win the next week. Then, Kotite reinstalled Cunningham as the starter. In the process, the Eagles offense scored 15 more touchdowns in 1992 than it did in 1991, and 69 more points overall, in large part due to the presence and ability of Cunningham. He ended up with 233 of 384 completions for 2,775 yards and 19 touchdowns, decent numbers for most mortals, but on the low end for a talent like Cunningham.

Running Back

Herschel Walker looked like the answer to Eagles fans' prayers, and performed like one for a while. But by the latter stages of the season, he had become involved in a minor running-back controversy with Heath Sherman. It seems that short of an O. J. Simpson-like performance, Walker will be deemed an underachiever wherever he plays. And while he did not lead the Eagles to the promised land, he did have a terrific season by anyone else's standards, rushing for 1,070 yards and 8 touchdowns. Only 8 NFL running backs who rushed for 1,000 yards had more rushing touchdowns than Walker in 1992, and he was the first Eagles back to rush for 1,000 yards since Earnest Jackson rushed for 1,028 of them in 1985. Yet he still received tons of negative press. Heath Sherman posted good numbers as well, rushing for 583 yards and 5 touchdowns, 497 of those yards and all 5 of the touchdowns in the second half of the season. The Eagles ended up with the highest-rated rushing offense in the NFC, but only the 13th-rated passing offense.

Receiver

Fred Barnett and Calvin Williams were reunited and combined to make one of the more potent receiving tandems in the league in 1992. In 1990, their rookie year, Barnett and Williams combined for 17 touchdowns. This twosome dipped precipitously in production in 1991, due to the injury to Cunningham and their own health problems. In 1992, they returned to rookie form, combining for 123 receptions, 1,681 yards, and 13 touchdown passes. Running back Keith Byars moved to tight end to fill the spot left by the free agency departure of Keith Jackson, and caught 56 passes for 502 yards and 2 touchdowns. Free agent Mark Bavaro will take over at tight end in 1993.

Kicker

Roger Ruzek disappointed Eagles fans terribly after his great performance in 1991. Ruzek kicked 28 of 33 field goals in 1991, on his way to a total of 111 points, seventh-best in the league. But he booted only 16 of 25 field goals in 1992, scoring a total of 88 points, his worst in three seasons as an Eagle.

Yardage Breakdown on Scoring Plays—1990

Touchdowns	1–10	11–20	21–30	31–40	41–50	+50	Total
Cunningham	10	8	4	5	2	1	30
Barnett	2	1	1	2	1	1	8
Williams	2	3	3		1		9

Field Goals	11–20	21–30	31–40	41–50	+50	Total
Ruzek	2	6	8	4	1	21

Yardage Breakdown on Scoring Plays—1991

Touchdowns	1–10	11–20	21–30	31–40	41–50	+50	Total
McMahon	3	4	1	1		3	12
Barnett		2				2	4
Williams	1	1	2			1	5

Field Goals	11–20	21–30	31–40	41–50	+50	Total
Ruzek	3	7	10	7	1	28

Yardage Breakdown on Scoring Plays—1992

Touchdowns	1–10	11–20	21–30	31–40	41–50	+50	Total
Cunningham	5	3	4	4	1	2	19
Walker	6	2					8
Barnett		2	1	1	1	1	6
Williams	2		2	2	1		7

Field Goals	11–20	21–30	31–40	41–50	+50	Total
Ruzek	2	3	5	6		16

DEFENSE

The old football bromide categorically states, "Defense wins championships." If that is the case, why have the Eagles, with their perennially powerful defense, only been to one Super Bowl (which they lost)? A look at the numbers shows that a good offense may be just as valuable as a good defense when it comes to winning the Lombardi Trophy, pro football's ultimate prize. Let's look back over the 27 Super Bowls, using "most points scored" and "fewest points allowed" as the benchmark for offensive and defensive strength in this particular model. Over the years there have been 19 teams in the Super Bowl who led their conference (or league, prior to the AFL-NFL merger) in scoring that particular season. Of those 19 teams, 10 won the Super Bowl. On the other hand, 21 teams with the fewest points allowed in their conference (or league) made it to the Super Bowl, and 11 of those teams won. So there doesn't seem to be any real advantage there. The balance shifts slightly when the offensive and defensive leaders go toe-to-toe in the Super Bowl. In those situations, the defensive leaders have beaten the scoring leaders five out of eight times. But there is no statistical trend strong enough using this model to justify the claim that "Defense wins championships."

While the Eagles' offense is hardly the soul of consistency, year in and year out the Eagles' defense excels. Last season it had 37 takeaways, and a differential of 9 more takeaways than giveaways, tying Philadelphia with New Orleans for the second-best differential in the NFC. Even with a mass exodus of free agent players, the Iggles' D remains a respectable choice on Draft Day. DT scores for 1992:

    37-yard fumble return
    Safety—punter tackled in end zone
    43-yard interception return

3-yard blocked punt return
87-yard punt return
24-yard interception return

Fantasy Rankings: 1992—32 points (Tied for 5th)
1991—24 points (Tied for 7th)
1990—24 points (Tied for 8th)
1989—32 points (Tied for 4th)

Past Performance Key: The Eagles' average of 28 fantasy points over the past four seasons is the fifth-best among defensive teams in the NFL.

1992 DT Game Summaries:

Shutouts	One
1–7 Points	Two
8–14 Points	Five
15–21 Points	Five
Over 21 Points	Three

PHOENIX CARDINALS

OFFENSE

It is the Phoenix Cardinals' great misfortune to play in the toughest division in football. If the Cards were in the AFC East (or West, or Central, for that matter) they might have battled for a playoff spot in 1992. As it is, they took several steps toward improvement in 1992. A few years from now, one game might be looked to as the watershed in franchise history, the Cards' defeat of the Washington Redskins in Week Five of the 1992 season. The media was abuzz with stories of the imminent departure of Coach Joe Bugel if the Cardinals, who at the time were 0–3, lost to the defending Super Bowl champs. Talk about pressure! Fortunately, the Redskins did their old pal Bugel a favor and turned the power off two quarters too soon. The Cards rallied and defeated the Skins with a great second-half comeback—a portent of the demise of the Super Bowl champs, by the way. The Cards went on to win three of their remaining 12 games, stunning the 49ers in Week Nine with a 24–14 victory, and losing by the slim margins of 7–3 to the Eagles in Philly in Week Eight and 16–10 to the eventual NFL champion Dallas Cowboys in Week Twelve. Joe Bugel went from goat to hero in the time it takes to run two interceptions back for touchdowns, and optimism blooms in the desert. Now if the Cardinals could just figure out a way to switch conferences.

Quarterback

Football's dreaded "quarterback controversy" may be brewing between Chris Chandler, Timm Rosenbach and free agent Steve Beuerlein. Rosenbach, the erstwhile Comeback Kid, was injured again in Week One after missing the entire 1991 season. Chandler took over for the injured Rosenbach and posted great numbers in 1992, completing 245 of 413 passes for 2,832 yards and 15 touchdowns. Faced with this performance, Rosenbach spent the season as Chandler's backup once he returned to health. Oh, well, Coach Bugel has plenty of experience with the quarterback controversy, having been the offensive line coach for Washington during the Theismann/Schroeder/Williams/Rypien era (Washington fans: first in war, first in peace, and last to be satisfied with a starting quarterback's performance). In Washington, though, it wasn't Bugel's problem, at least not directly. In Phoenix, that hot potato will be all his.

Running Back

Johnny Johnson came back from injuries to reclaim his starting role in the Cards' backfield in the team's stunning victory over the 49ers in Week Nine, and racked up 734 yards and 6 touchdowns in 1992, with four of his scores coming in the last four weeks of the season. Because of injuries, Johnson has yet to play a full schedule of 16 games in his three years in the league. If and when he does, with Johnson traded to the Jets, first-round draft pick Garrison Hearst becomes the Cards' hope to be that 1,000-yard rusher Phoenix has been looking for since 1985.

Receiver

Randal "Thrill" Hill joined Ernie "Indiana" Jones at wide receiver to make the position two-deep once again, in nicknames as well as skill, in the team's recent tradition of J. T. Smith and Roy Green. Hill led the team in passing yards, with 861 yards on 58 receptions, and scored three touchdowns. Ricky Proehl led the team in receptions with 60, for 744 yards and 3 touchdowns. Indiana Jones led the Cards with 4 touchdown passes, and his 72-yard touchdown pass in Week Six against the Giants was the longest scoring play for the Cardinals in 1992. First-year player Ivory Lee Brown rushed for 2 touchdowns during Johnson's absence, but averaged just 2.9 yards per carry.

Kicker

Greg Davis hit on only 13 field goals out of 26 attempts in 1992. He missed 3 field goal tries in the last game of the season in the sandlot-quality field that was Sun Devil Stadium by the end of December. (The other kicker in that game, the Bucs' Ed Murray, missed 3 field goals as well, so I guess you really could blame it on the field.) Davis ended up with 67 points, the lowest number of points in the NFC among those kickers who played a full 16-game schedule.

Yardage Breakdown on Scoring Plays—1990

Touchdowns	1–10	11–20	21–30	31–40	41–50	+50	Total
Rosenbach	3	3	4	3	2	1	16
J. Johnson	3		2				5
E. Jones			3			1	4

Field Goals	11–20	21–30	31–40	41–50	+50	Total
Del Greco	1	4	7	5		17

Yardage Breakdown on Scoring Plays—1991

Touchdowns	1–10	11–20	21–30	31–40	41–50	+50	Total
Chandler	1		1	1			3
J. Johnson	4						4
E. Jones		1	2		1		4

Field Goals	11–20	21–30	31–40	41–50	+50	Total
Davis		6	8	4	3	21

Yardage Breakdown on Scoring Plays—1992

Touchdowns	1–10	11–20	21–30	31–40	41–50	+50	Total
Chandler	8		3	1	1	2	15
J. Johnson	5				1		6
E. Jones	1				1	2	4

Field Goals	11–20	21–30	31–40	41–50	+50	Total
Davis	1	5	3	4		13

DEFENSE

The Cardinals' defense demonstrated the difference between NFL performance and fantasy results in both 1991 and 1992. For example, the Cards had the same number of takeaways as the Houston Oilers in 1991 (38), but just couldn't convert them into fantasy scores like the First Echelon Oilers, scoring 18 fewer fantasy points than Houston did in 1991. Conversely, 1992 was a subpar year for the Cardinals in terms of takeaways (their total of 28 was the third-lowest in the NFC), but they were more successful in converting them to scores. Robert Massey returned 3 interceptions for touchdowns in 1992, 2 of those coming in one game against the Redskins in Week Five. With Massey's big help, the Cardinals increased their fantasy point totals in 1992. Look for further improvement in 1993. DT scores in 1992:

31-yard interception return
41-yard interception return
46-yard interception return
Safety—quarterback tackled in end zone

Past Performance Key: Phoenix's 3 interception returns for touchdowns were all scored by the same player, Robert Massey. Massey was one short of the NFL season record for interception returns for touchdowns.

Fantasy Rankings:
1992—20 points (Tied for 13th)
1991—18 points (Tied for 10th)
1990—12 points (Tied for 22nd)
1989—14 points (Tied for 19th)

1992 DT Game Summaries:

Shutouts	One
1–7 Points	Two
8–14 Points	Two
15–21 Points	Three
Over 21 Points	Eight

SAN FRANCISCO 49ERS

OFFENSE

Coaches come and coaches go (Bill Walsh to NBC and then Stanford, offensive coordinator Mike Holmgren to the Pack), but the legacy of the 49ers offense is handed down to successive regimes like a family heirloom. And that legacy is perhaps the best-sustained offense in NFL history. Since Bill Walsh took over as the 49ers' head coach in 1979 and went 2–14 in his first season at the helm, they have gained at least 5,000 yards on offense each season (not counting the strike year of 1982), the longest such streak in the NFL. During that period, the 49ers have amassed over 6,000 total yards four times, a record surpassed only by the San Diego Chargers, who used Air Coryell to reach the 6,000-yard mark five times in the early 1980s. Starting with the 1983 season, the 49ers have scored over 400 points in a season six times and have *averaged* 414 points a year, a total bettered *in any one season* by only half of the teams in the NFL during those 10 years.

And the beat goes on. While the 49ers lost to the Cowboys in the NFC Championship Game, they still scored 431 points in 1992 to lead the league. The 49ers have the best of both worlds, a head coach who is a defensive guru and an offense that ranks with the best in the game, year after year. The parts may change, but the high-performance engine keeps humming right along.

Quarterback

Steve Young was given the opportunity to show what he could do as a starter for all 16 games in 1992, and the results were spectacular. He completed 268 of 402 passes, for 3,465 yards and 25 touchdowns, the most TD passes in the NFL in 1992. He posted the highest quarterback ranking this side of, well, Joe Montana, with a 107.0 mark, his second consecutive year with a quarterback rating higher than 100. He led the Niners to a 14–2 regular-season record, the best in the NFL in 1992. He was named the league's Most Valuable Player and the All-Pro quarterback by the Associated Press, and was a Pro Bowl starter. (Although I'm sure he would have much rather been the Super Bowl starter instead.) Speaking of Joe Montana, he came back from his elbow troubles and threw 2 touchdown passes against the Lions in the last game of the 1992 season, inspiring a national audience on the Monday Night Game. Even Steve "Sonny" Bono, the third quarterback on the roster, threw for 2 touchdowns, in the first week of the season game, and raising his value to the highest bidder, which proved to be Kansas City.

Running Back

To borrow an expression from baseball, the 49ers' backfield had a Tinkers-to-Evers-to-Chance theme in 1992. First Tom Rathman started the season hot, scoring 3 touchdowns in Week One against the Giants and 5 touchdowns in the first four weeks. But after Week Five, Ricky Watters took over the backfield scoring on the relay from Rathman. He scored 2 touchdowns, a rush and a pass, in the Niners' game against the Patriots in Week Six, and 3 rushing touchdowns in the 49ers' 56–17 romp over Atlanta in Week Seven. Watters scored an amazing 10 touchdowns during a seven-game stretch in the middle of the season, before getting injured and missing all or most of the last five games of the year. When Watters was sidelined with a bruised shoulder in Week Thirteen, rookie Amp Lee came on and rushed for 261 yards in the last four games. Lee scored 2 touchdowns against the Vikings in a pivotal victory in Week Fifteen, and 4 touchdowns total for the season. Overall, Watters emerged in 1992 as one of the best backs in the league.

Interestingly, the 49ers' longest scoot for a touchdown by a running back in 1992 was 8 yards. (Jerry Rice scored on a 26-yard run in Week Seven against Atlanta, and Young scored on a 39-yard run in Week Five against the Rams to post the longest touchdown runs from scrimmage for the team in 1992.)

Receiver

Jerry Rice (84 receptions, 1,201 yards, and 10 touchdowns in 1992) and anyone else, even Phil McConkey, maybe even your grandmother, might be the best pair of receivers in the NFL. John Taylor is assuredly better than McConkey, your grandmother, and maybe even NBA star Larry Johnson's Grandmama. Taylor missed much of the 1992 season with a broken leg, but still managed to average 17.1 yards per reception and score 3 touchdowns, including a 54-yard bomb. Throw in Mike Sherrard (38 receptions, 607 yards) and tight end Brent Jones (45 receptions, 628 yards, and 4 touchdowns), and you have the finest receiving corps in the NFL, even with Mike Sherrard's departure to New York. Rice passed Largent in Week Fourteen with his 101st career touchdown reception. To show you how talented Rice is, Largent compiled his record over 14 years in the NFL, while Rice did it in his eighth. Rice finished the season with 108 career touchdowns, only 18 short of Jim Brown's record. Perhaps next season, or certainly the season after, Rice will become the leading touchdown scorer of all time, a remarkable achievement in any case, but especially so in such a short period of time.

Kicker

Mike Cofer is a luxury the 49ers can afford. He is arguably one of the worst kickers in the NFL, yet he still trots out to boot for the team every Sunday. His field goal total in 1992 was better than it was in 1991, but that's only because his total was so low in 1991. Cofer kicked only 14 field goals in 1991, making only 50 percent of them, a horrid average. In 1992, he improved somewhat, kicking 18 field goals while making 67 percent of them. He finished with 107 points, and was again the weak link in the 49ers' powerful offensive machine.

Yardage Breakdown on Scoring Plays—1990

Touchdowns	1–10	11–20	21–30	31–40	41–50	+50	Total
Montana	7	6	5	1	3	4	26
Rathman	7						7
Rice	2	6	2	1		2	13
Taylor	1		2	1	2	1	7

Field Goals	11–20	21–30	31–40	41–50	+50	Total
Cofer	1	11	6	4	2	24

Yardage Breakdown on Scoring Plays—1991

Touchdowns	1–10	11–20	21–30	31–40	41–50	+50	Total
Young	4	2	3	1		7	17
Rathman	6						6
Rice	4	2	1	1	1	5	14
Taylor	2	3	2			2	9

Field Goals	11–20	21–30	31–40	41–50	+50	Total
Cofer		5	3	6		14

Yardage Breakdown on Scoring Plays—1992

Touchdowns	1–10	11–20	21–30	31–40	41–50	+50	Total
Young	8	5	5	3	2	2	25
Watters	9						9
Rathman	5						5
Rice	1	2	2	3	1	1	10
B. Jones	2	2					4

Field Goals	11–20	21–30	31–40	41–50	+50	Total
Cofer		7	8	3		18

DEFENSE

The 49ers' defense doesn't seem to get the good press it deserves, as it labors in the long shadow cast by the 49ers' offense. Management has pulled some questionable moves over the past two years, such as letting Ronnie Lott go as a Plan B free agent to the Raiders in 1991, and trading the team's top pass rusher, and team irritant, Charles Haley, to the Cowboys at the beginning of the 1992 season. While the 49ers may have turned the rules of mathematics topsy-turvy in their addition by subtraction, the move provided the missing piece of the Cowboys' defensive puzzle, helping to ensure a trip to the Super Bowl. (The real irony is that the Cowboys, with Haley, beat the 49ers to get their ticket to Pasadena.) But even without these two players, the 49ers defense still excels. As I pointed out earlier, only a handful of teams have held their opponents to fewer then 300 points in each of the last three seasons. Only two teams other than the 49ers have done it four years in a row, and no team has a longer streak than that—except the 49ers. They've managed to hold their opponents under 300 points every year since *1980*, a streak of 12 years!

Despite their overall excellence, the 49ers are a consistent fantasy disappointment, consistently ranking in the bottom of the league in fantasy scoring. In fact, in 1990, they were the lowest-scoring fantasy defense in the league. So don't let the marquee value of the 49ers' defense get in the way of a reasoned decision on Draft Day 1993. DT Scores in 1992:

56-yard interception return

39-yard fumble return

48-yard punt return

Fantasy Rankings: 1992—18 points (Tied for 17th)

1991—14 points (Tied for 15th)

1990—2 points (28th)

1989—12 points (Tied for 21st)

Past Performance Key: Only the Seattle Seahawks have averaged fewer fantasy points per season than the 49ers during the past four seasons.

1992 DT Game Summaries:

Shutouts	None
1–7 Points	Three
8–14 Points	Seven
15–21 Points	Three
Over 21 Points	Three

TAMPA BAY BUCCANEERS

OFFENSE

Former Cincinnati head coach Sam Wyche was brought in to make an instant impact on the Bucs' offense. He was to be the guiding hand that Vinny Testaverde needed all along to develop into a consistent NFL quarterback. The Bucs started well, winning their first two games for the first time in 12 years, and in the process posting a 3-game winning streak for the first time since 1982. However, the Bucs then woke up, realized who they were, and compiled a 3–11 record the rest of the way. While the best-laid plans often boomerang in the NFL, Bucs fans should be patient, because they are headed in the right direction with an offense-minded guru like Wyche. Wyche's teams in Cincinnati were unbelievable offensive machines in the mid-1980s, and he may not get the credit he deserves for having put that offense together. Cincinnati led the NFL in total yards gained in 1986 and 1988, and led the NFL in scoring in 1988. That's real good news for a franchise whose history, when it comes to offense, is, shall we say, offensive. Since its birth as an expansion team in 1976, Tampa Bay has never led the NFL in scoring, or even scored 400 points. It has never had a division rushing leader or a leading touchdown passer. The franchise high for a season is 335, and the Bucs have exceeded 300 points in a season only four times, while scoring fewer than 200 points three times, not counting 1982. This isn't ancient history we're talking about, either—the Bucs scored 199 points in a season as recently as 1991. It might take time for Wyche to bring in the players he needs, but once he does, the Bucs will have an offense more potent than any that's ever been seen in Tampa Stadium, at least in the Florida orange colors.

Quarterback

My Cousin Vinny, in case you missed it, was a movie released in the summer of 1992. It is charitable to describe it as a critical flop. My Cousin Vinny, NFL style, was no flop last season, as Vinny Testaverde made significant improvement, completing 206 of 358 passes for 2,554 yards and 14 touchdowns in 1992. Sam Wyche never had a starting quarterback with a completion average of less than 55 percent in his seven-year tenure at Cincinnati, so it's not surprising that Vinny had a completion average of 57.5 percent, the highest of his career. And, he surpassed Doug Williams as the Bucs' career passing leader in Week Two of the 1992 season.

Running Back

Reggie "Tex" Cobb had a fine season in 1992. He was the first Bucs back to rush for 1,000 yards since James Wilder did the trick in 1985. Cobb rushed for 1,171 yards and 9 touchdowns in 1992. Eight of those touchdowns were from the 1-yard line, the mark of a true designated scorer. A real workhorse, Cobb's 310 carries in 1992 were the fifth-highest total in the league. The Bucs' second-round pick, and 30th overall, in the 1990 draft, Cobb should be a fixture in the Tampa Bay backfield for years to come.

Receiver

Historically, the subpar performances of Tampa quarterbacks does not present a showcase situation for receivers. Still, the Bucs have some talent at this position. Lawrence Dawsey followed up his impressive rookie year with a solid sophomore season. He had 60 receptions for 776 yards, both team highs. But he scored only 1 touchdown in 1992, after 55 receptions for 818 yards and 3 touchdowns, with 1 bonus bomb, in 1991. Dawsey has now led the Bucs in receptions two years in a row. Mark Carrier made a mini-comeback in 1992. As recently as 1989, Carrier had 86 receptions for 1,422 yards, the third-highest yardage total in the NFL. He also scored 9 touchdowns that year, with 2 bonus bombs. In 1990 and 1991, Carrier disappeared into the shadows cast by his 1989 totals. But in 1992, Carrier had a respectable 56 receptions for 692 yards and 4 touchdowns. Tight end Ron Hall caught 39 passes for 351 yards, and scored 4 touchdowns, a career high for him, in the 1992 season. Still, Carrier's free agent signed with Cleveland weakens the Bucs at this position.

Kicker

In the perpetual game of musical kickers in the NFL, Plan B pickup Ken Willis left Dallas after the 1991 season to replace the departed Steve Christie, who had been lured northward to the Buffalo Bills as a free agent. Willis's luck and/or business judgment matched his kicking performance in 1992. Leaving the future Super Bowl champion Cowboys for the perennial NFC Central Division also-ran Bucs was as good a career move as that made by actor Ronald Reagan when he reportedly turned down the lead in some movie to be called *Casablanca.* This became especially evident when Willis was waived by the Bucs before Week Eleven, having made zero field goals in the five games, leading up to his release. Willis ended up with the New York Giants for the tail end of the season. Dame Fortune smiled on Reagan, who was given an opportunity to make up for his error later in life; let's hope Willis gets the same chance with the Giants. Ed Murray replaced Willis, and, perhaps in his swan song, disappointed Tampa fans, making only 4 of 8 field goal attempts in his seven weeks with the Bucs.

Yardage Breakdown on Scoring Plays—1990

Touchdowns	1–10	11–20	21–30	31–40	41–50	+50	Total
Testaverde	7	4	1	1	1	3	17
Cobb	2						2
Carrier	1		1	1		1	4

Field Goals	11–20	21–30	31–40	41–50	+50	Total
Christie		8	9	5	1	23

Yardage Breakdown on Scoring Plays—1991

Touchdowns	1–10	11–20	21–30	31–40	41–50	+50	Total
Testaverde	2	2	2			2	8
Cobb	5		1			1	7
Dawsey	1	1				1	3

Field Goals	11–20	21–30	31–40	41–50	+50	Total
Christie	1	5	8	1		15

Yardage Breakdown on Scoring Plays—1992

Touchdowns	1–10	11–20	21–30	31–40	41–50	+50	Total
Testaverde	4	7	1			2	14
Cobb	9						9
Carrier	1	2	1				4

Field Goals	11–20	21–30	31–40	41–50	+50	Total
Murray/Willis		3	6	3		12

DEFENSE

There was only one way for the Bucs' defense to go after posting zero fantasy points in 1991. And, the Bucs did show marked improvement in 1992 in the fantasy scoring department. But the Bucs must add some important features to their special teams, like a good kick returner, to increase their fantasy value. As I pointed out above, Tampa has never had a kickoff returned for a touchdown, and its date of birth is 1976. Until then, it has a long way to go before becoming a hot property on Draft Day. DT scores in 1992:

15-yard fumble return
42-yard fumble return
56-yard interception return
26-yard fumble return

Past Performance Key: The Bucs have not recorded a shutout since the 10th game of the 1985 season.

Fantasy Rankings: 1992—24 points (Tied for 11th)
1991—0 points (28th)
1990—18 points (Tied for 12th)
1989—22 points (Tied for 12th)

1992 DT Game Summaries:

Shutouts	None
1–7 Points	Three
8–14 Points	None
15–21 Points	Three
Over 21 Points	Ten

WASHINGTON REDSKINS

OFFENSE

The Washington Redskins' offensive scheme was about as successful as the Bush reelection campaign in 1992. On their way to a Super Bowl championship, the Redskins scored 485 points during the regular season in 1991, the fourth-highest total in league history. (The record is 541 points, held by the 1984 Redskins.) However, these same 'Skins scored only 300 points in 1992. Not only was it the team's lowest total since the 1985 season, it was close to the highest drop in scoring from one season to the next in NFL history. (The record is 207 points by the 1964 Giants and 1974 Falcons.) The unexpected departure of Coach Joe Gibbs, the architect of the Redskins' potent offense over the past 12 seasons, is not a great omen either. Washington fans should hope that sports does not once again imitate politics in RFK Stadium during the 1993 season.

Quarterback

Is Mark Rypien a stellar NFL quarterback or is he that common sports phenomenon, the mediocre player who has one great year in him? Judging by the boos that rained down on Rypien during the season at RFK Stadium, Washington fans are leaning toward the latter interpretation. Rypien dropped from 3,564 yards (most in the NFC) and 28 touchdowns in 1991 to 3,282 yards and only 13 touchdown passes in 1992. In all fairness, the offensive line was decimated by injuries early in the season. And once the Hogs, especially All-Everything Jim Lachey, returned to bolster the line late in the season, Rypien's and the Redskins' performances turned around. But the Washington faithful, famous for jumping off a bandwagon at the first whiff of trouble (do the names Zoe Baird or Kimba Wood ring a bell?), may not tolerate another substandard performance in 1993.

Running Back

In a word, the running-back position was a disappointment in 1992. Washington missed the presence of a big back in the Redskins tradition last season. First came the Diesel, John Riggins; then George Rogers; then Gerald Riggs, who was inexplicably released in preseason. In 1992, the team had its lowest rushing total since 1988, with 1,727 yards. The Redskins averaged just 3.6 yards per carry, Washington's lowest team average since 1988. Not surprisingly, Earnest Byner had his lowest rushing total in three seasons as well, rushing for 998 yards and 6 touchdowns he had 7 TDs overall). Ricky Ervins suffered from the proverbial sophomore jinx and did not develop in his second year as hoped, rushing for just 495 yards, an average of only 3.3 yards per carry, and 2 touchdowns. New head coach Richie Petitbon needs to find a big back for the 1993 season in the Redskins tradition, preferably with a last name that starts with *R*.

Receiver

The Posse's performance suffered as a result of Rypien's poor numbers in 1992. Gary Clark had his fewest receptions (64) and lowest yardage (912) since 1988, and his fewest touchdowns (5) since his first year in the league in 1985. Art Monk continued his trek to football immortality, passing the personal milestone of Steve Largent's total reception mark for a career in Week Six. Overall, though, Monk had only 46 receptions for 644 yards and just 3 touchdowns in 1992. Ricky Sanders had a good season, catching 52 passes for 707 yards and 3 touchdowns. New Posse member Desmond Howard was a victim of the mental problem that often afflicts members of the NFL coaching fraternity, freshman-o-phobia, and rarely saw action. Tight end Terry Orr added 3 touchdown catches on only 22 receptions. With Clark gone to Phoenix, Howard and free agent Tim McGee from Cincinnati, will need to step up to keep the posse at full strength.

Kicker

Chip Lohmiller, after a slow start, was his usual outstanding self in 1992. With only 10 field goals in the first seven weeks, he took the tonic indoors in Week eight of the season with 5 field goals against Minnesota, in his college arena, the Metrodome. Lohmiller is a remarkable dome kicker. In his five years in the league, he has played 10 games in a dome and has made 26 of 31 field goals during those, for an .838 accuracy percentage. He's 3 of 5 from 50 or more yards, 9 of 13 from 40 and beyond, and an almost-perfect 17 of 18 from inside the 40. On grass, his lifetime percentage is only .669. As you know, the Redskins play their home games on the natural grass of RFK Stadium in Washington. That didn't stop Lohmiller from kicking 30 field goals and scoring 120 points, tying Morten Andersen for second-best point total in the league, in 1992.

Yardage Breakdown on Scoring Plays—1990

Touchdowns	1–10	11–20	21–30	31–40	41–50	+50	Total
Rypien	9	3		2	1	1	16
Byner	5	1					6
Clark	2	1		1	3	1	8
Monk	3	1		1			5

Field Goals	11–20	21–30	31–40	41–50	+50	Total
Lohmiller	3	9	12	3	3	30

Yardage Breakdown on Scoring Plays—1991

Touchdowns	1–10	11–20	21–30	31–40	41–50	+50	Total
Rypien	6	6	6	2	3	5	28
Riggs	11						11
Byner	3		2				5
Clark	1	1	1	1	2	4	10
Monk	1	4	1	1		1	8

Field Goals	11–20	21–30	31–40	41–50	+50	Total
Lohmiller	1	8	11	9	2	31

Yardage Breakdown on Scoring Plays—1992

Touchdowns	1–10	11–20	21–30	31–40	41–50	+50	Total
Rypien	2	4	2	1	3	1	13
Byner	5	1					6
Clark	1	1	1	1	1		5
Monk	1				2		3

Field Goals	11–20	21–30	31–40	41–50	+50	Total
Lohmiller	2	9	10	7	2	30

DEFENSE

The former Super Bowl champions disappointed while defending their NFL crown. They suffered a crushing blow when they lost their great cornerback and interception returner, Darrell Green, in the second week of the season, and, under the burden of additional key injuries, Washington's pass defense never recorded. (Overall, Redskins starters missed a total of 51 games in 1992, most in the league. The two healthiest teams in 1992 were the Buffalo Bills, with nine games missed by starters, due to injury, and the Dallas Cowboys, with 11. Needless to say, good health goes a long way toward winning in the NFL.) This is demonstrated by the fact that the Redskins' defense pitched 3 shutouts in 1991, but none in 1992. Washington did add explosive 1991 Heisman Trophy winner Desmond Howard to a special-teams unit that already had an excellent kick returner in Brian Mitchell, and together they returned 2 punts for touchdowns in 1992. This well-coached unit should rebound in the fantasy scoring department in 1993. DT scores for 1992:

> 55-yard punt return
> 20-yard interception return
> 84-yard punt return
> 53-yard interception return
> Fumble recovered in end zone

Fantasy Rankings:	1992—30 points (Tied for 7th)
	1991—30 points (6th)
	1990—22 points (11th)
	1989—24 points (Tied for 10th)

1992 DT Game Summaries:

Shutouts	None
1–7 Points	Three
8–14 Points	Four
15–21 Points	Five
Over 21 Points	Four

DANNY SHERIDAN'S QUICK DRAFT TIPS: TEAM REPORTS

The following are more statistical summaries designed to help you evaluate factors affecting an NFL team's offensive and defensive potential in your preparation for Draft Day. The strength of schedule is intended to give fantasy owners an idea of the relative of an NFL team's upcoming matchups. It should also give a fantasy owner an idea about which offenses and defenses may have an easier or more difficult time than others in the 1993 season. For instance, both Kansas City and Houston had 10–6 records in 1992, yet because of scheduling quirks, these teams have the sixth- and seventh-easiest schedules in the NFL next year. On the other hand, Atlanta, which had a 6–10 record in 1992, must play a schedule that has a rating as the second-toughest in the NFL for the coming season.

Strength of Schedule for 1993 Season

Team	Opponents' Won-Lost Record	Winning Percentage
Tampa Bay	110–146	.430
New England	116–140	.453
Seattle	118–138	.461
LA Raiders	119–137	.465
Denver	121–135	.473
Kansas City	123–133	.480
Houston	124–132	.484
Detroit	125–131	.488
San Diego	125–131	.488
Indianapolis	126–130	.492
Pittsburgh	127–129	.496
Cincinnati	128–128	.500
Cleveland	129–127	.504
Buffalo	129–127	.504
Green Bay	130–126	.508
Miami	130–126	.508
Phoenix	130–126	.508
Chicago	131–125	.512
New Orleans	131–125	.512
Washington	131–125	.512
Minnesota	132–124	.516
San Francisco	132–124	.516
Dallas	135–121	.527
LA Rams	135–121	.527
NY Jets	135–121	.527
NY Giants	137–119	.535
Atlanta	138–118	.539
Philadelphia	146–110	.570

• • • • SEVEN • • • •

PLAYER SCOUTING REPORTS

QUARTERBACKS

THE FOLLOWING IS A LISTING of NFL quarterbacks, grouped according to my estimation of their value to the fantasy football owner. The players' fantasy scoring totals, and their prior rankings based on those points from the last four seasons, are provided with each player's report for easy reference. As you will see, the groupings are based on some subjective factors that go beyond mere statistics.

As I noted earlier, scoring in the NFL is down again in 1992 due to shorter games, and the quarterbacks' scoring numbers are clear evidence of that fact. For instance, Steve Young led the NFL with 25 touchdown passes. This is the lowest number of touchdown passes to lead the league since the NFL switched to the 16-game schedule in 1978 (not counting the strike year of 1982). For the second year in a row, only five quarterbacks had 20 or more touchdown passes. In fact, only six quarterbacks have averaged 20 touchdown passes per year over the past two seasons, and only one, Jim Kelly, has averaged 25 touchdown passes or more. On the other hand, nine quarterbacks had 20 or more touchdown passes in 1990, the first year of the new NFL rules regarding the running of the clock, and 10 quarterbacks reached the 20-touchdown mark in 1989 under the old rules of timekeeping.

It is interesting to note that for the second straight season the NFC dominated the NFL's quarterback ratings. The NFC had the three highest-rated quarterbacks in the NFL last season, with the 49ers' Young leading the pack by a country mile (Chris Miller and Troy Aikman were second and third, respectively). Young had a rating of 107.0, 16.3 points higher than his closest competitor. Overall, the NFC had five of the six top-rated quarterbacks, and six of the top nine. In the fantasy realm, the results were a little more balanced. Young was the fantasy scoring leader, of course, with Randall Cunningham second. But the AFC's Jim Kelly was a close third, and AFC quarterbacks ended up with four of the top eight spots.

Injuries also played a key part in NFL quarterbacks' success, or lack of same, in 1992. Only one quarterback, the durable Dave Krieg, played the entire season without missing a snap. Cunningham, recovered completely from his debilitating knee injury of 1991, might have played every down if he hadn't been benched by head coach Rich Kotite in the middle of the season. Otherwise, quarterbacks dropped like flies in 1992.

FIRST ECHELON

1. Steve Young, San Francisco 49ers   Young has demonstrated for two consecutive seasons that he is the most valuable fantasy quarterback in the league. In 1991, Young was on his way to a phenomenal year when he went down with a knee injury in Week Ten against Atlanta. His 96 fantasy points in 10 games translated into 154 points for a full season, a staggering amount. He threw 7 bonus bombs, the most by any quarterback, in 1991, and also rushed for 4 touchdowns, the second-highest total for a quarterback. In 1992, a year when league scoring was its lowest since 1978, Young led all quarterbacks in fantasy scoring by a relatively large margin. He led the league in touchdown passes with 25, and rushed for 4 touchdowns for the second straight season. He was named the league's Most Valuable Player and the All-Pro quarterback by the Associated Press, and a Pro Bowl starter. While his season ended too early to please 49ers fans, who are stuck in the mud somewhere in the swamps of Candlestick, Young's fantasy owners were ecstatic in 1992. They should be just as pleased in 1993.

    Fantasy Rankings: 1992—105 points (1st)
                          1991—96 points (3rd)
                          1990—0 points
                          1989—39 points (22nd)

    Past Performance Key: Young finished the season with a quarterback efficiency rating of 107.0. He is the first NFL player to post a rating of 100 or more for two consecutive seasons since the present rating system was established in 1973. Dan Marino has achieved a rating of 100 or better only once in his 10-year career. Young's 8 rushing touchdowns over the past two seasons ties him with John Elway for the lead among quarterbacks.

2. Jim Kelly, Buffalo Bills   Kelly's stats dipped slightly from his numbers in 1991, but that's to be expected, since 1991 was the best year in this star's NFL career, from a statistical perspective. Kelly set career highs in touchdowns, yardage, completion percentage, and completions in 1991. Kelly returned to earth in 1992 with 23 touchdown passes and only 3 bonus bombs. These numbers are more in line with Kelly's NFL career overall. His NFL career quarterback rating from 1986 to 1989 was 82.6. In 1990–91, he posted markedly improved ratings of 101.2 and 97.6, respectively. In 1992, his rating fell to 81.2, his lowest mark since 1988. Seen in this perspective, it may be asking too much to expect Kelly to throw 33 touchdown passes each year, with 6 bonus bombs, like he did in 1991. But he doesn't need to, as long as the Bills' rushing game keeps rolling along (the Bills led the NFL in rushing yards in 1991 and 1992) and they maintain their fine receiving corps, with the likes of James Lofton and Andre Reed. The Bills' offense remains the best in the AFC and, as long as there is no psychological hangover from Buffalo's third straight Super Bowl loss, it should roll on unimpeded in 1993. With his own ability and the skill of the offense surrounding him, there is no reason Kelly can't post strong numbers again this season and be a First Echelon quarterback for the third straight year.

Fantasy Rankings: 1992—84 points (3rd)
1991—123 points (1st)
1990—81 points (Tied for 4th)
1989—99 points (4th)

Past Performance Key: Kelly's 23 touchdown passes in 1992 was his lowest season total since 1988. He failed to notch the top quarterback rating in the AFC in 1992 after leading the AFC the two prior years. His 80 touchdown passes over the last three years, and 105 over the last four, are the highest totals among NFL quarterbacks. Kelly threw 83 touchdown passes in 32 games in the USFL during the 1984–85 seasons.

3. Randall Cunningham, Philadelphia Eagles Cunningham likes those even-numbered years. He was the highest-rated quarterback under my scoring system in 1988, but fell to the eighth spot in 1989. In 1990, he regained the top spot in fantasy scoring among quarterbacks, and he looked like he was the king of the hill settling in for a long and prosperous reign. Then, disaster struck early in the first game of the 1991 season, and he missed the entire year after reconstructive surgery on his knee. R.C. recovered fully and posted great fantasy numbers once again in 1992, despite the short-lived, but heated, quarterback controversy in the City of Brotherly Love. He threw for 19 touchdowns, with 2 bonus bombs, and, most important for fantasy owners, rushed for 5 touchdowns, the most by any quarterback in the NFL in 1992. Like Satchmo's Dolly, Cunningham's back where he belongs, in the First Echelon—even if 1993 *is* an odd-numbered year.

Fantasy Rankings: 1992—93 points (2nd)
1991—0 points
1990—129 points (1st)
1989—90 points (8th)

Past Performance Key: Cunningham scored 15 rushing touchdowns from 1988 to 90, including 1 bonus run in 1990. During that time, he also threw more touchdown passes than Joe Montana. Cunningham rushed for more touchdowns than either Dalton Hilliard, Marion Butts, Barry Word, or Eric Dickerson in 1992. He passed Fran Tarkenton as the NFL's career quarterback rushing leader in 1992: Cunningham now has 3,986 career rushing yards, while Tarkenton accumulated 3,674.

4. Dan Marino, Miami Dolphins   There is one quarterback you always want on your fantasy squad, and that's Dan Marino. Marino had another stellar season, fantasy and NFL, in 1992, as you would expect from one of the all-time greats. He tossed 24 touchdown passes, with 2 bonus bombs. Marino also continued to set or approach a bunch of records in his 10th year in the league. He tied Johnny Unitas's career total of 290 touchdown passes, second on the all-time list, and needs 53 to pass Fran Tarkenton's record total of 342. Marino kept his 3,000-yard-season streak alive, raising it to an NFL record nine straight. He became only the third player in NFL history with more than 3,000 completions in a career, joining Fran Tarkenton and Dan Fouts in that select group. As far as consistency goes, Marino threw touchdowns in 13 of the 16 Dolphin games in 1992. While he has never again scaled the lofty heights of his utterly incredible performances in 1986 (44 touchdown passes) and 1984 (48), he's one of the few NFL players who combines huge marquee value with fantasy value. He's especially valuable as NFL scoring totals drop, since he's guaranteed to post consistently high numbers from year to year. That's why he's in the First Echelon for the second straight year.

Fantasy Rankings: 1992—78 points (Tied for 4th)
1991—81 points (7th)
1990—69 points (9th)
1989—93 points (Tied for 6th)

Past Performance Key: After 10 NFL seasons, Marino is ranked third in both career attempts and completions, fourth in yardage, and tied for second in touchdown passes. Only Kelly and Moon have more touchdown passes over the last four seasons than Marino. Marino's 7.43 yards per attempt in 1992 was his best season mark since 1986.

5. Warren Moon, Houston Oilers   The 1992 season was the second big disappointment in a row for Moon's fantasy owners. Moon missed virtually all of the last six weeks of the season while recuperating from a broken shoulder he incurred in Week Eleven against the Vikings. (He played briefly in the Oilers' final game of the season.) As a result, he posted his lowest touchdown-pass total since 1988, when he played in only 11 games for the Oilers. He has now dropped from 33 touchdown passes and 2 bonus bombs in 1990, to 23 touchdowns and 1 bomb in 1991, to 18 touchdown passes and 1 bomb in 1992. Moon remained a consistent scorer, though. (He threw touchdown passes in each of the first seven games of the season, for a total of 16, and threw touchdown passes in nine of the 11 games in which he played.)

As long as the Oilers use their version of the run-and-shoot like a possession offense inside the red zone (14 of Moon's 18 touchdown passes, and *all 9* of backup Cody Carlson's, were shorter than 20 yards), Moon has the potential to lead NFL quarterbacks in touchdown passes, and to be one of the premier fantasy quarterbacks in the game. Past performance, and this potential for big numbers, keeps Moon in the First Echelon this year. But fantasy owners, who have now used an early pick on Moon two years in a row, may be running out of patience, as Moon's historic professional football career begins to wind down.

Fantasy Rankings: 1992—63 points (10th)
1991—84 points (Tied for 5th)
1990—117 points (2nd)
1989—96 points (5th)

Past Performance Key: Moon's total of 74 touchdown passes is second only to Kelly's 80 over the last three years, and Moon's total of 97 is second only to Kelly's 105 over the last four. He scored 4 rushing touchdowns in 1989; he's scored 5 since then. Moon was one of only two quarterbacks with 5 touchdown passes in one game in 1992 (Atlanta's, now New Orleans', Wade Wilson was the other).

SECOND ECHELON

1. Troy Aikman, Dallas Cowboys   Aikman continued to make great strides toward NFL stardom in 1992, improving his stats for the fourth straight year while leading the Cowboys to the Super Bowl. He posted career highs in completions, yardage, and touchdowns, with 23, which tied him with Jim Kelly for the third-highest total in the league in 1992. Overall team improvement was one factor in Aikman's numbers, certainly, but good health was a factor, too. After missing the last four weeks of the 1991 season due to injury, Aikman somehow avoided the injury epidemic plaguing the NFL in 1992. The sky's the limit for the first pick in the 1989 draft, as the young Cowboys continue to mature under the steady hand of innovative head coach Jimmy Johnson. Fantasy owners should have no hesitation in making the star quarterback of America's Team, and the MVP of Super Bowl XXVII, the quarterback of their fantasy teams this season.

Fantasy Rankings: 1992—78 points (Tied for 4th)
1991—39 points (19th)
1990—42 points (Tied for 24th)
1989—33 points (Tied for 25th)

Past Performance Key: Aikman has thrown only 2 bonus bombs over the past three seasons. He has rushed for a touchdown in each of the last three seasons. Aikman threw touchdown passes in 12 of the Cowboys' 16 games in 1992. His quarterback rating of 89.5 percent in 1992 was the highest of his career.

2. Chris Miller, Atlanta Falcons   Miller got his annual visit from the injury jinx in 1992. Since 1989, when Miller had 526 pass attempts, he has not thrown more than 413 times in any year, missing games in each of the 1990, 1991, and 1992 seasons due to injury. This was truly unfortunate last year, since he was well on his way to another stellar season for the Falcons. Miller threw 13 touchdown passes in the Falcons' first six games, and 15 overall, before blowing out his knee in Week Nine. Double Miller's number as an approximation of what he might have done over 16 games (or add on backup quarterback Wade Wilson's numbers), and you've got yourself some pretty hefty fantasy numbers for the season. These numbers are not unrealistic, since Miller threw 26 touchdown passes in 1991. Keep in mind that Miller might have the best receiving trio in football to throw to, with speed merchants Haynes, Rison, and Pritchard catching passes for him. This is becoming a lamentably regular comment, but if Miller stays healthy in 1993, he could post First Echelon numbers. Based on past history, however, and with eight games at home on the concrete carpet, his staying healthy for a full season is a mighty big if.

Fantasy Rankings: 1992—51 points (Tied for 14th)
1991—87 points (4th)
1990—66 points (Tied for 11th)
1989—57 points (Tied for 16th)

Past Performance Key: Miller and Wilson combined for 28 touchdown passes and only 10 interceptions in 1992. Miller has never played in all 16 games in one season in his six-year NFL career. He surpassed 12,000 career passing yards in Week One. Only Joe Namath, Dan Marino, Fran Tarkenton, and Bernie Kosar reached that figure faster than Miller, who turned 27 in August of 1992. Only Kelly, Moon, and Marino have more touchdown passes during the last three seasons than Miller, and only Kelly and Young have thrown more bonus bombs over the last three. Miller's 89-yard touchdown pass to Michael Haynes was the longest scoring play from scrimmage in the NFL in 1992.

3. Brett Favre, Green Bay Packers   Early in the season Mike Holmgren was quoted as saying about Brett Favre, "I think I know quarterbacks, and I know what I see and I know what I see in him. He's a talent. It's just, 'How soon will he be a total quarterback?' " The answer to that question became obvious by the middle of the 1992 season, and the answer was, "Right Now." Stolen from Atlanta in a trade for a No. 1 pick prior to the 1992 NFL draft, Favre thrived in new head coach Holmgren's offense, which he imported with him from San Francisco, and completed 302 of 471 passes for 3,227 yards and 18 touchdowns in 1992, the best numbers from a Packer quarterback since those put up by Don Majkowski in 1989. He was a big part of Green Bay's success in 1992, and this young player, who is still learning the NFL ropes, obviously has the tools to become a huge star in Holmgren's sophisticated passing offense. Favre, who pronounces his name "FAHRV," may be causing consternation among linguists and sports announcers around the country, but fantasy owners should have no problem pronouncing his name in the early rounds on Draft Day 1993.

Fantasy Rankings: 1992—66 points (Tied for 9th)
1991—0 points

Past Performance Key: Favre's 64.1% completion percentage was third-best in the NFL in 1992, and second only to Steve Young's among quarterbacks with more than 3,000 yards passing.

4. Jim Everett, Los Angeles Rams   In last year's edition of my book, I pointed out that since his two great seasons in 1988 and 1989, in which he led the league in touchdown passes both years, it had been all downhill for Everett. I noted that he had hit bottom in an abysmal season in 1991. I also said that Everett was too talented to repeat his dismal performance in 1992, and that if you didn't agree with me it wouldn't cost you a very high draft pick to prove me wrong. Well, those of you who sat back and took Everett in the late rounds of the 1992 draft should have done very well in league play in 1992. Everett very quietly was one of the fantasy Comeback Players of the Year in 1992. He jumped from 11 touchdown passes in 1991 to 22 in 1992, with 1 bonus bomb. While he may never repeat his fabulous performances in 1988–89, when he threw a total of 60 touchdown passes, it's not likely he will repeat his awful performance in 1991, either. Look for solid fantasy production from Everett again in 1993.

Fantasy Rankings: 1992—69 points (Tied for 7th)
1991—33 points (Tied for 21st)
1990—81 points (Tied for 4th)
1989—102 points (3rd)

Past Performance Key: Everett's completion percentage of 59.2% in 1992 was his best since 1988. He threw touchdown passes in 13 of the Rams' 16 games. The last NFC quarterback, going back to the old, pre-merger NFL, other than Everett to lead the league in touchdown passes two consecutive years was Y. A. Tittle of the New York Giants in 1962–63. Everett has thrown for at least 3,000 yards in five consecutive seasons.

5. John Elway, Denver Broncos   Elway is the classic example of NFL star quality (or "marquee value") obscuring a player's worth to fantasy owners. Elway's best qualities lie in the real NFL game, where he has the uncanny ability to pull out a close contest. As I pointed out in my discussion of Elway in the previous chapter, 31 times in his 10-year career Elway has brought the Broncos from behind in the fourth quarter, 30 times to victory and once to a tie. Elway worked his magic three times in 1992, against the Raiders in Week One, the Chiefs in Week Five, and the Oilers in Week Seven, before a bum shoulder virtually ended his season. This is a truly remarkable achievement, a testament to his skills as a competitive athlete. But his talents simply do not shine in the harshly objective realm of fantasy football, where scoring, or lack of same, is the sole criterion of ability, and no points for late-game heroics are awarded. Elway has thrown for 20 or more touchdown passes in a season only *once* in his 10-year career (in 1985, when he had a career-high 22). He pads his fantasy totals by scoring several rushing touchdowns every season. Elway rushed for 2 touchdowns in his injury-abbreviated 1992 season, and has rushed for 8 touchdowns during the past two seasons, the highest total among NFL quarterbacks over that time. Certainly, fantasy points are fantasy points, and it doesn't matter how they are scored. But the bottom line for fantasy owners is that Elway might have an uncanny knack for pulling out wins in big games, but he remains highly overrated for fantasy purposes.

Fantasy Rankings: 1992—48 points (Tied for 15th)
1991—84 points (Tied for 5th)
1990—66 points (Tied for 11th)
1989—75 points (Tied for 10th)

Past Performance Key: Elway's streak of seven consecutive 3,000-yard seasons was broken in 1992. He has rushed for at least 2 touchdowns in five of the last six years. Since 1985, Elway has thrown 13 fewer touchdown passes than Dave Krieg, and he has thrown 3 fewer touchdown passes than Vinny Testaverde over the last four years.

6. Stan Humphries, San Diego Chargers   You might call the Lightning Bolts "Washington Redskins West." General Manager Bobby Beathard moved over from Washington and brought lots of other front-office personnel with him. The Chargers have instituted a run-oriented offense under Bobby Ross, not unlike offenses usually seen in the NFC East. Perhaps the most fortuitous transplant is former Redskins quarterback Stan Humphries. Beathard stole Humphries from the Redskins for a third-round pick in late preseason when starter John Friesz was knocked out for the season with a ripped-up knee. Humphries, who had not thrown a pass in an NFL game since mid-1990, took over from Bob Gagliano in the third quarter of the first game and was an initial disappointment, to say the least. He passed for 658 yards with just 1 touchdown and 8 interceptions in the first four games. Then Humphries found his sea legs and caught fire, along with the rest of the team. He passed for 1,021 yards, 6 touchdowns, and only 4 interceptions in the next four games, when the Chargers became only the third team in NFL history to win four games after losing their first four. Overall, Humphries completed 263 passes for 3,356 yards and 16 touchdowns in 1992. He threw 2 bonus bombs and rushed for 4 touchdowns as well. Humphries is the perfect blend of a young but experienced quarterback with a great arm, and a brilliant future. As the song goes, "The future's so bright I gotta wear shades." Don't be blinded by the light, and the implications of the Chargers' tougher schedule, in 1993. If Humphries lasts past the first few rounds, grab him.

> **Fantasy Rankings:** 1992—78 points (Tied for 4th)
> 1991—0 points
> 1990—21 points (Tied for 31st)
>
> **Past Performance Key:** Humphries was the first San Diego quarterback to throw for 3,000 yards since Dan Fouts had 3,031 in 1986. Chargers quarterbacks averaged 5.84 yards per passing attempt in 1991, and 7.29 yards per attempt in 1992. Humphries's 4 touchdowns rushing tied him with Steve Young for the second highest total among quarterbacks in the league. This was a personal best, and was the most for a Chargers quarterback since Mark Malone rushed for 4 touchdowns in 1988. Prior to Humphries's 2 bonus bombs in 1992, San Diego quarterbacks had not tossed one in the previous two seasons.

7. Bobby Hebert, Atlanta Falcons Bobby Hebert had his best NFL season in 1992, achieving his highest single-season yardage total and quarterback rating. He threw 19 touchdown passes, just missing his personal best of 20, and threw 3 bonus bombs to the deceptively speedy receiving corps in New Orleans. He'd be a great selection if he were going to be the starter in Atlanta, but that job belongs to Chris Miller. Or it does until Miller gets hurt again, as he does every season. Hebert is an expensive insurance policy for the Falcons, but a dependable one. So if Miller goes down at some point in the season, Hebert will step right into the high-powered Atlanta offense. You should try to throw Hebert into your fantasy lineup at that point as well.

> **Fantasy Rankings:** 1992—66 points (Tied for 9th)
> 1991—33 points (Tied for 21st)

1990—0 points
1989—51 points (Tied for 19th)
Past Performance Key: Hebert threw 81 touchdown passes in his three years
(1983–85) in the USFL. He has thrown 85 in seven seasons in the NFL.
Hebert had been 15–0 against AFC teams prior to losing to Buffalo at home
in Week Sixteen of the 1992 season. His average of 7.79 yards per attempt
was the highest of his NFL career, and second only to Steve Young's in the
NFL in 1992.

BEST OF THE REST

1. Bernie Kosar, Cleveland Browns   Kosar, like John Elway, is an NFL
player whose star status—or "marquee value," as I put it—far exceeds
his value to fantasy owners. For instance, Kosar hasn't thrown more
than 18 touchdowns in a season in six years. And he has thrown more
than 18 touchdowns in a season only once in his eight-year career. Yet,
he is still regarded as one of the game's best by the pigskin cognoscenti.
Go figure. To add injury to insult, Kosar had a subpar season in 1992
due to a broken ankle. He missed nine weeks after surgery to repair it,
and as a result posted career lows in attempts, completions, yards, and
touchdowns passed. While his grade for 1992 was incomplete, Kosar's
career numbers are a true indication of his value to fantasy owners, and
they are not high enough for you to select Kosar as anything other than
a second quarterback or a backup under expanded-roster rules.
Fantasy Rankings: 1992—27 points (26th)
1991—66 points (8th)
1990—30 points (Tied for 27th)
1989—75 points (Tied for 10th)
Past Performance Key: Kosar's completion rate of 66.5 in 1992 was a personal
best, but he attempted only 155 passes, the lowest total of his career.

2. Dave Krieg, Kansas City Chiefs   Krieg was shown the Plan B door
after 12 fine years with the 'Hawks, but landed on his feet with the
Chiefs for the 1992 season. Still, he didn't do much to solve the Chiefs'
perennial weakness at the quarterback position. Ten NFL quarterbacks threw more touchdown passes than Krieg in 1992. His fantasy
totals were padded by his 4 bonus bombs and 2 rushing touchdowns.
There's no reason that Krieg's performance should improve dramatically in 1993, given the Chiefs' emphasis on the running game. (They
attempted only 413 passes in 1992, second-lowest total in the AFC and
third-lowest in the league.) Not to mention the presence of Joe Montana, who was not obtained by the Chiefs to warm the bench. Krieg is
playing for the record books as well at this point in his career, trying

to pad his resume for Canton. (Who do you think threw all those passes to Steve Largent—Stan Gelbaugh?) He should pass the 30,000-yard mark in 1993, a level reached by only 15 other quarterbacks in NFL history (three of them in 1992: Warren Moon, Phil Simms, and John Elway). He finished the season with 210 career touchdown passes, and needs only 5 more to move into 10th place on the all-time NFL list. All these fancy numbers demonstrate, unfortunately, is that Krieg's best years are behind him. At best, he is a decent second quarterback or backup for expanded-roster owners in 1993.

Fantasy Rankings: 1992—69 points (Tied for 7th)
1991—33 points (Tied for 21st)
1990—51 points (Tied for 20th)
1989—69 points (Tied for 12th)

Past Performance Key: Krieg reached the 200-touchdown mark for his career in Week Six of the 1992 season. He reached that mark in 135 games, faster than all but two NFL quarterbacks, Marino in 89 games and Unitas in 121. His 7.54-yard average per pass attempt was the best in the AFC in 1992. Krieg's 4 bonus touchdown passes were the most by an NFL quarterback in 1992. He has compiled more career yardage than either Len Dawson, George Blanda, Terry Bradshaw, or Joe Namath, all of whom are Hall of Famers and NFL legends.

3. Jim Harbaugh, Chicago Bears   Harbaugh took a giant step backward in 1992, after having the best season of his career in 1991. But so did the whole team. Now that Mike Ditka is gone and Dave Wannstedt is the new Big Bear, will things change much offensively in Chicago? Well, let's put it this way: The Bears franchise, at least in modern times, has never been—and as long as the ghost of George Halas peers down from football's Olympus (his grandson Mike McCaskey's efforts to transform the Bears' image to the contrary), probably never will be—a passing team. First, if you want to revamp the offense, you don't start by hiring a defensive coordinator like Wannstedt. Second, there's something in the collective consciousness of the team that just says "run the ball." As I pointed out in the previous chapter, the team record for passing yardage in a season was set by none other than Billy Wade in 1962, 31 years ago. That's right, 31 years ago, when the NFL season was 14 games long. The amount of Wade's record yardage is 3,172. That's right, only 3,172. Nine NFL quarterbacks passed that figure in 1992 alone. In fact, Wade's total is the lowest record for season passing yards of any team in the NFL. The Bears love to run the football, and who can argue with them? In 1985–86, the Bears averaged 423 pass attempts a season, and 608 rushing attempts. Their combined won-lost record those two years was 29–3. In 1987, the Bears temporarily lost their senses and actually passed more than they ran, but they got away with it, going 11–4. From the 1988 through the 1991 season, the Monsters of the Midway rushed more than they passed each year, compiling a record of 40–24 in the process. The Bears passed 52 more times than they rushed in 1992, and look what happened. Even if Wannstedt wants to remake the style of the Bears' offense, the talent may not be there in 1993. So, if you are a big fan of Da Bears, worship the memory of the departed Coach Ditka in private, but, in public, pass on Harbaugh on Draft Day 1993.

Fantasy Rankings: 1992—48 points (Tied for 15th)
1991—63 points (9th)
1990—30 points (Tied for 27th)

5. Vinny Testaverde, Cleveland Browns   This former Heisman Trophy winner was a bust as the Bucs' quarterback for six years. In a move that defies reason on both parties' behalf, Cleveland will pay millions of dollars to Vinny as Bernie Kosar's backup for the next few years. On second thought, maybe taking a few million bucks to sit on the Cleveland bench isn't such a crazy idea after all. Not that Vinny doesn't belong there. Testaverde has accurately been described by one NFL observer as an interception waiting to happen. All quarterbacks throw interceptions (George Blanda, Bobby Layne, Sammy Baugh, Y. A. Tittle, Joe Namath, and Norm van Brocklin all have at least two things in common: They all are in the Pro Football Hall of Fame, and they all have more career interceptions than touchdown passes), but Vinny's touchdown-to-interception ratio is buried so far in the negative that it's off the screen. In all fairness, he did show some improvement in his first year under Coach Sam Wyche's capable tutelage, posting the best completion rate of his six-year career and his second-highest quarterback rating for a season. Still, Testaverde bailed out before Wyche could make serious inroads into Vinny's professional problems. Draft Testaverde only if your league rules award points for completions to the opposing team.

Fantasy Rankings: 1992—60 points (11th)
1991—30 points (Tied for 27th)
1990—66 points (Tied for 11th)
1989—63 points (Tied for 13th)

Past Performance Key: In his six seasons in the NFL, Testaverde has thrown 77 touchdown passes and 112 interceptions. He has never thrown fewer interceptions than touchdown passes. He rushed for 2 touchdowns in 1992, a personal best.

6. Jim McMahon/Sean Salisbury, Minnesota Vikings   In last year's edition of my book, I said that Rich Gannon was not the answer to the Vikings' problems at quarterback. I guess Dennis Green agrees with me, because Coach Green sat Gannon down in favor of Sean Salisbury in the middle of the season and kept him there through the Vikings brief trip to the playoffs. Then the Vikings released Gannon in the offseason, replacing him with free agent Jim McMahon. Unfortunately, McMahon may not be the answer to the Vikings' problems at quarterback, either. (Vikings fans probably never thought they would see the day when they'd pine for Wade Wilson.) Gannon's fantasy owners could not have been too pleased with Coach Green's decision, since Gannon was not having such a bad season from a fantasy perspective when told to grab some bench. Gannon had thrown 12 touchdown passes in the Vikes' first eight games, including 1 bonus bomb. Salisbury threw only 3 touchdown passes in the last eight games for the Vikings. McMahon is a great leader on the field, but he's never thrown more than 15 touchdown passes in one season during his 11-year NFL career. Even so, surrounded with offensive talent in Minnesota, he's worth a look as a desperation pick later in the draft or as a backup quarterback in the expanded roster format.

Fantasy Rankings:

McMahon	1992—3 points (Tied for 51st)
	1991—51 points (12th)
	1990—0 points
	1989—36 points (Tied for 23rd)
Salisbury	1992—15 points (Tied for 33rd)

Past Performance Key: McMahon has thrown 29 touchdown passes in the 6 even-numbered years in his career. He has thrown 61 touchdown passes in the 5 odd-numbered years in his career. Salisbury had not played a game in the NFL prior to 1992 since 1987, when he had played in 2 games as a replacement player for the Colts in that strike year.

KEEP AN EYE ON

1. Joe Montana, Kansas City Chiefs   Yes, that does have a strange ring to it, Joe Montana of the Kansas City Chiefs. But it was a foregone conclusion that Montana would not be back wearing a 49ers uniform in 1993. Joe wanted to play, not sit as a backup, and who can blame him. I'm sure that Steve Young didn't mind seeing the darling of the 49ers fans leave as well. Common sense dictates that if Montana's healthy, he's your man at quarterback. The greatest quarterback of our time, and maybe of all time, looked good in the final game of the 1992 season and still should have a few touchdowns left in his surgically repaired arm. The Chiefs have plenty of offensive talent and a commitment to building an offense around Montana's skills. (The Chiefs have hired a new offensive coordinator, Paul Hackett, who is a Bill Walsh disciple. Say no more.) While it might be strange to see Montana in a uniform other than the 49ers' Gold and Scarlet, (and an AFC uniform at that), he should look right at home on your fantasy roster this season.

Fantasy Rankings: 1992—6 points (Tied for 46th)
1991—0 points
1990—96 points (3rd)
1989—114 points (2nd)

Past Performance Key: Montana has the highest pass rating of any quarterback in history with at least 1,500 career passing attempts. He set the single-season record for the highest pass rating, with a 112.4 in 1989.

2. Jeff George, Indianapolis Colts   George might get pounded into early retirement before Colts fans and fantasy owners ever get the chance to see what this strong-armed gunslinger can do. He missed three games in his first season, and missed the first four weeks in 1992 with a strained ligament in his right thumb that he suffered during preseason. Then George went down with a broken wrist in Week Eleven. In his brief time in the league, and on his feet, George has exhibited talent. But he must stay healthy before Ted Marchibroda can work on his star pupil and develop him like earlier protégés of his like Bert Jones and Jim Kelly. The potential may be there, but George must prove his worth—and his durability—before he gets much attention on Draft Day.

Fantasy Rankings: 1992—30 points (Tied for 25th)
1991—30 points (Tied for 27th)
1990—60 points (Tied for 17th)

Past Performance Key: Only one NFL quarterback, Browning Nagle, threw as many passes as George in 1992 with as few touchdown passes. George's 7 touchdown passes in 1992 was the lowest total of his three-year career. He has thrown 7 more interceptions than touchdown passes in his career.

3. David Klingler, Cincinnati Bengals   David Klingler, the Bengals' first-round draft pick in 1992, didn't have to wait long before getting his introduction to NFL football. He replaced Boomer in Week Twelve of Cincinnati's disappointing season in 1992. In his abbreviated stint at the end of the season Klingler completed 47 of 98 passes for 530 yards and 3 touchdowns. Despite the underwhelming results, the fans in Riverfront Stadium surely have seen the future at the quarterback position in Cincinnati, and with Boomer gone to the Jets, the future is now for Klingler.

Fantasy Rankings: 1992—points (Tied for 27th)

Past Performance Key: Klingler's 83-yard touchdown to Jeff Query in Week Fifteen was the longest touchdown pass in the AFC in 1992. It was the only bonus bomb of the season by a Bengal quarterback.

4. Timm Rosenbach/Chris Chandler/Steve Beuerlein, Phoenix Cardinals Rosenbach was a sleeper pick to be one of the top fantasy quarterbacks in 1992, after missing 1991 with a knee injury. But he was injured again early in the 1992 season, and Chris Chandler took over at the Cardinals' helm. After bouncing around the NFL for 4 years, Chandler did an outstanding job and enjoyed the best season of his career. He posted career highs in completions, completion percentage, yards passing, and touchdown passes, with 15, and added 2 bonus bombs. After Week Nine, the surprising Chandler had as many fantasy points as Jim Kelly, and more than Marino, Rypien, or Aikman! While he could not maintain that pace the entire season, Chandler still posted healthy fantasy numbers. In addition to a healthy Rosenbach, Chandler will now have to contend with free agent Beuerlein, signed to a $7.5 million contract in the offseason. There will be some dogfight in preseason for the starting job between three talented quarterbacks. The survivor could be a fantasy sleeper in 1993.

Fantasy Rankings:

Rosenbach	1992—0 points
	1991—0 points
	1990—69 points (Tied for 9th)
	1989—0 points
Chandler:	1992—57 points (12th)
	1991—15 points (Tied for 38th)
	1990—12 points (Tied for 38th)
	1989—15 points (Tied for 37th)
Beuerlein:	1992—0 points
	1991—21 points (Tied for 35th)
	1990—Did Not Play
	1989—42 points (21st)

Past Performance Key: Rosenbach passed for more than 3,000 yards and 16 touchdowns in 1990. He also rushed for 3 touchdowns. Chandler has rushed for at least 1 touchdown in four of his five NFL seasons. Beuerlein has a lifetime completion average of 48% during his four years in the league.

5. Rodney Peete/Andre Ware, Detroit Lions Wayne Fontes is faced this season with the old bugaboo of head coaches in the NFL, the dreaded quarterback controversy. Rodney Peete could make Fontes's life real simple by coming into camp healthy and staying that way, because he's the best quarterback the Lions have. Like Chris Miller, Peete was off to a great start before injuries slowed him down in 1992, tossing 9 touchdown passes in the Lions' first seven games, including 3 bonus bombs. But also like Miller, Peete seems to get hurt every year. Peete had missed 21 of 48 games in the three years prior to 1992, and then missed portions of several games before being benched for Andre Ware the final three weeks of last season. It is not much of an understatement to say that Ware didn't exactly set the world on fire in his brief stint in the starting lineup. Peete is worth a shot as a second quarterback, or a backup in the expanded-roster format, if you think he will stay healthy this season. You can steer clear of Motor City quarterbacks in all other respects on Draft Day 1993.

Fantasy Rankings:

Peete
1992—36 points (21st)
1991—30 points (Tied for 27th)
1990—78 points (7th)
1989—33 points (Tied for 25th)

Ware
1992—9 points (Tied for 41st)
1991—0 points
1990—3 points (Tied for 49th)

Past Performance Key: Peete's yardage average of 7.99 yards per attempt in 1992 was a career high. He has attempted more than 213 passes, his 1992 total, only one other season in his four-year career. Ware was the second-leading rusher on the Lions, with 124 yards, in 1992.

6. Phil Simms, New York Giants   The quarterback controversy that developed between Jeff Hostetler and Phil Simms over the last two seasons led directly to the downfall of former Giants coach Ray Handley. The Giants helped new head coach Dan Reeves avoid this problem by letting free agent Hostetler seek a new team while signing Simms to a multimillion-dollar contract last March. Offensive genius Reeves should bring out the best in Simms, as he performs his swan song for two more seasons at quarterback before packing it in and spending the next few years deciding whom he wants to introduce him at Canton. Simms might surprise as a second quarterback on your fantasy roster next season.

Fantasy Rankings: 1992—15 points (Tied for 33rd)
1991—30 points (Tied for 27th)
1990—57 points (19th)
1989—57 points (Tied for 16th)

Past Performance Key: Simms is one of only 12 NFL quarterbacks to throw for 4,000 yards in a season. He passed the 30,000-yard mark in 1993, a level reached by only 14 other quarterbacks in NFL history. He has thrown 36 more career touchdown passes than interceptions, a differential matched by only nine of the 22 quarterbacks with more career touchdown passes than Simms.

7. Wade Wilson, New Orleans Saints Wilson's NFL stock, which had plummeted after his release from the Vikings before the 1992 season, rose significantly as a result of his second-half performance with the Falcons in 1992. Filling in for the injured Chris Miller, Wilson threw 11 touchdown passes in the last four weeks of the 1992 season, and 13 overall. With Bobby Hebert gone, Wilson should be the starter in the Superdome this year. But New Orleans' offense will never be confused with the Red Gun, so don't expect a repeat performance of Wilson's great second half this year. Hebert may be gone, but his scoring numbers will live on in the person of Wade Wilson for fantasy owners in 1993.

Fantasy Rankings: 1992—42 points (Tied for 18th)
1991—9 points (Tied for 40th)
1990—30 points (Tied for 27th)
1989—33 points (Tied for 25th)

Past Performance Key: Wilson's 13 touchdowns in 1992 was his highest season total since 1988, and the third-highest season total of his 11-year career.

BIGGEST BUSTS

1. Mark Rypien, Washington Redskins I've given myself credit several times for perceptive predictions in last year's edition of this book. In the interests of fairness, here's what I had to say about Rypien last year. "Mark the Rypper's spectacular season in 1991 dispelled all doubts held by Redskins fans about his ability to lead Washington's offense. At the same time, he relegated the hallowed Washington tradition of the quarterback controversy to the trash heap. . . . With the Posse intact, the addition of Heisman Trophy Winner Desmond Howard, and one of the great offensive lines in NFL history protecting him (potential Hall of Fame tackle Jim Lachey allowed *no* quarterback sacks in 1991), Rypien should do as well or better in 1992." Well, nobody's perfect— and the same could certainly be said of Rypien and the Redskins in 1992. What a disappointment. Rypien went from career highs of 28 touchdown passes and 6 bonus bombs in 1991 to 13 touchdowns and

1 bonus bomb in 1992. The same man who threw 6 touchdown passes in one game in 1991 could manage to throw no more than 2 in any one game in 1992 (23 quarterbacks in the league had 3 or more TD passes in one game in 1992). In one game against Atlanta in 1991, he posted a total of 33 fantasy points; his entire total for the 1992 season was 54 points. His yardage average per attempt fell from 8.47 in 1991 to 6.85 in 1992. The Redskins did not fall that far in 1992 that they can't rebound in 1993, although the premature retirement of Joe Gibbs is a blow to their offense. But it looks like 1991 was a career year rather than a career norm for Rypien.

Fantasy Rankings: 1992—54 points (13th)
1991—108 points (2nd)
1990—51 points (20th)
1989—78 points (9th)

Past Performance Key: Rypien's quarterback rating fell from 97.9 in 1991 to 71.7 in 1992. In 67 NFL contests, Rypien has thrown 97 touchdown passes, an average of almost 1.5 per game. Joe Montana has averaged 1.5 touchdown passes per game over his career.

2. Boomer Esiason, New York Jets   Boomer hit bottom in 1992, with his second consecutive disastrous season. His yardage and touchdown totals, as well as his yardage average and quarterback rating, were his lowest since 1984. His yardage average per attempt had dropped from 9.21 in 1988 to 7.75 in 1989, 7.54 in 1990, and 6.98 in 1991. Then, in 1992, it had fallen to 5.08 by the time he was benched for Klingler. The last straw came in Week Twelve, when Boomer completed 12 passes for only 64 yards in a 19–13 loss against Detroit. Once one of the preeminent signal-callers in the league, Norman needed another chance to show that he was not done as an NFL quarterback. And the Jets have offered him that chance. Reunited with his old offensive coordinator, Bruce Coslet, and playing in front of his hometown fans (Boomer grew up in the New York metropolitan area), Esiason should demonstrate that there are still a few touchdown passes left in his arm. Don't risk an early draft pick to find out just how many, but don't be afraid to grab him as a second quarterback late in the draft, either.

Fantasy Rankings: 1992—33 points (Tied for 22nd)
1991—42 points (Tied for 16th)
1990—75 points (8th)
1989—93 points (6th)

Past Performance Key: In 1989–90, only Warren Moon threw more touchdown passes than Boomer's (and Jim Everett's) 52. But in the last two seasons, 13 quarterbacks have thrown more touchdown passes than Boomer's 24.

3. Jeff Hostetler/Todd Marinovich, Los Angeles Raiders What can you say? Not to put too fine a point on it, but the Raiders' quarterbacks were terrible, at least from a fantasy perspective. Even if you combined their fantasy totals in 1992, Schroeder and Marinovich would have managed only 54 fantasy points, tying Mark Rypien for the 13th-best mark. (Talk about terrible—but I've already ripped the Rypper.) Famous for being a shrewd judge of talent, Al Davis has invested a large chunk of his reputation in the eventual success of Todd Marinovich. You can be sure that the canny Davis will find some way to salvage this situation. Signing free agent Jeff Hostetler was a step in the right direction. So was letting free agent Schroeder sign with Cincinatti, where he will provide backup help for David Klinger. Even with Hostetler on board, though, you can skip selecting a quarterback wearing the Silver and Black on Draft Day 1993 with a clear conscience.

Fantasy Rankings:

Schroeder	1992—33 points (Tied for 22nd)
	1991—54 points (11th)
	1990—63 points (Tied for 14th)
	1989—33 points (Tied for 25th)
Marinovich	1992—21 points (Tied for 28th)
	1991—9 points (Tied for 40th)
Hostetler	1992—42 points (Tied for 18th)
	1991—27 points (Tied for 33rd)
	1990—21 points (Tied for 31st)
	1989—21 points (Tied for 35th)

Past Performance Key: Schroeder's 11 touchdown passes in 1992 was his lowest total since 1989, his first year with the Raiders, and the third-lowest total of his eight-year career. He failed to throw a bonus bomb for the first time in the four editions of this book. Schroeder's 5.83 yards per attempt was the lowest average of his career. Marinovich threw 4 more interceptions than touchdown passes in 1992. Hostetler rushed for 3 touchdowns in 1992, a career high. He had rushed for 2 touchdowns in the 1989, '90, and '91 seasons.

5. Stan Gelbaugh/Dan McGwire, Seattle Seahawks This duo is not dynamic, and any further explanation than that to even the casual observer of professional football during the 1992 season is not warranted. You can safely pass on these Seahawks quarterbacks in the 1993 draft.

Gelbaugh	1992—18 points (Tied for 30th)
	1991—9 points (Tied for 40th)
	1990—DNP
	1989—0 points

McGwire   1992—0 points
            1991—0 points
Past Performance Key: Gelbaugh completed less than half of his passes in 1992. Dan McGwire is the brother of Oakland A's first baseman Mark McGwire.

QUICK DRAFT TIPS: QUARTERBACKS

The following statistical summaries try to give a quick glimpse at those scoring abilities that might set a quarterback apart from the crowd in this year's fantasy draft.

Leaders in Touchdown Passes—1991–92

Kelly	56
Marino	49
Young	42
Moon	41
Rypien	41
Miller	41
Aikman	34
Everett	33
Harbaugh	28
Hebert	28
Kosar	26
Krieg	26
Schroeder	26
Esiason	24
Gannon	24
O'Donnell	24
Elway	23
Testaverde	22

Quarterback Leaders in Rushing Touchdowns
1992

Cunningham	5
Humphries	4
Young	4
Hostetler	3
Elway	2
Krieg	2
Rypien	2
Testaverde	2
Aikman	1
Carlson	1
Chandler	1
Favre	1
George	1
Harbaugh	1
Kelly	1
Moon	1
O'Donnell	1

Leaders in Bonus Bombs—1991–92

Kelly	9
Young	9
Rypien	7
Elway	5
Hebert	5
Kosar	5
Miller	5
Krieg	4
Peete	4
Testaverde	4
Harbaugh	3
Millen	3
Schroeder	3
Chandler	2
Cunningham	2
Favre	2
Marino	2
Moon	2
O'Brien	2
O'Donnell	2

1991–92

Elway	8
Young	8
Hostetler	5
Cunningham	4
Humphries	4
Harbaugh	3
Moon	3
Rypien	3
Aikman	2
Gannon	2
Hebert	2
Kelly	2
Krieg	2
Testaverde	2

RUNNING BACKS

Surprise, surprise. That was the theme of the performances by running backs in the NFL in 1992. While the usual high-scoring suspects generally dominated the other player categories found in my Scouting Reports, the high end of the running-back category was filled with new and unexpected names and faces last season. You expected great performances from the likes of Emmitt Smith, Thurman Thomas, and Barry Sanders. But the average fan could not have anticipated some of the other great performances in 1992. (If you did, you should be gazing into the future over a copy of the *Racing Form* somewhere along the homestretch.) Running backs like Barry Foster, Ricky Watters, and Terry Allen came out of NFL obscurity to have spectacular seasons for the Pittsburgh Steelers, the San Francisco 49ers, and the Minnesota Vikings, respectively. The Giants' Rodney Hampton, while certainly a heralded back (he was rated the sixth-best running back, third in the Second Echelon, in last year's edition of this book), raised his game up another level to become one of football's real stars. Cleveland Gary overcame a severe case of fumble-itis and returned from the NFL scrap heap to become a scoring force for the Rams. Herschel Walker, always deemed a perennial underachiever in the media, had another quietly spectacular NFL season, this time for his new squad, the Eagles.

Last year I ranked three running backs in the First Echelon: Barry Sanders, Thurman Thomas, and Emmitt Smith. This year Emmitt Smith stands alone in the coveted top ranking. Barry Sanders and Thurman Thomas drop down to lead what may be the strongest Second

Echelon of running backs in the four editions of this book. Several of them emerged in 1992 as talented backs, and some have the potential to move up into the First Echelon with Smith. But Smith is the premier running back in the NFL, fantasy or otherwise, as Draft Day 1993 approaches.

FIRST ECHELON

1. Emmitt Smith, Dallas Cowboys After an excellent rookie year in 1990, Smith performed like the second coming of Tony Dorsett in 1991. Then he made everyone forget Tony Dorsett in 1992, with a truly great season. Smith led the NFL in rushing for the second consecutive season, with 1,713 yards, fending off a strong challenge by Pittsburgh's Barry Foster. In leading the NFL in rushing for the second year in a row, Smith became the first back since Eric Dickerson in 1983–84, and one of only nine players in NFL history, to perform the feat. He scored 18 rushing touchdowns, tying him with two other NFL players for the sixth-highest single-season total in NFL history, and he caught a touchdown pass to boot. In the playoffs he rushed for 336 yards and scored 3 touchdowns in leading the Cowboys to their Super Bowl victory. He led all backs in fantasy scoring with 117 points, the highest total for a back in the four-year history of this book. Known as "Magic Man" in the Big D, Smith has demonstrated that he may dominate his sport like another Magic did in the NBA. If he isn't the first pick on Draft Day, 1993, the guy with the second pick pulled a Houdini.

Fantasy Rankings: 1992—117 points (1st)
1991—87 points (2nd)
1990—66 points (Tied 7th)

Past Performance Key: Smith's total of 41 rushing touchdowns over the past three years is the best in the league. He has 4,213 yards rushing over the last three seasons, best in the NFL by the slimmest of margins. (Barry Sanders has 4,204 yards, and Thurman Thomas has 4,191.) Smith was one of only two backs in the NFL with two games in which he scored 3 rushing touchdowns in 1992. (The Giants' Rodney Hampton was the other.) He recorded a bonus touchdown run for the second consecutive year, one of only five backs in the NFL to do so. His 68-yard touchdown run in Week Thirteen against the Giants in Dallas was the longest such run in the NFL from scrimmage in 1992.

SECOND ECHELON

1. Barry Sanders, Detroit Lions Sanders was my top-rated running back in the 1990 and 1991 editions of this book. He slipped a notch in

1992, just enough to tumble from the First Echelon, but not far from it. Only a Herculean effort by Emmitt Smith in 1992 allowed him to pull away, however slightly, from Sanders. To be fair, all of the blame for his dip in production cannot be laid at Sanders's feet. Even with his extraordinary talent, he could not overcome the personal tragedies that decimated his offensive line. Nevertheless, Sanders remains the second-best running back in the game. He rushed for 1,352 yards and 9 touchdowns in 1992, scoring 10 TDs overall—and this was his worst season in his four years in the league! Over the last three seasons, Sanders's 4,204 yards is second only to Smith's 4,213, and his 38 rushing touchdowns are right behind Smith's 41. In fact, the hairbreadth of difference between the two players might just be the quality of the team they each play for—specifically, the quality of their offensive lines. While that opinion might be an arguable proposition, it is safe to say that if Sanders isn't the first player selected on Draft Day 1993, he should be the second.

Fantasy Rankings: 1992—63 points (Tied for 5th)
1991—111 points (1st)
1990—87 points (Tied for 1st)
1989—84 points (Tied for 4th)

Past Performance Key: Sanders's 9 rushing touchdowns in 1992 was the lowest season total of his four-year career. His yards-per-carry average has dropped steadily each season, from 5.3 in his rookie year to 4.3 in 1992. Like Smith, Sanders recorded a bonus touchdown run for the second consecutive year. Only a measly 25 yards separated Sanders from three consecutive rushing titles in 1989–91. (He finished 10 yards behind Christian Okoye in 1989, 1,480 to 1,470, and 15 yards behind Emmitt Smith in 1991, 1,563 to 1,548. He won the rushing title with 1,304 yards in 1990.) Sanders's 5,674 yards rushing in his first four seasons in the league is third in NFL history behind Eric Dickerson's 6,968 yards and Earl Campbell's 6,457.

2. Rodney Hampton, New York Giants   Hampton emerged from the rubble of the Giants' disappointing season in 1992 as one of the premier backs in the NFL, as well as a hero to his fantasy owners. Hampton continued in the hallowed tradition of designated scorers in the Giants' backfield. He scored all but 3 of the team's rushing touchdowns in 1991, and 14 of the 17 rushing touchdowns by Giant backs in 1992, despite the presence of running mate Jarrod Bunch, a natural fullback and a potentially awesome designated scorer (6'2", 250, and timed at 4.6 in the 40). When I say "hallowed tradition," I mean that a Giants running back has scored at least 10 rushing touchdowns in six of the last eight seasons, including Hampton's 14 touchdowns in 1992, the second-highest total in the league. Hampton rushed for 1,141 yards in 1992, after racking up 1,059 yards in 1991. Regardless of the new offensive scheme installed by Giant Coach Dan Reeves, Hampton's here to stay as the Giants' feature back for years to come. He is a first-round pick on Draft Day 1993.

Fantasy Rankings: 1992—90 points (2nd)
1991—60 points (Tied for 6th)
1990—18 points (Tied for 45th)

Past Performance Key: Hampton's 24 rushing touchdowns over the last two years is topped only by Barry Sanders and Emmitt Smith. Before him, the last (and only) Giants back to post consecutive 1,000-yard rushing seasons was Joe Morris in 1985–86. Hampton is one of only two backs in the NFL in 1992 who scored 3 rushing touchdowns in one game twice, the other being Emmitt Smith.

3. Thurman Thomas, Buffalo Bills   It is with great reluctance that I do not include Thurman Thomas in the First Echelon in this edition of my book, for the first time in three seasons. It's a tough call, because Thomas is clearly a great running back. The problem is that he is a great back in the NFL game, but a little less than great in the fantasy game. Unless, of course, your league rules award points for yardage, too; then Thomas is as valuable as any back in the game. Thomas led the NFL in total yards from scrimmage for the fourth straight year in 1992, breaking Jim Brown's venerable record. He finished second in the AFC in rushing, and third in the league, with 1,487 yards, the highest season total of his career. He led the AFC in touchdown scoring for the second straight year, having tied Mark Clayton for the AFC high with 12 in 1991. His 9 rushing touchdowns in 1992 were the second-highest total of his career. These are great numbers—just not as great as Smith's.

One cautionary note with respect to Thomas is that the pounding he takes from constant use seems to be a growing concern of the Bills' coaching staff. As a result, Thomas has been much less effective as a fantasy performer over the second half of each of the last two seasons. For example, he scored 30 fantasy points in the first two weeks of the 1992 season, 36 in the first four weeks, and only 27 points in the last 13 weeks. (Thomas scored only 3 touchdowns from Week Three through Week Fourteen in 1992.) This is consistent with his performance in 1991, when Thomas scored 36 of his 60 fantasy points in the first half of the season. So think long and hard about whether you want to risk your top pick in the draft with a back whose value apparently will diminish significantly as the season progresses. It's a tough call, especially since Thomas will probably be gone by the time you get to use your second-round pick on Draft Day 1993.

Fantasy Rankings: 1992—63 points (Tied for 5th)
1991—60 points (Tied for 6th)
1990—78 points (Tied for 4th)
1989—57 points (Tied for 9th)

Past Performance Key: Thomas has scored 49 touchdowns over the last four years, third behind Barry Sanders's NFL-leading total of 57 and Jerry Rice's 55. He failed to record a bonus score for the first time in the four editions of this book. Thomas averaged 4.8 yards per carry in 1992, the highest average in the AFC and second only to Ricky Watters in the NFL among backs who rushed for 600 or more yards.

4. Barry Foster, Pittsburgh Steelers   Foster, a fifth-round pick from Arkansas in the 1990 draft, clearly demonstrated his football ability in his brief stints on the field under former head coach Chuck Noll. Apparently not to Coach Noll, however, which may be one reason Noll's gone. Foster had averaged 5.2 yards per carry during the 1990 and 1991 seasons, but on only 132 carries. Some might say, as I did in last year's edition of this book, that this impressive yardage average, combined with his bonus run of 56 yards in Week Two of 1991, was a pretty good indicator of his talent. But no one could have foreseen the quantum leap Foster took in 1992, when he, like Emmitt Smith, had one of the great rushing years in NFL history. His single-season total of 1,690 yards in 1992 has been exceeded by only eight backs in the history of the NFL (including Emmitt Smith last season). He shattered Franco Harris's team records for total yards, carries, and 100-yard games, and tied Eric Dickerson's NFL record of an even dozen 100-yard games, set in 1984. Foster rushed for 11 touchdowns, the highest total for a Steeler back since Harris did it in 1979. What's even more remarkable about Foster's achievement is that he skipped the preseason due to a contractual dispute, holding out until the eve of the regular season. If Foster does anything in 1993 that comes close to resembling his performance in 1992, he will move into the First Echelon in a hurry.

Fantasy Rankings: 1992—72 points (Tied for 4th)
1991—15 points (Tied for 52nd)
1990—6 points (Tied for 74th)

Past Performance Key: Foster is one of only five NFL backs with a rushing touchdown from bonus territory in both 1991 and 1992. He had scored only 2 rushing touchdowns in 132 carries over the two years prior to 1992. Foster led the NFL in rushing attempts, with 390, in 1992, tying him with Eric Dickerson (for the Rams in 1983) and Marcus Allen (for the Raiders in 1985) for the fourth-highest number of rushing attempts in one season in the history of the NFL. He had more carries than starting quarterback Neil O'Donnell had pass attempts for the Steelers in 1992.

5. Ricky Watters, San Francisco 49ers   Watters obliterated 49ers fans' collective memory of former star Roger Craig with his standout performance in 1992. The 49ers' second-round draft pick out of Notre Dame in 1991, Watters sat out that season due to injury. He started the 1992 season auspiciously, becoming the first NFL back to gain 100 yards in his NFL debut since Christian Okoye opened the 1987 season with 105 yards against the Chargers. Running mate Tom Rathman did most of the scoring early, scoring 5 touchdowns in the first four weeks of the season, but after Week Five Watters took over the backfield scoring. He tallied 2 touchdowns, 1 rushing and 1 receiving, in the Niners' game against the Patriots in Week Six, and 3 rushing touchdowns in Week Seven. After scoring just 12 fantasy points in the first five games of the season, Watters scored an amazing 48 in the next six, before getting injured and missing all or most of the last five games. Nevertheless, Watters posted some great numbers in his injury-abbreviated season. He scored 11 touchdowns, 9 of them rushing, tying him with three other players for the fifth-best touchdown total in the NFC. He accumulated 1,418 yards rushing and passing from scrimmage, also tying him for fifth-best in the NFC. As you readers of past editions of this book know, I usually don't rate a player very highly based on only one season's performance; I like to see him excel over the course of two or more seasons before conferring First or Second Echelon status. However, the talented Watters is the exception that proves the rule. With the 49ers' high-powered offense good to go in 1993, Watters is a first-round pick this season.

Fantasy Rankings: 1992—60 points (7th)
1991—0 points

Past Performance Key: Watters's yards-per-carry average of 4.9 yards was the best of any NFL running back with 1,000 yards in 1992. The last 49ers running back to rush for 9 touchdowns in one season was Roger Craig in 1988. Watters was one of only four NFL backs to rush for 3 touchdowns in one game in 1992. (No back rushed for 4 touchdowns in one game in 1992. The last NFL back to do so was Barry Sanders in Week Thirteen of the 1991 season against the Minnesota Vikings.)

6. Terry Allen, Minnesota Vikings   With the presence of new head coach Dennis Green, and the absence of Herschel Walker, Allen moved into the lineup as the featured back for the Vikings and blossomed into an NFL star in 1992. Allen gave some inkling of his capability for the perspicacious fantasy owner in 1991. He scored all 21 of his fantasy points in the last half of the 1991 season, including a 55-yard touchdown run against the Bucs in Week Ten. Allen blossomed in 1992, rushing for 1,201 yards and scoring 15 touchdowns, 13 on the ground.

He also was the second-leading receiver on the team, behind Cris Carter, catching 49 passes for 478 yards and 2 touchdowns. His combined yardage from scrimmage, 1,679 yards, was the fifth-highest total in the NFL in 1992. Only a ninth-round pick in 1990 draft, Allen appears destined for NFL greatness. Don't let him slip down to the middle rounds of your fantasy draft.

Fantasy Rankings: 1992—84 points (3rd)

1991—21 points (Tied for 42nd)

1990—0 points

Past Performance Key: Allen's 15 touchdowns was the second-highest total in the NFL in 1992, behind Emmitt Smith's 19. His 1,201 yards rushing broke Chuck Foreman's team record of 1,155 yards, set in 1976, and his 15 touchdowns was the highest total by a Viking since Chuck Foreman scored 22 in 1975. Allen scored a rushing touchdown and a passing touchdown in one game twice during the 1992 season. Only three other backs (Neal Anderson, who did it three times, Rodney Culver, and Thurman Thomas) accomplished that feat in 1992.

7. Lorenzo White, Houston Oilers   In last year's edition of this book, I told fantasy owners, "Watch for a big fantasy comeback for White in 1992." Lo and behold, White rebounded with a great season. The previous year had been a down one for this talented back, as contract problems resulted in his holdout at the beginning of the 1991 season and the lost time affected his performance on the field. His scoring totals dropped from 12 touchdowns in 1990 to only 4 in 1991. But it was clear early in the 1992 season that White was back, as he racked up more total yards in the first seven weeks than he accumulated the entire 1991 season. He also equaled his 1991 fantasy point total by Week Eight of the 1992 season. He reached the 1,000-yard rushing mark for the first time in his career on national television, in the Monday Night Game against the Bears in Week Fourteen, and ended the season with 1,226 yards and 7 rushing touchdowns. He also caught 57 passes for 641 yards and 1 touchdown. His combined yardage from scrimmage, 1,867 yards, was the fourth-highest total in the NFL in 1992. White's great talent is obscured by the Houston version of the run-and-shoot. Given the chance, through free agency or otherwise, White could prove to be a tremendous fantasy back in the proper offensive system. As it is, he's a great second back.

Fantasy Rankings: 1992—48 points (Tied for 11th)

1991—24 points (Tied for 32nd)

1990—60 points (9th)

1989—30 points (Tied for 26th)

Past Performance Key: White's 69-yard touchdown reception in Week Two was the longest for the Oilers in 1992. In fact, this scoring play was the only bonus bomb scored by a Houston player. white was one of only four running backs to catch a touchdown pass from bonus territory in 1992. His reception totals and yardage in 1992 were career highs. White had caught only 72 passes for 616 yards during his four years with Houston prior to 1992.

8. Herschel Walker, Philadelphia Eagles   The Sphinx has got nothing on Walker when it comes to the all-time-enigma category. The treatment of Walker, when it comes to his reputation around the league and among NFL fans, defies rational explanation. He is one of the most talented backs in the game, but you would never know it. Walker started the season with back-to-back 100-yard games for the first time since 1987. He rushed for more than 1,000 yards for only the second time in his seven-year NFL career, and scored 10 touchdowns for the second year in a row. Walker has scored 10 touchdowns in three of the last four seasons, and has a total of 39 touchdowns; only four other running backs have scored more touchdowns than him during this period. The Eagles had not had a back rush for 1,000 yards since the 1985 season. Moreover, the Eagles only had 8 rushing touchdowns total in 1991; Walker rushed for 8 touchdowns himself in 1992, and the team rushed for 19 overall. Yet, despite this tremendous contribution to the Eagles' offense, by the end of the season Walker was sharing time with a running back named Heath Sherman. Walker rushed for just 44 yards on 13 carries in Week Fourteen, and was reduced to waving towels on the sideline to pump up the hometown fans, while getting slammed in print and over the airwaves. It's almost sad that this enormously talented running back, whose combined USFL and NFL statistics rank him with the all-time greats, will always be considered a failure, a rank underachiever, in the NFL. (The low blows have started early. At least Franco Harris had been retired for several years before his reputation as a "soft" running back became popular. Walker's reputation as a "soft" type of runner is already making the media rounds.) This may be sad for Walker, but it's good for the shrewd fantasy owner, who will probably get a shot at the high-scoring Walker in the second or even third round on Draft Day 1993.

Fantasy Rankings: 1992—54 points (Tied for 8th)
1991—66 points (Tied for 3rd)
1990—48 points (Tied for 12th)
1989—54 points (Tied for 9th)

Past Performance Key: Walker has compiled 12,284 yards rushing and 4,761 yards receiving in his 10-year professional (USFL and NFL) career. His 12,284 yards would place him fifth on the all-time rushing list, and his combined yards from scrimmage of 17,045 would be surpassed only by

Walter Payton (21,264). Walker was one of seven backs who scored 2 rushing touchdowns in one game twice in 1992.

9. Cleveland Gary, Los Angeles Rams   You can't blame Gary if he's got a small dose of motion sickness, considering the career roller coaster he's been on lately. Gary had a spectacular year in 1990, rushing for 808 yards and 14 touchdowns and adding a touchdown reception in the bargain. He tied with Derrick Fenner for the fantasy scoring lead among running backs. So what happened in 1991? He fumbles a few times, and John Robinson plants him permanently on the bench, while the immortal Robert Delpino takes over in the backfield for him. See ya, Coach Robinson. New head coach "Ground" Chuck Knox liberated Gary from the bench in 1992, and Gary fumbled a few times again (9 times, to be exact). He also rushed for 1,125 yards; led the Rams in receptions with 52 catches; combined for 1,418 yards from scrimmage, tied for fifth-best in the NFC; and scored 10 touchdowns, 7 on the ground. In a word, a monster year. Knox, like his predecessor, employs a rushing system that requires a designated scorer each year. Robinson had plugged Charles White, Greg Bell, Cleveland Gary, and Robert Delpino into his system. While at Seattle, Knox turned first to Curt Warner, then to Derrick Fenner. All of these backs prospered in these offensive systems, which emphasized the running game with a designated scorer. Now, Gary's firmly ensconced in the Knox system's driver's seat in Los Angeles. However, trade rumors regarding Gary abound, the Rams having selected Jerome Bettis with their first pick and Russell White with their third in the NFL draft. If Gary remains in the Rams' fold, he should score plenty of touchdowns in the years to come, as long as his fumbling doesn't drive Knox to distraction, like it did Robinson. Gary should slip down to the second round on Draft Day 1993. If he falls any farther than that, then take the ride with him, because you will have yourself a bona fide bargain on your roster. One note of caution: Watch for first-round pick Jerome Bettis to see action at the goal line for the Rams this season.

Fantasy Rankings: 1992—51 points (10th)
1991—6 points (Tied for 71st)
1990—87 points (Tied for 1st)
1989—6 points (Tied for 78th)

Past Performance Key: Gary's 1,125 yards rushing was the most by a Ram since Greg Bell rushed for 1,137 yards in 1989. The last running back before him to lead the Rams in receptions was Wendell Tyler in 1982. Gary's 279 rushing attempts and 52 receptions were career highs. He was the only running back in the NFC to lead his team in receptions. Five of Gary's 7 rushing touchdowns were from the 1-yard line, and all 7 were from less than 10 yards.

10. Reggie Cobb, Tampa Bay Buccaneers   Cobb, the Bucs' first pick in the 1990 draft, paid large dividends in his third year in the league as he rushed for 1,171 yards and 9 touchdowns. He was the first Buccaneer back to rush for 1,000 yards since James Wilder did the trick in 1985. Cobb's yards-per-carry average (3.8 in 1992, 3.65 for his career) is not going to knock anyone's socks off, but he's a workhorse (310 carries in 1992, fifth-highest in the league) who piles up the yards and gets in the end zone. Cobb is a steal as a third back in 1993.

Fantasy Rankings: 1992—54 points (Tied for 8th)
1991—48 points (14th)
1990—12 points (Tied for 57th)

Past Performance Key: Cobb's 1,171 yards rushing was the highest total for a Buc since James Wilder rushed for 1,300 yards in 1985. His 9 rushing touchdowns were the highest total for a Buc since James Wilder rushed for 10 in 1985. Eight of Cobb's 9 touchdowns were from the 1-yard line in 1992, and all of them were from inside the 5.

11. Neal Anderson, Chicago Bears   While he isn't the First Echelon player he once was, Anderson has settled into a level of performance that is still head and shoulders above most NFL running backs from a fantasy perspective. Anderson scored 11 touchdowns in 1992, which tied for the fifth-best mark in the NFC. Still, Anderson appears to be paying the price for carrying the load of the Bears' rushing offense for the past five years. In 1991, Sweetness's successor in the Bears' backfield posted his lowest totals for rushing touchdowns and combined touchdowns since 1987, as well as his lowest amount of rushing yards since then. He recorded the lowest rushing average of his six-year career up to that point in 1991 as well (3.6 yards, the first time it had ever been below 4 yards in his career). Anderson rebounded in the scoring department in 1992, but his 582 yards rushing was his lowest total since his rookie year in 1986, when he carried the ball only 35 times. And he averaged less than 4 yards a carry in 1992 for the second consecutive season. Between the effect of the inevitable aging process of an NFL workhorse, and the questions raised by a new offensive scheme, it might be wise to lay off Anderson in the very early rounds of the draft, where he customarily is selected, on Draft Day 1993.

Fantasy Rankings: 1992—48 points (Tied for 11th)
1991—45 points (Tied for 15th)

1990—72 points (6th)
1989—90 points (Tied for 2nd)

Past Performance Key: Anderson failed to score a bonus touchdown in 1992 for the second straight season. He scored 6 touchdowns from bonus range in 1988 through 1990, but none in 1991 and 1992. His 5 rushing touchdowns were his lowest total since 1987. Only Barry Sanders and Thurman Thomas among NFL running backs have scored more touchdowns than Anderson over the past four seasons.

12. Marion Butts, San Diego Chargers   For the second straight season, injuries curtailed Butts's effectiveness for fantasy owners in 1992. He strained a knee ligament in the season opener. To his credit he played hurt the first five weeks, but, predictably, he was not effective, rushing for only 176 yards and no touchdowns. He did not score his first touchdown until Week Nine, and his 4 touchdowns for the season were a career low. Even with these injuries, though, the level of Butts's value to fantasy owners in the upcoming season increased significantly with the move of free-agent running mate Rod Bernstine to Denver. There is no getting around the fact that Butts's touchdown totals have now declined for the third straight year, from a high of 9 in his rookie year in 1989 to 4 last season. But if he is healthy, Butts, with Rod Bernstine gone to the Broncos, should be the designated scorer for the Chargers and return to his rookie-year scoring levels this season.

Fantasy Rankings: 1992—24 points (Tied for 27th)
1991—39 points (Tied for 17th)
1990—48 points (Tied for 12th)
1989—60 points (Tied for 7th)

Past Performance Key: Butts has led the Chargers in rushing in each of his four seasons in the league. His yards-per-carry average of 3.7 in 1992 was the lowest of his career. Butts scored a rushing touchdown from bonus territory (54 yards) against the Chiefs in the first round of the playoffs last season.

13. Kevin Mack, Cleveland Browns   Mack continued his role as the designated scorer for the Browns in 1992, scoring 6 rushing touchdowns, none of them from longer than 7 yards. He had a very strong season, considering that he missed the first four weeks of the season while on injured reserve. But the warning lights are flashing. The Browns drafted "Touchdown" Tommy Vardell with their first pick in the 1992 draft, and he got his share of carries, albeit not at the goal line. Mack averaged only 3.2 yards per carry in 1992, the lowest mark of his eight-year NFL career. He'll be 31 years old in August, ancient in pro football terms. Go slowly as you consider selecting the Big Mack Attack on Draft Day 1993.

Fantasy Rankings: 1992—36 points (Tied for 18th)
1992—60 points (Tied for 6th)
1990—36 points (Tied for 21st)
1989—6 points (Tied for 78th)

Past Performance Key: Mack failed to score a receiving touchdown for the first time in three seasons in 1992.

14. Earnest Byner, Washington Redskins   Byner was one of the few bright spots for Washington's offense in 1992. He led the team in touchdowns with 7, a meager total for the potent Redskins' offense, but a team-leading total nevertheless. Still, Byner remains a fantasy under-achiever. Of course, all this would change if Byner were installed as the designated scorer in the Redskins' goal line offense. But it hasn't happened yet in Byner's four years with the team, and, in all likelihood, will not happen in 1993. There is a lot of talk about the Redskins bringing in a big back in 1993 for their goal line offense—a la Gerald Riggs, who was released prior to the 1992 season for no apparent reason. (The Redskins were lackluster at the goal line all season as a result, desperately missing the 11 rushing touchdowns, 10 of them from the 1-yard line, that Riggs gave them in 1991.) If the Redskins finally import a big back to replace Riggs, Byner is a third back at best for fantasy owners.

Fantasy Rankings: 1992—42 points (Tied for 14th)
1991—33 points (Tied for 21st)
1990—42 points (Tied for 15th)
1989—48 points (Tied for 13th)

Past Performance Key: Only Barry Sanders, Emmitt Smith, and Thurman Thomas have rushed for more yards than Byner over the last three years. Byner missed by 2 yards becoming the first Washington player to rush for 1,000 yards three seasons in a row. He has rushed for a touchdown, caught a touchdown, and thrown for a touchdown in each of the last three seasons!

BEST OF THE REST

1. Derrick Fenner, Cincinnati Bengals   Fenner signed with Cincinnati as a Plan B free agent (remember them?) in 1992, and the change of scenery, after three years in Seattle, agreed with him. Fenner rebounded from a disastrous 1991 season (rushing 91 times for 267 yards, a ludicrous 2.9-yard average, and 4 touchdowns) with a solid season in 1992. New head coach David Shula seemed to be feeling his way early in the season in deciding which back to give the ball to at the goal line. But Fenner rushed for 5 touchdowns in the second half of the season, 2 in the last game of the season against the Colts. He could be the designated scorer for the Bengals at the goal line in 1993. Take advantage of this uncertainty and save Fenner for the later rounds of the draft.

Fantasy Rankings: 1992—45 points (Tied for 13th)
1991—24 points (Tied for 32nd)
1990—87 points (Tied for 1st)
1989—6 points (Tied for 78th)

Past Performance Key: Fenner scored 14 rushing touchdowns in 1990; he's scored 12 total in his other three seasons in the NFL. His 4.5-yards-per-carry average in 1992 was the best of his four-year career.

2. Tom Rathman, San Francisco 49ers Rathman has very quietly been a most valuable fantasy player during the last three years. He is stamped from the classic designated-scorer mold, since he has not had a touchdown run of longer than 2 yards in the last three years. (Rathman's 27-yard touchdown reception in Week Fourteen is a bonus romp in comparison.) Like a true designated scorer, Rathman needed only 57 carries in 1992 to score his 5 rushing touchdowns. It's hard to tell if Ricky Watters will relieve Rathman of all goal line responsibility in 1992, but if past form holds true, Rathman will get the call for the last, tough yard on a lot of 49ers touchdown drives in the upcoming season. He's still a valuable third back for fantasy owners in 1993.

Fantasy Rankings: 1992—42 points (Tied for 14th)
1991—36 points (Tied for 19th)
1990—42 points (Tied for 15th)
1989—9 points (Tied for 67th)

Past Performance Key: Rathman had 5 rushing touchdowns in 1986–89; he has scored 18 rushing touchdowns in 1990–92. Rathman and Watters combined for 20 touchdowns in 1992, second-highest total for a two-back combination from one team in the league. (Emmitt Smith and Daryl Johnston combined for 21.) Rathman has rushed for 18 touchdowns on only 221 rushing attempts during the last three seasons. His total of 9 touchdowns overall in 1992 was the highest single-season mark of his seven-year career, as was his 4 touchdown receptions. Rathman was one of only two NFL backs with 3 touchdown receptions in one game in 1992. (The other was Eric Metcalf.)

3. Chris Warren/John L. Williams, Seattle Seahawks Warren is one of those few players who slip through the cracks of the recruiting process and end up at schools far from the spotlight of NCAA football. He was a fourth-round pick in the 1990 draft from the football factory that is Ferrum College, a division III school in Ferrum, Virginia. As I'm sure many readers know, *ferrum* is the Latin word for iron, which is the type of will Warren must possess to have made it to this level of the game from such an obscure school. The one bright light in the darkness of the Seahawks' 1992 season, Warren rushed for 1,017 yards, the highest total for a Seattle back since franchise legend Curt Warner rushed for 1,025 in 1988. Warren's touchdown total (3) needs some work, but if he can rush for 1,000 yards again in 1993, his TD total is bound to increase.

Williams is primarily a pass receiver, but that's like saying Al Pacino is primarily an actor. Williams has been one of the best receiving backs in the game during his seven-year career. He has averaged 68 receptions per season during the last five years. Despite these numbers, Williams is a third back at best because of his scoring totals. While he posted 9 touchdown receptions in 1988–89 (and 14 touchdowns overall), he has scored only 3 touchdown receptions over the last three years. Overall, I would go slow in drafting either Warren or Williams on Draft Day 1993.

Fantasy Rankings:

Warren	1992—18 points (Tied for 37th)
	1991—6 points (Tied for 71st)
	1990—6 points (Tied for 74th)
Williams	1992—12 points (Tied for 48th)
	1991—27 points (Tied for 26th)
	1990—18 points (Tied for 45th)
	1989—12 points (Tied for 52nd)

Past Performance Key: Warren had a total of 17 rushing attempts in his first two years with the Seahawks; he carried the ball 223 times for them in 1992. Williams's 339 yards rushing in 1992 was a career low.

4. Roger Craig, Minnesota Vikings Craig made the most of his playing time in 1992, limited as it was by the great performance of teammate Terry Allen. Craig rushed for 4 touchdowns, the highest total for him in that category since 1989, when he rushed for 1,054 yards and 6 touchdowns for the world champion San Francisco 49ers. His excellent career is definitely on the decline, especially from a fantasy perspective. But Craig can contribute significantly to the Vikings' offense as Allen's backup again this season, and if he scores 4 or 5 touchdowns in 1993, Craig has some value as a third back.

Fantasy Rankings: 1992—24 points (Tied for 27th)
1991—6 points (Tied for 71st)
1990—6 points (Tied for 74th)
1989—12 points (Tied for 52nd)

Past Performance Key: Craig had only 2 rushing touchdown during the 1990–91 seasons. His 4 yards per carry in 1992 was his highest season average since 1988. Craig is the only active NFL running back with 1,000 yards receiving in one season (1985), and he is the only running back in NFL history to record 1,000 yards rushing and 1,000 receiving in one season (1985).

5. Steve Broussard/Tony Smith, Atlanta Falcons   This is an easy one. As long as the Falcons are coached by Jerry Glanville and rely on the Red Gun offense, any Atlanta running back will be almost superfluous to their scoring plans. There is a simple illustration to this principle. The Falcons rushed for 3 touchdowns *as a team* in 1992. (The next-lowest total for a team was Seattle with 4, then New England with 6. You might notice the similarity between the 1992 won-lost records of these teams and their very low total of rushing touchdowns. It's more than a coincidence, don't you think?) You certainly can't say the Falcons haven't tried to develop running-back talent. Broussard was their first-round pick (20th player selected) in the 1990 NFL draft, and Smith their first-round pick (19th player selected) in 1992. These players obviously have talent, but the Atlanta offensive scheme makes them virtually worthless to fantasy owners. Broussard and Smith are of interest only to rabid Falcons fans and owners who use my expanded-roster rules in 1993.

Fantasy Rankings:

Broussard   1992—9 points (Tied for 62nd)

1991—27 points (Tied for 26th)

1990—18 points (Tied for 45th)

Smith   1992—12 points (Tied for 48th)

Past Performance Key: Broussard's 363 yards rushing and 1 rushing touchdown in 1992 were career lows. Smith's 2 rushing touchdowns led the team.

6. Blair Thomas, New York Jets   Thomas has talent, but Coach Coslet's patience with this injury-prone back may be wearing thin. The second pick overall in the 1990 NFL draft, Thomas has averaged only 136 rushing attempts per season in his three years in the league. Even worse, he failed to score even a single touchdown in 1992. The B.T. Express remains a huge disappointment for the Jets and a third back at best for fantasy owners, especially with Johnny Johnson in the Jets fold for 1993.

Fantasy Rankings: 1992—0 points

1991—24 points (Tied for 32nd)

1990—9 points (Tied for 67th)

Past Performance Key: Thomas has averaged 4.37 yards per carry during his career. He has rushed the ball 409 times in three years in the league; Barry Foster had 390 carries in 1992 alone.

7. Carwell Gardner, Buffalo Bills This second-round draft pick for the Bills in the 1990 draft scored 4 touchdowns from close range for the Bills in 1991, and 2 more in 1992. Keep an eye on him early in the upcoming season, especially if it appears that the Bills want to reduce the load on Thurman Thomas and Kenneth Davis at the goal line.

Fantasy Rankings: 1992—12 points (Tied for 48th)

1991—24 points (Tied for 12th)

1990—0 points

Past Performance Key: All 5 of Gardner's career rushing touchdowns are from 3 yards or closer. (Gardner also recovered a fumble in the end zone for a touchdown in 1991.)

8. Keith Byars, Philadelphia Eagles Byars had been a wide receiver masquerading in running back's clothing until the Eagles lost Keith Jackson to Miami through free agency. The masquerade was dropped at that point, and Byars moved to tight end in Jackson's place. The irony is that Byars, who had been the Eagles' leading receiver in the three years prior to 1992, failed to lead the team in receptions in 1992, even though he spent most of his playing time lining up as a tight end. Even if Byars returns to the backfield in 1993, he has little or no value to fantasy owners in 1993.

Fantasy Rankings: 1992—12 points (Tied for 48th)

1991—15 points (Tied for 52nd)

1990—21 points (Tied for 39th)

1989—30 points (Tied for 26th)

Past Performance Key: Byars scored 11 rushing touchdowns for the Eagles during the 1988–89 seasons; he has scored 2 rushing TDs in the three seasons since then. Byars's 56 receptions in 1992 was his lowest total since the 1987 season.

KEEP AN EYE ON

1. Rod Bernstine, Denver Broncos What goes around comes around, I guess. Bernstine took advantage of injuries to former teammate Marion Butts to emerge as a fantasy force in 1991. After averaging 4.8 yards per carry in his transition year from the tight-end position in 1990, and rushing for 4 touchdowns, Bernstine again averaged 4.8 yards per carry and led the Lightning Bolts with 8 rushing touchdowns in 1991. But injuries to Bernstine forced him to the sidelines in the second half of the season. As a result, he scored only 1 touchdown after Week Seven of the 1992 season. Liberated through free agency from sharing the workload with Butts, another excellent runner, in the Chargers backfield, Bernstine could emerge as a star running back, and the Broncos' designated scorer, in 1993.

Fantasy Rankings: 1992—24 points (Tied for 27th)
                         1991—57 points (Tied for 9th)
                         1990—24 points (Tied for 34th)
                         1989—9 points (Tied for 67th)

Past Performance Key: Bernstine, drafted as a tight end by the Chargers in the first round of the 1987 NFL draft, has averaged nearly 5 yards per carry (4.93) on 407 career attempts.

2. Johnny Johnson, New York Jets Johnson's professional fortunes, and that of the Jets, took a decided turn for the better on the first day of the NFL draft. The Cardinals traded Johnson to the Jets to get a shot at Garrison Hearst. The Jets were happy to take the former Pro Bowler off the Cardinals' hands as part of their overall strategy to improve the team after a disappointing season in 1992. Johnson will certainly help the Jets' offense. Johnson had his third solid fantasy season in a row in 1992. Despite missing three games early in the season with injuries, Johnson came on to score 6 rushing touchdowns, a career high. Johnson was the Cardinals' leading rusher each of his three years in the league, and could easily assume that role for the Jets. The only problem is that Johnson may get most of the yards but Brad Baxter most of the touchdowns, in the Jets' offensive scheme. But Johnson will have the opportunity to get in the end zone at least as often as he did in Phoenix, if the marked offseason improvement made by the Jets is reflected by the team's actual performance on the field this season. If so, Johnson is a bargain as a third back for astute fantasy owners.

Fantasy Rankings: 1992—36 points (Tied for 18th)
                         1991—33 points (Tied for 21st)
                         1990—30 points (Tied for 27th)

Past Performance Key: Johnson scored 4 rushing touchdowns in the last eight weeks of the 1991 season, and all 6 of his rushing touchdowns in the last nine weeks of 1992. His 42-yard touchdown run in Week Fifteen against the Giants in 1992 was the longest touchdown run of his three-year career.

3. Rodney Culver, Indianapolis Colts The Colts had the worst rushing offense in the league in 1992. Despite this handicap, Rodney Culver had an impressive rookie year as their designated scorer. This fourth-round draft pick from Notre Dame scored 7 rushing touchdowns, and 9 TDs overall. This combined total was the best for a Colts back since Eric Dickerson's 15 touchdowns in 1988. It's too early to tell if Culver is the real deal for fantasy owners, especially with the state of the Colts' rushing offense, but it would be worth a late-round pick to find out.

Fantasy Rankings: 1992—48 points (Tied for 11th)

Past Performance Key: Culver's 7 rushing touchdowns were the most by a Colts rookie since Curtis Dickey rushed for 11 in his rookie season in 1980. Culver was one of four backs who scored a rushing touchdown and caught a touchdown pass in one game two or more times in 1992.

4. Kenneth Davis, Buffalo Bills Davis reprised his role as the premier understudy in the game, a role he created in 1991, as he posted a second consecutive career-best year in 1992. He rushed for 624 yards and scored 5 touchdowns, 4 of them rushing, in 1991, including a 78-yard TD run. Davis's 33 fantasy points in 1991 were a career best to that point. Then came his performance in 1992, as he rushed for 613 yards, jumped up to 6 touchdowns (including a 64-yard run), and scored a whopping 42 fantasy points, his career high. Davis actually caught Thurman Thomas in fantasy points for the season in Week Fourteen, only to drop back behind him in the last three weeks. For the second year in a row, almost all of Davis's scoring (36 of 42 fantasy points) occurred in the second half of the season. He is undeniably talented, and should become as valuable as almost any back in the league in the second half of the 1993 season, if form holds true.

Fantasy Rankings: 1992—42 points (Tied for 14th)
1991—33 points (Tied for 21st)
1990—27 points (Tied for 31st)
1989—12 points (Tied for 52nd)

Past Performance Key: Davis recorded a bonus touchdown run for the second consecutive year, one of only five backs in the NFL to do so. He failed to catch a touchdown pass in 1992 for the first time in four seasons.

5. Heath Sherman, Philadelphia Eagles Sherman had a banner year in 1992. He had career highs with 5 rushing touchdowns and 6 overall. By the end of the season, he had entrenched himself as the featured back in the Eagles' offense, edging Herschel Walker out of that position. Assuming that he gets to split time with Walker again, Sherman would be a pleasant addition to your fantasy roster as a second back, and a steal as a third back this season.

Fantasy Rankings: 1992—36 points (Tied for 18th)
1991—0 points

1990—15 points (Tied for 51st)
1989—12 points (Tied for 52nd)

Past Performance Key: Sherman was one of only four NFL backs with a bonus touchdown pass in 1992. His 75-yard touchdown reception in Week Eleven was the longest scoring play from scrimmage by an NFL running back in 1992.

6. Harold Green, Cincinnati Bengals   So many yards, so few touchdowns from Green in 1992. Green, the 38th pick in the 1990 draft, began to edge James Brooks out of the Bengals' backfield picture in 1991. He was the Bengals' leading rusher that year, the first time either Brooks or Ickey Woods hadn't led the team since 1987. With Brooks signed as a Plan B free agent by Cleveland, Green repeated as the Bengals' leading rusher in 1992, running for 1,170 yards, the best total for a Bengal back since 1989. As long as Derrick Fenner appears to be the designated scorer at the goal line, however, Green will keep piling up the yards, but not the scores, for his fantasy owners this season.

Fantasy Rankings: 1992—12 points (Tied for 48th)
1991—18 points (Tied for 45th)
1990—9 points (Tied for 67th)

Past Performance Key: Only one other back in NFL history has rushed for over 1,000 yards and scored only 2 touchdowns (Lawrence McCutcheon, Los Angeles Rams, 1973). And no NFL back in the history of the league has rushed for as many yards as Green did in 1992 and scored so few touchdowns.

7. Mark Higgs/Bobby Humphrey, Miami Dolphins   Higgs and Humphrey had clearly defined roles in 1992, sharing the responsibilities in the Dolphins' backfield. Higgs ran the ball, Humphrey caught the ball. Higgs rushed for 915 yards, a career high, and 7 touchdowns, also a career best. He was off to a tremendous start, and could have posted great numbers for the season and become the Dolphins' first 1,000-yard rusher since 1978, but he was injured during the second half of the season and missed a lot of playing time. As a result, Higgs did not score a touchdown the last seven weeks of the season. Humphrey, in a solid comeback from his lost year in 1991, led the Dolphins in receptions and also rushed for 471 yards. But he only scored 2 touchdowns, 1 of them rushing, in 1992. Higgs had originally seemed to be a stopgap measure while Humphrey returned to form, but he proved his mettle and talent in the first half of the season. A major problem with Higgs, though, is that no back in the league rushed for 600 or more yards in 1992 and had a worse yards-per-carry average than Higgs's mark of 3.6. If the Dolphins want to improve their rushing game, they might turn to Humphrey. He is a proven star who has averaged more than 4 yards per carry during his career, and could squeeze Higgs out of the starting lineup with a solid preseason. If so, Humphrey will be a steal as a second or third back in 1993. But Humphrey's off-season problems, well documented in the media, might have an affect on his performance with Miami in 1993.

Fantasy Rankings:

Higgs	1992—42 points (Tied for 14th)
	1991—24 points (Tied for 32nd)
	1990—0 points
	1989—0 points
Humphrey	1992—9 points (Tied for 62nd)
	1991—0 points
	1990—42 points (Tied for 15th)
	1989—48 points (Tied for 13th)

Past Performance Key: Higgs has rushed for 11 touchdowns during the last two seasons; he had no rushing touchdowns in his first three years in the league. Humphrey scored 15 touchdowns his first two years in the league, and has scored 2 in the two years since then.

8. Eric Metcalf, Cleveland Browns Eric Metcalf is another nominee for Fantasy Comeback Player of the Year in 1992. After a gradual decline from 54 fantasy points in 1989 to 21 in 1990 and then to absolutely zero in an injury-plagued 1991, the Browns worked a healthy Metcalf into the offense more efficiently in 1992. Metcalf had a fabulous game in Week Three of the season, when he scored 4 touchdowns, 1 rushing and 3 receiving. (Two of the 3 touchdown passes were bonus bombs.) He then leveled off, with no touchdowns until Week Thirteen, an eight-game drought. Metcalf finished with a crescendo, adding a punt return and 2 touchdown passes for 7 touchdowns on the season. Metcalf can score just about every time he gets his hands on the ball. As long as the Browns continue to use him in their regular offense, he's a steal as a third back.

Fantasy Rankings: 1992—33 points (Tied for 24th)
1991—0 points
1990—21 points (Tied for 39th)
1989—54 points (Tied for 9th)

Past Performance Key: Metcalf has now scored a touchdown in every fashion possible for an offensive player during his career. He has caught and thrown a touchdown pass. He has rushed for a touchdown, and returned both a punt and a kickoff for a touchdown. Metcalf was the only running back in the NFL with 2 bonus touchdown pass receptions last season. (He also was the only player to score 2 bonus touchdown receptions in one game in 1992.) Metcalf was one of only two NFL backs with 3 touchdown receptions in one game in 1992. (Tom Rathman was the other.)

9. Dalton Hilliard/Craig Heyward/Vaughn Dunbar, New Orleans Saints

Here's another tip you can use when searching through this book for the key to the upcoming draft. When one of my Scouting Reports includes more than one running back in the header, it probably doesn't include a fantasy star. Take the Saints' trio of running backs, for instance. Despite the emergence of 1992 first-round pick Vaughn Dunbar as the leading rusher for the Saints last season, Hilliard emerged as the main scorer for the Saints, Hilliard led the team with 7 touchdowns, 4 of them pass receptions. But each of these players scored 3 rushing touchdowns in 1992. Based on 1992 results, Coach Jim Mora seems to rotate these players at the goal line. This is great for team morale, but lousy for fantasy owners looking for a designated scorer out of the Saints' backfield. While Hilliard is the best bet to score the most touchdowns here, he won't score enough to risk anything but a late pick on him.

Fantasy Rankings:

Hilliard	1992—30 points (Tied for 25th)
	1991—33 points (Tied for 21st)
	1990—3 points (Tied for 97th)
	1989—99 points (1st)
Heyward	1992—18 points (Tied for 37th)
	1991—27 points (Tied for 26th)
	1990—24 points (Tied for 34th)
	1989—6 points (Tied for 78th)
Dunbar	1992—18 points (Tied for 37th)

Past Performance Key: Hilliard scored 37 touchdowns in his first four years with the Saints (30 rushing), but has scored only 13 touchdowns in the last three. Dunbar's 565 yards rushing were the most by an NFL rookie in 1992. (Ricky Watters was technically not a rookie under NFL personnel rules.) Heyward's 416 yards rushing in 1992 were the second-highest total of his five-year career.

10. Craig Heyward, Chicago Bears

Heyward moves to the Windy City to replace Brad Muster in the Bears' backfield. Always a great potential designated scorer, Heyward could get a chance to score a lot more than he has in the past (only three touchdowns in 1992) with his new team. Weight has always been a problem for Heyward, at least in his employers' eyes, but the Bears are old hands with weight problems. (Bears' management is reported to have inserted the "Fridge Clause" in Heyward's contract, providing him with monetary incentives to keep the weight off.) Fantasy owners who are looking to add a little heft to their scoring totals should say "Pass the Heyward" in the middle rounds on Draft Day 1993.

Fantasy Rankings: 1992—18 points (Tied for 37th)

1991—27 points (Tied for 26th)

1990—24 points (Tied for 34th)

1989—6 points (Tied for 78th)

Past Performance Key: Heyward's 416 yards rushing in 1992 was the second-highest total of his 5-year career.

11. John Stephens, Green Bay Packers As I've said in other editions of this book, Stephens is an enigma, sort of a poor man's Herschel Walker. He started brilliantly in his rookie year in 1988, rushing for 1,168 yards and 4 touchdowns, and posted even better scoring numbers in 1989. But after scoring 11 rushing touchdowns in his first two seasons (12 touchdowns overall), Stephens has now scored only 6 rushing touchdowns in the last three years (7 touchdowns overall). This is not the way you want a player's scoring totals to go. But Stephens now has the chance to become an integral part of a high-scoring team, a team definitely on the rise. If Stephens grabs the opportunity given to him in Green Bay, he could post numbers reminiscent of his early years in the league.

Fantasy Rankings: 1992—12 points (Tied for 48th)

1991—12 points (Tied for 59th)

1990—15 points (Tied for 51st)

1989—42 points (17th)

Past Performance Key: Stephens' 13-yard touchdown run against the Jets last season was longer than any touchdown run by a Packers' running back in 1992.

BIGGEST BUSTS

1. Brad Baxter, New York Jets The Jets might have been the biggest bust as a team in the NFL in 1992, especially after their undefeated preseason, and great things were expected of Baxter as well. What a letdown. Baxter appeared in 1991 to have become a classic designated scorer for the Jets. His 11 rushing touchdowns in 1991 led the AFC and tied him for third in the entire league. Baxter's longest touchdown run in 1991 was 4 yards, and 6 of his 11 touchdowns were from a yard out. But the expectations were too high, as 1991 may have been a career year. Baxter fell to 6 touchdowns in 1992, the same total he scored in

1990. On the other hand, he did post a career high 698 yards rushing, and averaged 4.6 yards per carry, a personal best as well. Baxter will continue to score at the goal line for the Jets in 1993. The big question is, How often? Assuming the Jets show any improvement in 1993, Baxter could rebound big time in 1993. If so, he's a steal as a third back, and has solid value as a second back for fantasy owners in 1993.

Fantasy Rankings: 1992—36 points (Tied for 18th)
1991—66 points (Tied for 3rd)
1990—36 points (Tied for 21st)

Past Performance Key: Baxter's 23 rushing touchdowns over the last three years are topped only by Thurman Thomas, Derrick Fenner, Barry Sanders, Rodney Hampton, and Emmitt Smith. The only backs in the NFL with more rushing yards than Baxter and a higher yards-per-carry average in 1992 were Thurman Thomas and Ricky Watters.

2. Eric Dickerson/Nick Bell, Los Angeles Raiders
Marcus Allen, Kansas City Chiefs   It might have looked like Dickerson and the Raiders were the perfect match before the 1992 season. The Raiders were always safe harbor for NFL veterans of the rebellious and disgruntled variety, and Dickerson, perpetually dissatisfied with his contract status, fit the bill. Maybe if this courtship had occurred during the 1980s, it would have had a happy ending. But the parties may be at that point of their relationship when they wonder what they ever saw in each other, with divorce proceedings sure to follow. Dickerson rushed for 729 yards in 1992, the third-lowest season total of his magnificent career. (Despite this low number, Dickerson passed Tony Dorsett to reach second place on the career rushing list behind Walter Payton.) Dickerson also rushed for only 2 touchdowns for the second straight year, a dismal total for a player who has rushed for 11 or more touchdowns five times in his career.

Speaking of divorce, how about that spat between Marcus Allen and Al Davis. Played out on national television, during halftime of the Raiders' Monday Night Game against Miami in Week Fifteen, no less. If this were a marriage, Allen and Davis would be at the point where all the locks in the house are changed and the divorce lawyers have been retained. All indications are, though, that, while Allen may not be the player he once was, he's still got some touchdowns left in him. Hooking up with Joe Montana in the Kansas City backfield, Allen should get the chance to show what, if anything, he's got left. After obtaining future Hall of Famers Montana and Allen in the offseason, I'm sure that the Chiefs hope they can somehow turn back the hands of NFL time in the upcoming season. With additional playing time, Nick Bell could prove to be a valuable fantasy back. He's obviously talented, being one of only seven backs in the NFL in 1992 with a bonus rushing touchdown. Someone has to emerge as The Man at the goal line. Be it Dickerson or Bell, one of them will be a solid third back in 1993.

Fantasy Rankings:

Dickerson	1992—15 points (Tied for 44th)
	1991—15 points (Tied for 52nd)
	1990—24 points (Tied for 34th)
	1989—45 points (16th)
Allen	1992—15 points (Tied for 44th)
	1991—15 points (Tied for 52nd)
	1990—75 points (5th)
	1989—12 points (Tied for 52nd)
Bell	1992—24 points (Tied for 27th)
	1991—18 points (Tied for 45th)

Past Performance Key: Dickerson failed to reach the 1,000-yard mark for the third straight season, after 1,000-yard seasons in his first seven seasons in the league. He has 8 rushing touchdowns over the past three seasons; before that, he averaged better than 11 touchdowns per season over seven years. Allen's season total of 2 rushing touchdowns tied his career low for the second consecutive year. He has rushed for exactly 2 touchdowns three of the last four seasons; in the other season, 1990, he rushed for 12. Allen needs 2 touchdowns to reach a career total of 100 touchdowns scored, and Dickerson needs 4 to reach that mark as well. Bell has now led the Raiders in rushing touchdowns two consecutive seasons.

3. Christian Okoye/Barry Word/Harvey Williams, Kansas City Chiefs - This bunch has the same crowded-backfield problem as the Raiders, but with a lot more talent involved. Still, there are only so many footballs to go around. Throw in some injuries, and you have a big disappointment for the Kansas City running backs in 1992. Let's start with Okoye. Plainly stated, the Nigerian Nightmare had the worst season of his six-year career in 1992. He held out in the preseason over a contract dispute, and, as usually happens, reported very late and didn't work into the offense until later in the season. As a result, he didn't score his first touchdown in 1992 until Week Ten of the season. Overall, he rushed for only 448 yards and just 6 touchdowns. Someone with Okoye's size and speed should be unstoppable on a football field, especially at the goal line. But for some reason, the coaching staff wants to spread the work around, and the Magic Christian's scoring totals suffer as a consequence.

Word had 4 touchdowns for the third straight year, but he's capable of much more. His presence adds to the confusion in the Chiefs' backfield. Then there's Harvey Williams, the heir apparent at the feature-back position, who scored just 1 touchdown in 1992, after rushing for 1 and catching 2 TD passes in his rookie year in 1991. Too many Chiefs spoil the stew, to mix metaphors. Okoye is the key in this equation, and is always worth selecting as a third back, just because of his scoring potential. But watch carefully what management does over the summer. If the Chiefs winnow some of the crowd from their backfield before the season, the survivors should be worth a look in an offense that favors the ground game.

Fantasy Rankings:

Okoye	1992—36 points (Tied for 18th)
	1991—54 points (Tied for 12th)
	1990—42 points (Tied for 15th)
	1989—72 points (6th)
Word	1992—24 points (Tied for 27th)
	1991—24 points (Tied for 32nd)
	1990—30 points (Tied for 27th)
	1989—0 points
Williams	1992—6 points (Tied for 68th)
	1991—12 points (Tied for 59th)

Past Performance Key: Okoye's 3.1 average per carry in 1992 was the lowest of his career. He has led the Chiefs (or tied for the lead) in rushing touchdowns in every one of his six years on the team. Word scored 2 of his 4 touchdowns in 1992 in the first two weeks of the season. Williams averaged 4.6 yards per carry in 1991; he averaged 3.4 in 1992.

4. Vince Workman, Green Bay Packers Workman came out of nowhere to post great scoring numbers in 1991. Just as quickly, he returned to the NFL obscurity from whence he had come in 1992. By obscurity, I mean that Workman had 4 carries and no pass receptions in his rookie year in 1989, and only 12 combined rushes and receptions for 1 touchdown in 1990. Then, in 1991, he not only led the Pack in scoring with 11 touchdowns, 7 of them rushing, but also scored more touchdowns than all but six other NFL players. With the former steward of the 49ers offense, Mike Holmgren, installed as the new head coach for the Packers, 1992 looked like it could be a banner year for Workman. Wrong. Like the San Francisco offense, Green Bay uses receivers, not running backs, to carry the scoring load. As a result, Workman scored only 2 touchdowns in 1992, both rushing, a minuscule amount after Workman's scoring bonanza in 1991. With Coach Holmgren's system in place, and former Patriot John Stephens added to the roster, Workman is a third back at best in the upcoming draft.

Fantasy Rankings: 1992—12 points (Tied for 48th)
1991—54 points (Tied for 12th)
1990—3 points (Tied for 97th)
1989—0 points

Past Performance Key: No back in the NFC rushed for as many yards as Workman in 1992 (631) and scored as few rushing touchdowns. Workman's 4 touchdown receptions in 1991 were the most by a Packer back since Vince Lombardi became the team's coach.

5. Brad Muster, New Orleans Saints Muster was a disappointment in 1992. His 3 rushing touchdowns were his lowest total since his rookie season in 1988, as were his overall total of 5, Muster had been described in these pages as Mr. Second Half, since he had scored 15 of his 21 touchdowns during the 1989–91 years in the second half of the season. In 1992, Muster turned the tables. He was off to a pretty good start, scoring 5 touchdowns in the first seven games of the season. But then he went into a tailspin, like the rest of the team, and didn't reach the end zone for the last nine games of 1992. I would be wary of drafting Muster much before the end of the draft.

Fantasy Rankings: 1992—24 points (Tied for 27th)
1991—39 points (Tied for 17th)
1990—36 points (Tied for 21st)
1989—39 points (Tied for 18th)

Past Performance Key: Muster's combination of 9 rushing touchdowns and 3 touchdown receptions over the last two years is topped in each category only by Neal Anderson, Thurman Thomas, and Tom Rathman.

6. Leroy Hoard, Cleveland Browns This second-round pick in the 1990 draft burst on the NFL scene with a vengeance in 1991. Only three running backs—Barry Sanders, Emmitt Smith, and Thurman Thomas—scored more touchdowns than Hoard did in 1991. Hoard's unusual speed for a big back was demonstrated by his 2 touchdown receptions from bonus territory in 1991, more than any other back scored from that distance in the NFL in 1991. But with Eric Metcalf back to form, and Tommy Vardell vying with Kevin Mack for playing time, Leroy Hoard was the odd man out in 1992, despite his brilliant season in 1991, and his touchdown total plummeted to just 1 score, a

46-yard touchdown pass. Don't count on this situation being much different for Hoard in the Cleveland backfield in 1993.

Fantasy Rankings: 1992—3 points (Tied for 80th)

                       1991—45 points (Tied for 15th)

                       1990—18 points (Tied for 45th)

Past Performance Key: Hoard's 9 touchdown receptions in 1991 were the most by a Brown since Ozzie Newsome caught 9 in 1979, and the most by an NFL back since Chuck Foreman scored 22 touchdowns, 9 of them pass receptions, for the 1975 Minnesota Vikings.

7. Leonard Russell/Jon Vaughn, New England Patriots   It would be easy to dismiss these two as just a bunch of Patsies and to warn you off on Draft Day 1993. But despite the lackluster numbers they put on the board in 1992, there's some real talent here. Russell, for example, was the 14th player selected in the 1991 NFL draft, and his 959 yards rushing that year was the highest total by a Pats' rookie since John Stephens posted 1,168 yards in his rookie season of 1988. But he dipped from 4 touchdowns in 1991 to only 2 in 1992. Vaughn is an NFL classmate of Russell's, taken by New England in the fifth round in the 1991 draft. Vaughn led the Pats in rushing in 1992 and led the NFL in kickoff returns, as he averaged 28.2 yards a return, with one touchdown return.

So what do fantasy owners do with this group on Draft Day 1993? Hold your nose and take a plunge on Russell or Vaughn as a reserve back, if you're using my expanded roster rules, and hope that Bill Parcells gets the maximum performance from these players.

Fantasy Rankings:

Russell   1992—12 points (Tied for 48th)

                       1991—24 points (Tied for 32nd)

Vaughn   1992—12 points (Tied for 48th)

                       1991—21 points (Tied for 42nd)

Past Performance Key: Russell has averaged 3.5 yards per carry in his two seasons in the league. Vaughn has returned a kickoff for a touchdown in both of his two years in the league. Former Patriot John Stephens's 13-yard touchdown run against the Jets was the longest touchdown run by a Pats' running back since Stephens posted a 35-yard touchdown run during the 1989 season.

8. Ricky Ervins, Washington Redskins   In last year's edition of this book, I said, "After just one season, it is clear that Ervins is an NFL star just waiting to happen." All I can say in my defense is, I didn't say how long a wait it was going to be. And by all indications given by

Ervins in 1992, it could be a while. Ervins was a huge disappointment. And it's not like he didn't get the opportunity to shine. He carried the ball 151 times, but he rushed for only 495 yards, a 3.3-yard average. And this from a back who was supposed to be a game breaker along the lines of a Barry Sanders or a Thurman Thomas, a back who averaged 4.7 yards on 145 carries in 1991. He's strictly expanded-roster material on Draft Day 1993.

Fantasy Rankings: 1992—12 points (Tied for 48th)
1991—27 points (Tied for 26th)

Past Performance Key: Ervins's 3.3 yards-per-carry average was the worst among running backs with more than 200 yards rushing in the NFC in 1992.

QUICK DRAFT TIPS: RUNNING BACKS

The following statistical summaries try to give a quick glimpse at those scoring abilities that might set a running back apart from the crowd in this year's fantasy draft.

Running Backs with Bonus Rushing Touchdowns—1992

Player	Number
Nick Bell	1
Kenneth Davis	1
Barry Foster	1
Gaston Green	1
Rodney Hampton	1
Barry Sanders	1
Emmitt Smith	1

Running Backs with Bonus Touchdown Receptions—1992

Player	Number
Eric Metcalf	2
David Lang	1
Heath Sherman	1
Lorenzo White	1

Running Backs with Two or More Rushing Touchdowns in One Game—1992

Player	Number of Touchdowns	Number of Times
Rodney Hampton	3	1
Emmitt Smith	3	1
Thurman Thomas	3	1
Ricky Watters	3	1
Terry Allen	2	3
Barry Foster	2	3
Earnest Byner	2	2
Kenneth Davis	2	2
Cleveland Gary	2	2
Rodney Hampton	2	2
Mark Higgs	2	2
Johnny Johnson	2	2
Herschel Walker	2	2
Neal Anderson	2	1
Brad Baxter	2	1
Rod Bernstine	2	1
Roger Craig	2	1
Derrick Fenner	2	1
Kevin Mack	2	1
Christian Okoye	2	1
Barry Sanders	2	1
Emmitt Smith	2	1
John Stephens	2	1
Thurman Thomas	2	1
Ricky Watters	2	1

WIDE RECEIVERS

As if you need further proof after the AFC's ninth consecutive loss in the Super Bowl last January, NFC dominance of the NFL is clear when you look at the performance of NFC versus AFC receivers in 1992. Of course, the NFC starts with a huge advantage as long as Jerry Rice suits up for the 49ers. But the leading receiver in football by a large margin in 1992 was Sterling Sharpe of the Green Bay Packers. Sharpe won the Triple Crown for NFL receivers going away in 1992. He set the NFL single-season record for receptions, with 108, while accumulating 1,461 yards and 13 touchdowns, the highest totals in both of those categories as well. Overall, six NFC receivers posted more than 1,000 yards, while only one AFC receiver reached that mark. Interestingly enough, two of the top four players in receptions in the AFC in 1992 were running backs, while you have to go all the way down to the 14th spot on the NFC list to find a running back. In fact, only one NFC team's leading receiver was a running back, while *five* AFC teams were led by them. While some NFL pundits feel that the AFC has the better quarterbacks, the results, at least with respect to the performance of receivers in 1992, show that the NFC has the better passing offenses.

There is one thing to keep in mind when reading my Scouting Reports on wide receivers. As I noted before, tight ends generally have less value to a fantasy owner, and they certainly do under my rules. They are less valuable for the simple reason that they don't score as often as their smaller, quicker counterparts out on the wings. As always, there are a couple of exceptions to the general rule, and these Scouting Reports will help you find them. Those of you readers whose league rules require you to draft at least one tight end should find the Scouting Reports on tight ends most useful as well.

Wide receivers should constitute the easiest part of the draft, after you have selected your first receiver. There are so many decent receivers, with equal, if unspectacular, value to fantasy owners, and there are a lot of marquee-value players to confuse the unprepared. If your fellow owners start snapping up a lot of receivers early in the draft, fine. Let them, while you snatch up valuable players from the other, more valuable player categories left for you as a result of this misguided strategy.

Another factor to keep in mind when drafting receivers is what I call my "Sophomore Sensation Theory." I have observed in the previous editions of this book that there appears to be a tendency for receivers with promising rookie years to break out in a big way in their sophomore year in the league. Examples from the last few years include the Falcons' Andre Rison, the Packers' Sterling Sharpe, and the Chargers' Anthony Miller. The 1992 season's paradigms are Mike Pritchard of the Falcons, Herman Moore of the Lions, and the Browns' Michael Jackson. It seems that very few receivers explode on the NFL scene in their first season. (Since a tight-end sensation named Mike Ditka caught 56 passes for 1,076 yards in his rookie season with the Chicago Bears in 1961, only five rookie receivers have accumulated 1,000 receiving yards in their first NFL season, and none since rookies Ernest Givins of Houston and Bill Brooks of Indianapolis both reached that figure in 1986.) It generally takes a season for top-notch receivers to get the hang of things in the NFL, and then, as John Madden might say, "Boom!"—Some will break out in a big way. I have pointed out some of those who could do this in 1993 in the following Scouting Reports.

FIRST ECHELON

1. Jerry Rice, San Francisco 49ers   Rice had a down year in 1992 from a fantasy perspective, but he's still the best in the game, arguably the best of all time. He broke Steve Largent's NFL record of 100 touchdown receptions with his 101st touchdown catch in Week Fourteen, and finished with 103, a total he should add to substantially over the rest of his brilliant career. To put that record in perspective, Rice needed only eight seasons to break the record set by Largent over the course of 14 seasons. Rice will probably shatter the all-time reception and yardage records as well, plus the all-time touchdown record (Rice is currently 18 TDs short of Jim Brown's mark of 126 career touchdowns), among others, by the time he's done. And despite all this, it still seems that the level of Rice's fame fails to reflect the absolutely staggering numbers he continues to pile up. For instance, he caught 84 passes for 1,201 yards in 1992. That yardage total was exceeded by no AFC receiver, and by only two NFL receivers, one of whom, Sterling Sharpe, had a season for the ages, and the other of whom, Michael Irvin, has now put together two consecutive phenomenal seasons. Yet, the 1,201 yards was Rice's *lowest* season total since the strike year, 1987, and the third-lowest of his eight-year career.

A few minor chinks in Rice's almost impenetrable armor turned up in 1992. By virtue of Sharpe's historic effort, Rice failed to lead all receivers in touchdowns and fantasy points for the first time in the four editions of this book. Rice scored only 1 bonus bomb in 1992, after tying Gary Clark for the NFL lead with 5 in 1991. Rice averaged 14.3 yards per catch in 1992, the lowest mark of his career. As good as Steve Young is, and he's as good as any quarterback in the league, Rice may still miss his old batterymate, Joe Montana. But despite these warning signs that Rice is mortal after all, you can't help but feel that, as was true of Reggie or The Mick in baseball, Rice has the chance to go downtown every time he touches the ball. Watch Rice every chance you get, because you may never see another NFL receiver like him again. And draft him early if you want him, because, to borrow an expression from the old Federal Express commercial, he absolutely, positively will go in the first two rounds.

Fantasy Rankings: 1992—39 points (2nd)
1991—57 points (1st)
1990—45 points (1st)
1989—63 points (1st)

Past Performance Key: Rice had his fourth consecutive season with 80 or more receptions in 1992, trying the NFL record set by Todd Christensen in 1983–86. He posted his seventh consecutive season with 1,000 or more yards, tying the NFL record of seven consecutive 1,000-yard seasons held by Lance Alworth. He scored 11 bonus bombs during the three years from 1989–1991, most in the NFL, but scored only 1 in 1992. He scored his first rushing touchdown since 1988 in 1992, the fifth of his illustrious career. He has averaged 1,284 yards per season over his eight-year career; only nine other NFL receivers have exceeded that mark *in one season* since Rice came into the league in 1985. He has averaged 1 touchdown every 5.9 receptions over his career. Rice became only the sixth receiver in NFL history to reach 10,000 career yards and 600 career receptions in 1992.

2. Sterling Sharpe, Green Bay Packers   Sharpe returns to the First Echelon on the heels of a season that was perhaps *the* greatest, and certainly one of the greatest, ever by an NFL receiver, and may have established himself as one of the all-time greats in the process. That's because in 1989 Sharpe had another magnificent season, matched by only one other player, Jerry Rice. In 1989, Sharpe had 90 receptions for 1,423 yards and 12 touchdowns, 2 of them bonus bombs. No player in NFL history up to that time had recorded as many receptions, yards and touchdowns in one season. Only one other player in NFL history since that time has posted as many receptions, yards, and touchdowns in one season, and that was Jerry Rice, in 1990. Sharpe fell prey to the poor quarterbacking situation in Green Bay in 1990 and 1991, and slumped to an average of 68 receptions, 1,033 yards, and only 5 touchdowns. Most NFL receivers would take those numbers in a New York minute, but, as the results from 1992 demonstrate, these were subpar statistics for Sharpe.

Sharpe had a season for the ages under new head coach Mike Holmgren's offensive system, which brought some of the 49ers' offensive magic to the Green Bay passing game in 1992. Sharpe set an NFL record with 108 receptions, besting Art Monk's single-season mark of 106. In the process Sharpe also shattered Roger Craig's record for the most receptions in the first five years of an NFL career. Craig, a running back, had totaled 358 receptions in his first five years in the league; Sharpe has accumulated 389 in his first five. In addition, Sharpe rolled up 1,461 yards and scored 13 touchdowns, 2 of them bonus bombs, in 1992. Holmgren set up his offensive system in Green Bay to substitute Sterling Sharpe for Jerry Rice. One season is all the evidence I need to say that plan is working just fine. Fantasy owners should follow Holmgren's lead, and plan to substitute Sharpe for every other receiver on their wish list of receivers, except Rice, in 1993.

Fantasy Rankings: 1992—45 points (1st)
1991—15 points (Tied for 27th)

1990—24 points (Tied for 11th)
1989—48 points (2nd)

Past Performance Key: Sharpe scored a bonus bomb for the fourth·straight year, one of only five NFL receivers with such a streak. He has 7 bonus bombs over the last four seasons, and 5 over the past three. Sharpe has scored 2 bonus bombs in three of the last four seasons. Only two other receivers in NFL history, Jerry Rice and Houston's Charley Hennigan (from the early AFL days), have accumulated 1,400 yards or more in two separate NFL seasons. (Michael Irvin missed tying this record by 4 yards in 1992; Rice has done it three times.)

3. Michael Haynes, Atlanta Falcons   Haynes broke out after three years in the league with a sensational season in 1991. He scored 8 touchdowns from 1988 to 1990; he scored 11 touchdowns in 1991. He maintained his exceptional level of performance in 1992, despite injuries that forced him to miss two games early in the season and the debilitating injury to Atlanta quarterback Chris Miller. Haynes scored 10 touchdowns in 1992, 2 of them bonus bombs. I said in last year's edition of this book that it would not surprise me to see Haynes move up to the First Echelon in 1992. And, despite his injuries, that's exactly what he did with his fine season. With the Red Gun offense in high gear in 1993, expect to find Haynes in this exclusive neighborhood again in next year's edition.

Fantasy Rankings: 1992—36 points (Tied for 3rd)
1991—45 points (Tied for 2nd)
1990—0 points
1989—15 points (Tied for 29th)

Past Performance Key: Haynes had 6 bonus bombs over the past two seasons, tying him with Jerry Rice for the best total in the NFL. His 89-yard touchdown in Week Two against the Washington Redskins was the longest scoring play from scrimmage in the 1992 season. Haynes's 21 touchdown receptions over the past two seasons is the third-highest total in the league, behind Rice's 24 and teammate Andre Rison's 23. His yardage average in the three years prior to 1991 was 16.1 per reception; for the two years since then, it's 19.7.

4. Michael Irvin, Dallas Cowboys   Irvin came back to earth somewhat in 1992 after an unearthly season in 1991, but it would have been tough to repeat exactly one of the great seasons ever by a wide receiver. Nevertheless, he came close. In 1991, he caught 93 passes for 1,523 yards and 8 touchdowns, with 2 bonus bombs. He led the NFC in catches and the NFL in receiving yardage. His 1,523 yards was the sixth-highest single-season total for a receiver in the history of the NFL. In 1992, Irvin had 78 receptions for 1,396 yards and 7 touchdowns, with 1 bonus bomb. His 6 catches for 114 yards and 2 touchdowns sparked the 'Boys to their Super Bowl XXVII victory, and was the best scoring performance by a Dallas receiver in the Super Bowl in the storied history of the franchise. For anyone else, these numbers would be spectacular, but for Irvin, they could be better. With the Cowboys continuing to improve—a scary thought to NFL opponents and the legions of Cowboy-haters across the country, after their great season in 1992—Irvin should be an offensive force at the wide-receiver position for the Cowboys for years to come. As long as Irvin avoids the injury problems that plagued him early in his career, he'll be a First Echelon regular.

Fantasy Rankings: 1992—24 points (Tied for 10th)
1991—30 points (9th)
1990—18 points (Tied for 20th)
1989—9 points (Tied for 57th)

Past Performance Key: Only two other receivers in NFL history have accumulated more than Irvin's consecutive two-year yardage total of 2,919 yards during 1991–92. (Jerry Rice (1989–90) and Lance Alworth (1965–66) each totalled 2,985 yards over two consecutive years). Irvin has scored a bonus bomb in each of his five NFL seasons. He had scored 12 touchdowns in only 78 career receptions prior to 1991; he has scored 15 touchdowns in the two seasons since then. Irvin scored 5 of his 7 touchdowns in 1992 in only two games.

5. Andre Rison, Atlanta Falcons   Rison cemented his First Echelon status on the strength of another superior season in 1992, as he caught 93 passes for 1,121 yards and 11 touchdowns. The number of both receptions and yards were career highs for this perennial All-Pro. In fact, only six receivers in NFL history have caught more than 93 passes in one season, and only two of those six, Jerry Rice in 1990 and Sterling Sharpe in 1992, scored as many as Rison's 11 touchdowns in the same season. There can be no doubt that the Falcons have gotten the best of the blockbuster deal that brought Rison from the Colts in a package for the No. 1 pick in the 1990 draft, which turned out to be Jeff George. While the jury is still out on the injury-plagued George's ability to anchor the wayward Indianapolis franchise, Rison is the skipper of what might be the best receiving corps in the NFL right now. (If you are skeptical about that, look how effective the Falcons receivers were during the last four weeks of the season with Vikings reject Wade Wilson at quarterback. Wade Wilson!) With a healthy Chris Miller returning to man the high-octane Red Gun offense, look for another First Echelon performance from Rison in 1993.

Fantasy Rankings: 1992—36 points (Tied for 3rd)
1991—36 points (Tied for 4th)

1990—36 points (2nd)
1989—15 points (Tied for 29th)

Past Performance Key: Rison's 33 touchdown receptions over the last three years are second in the NFL only to Jerry Rice's 37, and his 23 touchdown receptions in the last two are second only to Jerry Rice's 24. He has scored a bonus bomb in three of the his four NFL seasons, 1991 being the only year he did not. Rison did not repeat his 1990 "triple double" (2 touchdown receptions three games in a row) in 1992, but he did catch 6 touchdown passes in a three-game period from Week Four through Week Six in 1992.

SECOND ECHELON

1. Anthony Miller, San Diego Chargers   Miller returned to the ranks of the fantasy elite in 1992, after a brief period away for reasons not of his doing. In fact, several years of poor quarterbacking and injuries finally caught up with the fantasy stats of this talented receiver in 1991, arguably the worst season of his career. Miller had made the Pro Bowl two years running with first the 10th-rated and then the 12th-rated quarterback in the AFC tossing to him in 1989 and 1990. But Chargers quarterback John Friesz was only the 14th-rated signal-caller in the AFC in 1991, and something had to give. It finally did. Miller scored only 3 times in 1991, a career low. But then Bobby Beathard rescued Stan Humphries from the Redskins prior to the 1992 season when Friesz went down, and Miller, whether he knew it or not, was back. Miller had his best season since 1989 in 1992. He had 72 receptions for 1,060 yards and 7 touchdowns, adding another score on a fumble return. Miller was named to the Pro Bowl again after the 1992 season, a well-deserved honor, not only for his ability, but for his patience as well. Look for Miller to continue to shine in 1993.

Fantasy Rankings: 1992—30 points (Tied for 5th)
1991—9 points (Tied for 51st)
1990—21 points (Tied for 16th)
1989—42 points (3rd)

Past Performance Key: Miller scored his first bonus bomb in three seasons, after scoring 2 in 1989. He led the AFC with receiving yards in 1992, the second time in his five-year career he has posted more than 1,000 yards. Miller was the only AFC player with more than 1,000 yards receiving in 1992.

2. Haywood Jeffires, Houston Oilers   Jeffires had another spectacular season in 1992. In 1991, he became only the fifth receiver in NFL history with 100 receptions in a season, and led all NFL receivers in that category. He also led the AFC in both receptions and yardage for the second year in a row in 1991. In 1992, he failed to become the first NFL player to post back-to-back 100-reception seasons, but not for lack of trying. He caught 90 passes to lead the AFC for the third straight season. Nine of those receptions were for touchdowns, a career-high total. Make no mistake, Jeffires did miss the injured Moon, since he posted his lowest yardage total in three seasons, and the lowest yardage average of his career. Jeffires's yardage figures are also affected by the fact that the Oilers' offense uses the passing game heavily in the red zone, as evidenced by the fact that 7 of Jeffires's 9 touchdown passes in 1992 were less than 9 yards in length. Assuming Moon is back and healthy this season, Jeffires is solid gold as a second receiver on Draft Day 1993.

Fantasy Rankings: 1992—27 points (Tied for 7th)
1991—21 points (Tied for 15th)
1990—30 points (Tied for 3rd)
1989—6 points (Tied for 75th)

Past Performance Key: Jeffires caught 3 touchdown passes in Week Six, the first time an Oiler receiver had 3 touchdowns in one game in at least four seasons. It was also the first multiple-touchdown game for Jeffires in his career. Only two other NFL receivers, Michael Irvin and Andre Rison, caught 3 touchdown passes in one game in 1992. Jeffires's longest touchdown pass in 1992 was 17 yards. His yardage average on his 9 touchdown passes was only 7 yards in 1992, the second-lowest mark among receivers with 4 or more touchdown passes in 1992. (Dallas's Jay Novacek had the lowest average, 6.3 yards per touchdown catch.)

3. Ernest Givins, Houston Oilers   After a somewhat disappointing season from a fantasy perspective in 1991, Givins pumped it up a notch and had a stellar year in 1992. He scored 10 touchdowns (a career high) in 1992, after his touchdown total fell from 9 in 1990 to 5 in 1991. But the football gods giveth and the football gods taketh away, and while he posted the most touchdowns of his career, Givins's reception yardage (787) and yardage average (11.7 yards per reception) in 1992 were career lows. But for most fantasy owners, this is not a concern. So, as long as Givins is a main cog in the Oilers' high-octane offense, he is going to score, and will be a valuable second or third receiver in 1993.

Fantasy Rankings: 1992—30 points (Tied for 5th)
1991—15 points (Tied for 27th)
1990—30 points (Tied for 3rd)
1989—9 points (Tied for 57th)

Past Performance Key: Givins has not reached 1,000 yards in a season since his rookie year in 1986. He has not scored a bonus bomb since Week One of the 1990 season.

4. Andre Reed, Buffalo Bills   Reed is one of the finest receivers in the game, playing in one of the best offenses in the NFL. But, like teammate Thurman Thomas, he drops from the First Echelon in this edition of my book, after residing there for two straight years. He drops for the same reason as Thomas, a disappointing scoring performance in 1992. Reed caught 65 passes for 913 yards, which are fairly impressive totals, but he scored only 3 touchdowns in 1992, the lowest touchdown total of his eight-year career. He complained about his low production after Week Fifteen, having caught only 20 passes in the previous eight games. His fantasy owners were ticked off, too, as Reed's fantasy scoring totals remained well below his normal totals all season long. But 1992 was an aberration for this talented receiver. Look for Reed's scoring totals to rebound this season.

> **Fantasy Rankings:**   1992—9 points (Tied for 57th)
> 1991—33 points (Tied for 6th)
> 1990—27 points (Tied for 7th)
> 1989—33 points (Tied for 5th)

> **Past Performance Key:**   Reed led the Bills in receptions for the seventh consecutive year in 1992, but failed to score a bonus bomb after scoring 1 in each of the three prior seasons. His 14.0 yardage average was the second-highest of his career. Reed was a member of the AFC's Pro Bowl squad for the fifth straight year in 1992.

5. Fred Barnett, Philadelphia Eagles   After recovering quickly from a separated shoulder in preseason, Barnett moved to the head of the receiving line with a terrific year in 1992. He had the most receptions of his career, 67, and cracked the 1,000-yard barrier for the first time as well. After scoring only 4 touchdowns in 1991, Barnett posted 6 in 1992, with a bonus bomb. After a tremendous rookie year (8 touchdown catches on only 36 receptions in 1990), Barnett's scoring totals dipped in 1991. But that can be attributed to the absence of Randall Cunningham, who missed the year with a knee injury. The return of a healthy R.C. in 1992 was a tonic to Barnett. Look for more of the same from him in 1993, as he becomes a fixture in the upper ranks of NFL receivers.

> **Fantasy Rankings:**   1992—21 points (Tied for 13th)
> 1991—18 points (Tied for 21st)
> 1990—27 points (Tied for 7th)

> **Past Performance Key:**   Barnett has scored 4 bonus bombs in his three-year NFL career, and at least 1 in each season. He was the Eagles' leading receiver for the second straight year, but the undisputed leader for the first time in his three-year career. (He tied with Keith Byars for the team lead in receptions in 1991.)

6. Tim Brown, Los Angeles Raiders   What a long, strange trip it's been for this talented receiver. In 1988, he set an NFL record for most combined yards gained in a rookie season. Then, disaster struck in the first game of the 1989 season, and he missed almost the entire year after doctors reconstructed his knee. On the comeback trail, he only caught 18 passes for 3 touchdowns in 1990. In 1991, he started slowly, scoring only 1 touchdown in the first 10 weeks. But then Brown caught fire, and he ended up with 36 pass receptions for 5 touchdowns, with 1 bonus bomb. In addition, he returned a punt 75 yards for a touchdown in Week Thirteen. In 1992, Brown asserted himself as The Man in the Raiders' receiving corps, leading their receivers in receptions and yardage, while leading the team in touchdowns. This former Heisman Trophy winner is a true NFL star, and assuming the Raiders' quarterback situation improves in 1993, Brown should be a top fantasy performer this season.

> **Fantasy Rankings:**   1992—27 points (Tied for 7th)
> 1991—24 points (Tied for 12th)
> 1990—15 points (Tied for 32nd)
> 1989—0 points
>
> **Past Performance Key:**   Brown's 49 receptions and 7 touchdown receptions were career highs. He was one of only seven NFL receivers with 2 bonus bombs in 1992, and has now scored at least 1 bonus touchdown two years in a row.

7. Mark Clayton, Green Bay Packers   The 1992 season was another injury-plagued one for Mark Clayton. In 1990, injuries limited Clayton to only 32 receptions and 3 touchdowns. He rebounded in 1991 with the third-best year of his Hall of Fame career, catching 70 passes for 1,053 yards and 12 touchdowns. Clayton was hampered with a sore neck in 1992, and as a result missed three games and was slowed in parts of others, giving him 1990-like numbers: only 43 passes caught, for 619 yards and 3 touchdowns. These low numbers (for Clayton, that is) can be directly attributed to Clayton's subpar health in 1992. Clayton should be used as more than a decoy for Sterling Sharpe in Green Bay's passing game. (The next highest number of receptions by a Green Bay wide receiver in 1992 after Sharpe's record-setting 108 was only 17). If so, look for a healthy Clayton to rebound in a big way in 1993.

> **Fantasy Rankings:**   1992—9 points (Tied for 57th)
> 1991—36 points (Tied for 4th)
> 1990—9 points (Tied for 66th)
> 1989—33 points (Tied for 5th)
>
> **Past Performance Key:**   The 1992 season was the first that two Miami running backs caught more passes than Clayton since his rookie year in 1983, when

Clayton had only 6 receptions. Clayton has not scored a bonus bomb since 1989, when he scored 2.

8. Willie "Flipper" Anderson, Los Angeles Rams   In last year's edition of this book, I said that if you thought the Flipper of the 1989–90 seasons would be back in 1992, Anderson could be a steal of a fourth receiver. While not the most uncategorical prediction you have ever seen, it is still worth recounting, because fantasy owners who drafted Anderson late in last year's draft are still gloating. Obviously, you can throw out 1991 as an aberration, because everyone on the Rams was bad in that miserable season. Under head coach Chuck Knox, the Rams, and the offense in particular, are on the road to recovery. Exhibit A is Anderson, who posted a career-high 7 touchdowns on only 38 receptions in 1992. The speedy Anderson remains a deep threat as well. Anderson had averaged 24.1 yards his first three years in the league before dipping to 16.6 in 1991. His yardage average rose to 17.3 in 1992. Although it might be too much to expect Anderson to post the spectacular NFL numbers of his early seasons in the league, it is reasonable to expect him to post the same total of fantasy points, as he continues to assume the reins from Henry Ellard as the Rams's number one receiver.

Fantasy Rankings: 1992—21 points (Tied for 13th)
1991—3 points (Tied for 110th)
1990—15 points (Tied for 32nd)
1989—21 points (Tied for 22nd)

Past Performance Key: Anderson has averaged 21.3 yards per catch in his five-year career. He set the NFL record for most yards receiving in one game in 1989, with 336 yards against the New Orleans Saints, and averaged an even 26 yards per reception that season. Anderson failed to score a bonus bomb for the second straight season in 1992.

9. Mark Duper, Miami Dolphins   Duper's middle name could easily be Lazarus, instead of Super, after his miraculous return from the brink of fantasy oblivion the last three years. After 1 touchdown each in 1988 and 1989, Duper scored 5 in both 1990 and 1991, and in 1991 he accumulated over 1,000 yards for the first time since 1986. Duper continued his impressive comeback in 1992, scoring 7 touchdowns, his highest total since 1987, and scoring his first bonus bomb since 1990. These results may be attributable to lots of things, but probably not to the best off-season training practices. Duper reported to training camp about 12 pounds overweight and failed the 12-minute run at the Dolphins' training camp, according to published reports. But July isn't September, and he was ready to play by the start of the season, as his statistics for 1992 show. Duper has proven once again that he can put solid numbers on the board and is a solid bet as a third or fourth receiver in 1993.

Fantasy Rankings: 1992—24 points (Tied for 10th)
1991—15 points (Tied for 27th)
1990—18 points (Tied for 20th)
1989—3 points (Tied for 111th)

Past Performance Key: Duper's 17.3-yard average was his best since 1987. Duper and Clayton combined for 10 touchdown receptions in 1992. They have failed to combine for at least 10 touchdowns in a season only twice since 1984.

10. Webster Slaughter, Houston Oilers Webster Slaughter, ruled a free agent by Judge David Doty in the "Jackson Four" decision on September 24, 1992, signed with Houston immediately thereafter, prior to Week four, and, once he became familiar with the run-and-shoot offense, had a solid year. He scored 4 touchdowns on only 39 receptions. Unfortunately, his days as a deep threat may be over, especially in the conservative Oilers passing offense. His 14.2-yard average in 1991 was the lowest of his career up to that point, and was surpassed, if that's the right word, by his 12.5-yard average in 1992. That's too bad, because Slaughter used to be a bona fide deep threat. Three of his 6 touchdowns in 1989 were bonus bombs, and he scored 1 in 1991 for the Browns as well. While he may not "drop the bomb" like he once did, Slaughter should prosper in his second season in Houston. He is a steal as a fourth receiver on Draft Day, if he even slides that low.

Fantasy Rankings: 1992—12 points (Tied for 37th)
1991—12 points (Tied for 39th)
1990—12 points (Tied for 53rd)
1989—27 points (Tied for 15th)

Past Performance Key: Slaughter's 486 yards receiving in 1992 was his lowest total for a season since 1988, when he accumulated just 462—but he played in only eight games that year.

11. James Lofton, Los Angeles Raiders Without much fanfare, Lofton, with a solid season in 1992, added to his credentials as one of the greatest receivers in NFL history. He passed Steve Largent as the receiver with the most career yardage in NFL history in Week One, bettering Largent's mark of 13,089 yards. Lofton finished the season with 13,821 career yards, a total that should hover around the 15,000 mark by the end of his career, now that Lofton has signed with his old team, the Raiders, for whom he played during the 1987–88 seasons. (Buffalo announced on April 29, 1993, that they would not renew

Lofton's contract.) His 51 receptions tied him with Charlie Joiner for third on the career list, with 750. On the scoring ledger, Lofton followed his 8 touchdown receptions in 1991, tying his career high, with 6 in 1992. If Lofton is showing his age at all, it might be revealing that his yardage average per reception of 15.4 was his lowest since 1986, and the second-lowest of his career. But, as Lofton enters his 16th NFL season, he and Andre Reed still constitute one of the finest pairs of receivers in the NFL. On a warm summer afternoon in the not-too-distant future, you will see Lofton front and center at the annual induction ceremonies in Canton. If you are given the opportunity to snag, Lofton who will be a primary receiver in the Raider's offense, in the middle to late rounds of your fantasy draft, you should induct Lofton into your receiver corps.

Fantasy Rankings: 1992—18 points (Tied for 19th)
1991—33 points (Tied for 6th)
1990—18 points (Tied for 20th)
1989—9 points (Tied for 57th)

Past Performance Key: Lofton has averaged 18.1 yards per catch in his four years with the Bills, and 18.4 yards per catch over his career. He has compiled his remarkable career yardage total while never catching more than 71 passes in one season. After being one of only three NFL receivers with 2 or more bonus bombs in each of the two seasons prior to 1992, Lofton failed to post even 1 in 1992. It was the first time Lofton had failed to do so since 1989.

12. Cris Carter, Minnesota Vikings   This Carter has supplanted the other Carter as the premier receiver on the Vikings. For the second consecutive year, Cris Carter led Minnesota receivers in receptions and yardage, in addition to tying for the lead with Anthony Carter for touchdowns in 1991. And he accomplished this despite missing several games due to injury later in the season. Carter caught 53 passes for 681 yards and 6 touchdowns in 1992, after hauling in 72 passes for the Vikings in 1991, for 962 yards and 5 touchdowns. He should go early on Draft Day.

Fantasy Rankings: 1992—18 points (Tied for 19th)
1991—15 points (Tied for 27th)
1990—12 points (Tied for 53rd)
1989—33 points (Tied for 5th)

Past Performance Key: Prior to 1991, Carter had averaged a little more than 1 touchdown every 5 receptions in his four years in the league. Since then he has averaged a touchdown every 11 receptions. His 6 touchdowns in 1992 were his highest season total since 1989, when he caught 11 for the Eagles (and was promptly released).

13. Willie Green, Detroit Lions   Green has emerged as one of its better receivers. He scored 7 touchdowns in the 1991 season for Detroit, on only 39 receptions. He added 5 touchdowns (with 2 bonus bombs) on only 33 receptions in 1992. Green could produce similar numbers if Rodney Peete stays healthy and develops further at the quarterback slot this season.

Fantasy Rankings: 1992—21 points (Tied for 13th)

1991—24 points (Tied for 12th)

1990—0 points

Past Performance Key: Green led the Lions' receivers in touchdown catches for the second straight season in 1992. He has now scored at least 1 bonus bomb in both of his NFL seasons.

14. Anthony Carter, Minnesota Vikings   Last year I observed that 1991 was arguably Carter's worst year in his seven with the Vikings. I also warned fantasy owners to keep in mind that A.C. would be 32 years old in September of 1992, and that Father Time was starting to hit him with the old bump-and-run at the line of scrimmage. The bad news for Carter fans is, I was right. The 1992 season was A.C.'s worst as a Viking. It was the second year in a row he failed to lead the Vikings in receptions, after leading them every year from 1987 through 1990. He also posted the lowest season touchdown total of his career. A.C. had enjoyed Second Echelon status in each of the first three editions of this book. Sorry to say, Carter is in danger of becoming just one of the best of the rest from now on.

Fantasy Rankings: 1992—6 points (Tied for 80th)

1991—21 points (Tied for 15th)

1990—30 points (Tied for 3rd)

1989—12 points (Tied for 42nd)

Past Performance Key: Carter had never had fewer than 4 touchdown receptions in any one season in his 10-year professional career (three years in the USFL) prior to 1992. He failed to accumulate 1,000 yards receiving for the second consecutive year in 1992, after three straight seasons above 1,000 yards. Carter became the eighth player in NFL history to achieve a 100-game reception streak in 1992. He ended his consecutive game streak at 105 later in the season.

15. Ernie Jones, Phoenix Cardinals   Jones might go by the flashy nickname "Indiana" in certain circles, but he's just plain Ernie when it comes to his status as a fantasy receiver. Over the course of his five-year career, he scored 3 touchdowns in each of the first two years and 4 in each of the last three. He has not scored more than 15 fantasy points in any of the last four seasons, and has not ranked higher than 26th among fantasy receivers during that time. There is no doubt he remains a deep threat, as evidenced by his lifetime yardage average per catch of 17.0. But his average per catch in 1992, 14.7 yards, was the lowest of his career, and it has declined every year he's been in the league. Add this to the overall quality of the Cardinals' offense, and you don't come up with boffo box office from a fantasy perspective. Fantasy owners might as well search for the Lost Ark if they draft Jones much before the last rounds of the draft.

Fantasy Rankings: 1992—15 points (Tied for 26th)
1991—12 points (Tied for 39th)
1990—15 points (Tied for 32nd)
1989—12 points (Tied for 42nd)

Past Performance Key: Jones's 38 receptions and 559 yards in 1992 were his lowest totals since his rookie year of 1988. He scored a bonus bomb in 1992 after failing to score one in 1991 for the first time in three seasons.

16. Eric Martin, New Orleans Saints   Martin's career in the Big Easy rebounded in 1992 after a mild slump the prior two seasons. He had the most receptions and yards in a season since 1989, and scored 5 touchdowns after his 4 in 1991, which was his lowest total since his rookie year in 1985. Martin is nothing if not consistent (he has 68, 66, 63, and 68 receptions over the last four seasons, for example, with 5, 4, and 5 touchdowns over the last three). But it will be interesting to see how the return of Floyd Turner after a year on injured reserve affects Martin's status as The Man at wide receiver for the Saints. Because of this uncertainty, the steady Martin should not rate higher than a third or fourth receiver for fantasy owners in the upcoming season.

Fantasy Rankings: 1992—18 points (Tied for 19th)
1991—12 points (Tied for 39th)
1990—15 points (Tied for 32nd)
1989—27 points (Tied for 15th)

Past Performance Key: Martin has been the leading Saints receiver for the past six seasons. He has accumulated more than 1,000 receiving yards in three of the last five years.

17. Irving Fryar, Miami Dolphins   Fryar is one of those players who enters the league accompanied by huge fanfare, and of whom success is expected immediately, but whose career really doesn't blossom until later on down the road. Talk about great expectations: Fryar was the first player chosen in the 1984 NFL draft. (Jerry Rice was the first pick overall by the Birmingham Stallions in the USFL draft in 1985, but only the 16th pick overall by the 49ers in the 1985 NFL draft.) However, Fryar did not catch more than 50 passes in one season until 1990, and he did not exceed 1,000 yards in a season until 1991. In fact, 1991, his eighth year in the league, was arguably his best, as Fryar posted the highest number of receptions and yards of his career. And 1992 was another solid year. He caught 55 passes, the second-highest total of his career, for 791 yards, third-best in his career. But Fryar's touchdown totals continue to disappoint. From 1985 to 1988, Fryar scored 27 touchdowns, 23 of them receptions. In the four years since that time, Fryar has scored only 14 touchdowns, 4 of them last season. Fryar has not knifed in to the end zone on scoring passes more than 4 times in a season since 1988. That should change with Fryar's move to the Dolphins. Look for Fryar to increase his touchdown totals this season with his new team.

Fantasy Rankings: 1992—15 points (Tied for 26th)
1991—15 points (Tied for 27th)
1990—12 points (Tied for 53rd)
1989—9 points (Tied for 57th)

Past Performance Key: Nearly 50 percent of Fryar's touchdown catches (3 of 7) during the past two seasons were bonus bombs; he scored no bonus bombs during the 1988–90 seasons. Fryar averaged 37 yards per touchdown reception in 1992, tying him with Cleveland's Michael Jackson for the fourth-best mark in the league.

18. Henry Ellard, Los Angeles Rams   Ellard, who posted some of the best yardage numbers in NFL history during the 1988–90 seasons, continued to slip in 1992. His number of receptions, 47, slipped for the third straight year, to his lowest number since 1986. His yardage dropped for the fourth straight year, down to 727 yards, also his lowest mark since 1986. Most important, Ellard scored only 3 touchdowns in 1992, the same as he did in 1991, but still way below his career best. Once a First Echelon player, his best years may be behind this 10-year pro. However, his career is not yet over by a long shot, and with the talent that he's still got, he is a steal as a fourth receiver.

Fantasy Rankings: 1992—9 points (Tied for 57th)
1991—9 points (Tied for 51st)
1990—15 points (Tied for 32nd)
1989—24 points (Tied for 19th)

Past Performance Key: Ellard ended his four-year streak of 1,000 yards in 1992. Only three receivers in NFL history other than Ellard (Jerry Rice, Steve Largent, and Lance Alworth) have ever put together four consecutive 1,000-yard seasons at the wide-receiver spot. (Lofton has five seasons in a row if you do not count the abbreviated strike year of 1982.) Ellard's 15.5-yard average in 1992 was his lowest since 1986. He has averaged more than 1,000 yards per season over the past seven seasons. Ellard had 2 bonus bombs in 1988; he has scored only 1 since then.

19. Calvin Williams, Philadelphia Eagles   After leading all NFL rookie wide receivers in touchdowns with 9 in 1990, Williams's stats dropped precipitously without Cunningham at the Eagles' throttle in 1991, and because of his own injuries. He scored only 3 touchdowns in 1991. Like Cunningham, though, Williams was back with a vengeance in 1992, racking up 42 receptions, a career-high, and 7 touchdowns. After the results from 1992, it is safe to say that with Fred Barnett, Calvin Williams forms one of the most potent receiving duos in the NFL. Williams is back, and would be a real bargain as a third receiver in 1992.

Fantasy Rankings: 1992—21 points (Tied for 13th)
1991—9 points (Tied for 51st)
1990—27 points (Tied for 7th)

Past Performance Key: Williams has led the Eagles in touchdown receptions two of the last three years. His 9 touchdown passes in 1990 was the most by a rookie wide receiver in the NFL since Daryl Turner scored 10 for the Seahawks and Louis Lipps scored 9 for the Steelers in 1984.

20. Mark Jackson, New York Giants   Jackson had a great year for his fantasy owners in 1992, after a string of subpar performances the last few years. For example, although he was the team's leading receiver in 1991 when he went down with a wrist injury in Week Thirteen, he had caught only 33 receptions at that point, for only 1 touchdown. Jackson had 48 receptions in 1992 for 745 yards, plus 8 touchdowns, a career high. And all this with Elway sidelined most of the season with a bad shoulder. Jackson followed his former coach, Dan Reeves, to the Meadowlands in the offseason to replace Mark Ingram, who took his free agent act south to Miami. Jackson will now be catching passes from another NFL quarterback star, Phil Simms. Look for another solid year for this fine wide receiver in 1993.

Fantasy Rankings: 1992—27 points (Tied for 7th)
1991—3 points (Tied for 110th)
1990—18 points (Tied for 20th)
1989—6 points (Tied for 75th)

Past Performance Key: Jackson scored 6 touchdowns in 1988, but only a total of 11 touchdowns in his other five seasons in the NFL prior to 1992. He scored a bonus bomb for the first time in four editions of this book last season.

21. Mike Pritchard, Atlanta Falcons   This former Colorado Buffalo star and the Falcons' first pick in the 1991 NFL draft followed a good rookie year with a terrific sophomore season. After posting 50 receptions for 624 yards and 2 touchdowns in 1991, Pritchard improved to 77 receptions for 827 yards and 5 touchdowns in 1992, jumping 50 spots in the fantasy rankings. He has the talent to be a deep threat on any other team, but the presence of Haynes and Rison will relegate him to shorter-yardage duty in the foreseeable future. Still, expect to see the talented Pritchard continue to blossom in 1993.

Fantasy Rankings: 1992—15 points (Tied for 26th)

1991—6 points (Tied for 76th)

Past Performance Key: Haywood Jeffires was the only NFL player who had as many as or more receptions than Pritchard, but who averaged fewer yards per reception than Pritchard in 1992. Pritchard had 29 more receptions than teammate Michael Haynes, but only 19 more yards, and 5 fewer touchdowns, in 1992.

22. Brett Perriman, Detroit Lions   Perriman has blossomed in the run-and-shoot offense in Detroit. After averaging 24 receptions a year in three seasons in New Orleans, Perriman has caught 121 balls in Detroit in only two seasons. In fact, he had his best year as a pro in 1992, leading the Lions in receptions with 69, and scoring 4 touchdowns in the bargain. Perriman is a solid fourth receiver in 1993.

Fantasy Rankings: 1992—12 points (Tied for 37th)

1991—3 points (Tied for 110th)

1990—6 points (Tied for 84th)

1989—0 points

Past Performance Key: Perriman's reception, yardage, and touchdown totals in 1992 were all career bests.

BEST OF THE REST

1. Alvin Harper, Dallas Cowboys   Harper, the 12th selection in the 1991 NFL draft, made huge strides in 1992 toward making Michael Irvin and himself the most potent receiving duo in the league. Harper caught 4 touchdown passes on only 35 receptions in 1992, averaging 16.1 yards per catch. His slam-dunk of the football after his touchdown receptions in Super Bowl XXVII will make the highlight films for years. As Harper enters his third year in the league, he has begun to fulfill his potential to be one of the NFL's most exciting receivers. He is a steal as a fourth receiver on Draft Day 1993.

Fantasy Rankings: 1992—12 points (Tied for 37th)

1991—3 points (Tied for 110th)

Past Performance Key: Harper has averaged 16.2 yards per reception in his two years with the Cowboys.

2. Rob Moore, New York Jets   Moore had a solid season despite the Jets' otherwise disappointing year and confusion at quarterback. He scored 4 touchdowns in 1992, after scoring 5 in 1991 and 6 in his rookie year in 1990. His drop in receptions in 1992 was more pronounced, from 70 in 1991 to 50 in 1992. Moore is an obvious talent whose value to fantasy owners is restricted only by the Jets' quarterback situation. With Boomer Esiason taking over for the Jets at quarterback, Moore could get back on track to reach his full fantasy potential. He's a steal in the later rounds on Draft Day 1993.

> **Fantasy Rankings:**   1992—12 points (Tied for 37th)
> 1991—15 points (Tied for 27th)
> 1990—24 points (Tied for 11th)

> **Past Performance Key:**   Moore led the Jets in total yardage, with 726, and in yards per reception, at 14.5, in 1992. He had 2 bonus bombs in 1990, but has scored none in the two seasons since then.

3. Tim McGee, Washington Redskins   McGee was a victim of the Bengals' disastrous season in 1992. The Bengals' quarterbacks threw for only 1,943 net passing yards, the second lowest total in the NFL, and 16 touchdowns. So it comes as no surprise that McGee had a disappointing season in 1992. He had 35 receptions for only 408 yards, the lowest total for him in both categories since 1987, his second year in the league. He scored only 3 touchdowns in 1992, his lowest total since 1990. But all this should change in 1993, as McGee replaces Gary Clark in the Redskins' Posse. Plugged into the Redskins' potent passing game, McGee is a steal as a third or fourth receiver this season.

> **Fantasy Rankings:**   1992—9 points (Tied for 57th)
> 1991—15 points (Tied for 27th)
> 1990—3 points (Tied for 109th)
> 1989—27 points (Tied for 15th)

> **Past Performance Key:**   McGee scored 14 touchdowns in 1988–89. He has scored only 8 touchdowns in the three seasons since then. McGee's yardage average of 11.7 in 1992 was the lowest of his seven-year career, a precipitous drop of 4 yards per reception from his previous low.

4. Ricky Sanders, Washington Redskins   Like Tampa Bay's Mark Carrier, discussed a little further on in these reports, Sanders is a receiver whose performance expectations may have been raised too high by one career season. Sanders caught 12 touchdown passes in 1988, including a bonus bomb, but has caught only 20 touchdown passes over his other six NFL seasons. Like the other members of the Redskins' Posse, he had a disappointing season in 1992, scoring only 3 touchdowns, after scoring 6 in 1991. With free agent and fellow Posse member Gary Clark off to Phoenix, Sanders should see more passes thrown his way in 1993. As long as fantasy owners don't get their hopes up too high, Sanders should do a creditable job as a third or fourth receiver this season.

Fantasy Rankings: 1992—12 points (Tied for 37th)
1991—21 points (Tied for 15th)
1990—9 points (Tied for 66th)
1989—12 points (Tied for 42nd)

Past Performance Key: Sanders's bonus bomb in 1992 was his first since the 1988 season.

5. Dwight Stone, Pittsburgh Steelers The Steelers' deep threat was a disappointment in 1992. In fact, his year in 1992 was almost a complete turnaround from 1991. Three of Stone's 5 touchdowns in 1991 were bonus bombs; none of his 34 receptions in 1992 were. The only receiver with more catches and a better yardage average than Stone in the entire NFL in 1991 was Michael Haynes, who had a sensational year for the Falcons; Stone was third in receptions and second in yardage on the Steelers in 1992, never mind in comparison to the rest of the league. Stone's shortest touchdown catch in 1991 was 40 yards; in 1992 his longest was 24 yards. Stone seems too talented to languish in the Pittsburgh offense as a possession receiver, but he has languished in Pittsburgh before (only 70 receptions in his first five years with the team), so history could definitely repeat itself in this case. If this trend continues, then Stone, despite his obvious ability, should be no more than a late-round pick on Draft Day 1993.

Fantasy Rankings: 1992—9 points (Tied for 57th)
1991—24 points (Tied for 12th)
1990—3 points (Tied for 109th)
1989—0 points

Past Performance Key: Stone had an 18.4-yard-per-reception average for his five-year career prior to the 1992 season. His 14.7-yard average in 1992 was the second-lowest of his career.

6. Quinn Early, New Orleans Saints Early picked up the slack from the injured Floyd Turner, who spent the season on injured reserve. He had the best season of his five-year career, scoring 5 touchdowns, with 1 bonus bomb, and averaging 18.9 yards a catch. This yardage average tied Herman Moore of the Lions for the best mark in the NFC for receivers with 20 or more receptions, and was a personal best. He has talent, but fantasy owners' enthusiasm must be dampened by the return of Turner and the effect this will have on Early's performance. No matter how that works out, Early remains a steal as a fourth receiver.

Fantasy Rankings: 1992—18 points (Tied for 19th)
1991—6 points (Tied for 76th)
1990—3 points (Tied for 109th)
1989—0 points

Past Performance Key: Early's 566 yards in 1992 were a career high, as was his touchdown total. He has never had more than 32 receptions in one season during his five-year NFL career. Early's bonus bomb in 1992 was his first in the four editions of this book.

7. Ricky Proehl, Phoenix Cardinals   Proehl, a third-round pick in the 1990 NFL draft, was a "Keep Your Eye On" special in the last two editions of this book. That's because he was a prime candidate for the sophomore sensation trend in 1991, after a terrific rookie season. But Cardinals quarterback Timm Rosenbach was injured and missed the whole season. It is difficult for a wide receiver to excel when his signal-caller is the 15th-rated quarterback in his conference, which was the case for Proehl in 1991. So, Rosenbach comes back in 1992, and what happens? He gets hurt again, and Proehl puts up solid numbers anyway, with backup quarterback Chris Chandler having an excellent season. His 60 receptions were a personal best, and 1 of his 3 touchdowns was a bonus bomb. Still, fantasy owners eagerly await the breakout performance in the scoring department for this talented receiver. If you think 1993 is the year, then make sure you grab Proehl in the latter rounds of the draft. He should be waiting for you when you make your move.

Fantasy Rankings: 1992—12 points (Tied for 37th)
1991—9 points (Tied for 51st)
1990—12 points (Tied for 53rd)

Past Performance Key: Proehl scored a bonus bomb for the **second** year in a row in 1992. He led the Cards in receptions for the second time in his three-year career.

8. Don Beebe, Buffalo Bills   After a slow first half, this speedy receiver from that football powerhouse in Nebraska, Chadron State, posted some solid numbers in 1992. Beebe's 33 receptions and 554 yards were career highs. His touchdown total did drop, however, as he scored only 2 TDs, after scoring 6 in 1991. (His 6-touchdown total in 1991 is deceptive, since 4 of them came in one game.) But his overall fantasy scoring total dropped only a notch, because *both* of his touchdowns were bonus bombs. He's also no quitter, as his come-from-behind snatch of the football away from the showboating Leon Lett at the goal line in Super Bowl XXVII demonstrated. Beebe could be a steal as a fourth receiver in 1993, especially if he assumes a greater portion of the receiving load with the release of James Lofton.

Fantasy Rankings: 1992—12 points (Tied for 37th)

1991—18 points (Tied for 21st)

1990—3 points (Tied for 109th)

1989—12 points (Tied for 42nd)

Past Performance Key: Beebe's 16.8-yard average led the Bills' primary receivers in 1992. He has scored 11 touchdowns on only 93 receptions in his four years with the Bills. Four of his 11 career touchdowns are bonus bombs. His 4 touchdown catches in one game in Week Four was a league-leading mark for receivers in 1991. No NFL receiver duplicated that feat in 1992, and in fact, only three receivers even caught 3 touchdown passes in one game last year.

9. Jeff Query, Cincinnati Bengals Query came on strong in the second half of the 1992 season after David Klingler was promoted to the starting job at quarterback. He scored all his fantasy points in the last four weeks of the season, hooking up with Klingler on 2 of his 3 scoring passes, including a bonus bomb. As a result, Query tied Tim McGee for the team lead in touchdown catches. His total of 12 fantasy points led Bengals receivers in 1992. If you think Query and Klingler will hook up for more than 16 passes in 1993 (Query's reception total in 1992), then grab the speedy Query as a fourth receiver late in the draft.

Fantasy Rankings: 1992—12 points (Tied for 37th)

1991—0 points

1990—12 points (Tied for 53rd)

1989—6 points (Tied for 75th)

Past Performance Key: Query's 3 touchdown receptions were a career high. His bonus bomb in Week Fifteen was the only one scored by a Bengals receiver in 1992. Query was the only veteran player in the NFL at the start of the 1992 season whose last name began with the letter Q.

10. Mark Carrier, Cleveland Browns There is a regular but nevertheless baffling phenomenon in the cosmos of professional sports, from which no sport is immune, and for which there is no explanation. I'm talking about the phenomenon known as the "career year." Every season, in virtually every professional sport, some athlete, usually of some talent, throws off the shackles of mediocrity and puts up numbers that belong chiseled on a plaque in a Hall of Fame somewhere. Then, having spent himself in this titanic struggle against the sporting fates, the athlete in question sinks to the level of his preceding seasons, never to have such a great year again. I've already mentioned several examples of players who may have had career years, but Mark Carrier's season in 1989 is a prime example if there ever was one. Carrier's numbers in 1989 were spectacular (86 receptions, 1,422 yards, 9 touchdowns, 2 bonus bombs.) Prior to 1989, only one other receiver in NFL history, Charley Hennigan for the 1964 Houston Oilers, had caught as many passes for as many yards in one season as Carrier did that year. (Sterling Sharpe also reached those totals in 1989, and again in 1992, as did Jerry Rice in 1990 and Michael Irvin in 1991.) But Carrier's performance in his other five years in the league strongly suggests that 1989 was a career year. Over those other five years, he has averaged 47 receptions, 719 yards, and 3.6 touchdowns. Part of that problem might have been the fact that Vinny Testaverde was the Bucs' quarterback during most of that time. So what happens? Carrier signs as a free agent with Cleveland, and shortly thereafter, so does Vinny. Even with a healthy Bernie Kosar at quarterback for the Browns (heaven forfend Vinny should win the starting job), fantasy owners should not expect Carrier to post more than his average numbers in the upcoming season.

> 1991—6 points (Tied for 76th)
> 1990—15 points (Tied for 32nd)
> 1989—33 points (Tied for 5th)

Past Performance Key: Carrier did not score a bonus bomb in 1992 for the second straight year, after three consecutive seasons with bonus bombs. Carrier's 12.4 yards per catch in 1992 was the lowest average of his career.

11. Jessie Hester, Indianapolis Colts

Hester slumped big time for his fantasy owners in 1992. After managing a more than respectable 11 touchdowns over the 1990–91 seasons, he scored only 1 in 1992. Some of Hester's numbers are indicative of the fundamental problem with the passing game in the Hoosier Dome. Hester averaged 23.7 yards per catch in his first three years in the league with the bomb-oriented Los Angeles Raiders; he has averaged 14.8 yards in the four years with the Falcons and Colts since then. Hester has talent, but it looks like it's all or nothing in terms of scoring for him in the Colts' shaky passing offense.

> **Fantasy Rankings:**   1992—3 points (Tied for 116th)
> 1991—15 points (Tied for 27th)
> 1990—21 points (Tied for 16th)
> 1989—0 points

Past Performance Key: Hester scored 10 touchdowns in the 1985–86 seasons, no touchdowns in the 1987–88 seasons, and 11 touchdowns in the 1990–91 seasons. Hester's total of 792 yards in 1992 was the second-highest of his seven-year career.

12. Lawrence Dawsey, Tampa Bay Buccaneers

Dawsey disappointed his fantasy owners with a sophomore slump in 1992, after an impressive rookie year in 1991, in which he led all NFL rookie receivers in receptions and yardage, while leading the Bucs in those categories as well. He also caught 3 touchdown passes and scored a rushing touchdown. Despite leading the Bucs in receptions for the second straight year, Dawsey scored only 1 touchdown in 1992. Sam Wyche is going to have to raise the performance level of Tampa Bay's passing game in 1993 for Dawsey to deliver on the promise of his rookie season.

Fantasy Rankings: 1992—3 points (Tied for 116th)
1991—18 points (Tied for 21st)

Past Performance Key: Dawsey failed to score a bonus bomb in 1992 after scoring 1 in his rookie season. He was the first Tampa Bay rookie wide receiver in franchise history to lead the team in receptions.

13. Vance Johnson, Denver Broncos   Johnson had his third disappointing fantasy season in a row in 1992. He had only 2 touchdowns in 1992, after scoring only 3 in 1990 and 3 in 1991. I say that these scoring totals are disappointing because Johnson had 76 receptions for 1,095 yards and 7 scores in 1989. Until Johnson recaptures the glory of days gone by in his career, he is a fourth receiver at best.

Fantasy Rankings: 1992—6 points (Tied for 80th)
1991—9 points (Tied for 51st)
1990—9 points (Tied for 66th)
1989—24 points (Tied for 19th)

Past Performance Key: Johnson scored 19 touchdowns in three seasons from 1987–89; in the three seasons since then he has scored 8. He has not scored a bonus bomb since 1989.

14. Reggie Langhorne, Indianapolis Colts   "Foghorn" Langhorne came over from Cleveland as a Plan B free agent in 1992 and surprised everyone by ending up as the Colts' leading receiver and posting career highs in receptions (65) and yards (811). Langhorne had more receptions and yardage than such more famous AFC counterparts as James Lofton, Tim Brown, and Mark Duper. Of course, the touchdown numbers (only 1 in 1992) must improve for fantasy owners to get too excited about Reggie, but it certainly appears he will get his chance in 1993.

Fantasy Rankings: 1992—3 points (Tied for 116th)
1991—6 points (Tied for 76th)
1990—6 points (Tied for 74th)
1989—9 points (Tied for 57th)

Past Performance Key: Langhorne had 7 touchdown receptions with Cleveland in 1988. He has never caught more than 2 in any of his other seven seasons in the NFL. He has never averaged less than 12 yards per catch in any of his eight NFL seasons.

15. Tony Martin, Miami Dolphins   Martin had his best season in his third year in the league in 1992. He posted personal bests in receptions and yardage, and scored 2 touchdowns for the third straight season. If you're casting about for a fourth receiver at the end of the draft, you might try Martin.

Fantasy Rankings: 1992—9 points (Tied for 57th)
1991—6 points (Tied for 76th)
1990—6 points (Tied for 74th)

Past Performance Key: Martin averaged 16.8 yards a catch in 1992, second on the Dolphins only to Duper's 17.3 average. Martin had a bonus bomb for the first time in his three-year career in 1992.

16. Tom Waddle, Chicago Bears   Waddle continued to post satisfactory numbers for his fantasy owners in 1992. He scored a career-high 4 touchdowns, and threw in a bonus bomb to boot. Waddle averaged 35.7 yards per touchdown, the seventh-highest mark in the league for those receivers with 4 or more touchdown receptions in 1992. For someone whose name hardly conjures up the image of one who is swift afoot, that isn't half bad. Still, Waddle is only a fourth receiver at best.

Fantasy Rankings: 1992—15 points (Tied for 26th)
1991—9 points (Tied for 51st)
1990—0 points
1989—0 points

Past Performance Key: Waddle caught 3 passes his first two years in the league; he has caught 101 in the two years since then.

17. Hassan Jones, Minnesota Vikings   Jones rebounded from a dismal year in 1991 with a solid season in 1992. While he caught only 22 passes, he scored 4 touchdowns. Be careful in 1993, though: Jones appears to be another one of those occasional players whose careers are marked by the bizarre quirk of calendar numerology. In the three odd years of his career, he had 4 touchdown receptions; in the four even years, he had 20. And 1993 is an odd year, in case you didn't notice. I'm not a great advocate of tempting fate, so you might want to steer clear of Jones in 1993.

Fantasy Rankings: 1992—12 points (Tied for 37th)
1991—3 points (Tied for 110th)
1990—24 points (Tied for 11th)
1989—3 points (Tied for 111th)

Past Performance Key: Jones's 22 receptions in 1992 were his lowest total since 1987.

18. Ed McCaffrey, New York Giants   McCaffrey came out of nowhere (Palo Alto, California, and Stanford University, actually) to lead the Giants in receptions and touchdown passes in his second year in the league in 1992. With a new coaching regime installed for 1993, all of the Giants' offensive performers, with the exception of Rodney Hampton, are loaded with question marks. This receiver is a Giants' season-ticket-holder-only special.

Fantasy Rankings: 1992—15 points (Tied for 26th)
1991—0 points

Past Performance Key: McCaffrey had only 16 receptions in his rookie season with the Giants in 1991.

KEEP AN EYE ON

1. John Taylor, San Francisco 49ers   With all due respect to Atlanta, Houston, and Dallas fans, Taylor and Rice flat out constitute the best receiving duo in the NFL. And I can say this despite the fact that Taylor missed most of last season with a broken leg. The injury was a real shame, especially in light of the fact that Taylor was coming off an exceptional year in 1991, when he had the most receptions of his career (64) and broke the 1,000-yard barrier for the second time in his five years in the league. His 9 touchdown catches in 1991 were the second-highest total of his career as well. As I said, an exceptional year. Then Taylor started like gangbusters in 1992. He scored 2 touchdowns, with 1 bonus bomb, in Week Two, and was averaging 24 yards a catch when he broke his left fibula against the Jets in Week Three. Taylor and Rice are a good match, since they both run so well after catching the ball. The only obstacle to Taylor's ascendancy to superstardom is the presence of the best receiver in football on the opposite wing. Still, look for a healthy Taylor to return to First Echelon status in 1993.

Fantasy Rankings: 1992—12 points (Tied for 37th)
1991—33 points (Tied for 6th)
1990—24 points (Tied for 11th)
1989—39 points (4th)

Past Performance Key: Taylor has scored bonus bombs five years in a row, with 7 over the last four years and 9 over five. He has averaged 16.92 yards per catch over his six-year career; Rice has averaged 16.84 yards in his eight years.

2. Michael Jackson, Cleveland Browns   The Browns' sixth-round pick in the 1991 NFL draft was the first offensive player Cleveland selected that year. "Thriller" justified this selection with a sophomore sensation year in 1992. Discerning fantasy owners could see that the talent was there. In 1991, Jackson only caught 17 passes, but he averaged 15.8 yards a catch, the best mark on the team. And he scored 2 touchdowns, including a bonus bomb. Having set the stage, Jackson broke out big in 1992, leading Browns receivers in receptions, yardage, and touchdowns (if you don't consider Metcalf a receiver, which I don't.) Jackson posted these impressive numbers despite the injury-riddled quarterback situation for the Browns. Look for Thriller to be Dangerous with a healthy Kosar throwing to him in 1993.

Fantasy Rankings: 1992—24 points (Tied for 10th)
1991—9 points (Tied for 51st)

Past Performance Key: Jackson has caught a bonus bomb two seasons in a row. He averaged 37 yards a touchdown reception in 1992, which tied for fourth-highest in the league for those receivers with 4 or more TD receptions.

3. Herman Moore, Detroit Lions   The Lions' first-round pick from the University of Virginia in the 1991 NFL draft, and the 10th pick overall, Moore was another example of the Sophomore Sensation Theory in 1992. Given a chance to start after riding the pines (only 11 receptions) in 1991, Moore exhibited his incredible athletic skills last season. He caught 51 passes for 966 yards, averaging 18.9 yards per catch, and scored 4 touchdowns. Amazingly, Moore averaged 49.5 yards per touchdown, the highest mark in the league for those receivers with 4 or more TD receptions in 1992. The Top Ten in this category were:

Player	Average Per Touchdown
H. Moore	49.5
W. Green (Lions)	42.8
Barnett (Chiefs)	40
Fryar (Pats)	37
Jackson (Browns)	37
Duper (Dolphins)	36.7
Waddle (Bears)	35.7
Barnett (Eagles)	34.5
Jones (Cards)	32.2
Rice (49ers)	31.4

Moore emerged as one of the true deep threats in the league in 1992, and if by some fluke the other owners in your league don't see this Scouting Report and he lasts until the middle or the late rounds on Draft Day 1993, grab him.

Fantasy Rankings: 1992—18 points (Tied for 19th)
1991—0 points

Past Performance Key: Moore's yardage average of 18.9 in 1992 (Tied with the Saints' Quinn Early) was second only to the 21.0 average of Willie Davis of Kansas City among receivers with 30 or more receptions, and fifth-best among receivers with 17 or more. No receiver with at least as many receptions as Moore averaged more yards per catch than he did in 1993. Two of Moore's 4 touchdown receptions in 1992 were bonus bombs.

4. Tim Barnett/Willie Davis, Kansas City Chiefs Like the Brothers Sharpe, Sterling and Shannon, the Cousins Barnett were another family receiving act that did very well in the NFL in 1992. Tim Barnett, the Eagles' Fred Barnett's cousin, caught 5 touchdowns in his rookie season for the Chiefs in 1991. Since he had averaged 20 yards per catch in his college career at Jackson State, and had done well in his rookie season, it was reasonable to expect Barnett to perform well in 1992. And, once he recovered from an early-season injury, he was great. He did not catch a touchdown pass until Week Eleven, but then busted out for 4 in the last seven games for the Chiefs. He may rival his cousin's impressive stats if he can stay healthy in 1993.

Willie Davis was one of those rare NFL birds in 1992, a rookie free agent who makes an impact his first year in the league. (Davis was a "first-year player" and not a true rookie in the NFL sense of the term. He did spend 1990 and 1991 on the Chiefs' practice squad, although he was activated for only one game during that period. So he was a little older than the rest of the Chiefs' rookies in 1992.) This speedster (4.4 in the 40) had only 3 touchdown catches, but the yardage average for them was over 55 yards. His yardage average for the season was 21.0 per catch, best in the NFL in 1992. Look for more bonus-bomb activity from Davis in 1993.

Fantasy Rankings:

Barnett	1992—15 points (Tied for 26th)
	1991—15 points (Tied for 27th)
Davis	1992—15 points (Tied for 26th)
	1991—0 points

Past Performance Key: Barnett's 77-yard touchdown pass in Week Sixteen against the Giants was the Chiefs' longest scoring play from scrimmage in 1992. Two of Davis's 3 touchdowns in 1992 were bonus bombs.

5. Nathaniel Lewis, San Diego Chargers This seventh-round pick in the 1990 draft has turned out to be another one of General Manager Bobby Beathard's patented late-round finds. Lewis scored 3 touchdowns, as well as returning a kickoff for a touchdown, in 1991, then upped the ante in 1992. While slipping slightly in total receptions, he posted career highs in receiving yards (580) and touchdown receptions

(4). With San Diego on the move, Lewis is a solid fourth receiver for fantasy owners in 1993.

Fantasy Rankings: 1992—15 points (Tied for 26th)
1991—15 points (Tied for 27th)
1990—15 points (Tied for 32nd)

Past Performance Key: Lewis scored the first bonus bomb of his three-year career in 1992, which was the first season in his career he failed to return either a kickoff or a punt for a touchdown. Only two AFC receivers with 34 or more receptions (Willie Davis and Mark Duper) had a better yardage average per catch than Lewis (17.1).

6. Randal Hill, Phoenix Cardinals   The Thrill is a burner who has yet to tap the full potential of his skills in the NFL. The 23rd pick in the 1991 NFL draft by the Dolphins, Hill apparently did not see eye to eye with Coach Shula early on, and Miami shipped him to Phoenix after the first game of the 1991 season. Hill seems to have found his niche in Phoenix, and has posted some decent numbers in his two years in the league, including a total of 101 receptions. And he jumped from 1 touchdown in 1991 to 3 in 1992. But fantasy owners should expect more from him based on his ability. If Hill doesn't bust a move and move up in the scoring column in 1993, he might be chillin', not thrillin', for fantasy owners in 1993.

Fantasy Rankings: 1992—9 points (Tied for 57th)
1991—3 points (Tied for 110th)

Past Performance Key: Hill gained 3.3 yards more per reception in 1992 than he did in his rookie season in 1991. He led the Cardinals' receivers in yards gained in 1992. After two years in the league, Hill has yet to score a bonus bomb.

7. Kelvin Martin, Seattle Seahawks   While with Dallas, Kelvin Martin rounded out what was one of the two or three finest receiving corps in football. In addition to catching 3 touchdown passes, Martin also returned 2 punts for touchdowns in 1992, tying three other players for the league lead in that category. The good news about his signing with Seattle is that Martin should move right into the starting lineup. The bad news is that, other than the fact that they both field 11 players, the Seahawks' offense bears no relation to the Cowboys'. Because of his added ability as a punt returner, though, Martin is worth a look as a fourth receiver in 1993.

Fantasy Rankings: 1992—21 points (Tied for 13th)
1991—6 points (Tied for 76th)

1990—0 points
1989—6 points (Tied for 75th)

Past Performance Key: Martin was the second-rated punt returner in the NFL, behind Phoenix's Johnny Bailey, in 1992. He has returned 3 punts for touchdowns in the last two seasons. His 11.2-yard average per reception was the lowest of his career. His 3 touchdown catches in 1992 tied his career best.

8. Mark Ingram, Miami Dolphins Free agency paid off big time for Ingram, who moved south from New York to replace Mark Clayton in the Marks Brothers configuration. While Clayton's shoes are mighty big ones to fill, Ingram has the talent to be an excellent receiver for the Dolphins. Admittedly, Ingram slumped badly in 1992 in terms of scoring, with his lowest touchdown total since 1989. But that can be attributed to the dismal quarterback situation in the Meadowlands, and to Ingram's injuries. (He missed four games due to a knee injury.) To truly evaluate his talent, look at Ingram's yardage numbers. He averaged 15.1 yards per catch on 27 receptions in 1992, a mark that exceeded Clayton's. With Marino tossing, Ingram should be catching lots more passes, and scoring more touchdowns, in the upcoming season.

Fantasy Rankings: 1992—3 points (Tied for 116th)
1991—9 points (Tied for 51st)
1990—18 points (Tied for 20th)
1989—3 points (Tied for 111th)

Past Performance Key: Ingram has a 16.3-yard-per-catch average for his six-year career, spent entirely with the Giants.

9. Terance Mathis, New York Jets Mathis deserves a look as a fourth receiver, since he is not only a capable receiver with deep-threat potential, but also the Jets' kickoff-return specialist. His 14.4-yard-per-reception average was second-best on the team in 1992, illustrating his ability to get downfield with the ball. With Boomer Esiason at quarterback for the Jets in 1993, Mathis could surprise as a fourth receiver.

Fantasy Rankings: 1992—18 points (Tied for 19th)
1991—3 points (Tied for 110th)
1990—6 points (Tied for 84th)

Past Performance Key: Mathis was one of only three NFL receivers with a rushing touchdown in 1992. His 14.4-yard average and his 4 TDs overall in 1992 (3 touchdown receptions) were both career highs. He returned a punt 98 yards for a touchdown against Dallas in 1990, tying the NFL record for the longest punt return for a touchdown.

10. Carl Pickens, Cincinnati Bengals   The Bengals' second-round pick in the 1992 NFL draft (31st selection overall) impressed in his rookie year. He returned a punt 95 yards for a touchdown in Week Three (missing the just-mentioned NFL record by only 3 yards), and averaged 12.7 yards a return on 18 punt returns overall. (Rod Woodson led the AFC with an 11.4 average, but Pickens did not have enough returns to officially qualify.) Pickens added another score on a touchdown reception. With any support at all, he should be a prime example of the Sophomore Sensation Theory in 1993.

Fantasy Rankings: 1992—9 points (Tied for 57th)

Past Performance Key: Pickens tied with Arthur Marshall of Denver for most receptions by an NFL rookie receiver. His 95-yard punt return in Week Three against the Packers was the longest punt return for a score, and the second-longest scoring play, in the AFC in 1992.

11. Brian Blades, Seattle Seahawks   Blades continues to fail to live up to the promise he exhibited in his rookie season in 1988, at least as far as fantasy owners are concerned. His scoring has steadily decreased each year since then:

Year	Touchdowns
1988	8
1989	5
1990	3
1991	2
1992	1

Shortened due to injuries, Blades's 1992 season was the worst of his NFL career, as well as in the fantasy realm. With the state of the Seahawks such as it is, even a healthy Blades is no more than a fourth receiver in 1993.

Fantasy Rankings: 1992—3 points (Tied for 116th)
1991—6 points (Tied for 76th)
1990—9 points (Tied for 66th)
1989—18 points (Tied for 24th)

Past Performance Key: Either Blades or John Williams has been the leading Seahawks receiver every year since Blades has come into the league.

12. Lawyer Tillman, Cleveland Browns   Tillman had no fantasy points in 1992, but averaged an amazing 19.9 yards per catch, the second-highest mark in the NFL among receivers with 17 or more receptions. How he failed to get into the end zone while piling up those yards is a mystery, but it shouldn't happen two years in a row. His ability to go deep earns him a look late in the draft.

Fantasy Rankings: 1992—0 points

1991—0 points

1990—0 points

1989—12 points (Tied for 42nd)

Past Performance Key: Tillman was one of only two NFL receivers who had more than 400 yards in receptions in 1992 and did not catch a touchdown pass. (The 49ers' Mike Sherrard was the other one.) He spent the 1990 and 1991 seasons on injured reserve.

13. Alexander Wright, Los Angeles Raiders   Despite the fact that Wright was the first wide receiver (26th pick overall) selected in the 1990 NFL draft, he never seemed to fit into the Cowboys' plans. The Raiders obtained him in the middle of the 1992 season, and put him and his speed to work right away. Wright paid dividends by the end of the year, catching 1 touchdown pass in each of the Raiders' last two games. Look for his numbers to improve as he is worked into the Raiders' offense more significantly in 1993.

Fantasy Rankings: 1992—6 points (Tied for 80th)

1991—6 points (Tied for 76th)

1990—6 points (Tied for 74th)

Past Performance Key: Wright failed to return a kickoff for a touchdown in 1992 for the first time in his three-year career. He caught his 2 touchdown passes in 1992 on only 12 receptions.

14. Tommy Kane, Seattle Seahawks   Kane had his fewest number of receptions, 27, since 1989, but still scored 3 touchdowns. For a wide receiver on the Seahawks, that's pretty good. You could do worse for your fourth receiver in 1993, especially if the quarterback situation in Seattle improves at all.

Fantasy Rankings: 1992—9 points (Tied for 57th)

1991—6 points (Tied for 76th)

1990—15 points (Tied for 32nd)

1989—0 points

Past Performance Key: Kane's 27 receptions in 1992 was second to John L. Williams's 74 on the Seahawks. Only one team had a larger gap in the number of passes between the leading and second-leading receiver. (Green Bay—53.)

15. Arthur Marshall, Denver Broncos   Another free agent rarity, this receiver from the University of Georgia had an excellent rookie year in 1992. He caught 26 passes for 493 yards and 1 touchdown, an 80-yard bonus bomb, and his average of 19.0 yards per catch led the team. Look for him to add to his fantasy scoring totals with a healthy John Elway back in action in 1993.

Fantasy Rankings: 1992—12 points (Tied for 37th)

Past Performance Key: Marshall was the only player in the NFL in 1992 to both catch and throw a bonus bomb. He completed an 81-yard touchdown pass to fellow rookie Cedric Tillman in Week Fourteen against Dallas in 1992.)

16. Eddie Brown, Cincinnati Bengals   Not to be confused with MTV's "Downtown" Julie Brown, "Downtown" Eddie Brown spent the entire 1992 season on injured reserve as a result of a neck injury, which threatens his career. If Brown doesn't retire and returns to the Bengals in 1993, he is worth a long look in the middle and late rounds of the draft, based on his demonstrated talent in years past.

Fantasy Rankings: 1992—0 points

1991—6 points (Tied for 76th)

1990—30 points (Tied for 3rd)

1989—18 points (Tied for 24th)

Past Performance Key: Despite Brown's reputation as a deep threat, he has only accumulated 1,000 yards in a season once in his career. He shares the same middle name (and, unfortunately, not much else in the way of fantasy numbers) with Jerry Lee Rice.

17. Floyd Turner, New Orleans Saints   Turner had the best year of his career in 1991, raising expectations for fantasy football owners, and then missed the 1992 season on injured reserve with a bad leg. He had 64 receptions, with 927 yards and 8 touchdowns, in 1991. Turner's career stats show a rather uncanny ability to get into the end zone—he has averaged a touchdown every 8 catches. To put that in perspective, Jerry Rice has averaged a touchdown every 5.9 catches over his eight-year career. If Turner returns healthy in 1993, he's worth a look as a fourth receiver on Draft Day 1993.

Fantasy Rankings: 1992—0 points

1991—27 points (Tied for 10th)

1990—15 points (Tied for 32nd)

1989—6 points (Tied for 75th)

Past Performance Key: Turner scored 2 touchdowns in a game three times in 1991. He had scored a bonus bomb in each of his three years in the league prior to 1992.

18. Desmond Howard, Washington Redskins   The 1992 Heisman Trophy winner saw almost no action in his rookie season with the Redskins. But Howard is a sophomore sensation waiting to happen for several key reasons as a result of events in the nation's Capital during the offseason. First, Coach Joe Gibbs, who kept him firmly rooted on the bench in 1992, retired. Second, Gary Clark, the main member of the Posse, signed with Phoenix. Third, Art Monk has been benched by the Redskins' brass in what may be his last season in the league. Even with the signing of wide receiver Tim McGee from the Bengals, all this translates into more playing time for Howard in 1993. And more playing time means that this mercurial receiver could see the end zone early and definitely more often in the upcoming season.

Fantasy Rankings: 1992—6 points (Tied for 80th)

Past Performance Key: Howard's only score in 1992 was on a crossfield lateral from fellow punt-return man Brian Mitchell to score a 55-yard touchdown in Week Two against Atlanta.

TIGHT ENDS

The following are Scouting Reports on those tight ends who are most likely to make significant contributions to fantasy owners in 1993, especially those owners whose rules require that they draft a tight end.

1. Keith Jackson, Miami Dolphins   No matter what the ex-Eagle does on the playing field the rest of his career, he will always be known as one of the pioneer free agents whose successful lawsuit led directly to a labor agreement establishing true free agency for the NFL's rank and file. Not that what he has done and will continue to do on the field isn't memorable in its own right. Jackson added to his credentials as the premier tight end in football with another excellent season in 1992. After sitting out the first four weeks of the season until his lawsuit was resolved, Jackson caught 4 passes for 64 yards and 1 touchdown in his first game with the Dolphins, their 37–10 blowout of the Buffalo Bills in Week Five. Despite missing the first three games of the season, he led Miami receivers with 48 receptions, and his 5 touchdown passes were second only to Mark Duper's 7 on the team. With a whole preseason to acclimate himself further to Marino and the Dolphins' offense in 1993, look for Jackson to maintain his standard of excellence at the head of the tight-end class in the upcoming season.

Fantasy Rankings: 1992—15 points (Tied for 26th)

1991—18 points (Tied for 21st)

1990—18 points (Tied for 20th)

1989—9 points (Tied for 57th)

Past Performance Key: Jackson leads all tight ends with 25 touchdowns over the last five years. His yardage average was 12.4 in 1992, second-highest in his five-year career.

2. Jay Novacek, Dallas Cowboys   Novacek raised his already impressive game another level in 1992 with the best season of his eight-year career. Prior to last season, Novacek's consistency had been amazing. In 1990, Novacek had 59 receptions for 657 yards, an average of 11.1 yards, and 4 touchdowns. In 1991, Novacek had 59 receptions for 664 yards, an 11.3-yard average, and 4 touchdowns. Well, in 1992, Novacek had career highs in receptions, with 68, and touchdowns, with 6, as he became Troy Aikman's second-favorite target. Novacek has quietly emerged as one of the most valuable tight ends in the league for fantasy purposes, and should maintain the status quo in 1993.

Fantasy Rankings: 1992—18 points (Tied for 19th)
1991—12 points (Tied for 39th)
1990—12 points (Tied for 53rd)
1989—3 points (Tied for 111th)

Past Performance Key: Novacek's 68 receptions led NFL tight ends in 1992. His 186 receptions over the past three years lead all NFL tight ends as well. Novacek scored 8 touchdowns the first five years of his career; he has scored 14 the last three. His 9.3-yard average per reception in 1992 was the lowest for any of the six years in his career when he caught more than 1 pass. His 6.3-yard average per touchdown reception in 1992 was the lowest for any receiver who caught more than 4.

3. Brent Jones, San Francisco 49ers   Jones had a big comeback year in 1992, after a subpar season in 1991 due to injury. He scored 4 touchdowns in 1992, a typical scoring level for this talented tight end, when he's healthy. Jones is one of the few tight ends in the league you'd consider drafting as a fourth receiver under my regular rules—that is, in those leagues where an owner is not required to draft a tight end.

Fantasy Rankings: 1992—12 points (Tied for 37th)
1991—0 points
1990—18 points (Tied for 20th)
1989—12 points (Tied for 42nd)

Past Performance Key: Jones scored 9 touchdowns during the 1989–90 seasons. He averaged 14.0 yards per reception in 1992. (Jerry Rice averaged 14.3.)

4. Shannon Sharpe, Denver Broncos   The Sharpe family had quite a year. Sterling Sharpe posted the best numbers of any receiver in the

NFL in 1992, and his brother Shannon was one of the top tight ends in the league. Sharpe was drafted as a wide receiver out of Savannah State, but with his size and speed, he has flourished at tight end for the Broncos. He had a career year in 1992, with career highs in receptions (53), yards (640), and touchdowns (2). Look for the Sharpes' brother act to continue to knock 'em dead in 1993.

Fantasy Rankings: 1992—6 points (Tied for 80th)

1991—3 points (Tied for 110th)

1990—3 points (Tied for 109th)

Past Performance Key: Sharpe's 53 receptions led the Broncos in 1992, and he was the only tight end to lead his team in that category.

5. Pete Metzelaars/Keith McKeller, Buffalo Bills

Metzelaars, a former basketball star for the Division III Wabash College Little Giants, in Crawfordsville, Indiana, had an excellent season for the Bills in 1992. Pressed into service in the absence of the injured Keith McKeller, this 11-year veteran caught 30 passes for 298 yards and 6 touchdowns. His touchdown total was a career high, and tied Jay Novacek for the highest total among NFL tight ends. As for McKeller, after two impressive seasons in which he scored a total of 8 touchdowns, he tore knee cartilage in the first game of 1992, was out for five games, and never regained his 1990–91 form. As a result, he spent most of 1992 watching from the bench as Metzelaars stepped up and had a terrific season. As the touchdown totals I have just talked about demonstrate, the tight end plays a key role in the Buffalo passing game. So, while a healthy McKeller presumably will reclaim his starting role for the Bills in the upcoming season, Metzelaars deserves a look late in the draft if it appears he will get any playing time at all in 1993.

Fantasy Rankings:

Metzelaars   1992—21 points (Tied for 13th)

1991—9 points (Tied for 51st)

1990—3 points (Tied for 109th)

1989—6 points (Tied for 75th)

McKeller   1992—0 points

1991—9 points (Tied for 51st)

1990—15 points (Tied for 32nd)

1989—9 points (Tied for 57th)

Past Performance Key: Metzelaars exceeded his reception, yardage, and touchdown totals for each of the prior two seasons after Week Three of the 1992 season. He scored a bonus bomb for the second year in a row in Week Two, the only tight end in NFL who has accomplished this feat. His 21 fantasy points in 1992 led all NFL tight ends. McKeller scored a total of 10 touchdowns in the three seasons prior to 1992.

6. Marv Cook, New England Patriots   I said it last year and I'll say it again this year: "Cook might be the best tight end no one has ever heard of, mired as he is in the media wasteland that is Foxboro." Someone recognizes his ability, though, since he was named to the Pro Bowl for the second straight year in 1992. Cook led all tight ends with 82 receptions in 1991, the fourth-highest total in the NFL that season. He dropped to 52 receptions in 1992, with only 2 touchdowns, one less than in his fine 1991 season. If new head coach Bill Parcells uses him in the Pats' offense like he used Mark Bavaro with the Giants, Cook might finally get the media recognition he deserves as one of the premier tight ends in the league.

    Fantasy Rankings: 1992—6 points (Tied for 80th)
                                     1991—9 points (Tied for 51st)
                                     1990—15 points (Tied for 32nd)
                                     1989—0 points

    Past Performance Key: Cook has scored 10 touchdowns over the past three seasons. He has 185 receptions over the last three years, a single catch less than Jay Novacek, the leader among tight ends in this category. His 7.9 yards per reception were the least of any receiver with 50 or more receptions in the NFL in 1992.

7. Kerry Cash, Indianapolis Colts   This second-year tight end and former Texas Longhorn demonstrated a modified version of the sophomore sensation, tight-end style. Cash jumped from 1 reception in his rookie season of 1991 to 43 receptions in 1992 for 521 yards, an impressive 12.1 yards per catch. He also got in the end zone with 3 touchdown receptions in 1992. Look for Cash to catch and carry the pigskin to improved numbers in 1993.

    Fantasy Rankings: 1992—9 points (Tied for 57th)
                                     1991—0 points

    Past Performance Key: Cash's 3 touchdown receptions were the most for a receiver on the Colts in 1992.

8. Steve Jordan, Minnesota Vikings   Jordan has been a solid performer at the tight end position for years. But, after some high-scoring seasons in the latter half of the 1980s, his scoring total has decreased significantly, and he has scored only 2 touchdowns in each of the last two seasons. After 11 years in the league, Jordan is clearly on the downside of his career. Fantasy owners should only draft Jordan if they need a tight end toward the end of the draft.

    Fantasy Rankings: 1992—9 points (Tied for 57th)
                                       1991—6 points (Tied for 76th)

1990—9 points (Tied for 66th)

1989—9 points (Tied for 57th)

Past Performance Key: Jordan scored a bonus bomb for the first time in the four editions of this book in 1992. He has never averaged less than 10.9 yards per catch in any season in his 11-year NFL career.

9. Rodney Holman, Detroit Lions   It was a third straight disappointing season for Holman. After scoring a career-high 9 touchdowns in 1989, Holman saw his touchdown total sink to a measly 2 for the second straight year in 1992. His 26 receptions for 266 yards were his lowest totals since the 1984 season. After 11 years in the league he was not part of David Shula's rebuilding program, so he signed as a free agent with Detroit. The change of scenery might do his career some good, especially if Detroit continues to develop a more traditional passing offense. But I still would not place him too high on my list of tight ends for Draft Day 1993.

Fantasy Rankings: 1992—6 points (Tied for 80th)

1991—6 points (Tied for 76th)

1990—15 points (Tied for 32nd)

1989—33 points (Tied for 5th)

Past Performance Key: Holman scored 14 touchdowns in the 1989–90 seasons; he has scored 4 in the two seasons since then. His 33 fantasy points in 1989 are the highest total for a tight end in the four editions of this book.

10. Derrick Walker, San Diego Chargers   Walker had the best year of his three-year career in 1992. He caught 34 passes for 393 yards and 2 touchdowns, all career highs. Look for even better things from this tight end as the Chargers continue to roll in 1993.

Fantasy Rankings: 1992—6 points (Tied for 80th)

1991—0 points

1990—3 points (Tied for 109th)

Past Performance Key: Walker's average of 11.6 yards per reception in 1992 was the best of his career.

11. Jim Price, Los Angeles Rams   Price had his second solid season in a row in 1992. He caught 35 passes and scored 2 touchdowns in 1991, and followed that up with 34 receptions and 2 touchdowns in 1992. Price's scoring consistency in his first two years in the league bodes well for fantasy owners. This Price may be right for those of you who need to draft a tight end on Draft Day 1993.

Fantasy Rankings: 1992—6 points (Tied for 80th)

1991—6 points (Tied for 76th)

Past Performance Key: Price caught Mike Pagel's only touchdown pass of 1992 in Week Thirteen in the Rams' loss against the Vikings.

12. Ron Hall, Tampa Bay   Ron Hall had an average year for him in every category except scoring, as he scored 4 touchdowns, a career high. If you must draft a tight end, and it's late in the draft, close your eyes and go for Hall, and hope he returns to the end zone just as often in 1993.

Fantasy Rankings: 1992—12 points (Tied for 37th)
1991—0 points
1990—9 points (Tied for 66th)
1989—6 points (Tied for 75th)

Past Performance Key: Hall had 5 career touchdown receptions in his five years in the league prior to 1992. He posted a yardage average of only 9.0 in 1992, the lowest of his six-year career. Hall scored a bonus bomb in 1990. His 4 touchdown catches tied Mark Carrier for the team lead in that category.

13. Keith Cash/Jonathan Hayes, Kansas City Chiefs   The bad news for the fantasy owners of the Chiefs' tight ends last season was that they were largely invisible in the team's offense, combining for only 21 receptions and 190 yards between them. The good news is that Cash and Hayes each caught 2 touchdown passes. If the Chiefs look to the tight ends in the red zone more often in 1993, one of these guys could make his fantasy owners very happy.

Fantasy Rankings:
Cash   1992—6 points (Tied for 80th)
1991—3 points (Tied for 110th)
Hayes   1992—6 points (Tied for 80th)
1991—6 points (Tied for 76th)
1990—3 points (Tied for 109th)
1989—6 points (Tied for 75th)

Past Performance Key: Both of Cash's touchdown catches in 1992 were from the 2-yard line. Hayes scored both of his touchdowns in the last game of the season.

14. Terry Orr, Washington Redskins   Tight ends are generally not a big part of the Redskins' passing game, but Orr caught 3 touchdown passes in 1992, after scoring 4 in 1991. Orr may not have that many receptions overall, but the name of the fantasy game is getting in the end zone, and for a tight end Orr does a pretty good job of it. Orr is a good pick for fantasy owners who must draft a tight end in 1993.

Fantasy Rankings: 1992—9 points (Tied for 57th)

1991—12 points (Tied for 39th)

1990—0 points

1989—0 points

Past Performance Key: Orr scored 3 touchdowns during the 1986–90 seasons; he has scored 7 in the two seasons since then.

15. Mark Bavaro, Philadelphia Eagles Bavaro made a remarkable return from his one-year "retirement" with the Cleveland Browns in 1992, bad knees and all. He caught 25 passes for a 12.6-yard average, and scored 2 touchdowns. If determination to overcome physical adversity were the only criteria for fantasy success, Bavaro would be one of the first players selected. But Bavaro's bad knees could go at any time. That makes him a risky proposition for the Philadelphia Eagles, who signed him as a free agent to fill the void left by Keith Jackson, and that makes him a risky proposition for fantasy owners on Draft Day 1993. If healthy, though, Bavaro could make an inviting target for Randall Cunningham's passes.

Fantasy Rankings: 1992—6 points (Tied for 80th)

1991—0 points

1990—15 points (Tied for 32nd)

1989—9 points (Tied for 57th)

Past Performance Key: Bavaro missed all of 1991, retiring after being cut by the Giants prior to the season (the Giants released him on July 15, 1991, after he failed a physical).

16. Howard Cross, New York Giants Cross had his best year in four as a pro, catching 27 passes for 357 yards and 2 touchdowns in 1992. But the numbers certainly aren't staggering. He's a late-round pick for those who must draft tight ends.

Fantasy Rankings: 1992—6 points (Tied for 80th)

1991—6 points (Tied for 76th)

1990—0 points

1989—3 points (Tied for 111th)

Past Performance Key: Cross has now scored 2 touchdowns in two consecutive seasons.

KEEP AN EYE ON

1. Johnny Mitchell, New York Jets   Mitchell, the first-round pick of the Jets, and 15th selection overall, in the 1992 draft, was injured early in the year and did not catch his first (and only) NFL touchdown pass (a 37-yarder) until the ninth week of the season. Nevertheless, Mitchell showed ability during his rookie year by averaging 13.1 yards per catch on 16 receptions. Mitchell has the talent to become a potent weapon. If your rules require you to select a tight end, you could do a lot worse than selecting him toward the later rounds of your fantasy draft.

> **Fantasy Rankings:**   1992—3 points (Tied for 116th)
>
> **Past Performance Key:**   Mitchell's 13.1-yard average was the best for a Jets tight
> end with 16 or more receptions since Jerome Barkum averaged 14.9 yards
> per catch in 1979.

2. Jackie Harris, Green Bay Packers   Harris benefited almost as much as Sterling Sharpe from the new offensive package imported out of San Francisco by head coach Mike Holmgren in 1992. Harris's third year in the league was his best by far. He had 55 receptions for 595 yards, both career highs, and 2 touchdowns in 1992. If Sterling Sharpe took the Jerry Rice position in the Green Bay offense, then Harris is Brent Jones. You could do a lot worse than that in selecting a tight end on Draft Day 1993.

> **Fantasy Rankings:**   1992—6 points (Tied for 80th)
> 1991—9 points (Tied for 51st)
> 1990—0 points
>
> **Past Performance Key:**   Harris had caught only 36 passes in his two years in the
> league prior to 1992. He has caught 5 touchdown passes over the past two
> seasons.

3. Ferrell Edmunds, Seattle Seahawks   Buried behind Keith Jackson on the depth chart in Miami, this talented tight end flew the coop to the Great Northwest courtesy of free agency. While he doesn't have Dan Marino throwing to him anymore, Edmunds fills a big gap in the Seahawks' offense. He is a sleeper pick for those of you who must take tight ends in your draft.

> **Fantasy Rankings:**   1992—3 points (Tied for 116th)
> 1991—6 points (Tied for 76th)
> 1990—3 points (Tied for 97th)
> 1989—9 points (Tied for 56th)
>
> **Past Performance Key:**   Edmunds averaged 32 receptions a season in 1988–
> 90; he has averaged 10.5 receptions a season the last two years.

BIGGEST BUSTS

1. Gary Clark, Phoenix Cardinals   When you look up the definition of "biggest bust" in the sports dictionary, you will see the notation "Football department, Rypien to Clark, 1992 season." Clark's sore hamstrings gave his fantasy owners sore pocketbooks this season, as the Rypien-Clark double-down combo that was so potent in 1991 fizzled in 1992. Clark's troubles started in training camp, when he stopped talking to the press due to repeated questions about off-the-field problems. But Clark talked plenty to former head coach Joe Gibbs just before the end of the first half of the Redskins' playoff victory over the Vikings, screaming at him in front of a national audience about Gibbs's perceived lack of confidence in the wide receiver. In between these two events at the beginning and the end of the season, Clark caught only 5 touchdowns, with no bonus bombs, and dropped balls all season long. This was a far cry from 1991, when Clark had the best year of his distinguished pro career, scoring 10 touchdowns, half of them bonus bombs. Fantasy owners might want to take a page from Clark's playbook and get right in his face with their own temper tantrums if he doesn't return to form this season with his new team the Phoenix Cardinals. Besides money, the Cardinals lured free agent Clark with the promise of building their offense around him, like San Francisco does with Jerry Rice, and Green Bay with Sterling Sharpe. Whether the team can keep that promise, especially with the talent that Phoenix has, remains to be seen.

Fantasy Rankings: 1992—15 points (Tied for 26th)
1991—45 points (Tied for 2nd)
1990—27 points (Tied for 7th)
1989—30 points (Tied for 12th)

Past Performance Key: Clark's 5 touchdown passes in 1992 were his lowest season total since 1985, his first year in the NFL. He was the only receiver in the NFL who scored 2 bonus touchdowns in one game *twice* in 1991; no one did it even once in 1992. Clark scored no bonus bombs in 1992, after scoring 5 in 1991, and failed to reach 1,000 yards for the first time in four seasons. Clark has averaged 1,093 yards per season in his eight years in the league.

2. Art Monk, Washington Redskins   The elder statesman of the Posse is another all-time great who will end up in Canton shortly after the end of his career. In Week Six of the 1992 season he passed Steve Largent as the leading receiver in NFL history with his 820th reception, and ended the year with 847 receptions, and counting. He has compiled

11,628 career yards during his 13 seasons in the league. He ended the 1992 season with a reception streak of 148 consecutive games, third-best in NFL history behind Steve Largent's 177-game and Ozzie Newsome's 150-game streaks, and then caught passes in both of the Redskins' playoff games. This is all great, but you don't get fantasy points for setting all-time records, at least under my rules, and Monk is less than stellar as a fantasy receiver. Monk scored only 3 touchdowns in 1992, after scoring 8, with 1 bonus bomb, in 1991 (his first bomb since 1989). Monk was never that big a scoring threat anyway. (He has the most catches all-time, but only 63 career touchdowns, well down on the all-time receiver list. Former teammate Gary Clark accumulated 58 touchdown catches in his eight years with the Redskins, for example.) As revered as he is among Washington fans, Monk's 46 receptions was his lowest total for a full, nonstrike season in his 13 years in the league. The Redskins signed Monk to a one-year (and probably final) contract in the offseason and announced at the same time that Monk would not be in the starting lineup in the upcoming season. As a result, Monk's value as a fantasy receiver is almost the opposite of his historic status in the NFL.

Fantasy Rankings: 1992—9 points (Tied for 57th)
1991—27 points (Tied for 10th)
1990—15 points (Tied for 32nd)
1989—27 points (Tied for 15th)

Past Performance Key: Monk's 644 yards in 1992 was his lowest total ever for a full, nonstrike season. His 3 touchdowns were his lowest season total since 1985.

3. Drew Hill, Atlanta Falcons   Hill is another venerable receiver who keeps building a credible case for his eventual induction at Canton, but has lost some of his luster for fantasy owners. In fact, he was a big disappointment to his fantasy owners in 1992. His 60 receptions were certainly a respectable total, but his 3 touchdowns were not. This comes on the heels of the 1991 season, when Hill's 4 touchdowns were his lowest season since leaving the Los Angeles Rams in 1984. There is only one football to go around in the pass-oriented offense in Atlanta, and I'd say Hill was fourth at best in the pecking order for touchdowns among the receivers there, behind Rison, Haynes, and Pritchard. Don't let Hill's marquee value from his days as the leading receiver of the Houston Oilers confuse you on Draft Day 1993—his fantasy value as an Atlanta Falcon isn't much.

Fantasy Rankings: 1992—9 points (Tied for 32nd)
1991—15 points (Tied for 27th)

1990—15 points (Tied for 32nd)
1989—24 points (Tied for 19th)

Past Performance Key: Hill's 623 yards in 1992 was his lowest total since 1984. His 10.4 yards per reception was the lowest average of his 13-year career. Hill needs only 553 yards to reach 10,000 for his career, a total achieved by only nine other receivers in NFL history. Hill now has 600 career receptions, and is only the 10th player in NFL history to reach that mark.

4. Bill Brooks, Buffalo Bills   The law of averages finally caught up with Brooks in 1992. In last year's edition of this book I noted that Brooks's ability to post such solid numbers over his six-year career while playing with the offensively inept Colts was a testament to his tremendous skills. Through 1991, Brooks had averaged 61 receptions, 891 yards, and over 4 touchdowns a year, and had been the leading receiver on the Colts four of his six seasons with them. But a receiver still needs the quarterback to get the ball to him, no matter how talented that receiver is. In 1991, Jeff George was the 10th-rated quarterback in the *AFC*, and Brooks still managed to catch 72 passes, the highest number of his career, for 888 yards and 4 touchdowns. In 1992, Jeff George once again was the 10th-rated quarterback in the AFC. However, this time Brooks's luck ran out, and he could manage to snare only 44 passes, for 468 yards and just 1 touchdown. But good fortune in the form of free agency has smiled on Brooks, who was signed by the Buffalo Bills in the off-season. Now, with Jim Kelly instead of Jeff George throwing to Brooks in 1993, fantasy owners should see him return to the ranks of the top receivers in the AFC.

Fantasy Rankings: 1992—3 points (Tied for 116th)
1991—12 points (Tied for 39th)
1990—18 points (Tied for 20th)
1989—15 points (Tied for 29th)

Past Performance Key: Brooks's reception, yardage, and touchdown totals in 1992 were all career lows. His yard average per reception declined for the fifth straight year in 1992.

5. Mervyn Fernandez, Los Angeles Raiders   What in the world has happened to this guy? "Swervin' " Mervyn looked like a budding star in 1989, when he had 57 receptions for 1,069 yards, an 18.8 average, and 9 touchdowns, with 2 bonus bombs. His totals in each category have decreased every year since then. And in 1992, Fernandez caught only 9 balls for just 121 yards and zero touchdowns. It looks like Father Time has caught up to this talented receiver, after 11 years in professional football. (He spent the first five years of his career with the

British Columbia Lions in the Canadian Football League.) I said last year that 1992 might be his last chance to shine with the Raiders. Barring a miraculous comeback, it was.

Fantasy Rankings: 1992—0 points
1991—3 points (Tied for 110th)
1990—18 points (Tied for 20th)
1989—33 points (Tied for 5th)

Past Performance Key: Fernandez had failed to score a touchdown in only one season during his career prior to 1992.

6. Wendell Davis, Chicago Bears   As was typical of the entire Bears season in 1992, Davis had a poor year for his fantasy owners in 1992, after a terrific one in 1991. In 1991, Davis had the best year of his career, with 61 receptions and 6 touchdowns. He had solid totals in receptions (54) and yards (734) in 1992, but his 2 touchdowns were his lowest mark since his rookie year in 1988, when he scored none. Davis is certainly talented, but it remains to be seen how much value he will have to fantasy owners in 1993 as the Bears rebuild under new head coach Dave Wannstedt.

Fantasy Rankings: 1992—6 points (Tied for 80th)
1991—21 points (Tied for 15th)
1990—9 points (Tied for 66th)
1989—12 points (Tied for 42nd)

Past Performance Key: Davis's 13.6-yard average was the lowest of his five-year career. After scoring a bonus bomb in two of the three years prior to 1992, his longest touchdown reception in 1992 was 14 yards. Davis led the Bears in receptions for the second straight year.

7. Willie Gault, Los Angeles   The 1992 season was another disappointing one for this Raiders star (or should I say, "former star"). He followed his 20 catches in 1991, his lowest total since 1988, with only 27 receptions in 1992. Admittedly, Gault has never been the primary receiver for either the Bears or the Raiders. (He has caught more than 40 passes in a season only twice in his 10-year NFL career.) And his 4-touchdown total is impressive in light of the fact that he had only 27 receptions (in the NFL's wide-receiver category, only the Vikings' Hassan Jones and the Chiefs' Tim Barnett had fewer catches and scored as many touchdowns as Gault, and no receiver had fewer catches and more scores). But if Gault is going to play second or third banana in the Raiders' passing game, and he's not going to get the call deep (he failed to score a bonus bomb in 1992), then fantasy owners must adjust accordingly. Gault slips down to the fourth-receiver slot for fantasy owners, despite his scoring ability, on Draft Day 1993.

Fantasy Rankings: 1992—12 points (Tied for 37th)
1991—15 points (Tied for 27th)
1990—12 points (Tied for 53rd)
1989—15 points (Tied for 29th)

Past Performance Key: Gault failed to score a bonus bomb for the first time in four seasons in 1992. His longest touchdown pass in 1992 was 31 yards. Gault has scored exactly 4 touchdowns in three of the last four seasons.

8. J. J. Birden, Kansas City Chiefs   This is another receiver who raises expectations because of his ability as a bona fide deep threat. He has scored 8 touchdowns in his three seasons in the league, and 5 of them are bonus bombs, a 62.5 percent average. But it's one thing to be a deep threat, and another to be a scoring threat. Because of Birden's talent, he must score more often to avoid becoming a perennial fantasy disappointment. He certainly is worth drafting as a fourth receiver, but until he gets in the end zone more often than a Kerry Cash or a Terry Orr, he is not worth taking any earlier.

Fantasy Rankings: 1992—12 points (Tied for 37th)
1991—12 points (Tied for 39th)
1990—15 points (Tied for 32nd)

Past Performance Key: Birden has averaged 17.4 yards a reception during his three-year career. He is one of 11 NFL receivers with at least a single bonus bomb in each of the last three seasons.

9. Stephen Baker, New York Giants   I keep saying this every year—and it gets more difficult to make this argument every year—but this Giants receiver really has talent. While his scoring totals were low in 1992, Baker averaged a whopping 19.6 yards on 17 receptions, the best mark in the NFC for a player with 17 or more receptions. With Dan Reeves on board to rebuild the Giants' offense, and Phil Simms secure at the quarterback position, look for "The Touchdown Maker" to live up to his nickname more often this season.

Fantasy Rankings: 1992—6 points (Tied for 80th)
1991—12 points (Tied for 39th)
1990—15 points (Tied for 33rd)
1989—6 points (Tied for 75th)

Past Performance Key: Baker has an 18.3-yard-per-reception average for his six-year career. His nickname, "The Touchdown Maker," isn't a misnomer; Baker has averaged 1 touchdown every 6.7 receptions over his career. (Jerry Rice has averaged 1 every 5.9 receptions over his.)

10. Curtis Duncan, Houston Oilers   Duncan set an NFL record in the "dubious distinction" category in 1992: He broke Raymond Berry's

single-season league record of 75 receptions without a touchdown in
Week Sixteen against Cleveland in the 4th quarter, and set an overall
NFL record of 109 catches without a touchdown reception the same
week, before catching a TD pass in the 4th quarter to break his streak.
Every player worth his salt wants to be in the record books, but not
with those kinds of statistics. And for whatever astrological reasons,
Duncan has now scored 14 touchdowns in the three odd-numbered
years in his career, but only 3 in the three even years, scoring exactly 1
touchdown each season in 1988, 1990, and 1992. Duncan was named to
represent the AFC in the 1993 Pro Bowl, the first time he had received
this honor. For all his good numbers in the real world of NFL football,
Duncan will not be an All-Pro fantasy receiver until he begins to visit
the end zone on a regular basis.

Fantasy Rankings: 1992—3 points (Tied for 116th)
1991—12 points (Tied for 39th)
1990—3 points (Tied for 109th)
1989—18 points (Tied for 24th)

Past Performance Key: Duncan's 82 receptions for 954 yards were career
highs. Duncan has not scored a bonus bomb since the 1989 season. No
other receiver in NFL history with as many receptions and yards as Duncan
had in 1992 has ever scored as few as 1 touchdown in a season.

11. Eric Green, Pittsburgh Steelers   Green was the one blemish in an
otherwise sterling season for the Steelers in 1992. First, he missed the
first four weeks on injured reserve after bruising a rotator cuff on the
initial play of the season. Then, to add insult to injury, Green was
suspended on November 9 for six weeks after violating the NFL's
substance abuse policy. This was apparently his second violation, since
a player receives counseling and treatment after a first offense, and no
announcement is made. As a result of his shortened season, Green
scored only 2 touchdowns in 1992, his lowest total in three years in the
league. With his various injuries and now his personal problems, Green
still has not put together a full season in the NFL. (For instance, he
missed the last five weeks of the 1991 campaign with a broken ankle.)
Fantasy fans everywhere should wish Green the best of luck in his
recovery. Assuming he is healthy in every respect in 1993, he could be
one of the first tight ends drafted.

Fantasy Rankings: 1992—6 points (Tied for 80th)
1991—18 points (Tied for 21st)
1990—21 points (Tied for 16th)

Past Performance Key: Green scored 13 touchdowns during his first two years
in the league, which leads all tight ends in that category during that time

(1990–91). Nine of his 15 career touchdown receptions have been 10 yards or less.

12. Ethan Horton, Los Angeles Raiders   When Horton came out of nowhere to have a big year for the Raiders in 1991, lots of fantasy owners said, Who? But Horton heard lots of boos, not who's, from his fantasy owners in 1992, after his big year in 1991 had raised expectations for this tight end. In 1991 he led the Raiders in receptions with 53 and posted 5 touchdowns, including 1 bonus bomb. Horton fell to only 33 receptions for 409 yards and 2 touchdowns in 1992. Amazingly, these numbers are almost identical to his 1990 performance (33 receptions, 404 yards, 3 touchdowns). Based on this, Horton's performance in 1991 looks like it may have been a career year. Don't expect much more than last season's numbers from Horton in 1993.

Fantasy Rankings: 1992—6 points (Tied for 80th)
1991—18 points (Tied for 21st)
1990—9 points (Tied for 66th)
1989—3 points (Tied for 111th)

Past Performance Key: Horton's 2 touchdowns in 1992 were his lowest total since the 1989 season. His yardage average per reception the last three seasons are 12.2 (1990), 12.3 (1991), and 12.4 (1992).

QUICK DRAFT TIPS: WIDE RECEIVERS

The following statistical summaries try to give a quick glimpse at those scoring abilities that might set a wide receiver apart from the crowd in this year's fantasy draft, by his ability to score the all-important bonus bomb.

Receiver Leaders in Bonus Touchdowns, 1992

Beebe (Bills)	2
Davis (Chiefs)	2
Brown (Raiders)	2
Green (Lions)	2
Haynes (Falcons)	2
Moore (Lions)	2
Sharpe (Packers)	2

Receiver Leaders in Bonus Touchdowns, 1991–92

Haynes (Falcons)	6
Rice (49ers)	6
Clark (Redskins)	5
Barnett (Eagles)	3
Birden (Chiefs)	3
Brown (Raiders)	3
Fryar (Patriots)	3
Green (Lions)	3
Irvin (Cowboys)	3
Lofton (Bills)	3
Sharpe (Packers)	3
Stone (Steelers)	3
Taylor (49ers)	3

KICKERS

Obviously, you want to draft a kicker with the ability to put lots of fantasy points on the board for you each week. In fact, since overall scoring in the NFL was down again last season, placekickers have assumed a more important role than ever in the performance of your fantasy team.

There will always be the dominant kickers who are consistent fantasy scorers from year to year. But if history is any indication, some kicker will jump up in scoring in 1993, simply because he will get many more opportunities to boot field goals than he had in 1992. For instance, in 1990, Nick Lowery kicked the second-highest number of field goals in an NFL season in history (34). Prior to 1990, Lowery had never kicked more than 27 in a season. He's kicked 25 and 22 field goals in the two seasons since then. In 1991, two kickers, the Raiders' Jeff Jaeger and the Cowboys' Ken Willis, had 14 more attempts than the year before, and both, not surprisingly, jumped way up in the fantasy rankings. Both kickers fell back to the pack with a vengeance in 1992. In 1992, rookie Lin Elliott stepped in for the Cowboys and picked up where Ken Willis left off, and San Diego's John Carney kicked 7 more field goals than he had in any one season previously.

Here's one hint to help you draw up your list of desirable kickers: No AFC kicker has had as many field goal attempts as the NFC leader in that category since New England's Tony Franklin matched Chicago's Kevin Butler in 1986, and no AFC kicker has had more attempts than all his NFC counterparts since Pittsburgh's Gary Anderson led the league with 42 attempts in 1985. Here's another hint: The Redskins designated Chip Lohmiller as one of their two transitional players under the new free agent rules. You should designate Lohmiller as your fantasy kicker early on Draft Day 1993.

Speaking of Lohmiller, he is rated as the top fantasy kicker for the second season in a row. In fact, he and Pete Stoyanovich are First Echelon repeaters. They were the only kickers who merited First Echelon status in last year's edition of this book, but they are joined this year by the old war-horse, Morten Andersen. The Saints' Andersen, whom I ranked as the fourth-best kicker in last year's book, had a spectacular scoring year in 1992. These three kickers are a cut above the rest of the field, and take the worry out of drafting kickers if you are lucky enough to snag one of them.

FIRST ECHELON

1. Chip Lohmiller, Washington Redskins   Lohmiller was the one ray of offensive sunshine in an otherwise dark and dreary season for the Redskins' offense in 1992. He kicked 30 field goals, which tied him with Pete Stoyanovich for the league lead for the second consecutive year. His fantasy total of 135 points, although fourth-best among NFL kickers, was still a mild disappointment, especially in light of the staggering numbers he posted in 1991. His 173 fantasy points in 1991 were the best total for a kicker in the four editions of this book. His 31 field goals in 1991 tied Miami's Pete Stoyanovich for the most in the league, and his record of 8 bonus boots were the league high. The Chipster also tied Buffalo's Scott Norwood for the most extra points in the league in 1991, with 56. And therein lies Lohmiller's lower fantasy total in 1992: Because of the surprising futility of the Redskins' offense in 1992, Lohmiller kicked only 30 extra points, 26 fewer than the prior year. Despite the lower numbers in 1992, Lohmiller remains a fantasy scoring machine, averaging 145.5 fantasy points over the last four years. No kicker other than Lohmiller has even *reached* that total in the four editions of this book. Lohmiller's mark of at least 30 field goals in three consecutive years had never been accomplished by an NFL kicker before. Most important to fantasy owners, he has also led the league in field goal attempts each of the last four seasons. With his skill and leg strength, if this guy kicked indoors, for a team with normal offensive capability, he would be illegal. As it is, assuming that the Redskins' offense returns to some semblance of its normal prowess in 1993, Lohmiller has to go in the first or second round of the draft.

Fantasy Rankings: 1992—135 points (4th)
1991—173 points (1st)

1990—143 points (2nd)

1989—131 points (2nd)

Past Performance Key: Lohmiller has 40 or more field goal attempts in each of the last four seasons, an NFL record. In five seasons in the NFL Lohmiller has kicked 139 field goals, which is more than a third of the way to Jan Stenerud's all-time-leading total of 373, a mark that Stenerud needed 18 years to achieve. After five seasons, Lohmiller is already among the top 40 career field goal kickers in points scored. Lohmiller has missed 10 or more field goals in each of the last four seasons. He failed to kick a field goal in only two of the Redskins' 16 games in 1992. Lohmiller's 149 NFL points in 1991 were more than the Colts scored. Lohmiller did not kick a single bonus boot in the last nine games of the 1992 season.

2. Pete Stoyanovich, Miami Dolphins   In last year's edition of this book, I remarked that I expected a lengthy stay for Stoyo in the First Echelon, and he did nothing to disappoint me or, more important, his fantasy owners in 1992. Stoyo had another terrific season in 1992, after a huge year in 1991. In 1991, he tied Lohmiller for the most field goals in the league (31) and led the AFC in scoring, finishing second in the NFL to the Redskins' star. More to the point, he finished second in my fantasy rankings for kickers in 1991, even after missing the first two games of the season. In 1992, Stoyo moved up a notch, tying Lohmiller again for the most field goals in the league (30), but this time leading the entire NFL in scoring. His fantasy total of 136 points was the third-highest in the league. He and Lohmiller are charter members of the "big foot" breed of kickers, with the leg strength to instill confidence in their respective coaches to let them bomb away from 50 yards or more without anxiety. Few kickers are worth taking early in the draft. Stoyo's an exception that proves the rule against drafting kickers early, as Draft Day 1993 should prove.

Fantasy Rankings: 1992—136 points (3rd)

1991—139 points (2nd)

1990—112 points (9th)

1989—104 points (15th)

Past Performance Key: Stoyanovich now has 37 field goal attempts for two consecutive seasons, the most by an AFC kicker during those two years. The 37 attempts in each season are the most by a Dolphin since famous tie salesman Garo Yepremian attempted 37 for the Dolphins in 1973. Stoyo's 10 bonus kicks over the past two seasons tie him with Roger Ruzek for the fourth-highest total in the league. His 82 field goals during the last three years is the second-highest total in the league. Stoyo was the only kicker to boot 4 field goals in a game three times in 1992.

3. Morten Andersen, New Orleans Saints   Arguably the best kicker in the game during the mid-1980s, Andersen slumped in 1989–90. But he's back, with two strong seasons in a row. He's the perfect illustration of why a "Home in the Dome" kicker is so valuable to a fantasy owner. It's not enough that the Saints' conservative offense and good defense allow him ample opportunity to accumulate field goals and fantasy points year after year; on top of that advantage, Andersen doesn't have to worry about the effect of Mother Nature on his footing and the flight of the ball in 50 percent of his games. It's almost not fair. And when I say ample opportunity, I mean ample opportunity. Andersen has had fewer than 30 field goal attempts in a season in only two of the last eight years, and in those years he attempted 29 and 27. By contrast, only six other NFL kickers attempted 30 or more field goals in 1992. Coach Jim Mora also lets him boot away from long distance. Andersen's 7 bonus boots in 1992 tied him with Norm Johnson for the league lead. He kicked field goals in 14 consecutive games in 1992, and went only one game without a field goal. He ended the season hot, with 16 field goals in the last seven games, including 5 in Week Fourteen against Atlanta. Let's hope he stays hot for the wise fantasy owner who goes for Andersen early in the upcoming fantasy draft.

Fantasy Rankings: 1992—141 points (1st)
1991—128 points (6th)
1990—110 points (10th)
1989—107 points (14th)

Past Performance Key: Andersen has 18 bonus boots over the past three years, the highest total in the league over that time. He has 12 bonus boots over the past two years, second only to Chip Lohmiller during that time. Andersen broke the Chiefs' Nick Lowery's record of 19 field goals of 50 or more yards in 1992, ending the season with 21 field goals of 50 yards or more in his 11-year NFL career. He was one of only three NFL kickers with 5 field goals in one game in 1992.

SECOND ECHELON

1. Steve Christie, Buffalo Bills   The Bills improved their kicking game immensely by signing former Tampa Bay kicker Steve Christie as a Plan B free agent in February 1992. Christie's predecessor, Scott Norwood (he of "the missed kick in Super Bowl XXV" fame), had made only 65.5 percent of his field goal tries during the 1990–91 seasons, while Christie was 24 of 30 in field goal attempts in 1992, an 80 percent average, a tad below his career mark. Freed from the low-scoring Bucs, Christie had the best year of his career in 1992. He scored 130 fantasy points, the fifth-best total in the league, and a personal best as well. Christie should continue to rack up points kicking for the potent Buffalo offense in 1993.

Fantasy Rankings: 1992—130 points (5th)
1991—70 points (26th)
1990—105 points (Tied for 13th)

Past Performance Key: Christie missed the first PAT of his three-year career in 1992. He kicked 43 extra points in 1992. His career total in two years with the Bucs was 49.

2. Nick Lowery, Kansas City Chiefs   With the retirement of the Jets' Pat Leahy, Lowery has inherited the mantle of dean of NFL kickers (along with the Bengals' Jim Breech and, if he returns to the NFL in 1993, Matt Bahr). As befits such a lofty status, Lowery added to his record-breaking career statistics in 1992 with another solid season. He moved past Lou Groza into eighth place on the all-time scoring list in Week Fifteen, and past Fred Cox into seventh place in Week Seventeen. Lowery ended the season with 1,367 career points. He needs just 14 more to move past Jim Bakken and 16 to move past Mark Mosely into fifth place on the NFL's all-time scoring list, a position he should occupy by the end of the first month of the 1993 season. With another typical Lowery season, the Chiefs kicker could move past Jim Turner and his 1,439 career points into fourth place among career scorers by the end of 1993—and even past Pat Leahy (1,470 points) into third place. This future Hall of Famer (there is only one pure placekicker in the Hall of Fame, Jan Stenerud, so this process might take a while) would have returned to the First Echelon this year except for the fact that he seems to have lost the long-ball talent that in the past set him apart from the placekicking crowd. (Lowery started the 1992 season tied with Morten Andersen as the NFL record holder for most field goals from 50 yards or more in a career, 18. Morten Andersen passed him in this category in 1992, making 3 kicks from that distance during the season to Lowery's 1. Lowery had not kicked a 50-yard field goal in the two seasons prior to 1992. He finally did, in the third week of 1992.) Despite this drawback, Lowery still rates among the best field goal kickers because of his accuracy and because he kicks for Marty Schottenheimer's field goal offense. (Lowery had a streak of four consecutive years with 30 or more field goal attempts going into 1992. It ended as he attempted only 24 field goals last season.) The venerable Nick Lowery is a solid selection for your fantasy team in 1993.

Fantasy Rankings: 1992—111 points (Tied for 12th)
1991—113 points (10th)

1990—145 points (1st)
1989—112 points (13th)

Past Performance Key: Lowery had 7 bonus kicks in 1988, but has kicked only 7 since then. He has missed only 10 field goals the last three years, for a field goal percentage of 89 percent, the best in the league during that time. Only Lohmiller and Stoyanovich have more field goals than Lowery over the last three seasons. His 306 career field goals is the third-best mark of all time. His 80.1 percent field goal average during his 14-year career is the highest NFL career mark. His 22 field goals in 1992 were his lowest total for one season since he kicked 19 in 1987.

3. Norm Johnson, Atlanta Falcons After spending nine seasons in the cold, damp climate of the great Northwest with the Seahawks, Johnson has been revitalized in his two seasons with Hot-lanta. His field goal percentage in 1991 (82.6 percent) was his best since 1984, and he followed that by making 18 of 22 field goals in 1992, an 81.8 percent percentage. He also kicked 7 bonus boots in 1992, tying Morten Andersen for the league lead in that category. A "Home in the Dome" kicker, and one of the few good ones at that, he is a steal if he's still hanging around in the late rounds of the draft.

Fantasy Rankings: 1992—114 points (Tied for 8th)
1991—101 points (17th)
1990—105 points (13th)
1989—81 points (24th)

Past Performance Key: Johnson kicked a bonus field goal in five consecutive games in 1992, a league high. His average of 38.7 yards per successful field goal in 1992 was second only to the Raiders' Jeff Jaeger's mark of 39.2 yards. His 39 PATs in 1992 were his highest total since 1988. Johnson has never kicked more than 23 field goals in one season in his 11-year NFL career.

4. Gary Anderson, Pittsburgh Steelers Barry Foster got all the headlines, but Anderson had a quietly spectacular season for his fantasy owners in 1992, kicking 28 field goals and scoring 119 fantasy points. He had his best season since 1988, when he also kicked 28 field goals. If consistent scoring is the hallmark of a valuable fantasy kicker, then Anderson was Mr. Value in 1992. He kicked field goals in 14 of the Steelers' 16 games in 1992, and added 2 bonus boots. Anderson is another solid fantasy kicker who will be waiting for patient, and well-informed, fantasy owners in the later rounds of the upcoming draft.

Fantasy Rankings: 1992—119 points (7th)
1991—112 points (11th)

1990—104 points (15th)
1989—103 points (16th)

Past Performance Key: Anderson's 28 field goals in 1992 were his personal best since 1988. He broke his string of three years with a perfect PAT record by missing 2 extra points in 1992. Only Murray and Lohmiller are perfect with PATs during the last four seasons. Anderson has 30 or more field goal attempts in four of the last five seasons.

5. Lin Elliott, Dallas Cowboys   This free agent rookie from Texas Tech had a rocky start in the NFL, missing 8 field goals in the first eight games of the 1992 season, and was staring the NFL's unemployment line in the face. But then he kicked 10 field goals without a miss during Weeks Ten through Thirteen, ending up with only 3 missed attempts in the last eight weeks of the season, while kicking 16 field goals during that stretch. Elliott has a strong leg, as evidenced by his 6 bonus boots in 1992, second only to Morten Andersen and Norm Johnson. He also plays on a team that many pundits are predicting will have a longer reign than the Ming Dynasty. Whether or not the Cowboys repeat as Super Bowl champions, Dallas's young and loaded offense figures to give Elliott plenty of field goal opportunities in the future. As long as he stays as accurate as he was in the second half of the 1992 season, Elliott will be a top fantasy kicker for years to come.

Fantasy Rankings: 1992—137 points (2nd)

Past Performance Key: Elliott's 137 fantasy points were the highest total for a rookie kicker in the four editions of this book. His 35 field goal attempts were the fourth-highest total in the NFL in 1992.

6. Mike Cofer, San Francisco 49ers   This guy must have some goods on somebody in the 49ers' management, because he is absolutely one of the worst field goal kickers in the NFL. But he's not a total bust as a fantasy kicker—in fact, quite the opposite, because he generally has a huge number of extra points, which eventually add up for fantasy owners. Cofer made only two-thirds of his field goals in 1992, after making only 50 percent in 1991, which is disgraceful for a professional placekicker. The same kicker who scored 145 fantasy points, good for first place in my fantasy rankings in 1989, scored 103 fantasy points in 1991 and 113 in 1992. For a team that prides itself on its excellence in every area of the game, the reason for Cofer's continued presence on the 49ers' squad remains a complete and total mystery, right up there with what causes holes in the ozone layer. Cofer is a good selection with your last-round pick on Draft Day 1993.

Fantasy Rankings: 1992—113 points (Tied for 10th)
1991—103 points (15th)

1990—123 points (5th)

1989—145 points (1st)

Past Performance Key: Cofer's field goal percentage over the last three seasons is 61.5%. He has the highest number of PATs in the league over the past two, three, four, and five years. Cofer has kicked 10 bonus field goals over the past three years.

BEST OF THE REST

1. Al Del Greco, Houston Oilers Del Greco has a tendency to choke under pressure. His missed field goal against the Broncos in the 1991 playoffs ultimately cost the Oilers the game and perhaps their shot at getting into the Super Bowl. In 1992, Del Greco missed what would have been the winning kick, a 39-yard attempt, with six seconds left against Pittsburgh in Week Nine, and missed a 41-yarder with 1:49 left against the Dolphins in Week Twelve, which would have put the Oilers ahead by 3 points. (The Oilers lost the game when Pete Stoyanovich made a 52-yard field goal with two seconds remaining in the game.) But he's worth having even though he's not such a great clutch kicker. Why? The potent Houston offense, and eight games kicking in the 'Dome. Just don't clutch and waste an early pick on him.

Fantasy Rankings: 1992—113 points (Tied for 10th)

1991—52 points (28th)

1990—91 points (19th)

1989—91 points (Tied for 20th)

Past Performance Key: Del Greco has not missed a PAT in three years. He has a lifetime field goal percentage of 68% over his nine-year career.

2. Fuad Reveiz, Minnesota Vikings Reveiz had a good year in 1992, after being a major disappointment for fantasy owners in 1991. He had pumped up the fantasy crowd with a good half-season for Minnesota in 1990. But the Vikes fizzled in 1991, victims of a befuddled coaching staff, and Reveiz followed the crowd. The 1992 season was a different story, though, as Reveiz rode the crest with the whole team to a very successful year under new head coach Dennis Green. Reveiz's 19 field goals were his best season total since his rookie year with Miami in 1985. His 4 bonus boots were his highest season total in the four editions of this book. Last year I wrote that, for both Reveiz and the Vikings, the only direction for them to go was up. Even after a big jump in 1992, I still feel that way.

Fantasy Rankings: 1992—114 points (Tied for 8th)

1991—94 points (21st)

1990—68 points (28th)
1989—0 points
Past Performance Key: Reveiz kicked field goals in the Vikes' last seven games in 1992. His 25 field goal attempts in 1992 were his highest season total since his rookie year with Miami in 1985.

3. David Treadwell, Denver Broncos   After three solid years, Treadwell's fantasy scoring totals slumped badly in 1992, as the Broncos had one of their poorest seasons in years. Perhaps no other person at any other position on a football team is so dependent on the overall performance of a team for his numbers to be consistent. As the team goes, so goes the kicker, in other words. And this was certainly true for Treadwell and the Broncos in 1992. With quarterback John Elway injured, the whole Broncos offense went into the Dumpster. Denver failed to score 300 or more points in a full season for the first time since 1979, and Treadwell's production suffered directly as a result. In his first three years in the league Treadwell kicked 27, 25, and 27 field goals. He kicked 20 in 1992. More revealing, perhaps, is the fact that Treadwell had 33, 34, and 36 field goal attempts during the 1989–91 seasons, while he had only 24 in 1992. Because of his off year in 1992, Treadwell should drop down in the draft. If he drops too far, he will be a steal for some lucky fantasy owner in the late rounds of the 1993 fantasy draft.
Fantasy Rankings: 1992—94 points (Tied for 16th)
1991—115 points (8th)
1990—119 points (6th)
1989—124 points (Tied for 7th)
Past Performance Key: Treadwell's field goal percentage of 83% in 1992 was the best of his four-year career. It was also the first year in his career that Treadwell made all of his PATs.

4. Jason Hanson, Detroit Lions   Hanson, the Lions' second-round pick from Washington State, in the 1992 NFL draft, had a decent rookie season. Like the Cowboys' Lin Elliott, another rookie kicker, it took him a little while to settle in to kicking in the big leagues. He missed 4 field goals in the first four weeks, including a 49-yarder with 1:41 left that would have tied the game against Washington in Week Three. But his only miss the rest of the season was a 57-yard attempt in Week Fifteen. Overall, he missed just 5 of 26 field goals, for an impressive field goal percentage of 81%. He should post better fantasy numbers in 1993 with a year in the league under his belt, especially if the Lions' offense returns to form after a subpar year.

Fantasy Rankings: 1992—71 points (24th)

Past Performance Key: Hanson's shortest missed field goal in 1992 was from 45 yards, and the other 4 misses were from 49 yards or longer. He was the only NFC kicker with exactly 4 field goals in one game in 1992.

5. Kevin Butler, Chicago Bears   After two mediocre seasons in a row, it's clear that Butler's fabulous fantasy year of 1990 appears to have been an aberration, another example of the kicker who jumps up in attempts and has a great season, then falls back to the pack from whence he came. While Butler had a remarkable 135 fantasy points in 1990, the result of 26 field goals and 7 bonus boots, he has not broken the century mark in fantasy points in the two years since then, or in three of the last four seasons. So, putting aside 1990's numbers, what you see is what you get from Butler. To top it off, he kicks on a grass field, under bad weather conditions later in the year, and he's getting a bit long in the tooth in NFL years. Draft him only if you must.

Fantasy Rankings: 1992—94 points (Tied for 16th)

1991—98 points (19th)

1990—135 points (3rd)

1989—91 points (Tied for 20th)

Past Performance Key: Butler had 7 bonus boots in 1990, but has had only 5 since. He missed 6 of his 7 field goal attempts from beyond the 40-yard line in 1992. He was 0 for 4 from 40—49 yards, while making 1 of 3 from 50 or more yards. Butler has only one season with 20 or more field goals in the last six years. Since setting the NFL record for most consecutive field goals during the 1988–89 seasons (24), Butler's field goal percentage is 67%.

6. Jim Breech, Cincinnati Bengals   Along with Lowery (and Matt Bahr, if he's back) the dean of NFL kickers, Breech enters his 15th season in the NFL as the 10th-highest career scorer in the NFL. He now has accumulated 1,246 points in his career, which moved him past Chris Bahr into the Top Ten in 1992. Breech had one of the more remarkable streaks in NFL history, if not sports history, come to an end in Week Seven of the 1992 season—his 186-game consecutive scoring streak. That's right—Breech had scored in every Bengals game since Cincinnati's last shutout defeat, a 14–0 loss to the Buffalo Bills in the 11th game of the 1980 season. (Breech did not play in the 1987 replacement games.) But all good things must come to an end, and 229 field goals, 498 extra points, and 1,185 points later, the streak was snapped by the Steelers in the Monday Night Game. Breech will go down in the history books, but he shouldn't go down on your list of fantasy kickers, for a variety of reasons. One, Breech has kicked 20 or more field goals in a season only twice in the last seven years. Two, Breech had only 1 bonus boot last year, and has kicked only 7 over the last three years. And three, the Cincinnati offense is suspect as it rebuilds with young players like David Klinger at quarterback. You can do a lot better than Breech on Draft Day 1993.

Fantasy Rankings: 1992—91 points (18th)
                        1991—111 points (12th)
                        1990—95 points (Tied for 17th)
                        1989—73 points (Tied for 26th)

Past Performance Key: Despite the incredible length of Breech's scoring streak, he has never kicked more than 24 field goals in a season in his 14-year career. He has not missed a PAT during the last two years. Breech kicked only 3 field goals in 1992 from beyond the 40-yard line.

7. Matt Stover, Cleveland Browns   Stover showed mild improvement in his second year in the league. He kicked 5 more field goals than he did in 1991, and scored 5 more fantasy points. But the Browns' brain trust has still not exhibited real confidence in Stover's long game, and perhaps with good reason. Only 3 of Stover's 21 field goals were from beyond the 40-yard line in 1992, and Stover was only 3 of 9 from that distance. It might help his rating if he didn't kick in eight games a season on one of the worst playing surfaces in the NFL. Only charter members of the Dawg Pound need draft Stover earlier than the last round of the draft, because he'll be waiting when you come barking.

Fantasy Rankings: 1992—95 points (15th)
                        1991—90 points (23rd)

Past Performance Key: Stover missed only 2 field goals in the last seven weeks of the 1992 season. He made 4 field goals, and missed 3, in Week Eight. (The one-game NFL record for field goals is 7.) No kicker had as many as or more field goals than Stover and kicked fewer bonus boots in 1992.

8. Greg Davis, Phoenix Cardinals   Davis may not be long for this league if he continues to kick like he did in 1992. Granted, the playing surface in Sun Devil Stadium was a disaster by the end of the season, but that's no excuse for his having missed half his field goal attempts last year. Accuracy has never been a strong point with Davis, anyway. He posted his best field goal percentage for a full season in 1991, and it was only 70%. The justification for Davis's inaccuracy was the fact that he tried, and made, so many long field goals. Davis did make 10 bonus boots during the 1990–91 seasons. But he only made two field goals from 45 yards or more in 1992, neither of which was from 50 yards or more. It no longer looks like the risk is worth the reward for those of you who are thinking of tabbing the strong-legged Davis on Draft Day 1993.

Fantasy Rankings: 1992—73 points (23rd)

1991—100 points (18th)

1990—118 points (7th)

1989—118 points (8th)

Past Performance Key: Davis's field goal percentage of 50% was the lowest in the league in 1992. He led the league with 3 missed PATs in 1989; he's been perfect since. He's never kicked more than 23 field goals in a season. He has 12 bonus boots over the past three years.

9. Cary Blanchard, New York Jets   Blanchard joined the Jets in Week five, after Jason Staurovsky booted his way out of a kicking job in the first four weeks of the season. Blanchard, like the Jets, did nothing to truly recommend himself in 1992. One interesting thing about the Jets, though: They have used five placekickers over the past two seasons, so it's hard to get a clear picture of the team's kicking situation. But the Jets attempted 43 field goals in 1991, and 30 in 1992. So, if form holds true, the Jets' kicker could put up a lot of field goal attempts in 1993, especially if all of the free agents signed by the Jets perform up to expectations, especially on defense. If the Jets use only one kicker, and it's Blanchard, he could move up in fantasy points in a big way in 1993.

Fantasy Rankings: 1992—71 points (24th)

Past Performance Key: Blanchard kicked 10 field goals in his first five games with the Jets; he kicked 6 in the last seven.

10. Ken Willis/Matt Bahr, New York Giants   In one of the strangest career moves in recent memory, Willis jumped from the up-and-coming Cowboys, for whom he kicked in 1990 and 1991, to the lukewarm Bucs. Of course, the Cowboys' free agent pickup in 1990 from the University of Kentucky had paid handsome dividends for them before they left him an unrestricted Plan B free agent and he signed on with the Bucs in February 1992, for what I hope was not an inconsiderable amount of money. But as he quickly found out, the Bucs ain't the Cowboys, either in talent or temperament. After failing to kick a field goal for five straight games, Willis was waived in Week Ten, an expensive experiment in free agency for the Bucs. Willis caught on with the Giants to fill in for the injured Bahr in Week Fourteen. Bahr had been his usual steady but unspectacular self up to that point in the season, as he had been for many years in his lengthy career. This situation should develop into the classic matchup between Youth and Age in preseason, the survivor of which should post decent fantasy numbers in 1993. But with

DANNY SHERIDAN'S FANTASY FOOTBALL 1993

a new coaching staff, the entire Giants situation is in a state of flux, and I would tread carefully here on Draft Day 1993.

Fantasy Rankings:

Willis
- 1992—60 points (25th)
- 1991—133 points (4th)
- 1990—89 points (21st)

Bahr
- 1992—80 points (22nd)
- 1991—102 points (16th)
- 1990—86 points (22nd)
- 1989—95 points (18th)

Past Performance Key: Willis dropped from 27 field goals in 1991 to 10 in 1992. He has not missed a PAT in his three-year NFL career. Bahr has not played a full 16-game season since 1989.

11. Charlie Baumann, New England Patriots
The record of this refugee from the World League speaks for itself. Charlie has not impressed in his two seasons in the league. Unless Bill Parcells works a miracle all the way around the franchise in 1993, Baumann is of little value to fantasy owners.

Fantasy Rankings:
- 1992—55 points (27th)
- 1991—51 points (29th)

Past Performance Key: Baumann has made 20 of 29 field goals in his two years in the NFL. He did not kick his first field goal of 1992 until the sixth week of the season. Baumann attempted only 1 field goal from beyond the 45-yard line in 1992 (and missed it); Chip Lohmiller attempted 7.

12. Eddie Murray, Tampa Bay Buccaneers
Murray got the boot from the Lions after losing his job to rookie Jason Hanson in the 1992 preseason. He filled in for the injured Nick Lowery and booted a 52-yard field goal for the Chiefs in Week Eight. However, there was no chance of long-term employment there, so he tried to catch on later in the season with the Bucs. But the normally accurate Murray made only 4 of his 8 field goal attempts with them. Murray may be at the end of his very successful, 13-year career. Even if he fends off the challenge of a young gun in training camp, there still is not much value here for fantasy owners in 1993.

Fantasy Rankings:
- 1992—34 points (28th)
- 1991—109 points (13th)
- 1990—79 points (Tied for 25th)
- 1989—114 points (Tied for 11th)

Past Performance Key: Murray has not missed a PAT in four years, and only 5 in 13 years (394 attempts) in the NFL. He tied the NFL record for the highest field goal percentage in a season in both 1988 and 1989, with two consecutive marks of 95.24%. But his percentage in his other 11 seasons in the league is only 71.5%.

KEEP AN EYE ON

1. Chris Jacke, Green Bay Packers   Jacke rebounded in 1992 after two consecutive seasons of fantasy point decline. He posted his highest fantasy total since his rookie year in 1989, kicking 22 field goals, plus 5 bonus boots, the most in his career. Jacke was a consistent scorer last season, kicking field goals in 13 of the Packers' first 14 games. Jacke's fantasy total would have been higher, save for the fact that he had no field goal attempts in either of the Packers' last two games in 1992. With the Pack, by all appearances, well on the way Back, Jacke could post even better fantasy numbers in 1993.

Fantasy Rankings: 1992—111 points (Tied for 12th)
1991—91 points (22nd)
1990—106 points (12th)
1989—117 points (9th)

Past Performance Key: Jacke's 29 field goal attempts in 1992 were the second-highest season total in his four-year career. He missed only 1 field goal in the last seven games of the season.

2. Tony Zendejas, Los Angeles Rams   Zendejas is one of the most accurate kickers in the game. Now, if the Rams' brain trust could just do something about getting him more field goal attempts in a season. Zendejas did not miss a field goal in all of 1991, setting the NFL record for the highest field goal percentage in a season, and missed just 5 of 20 in 1992. But his 17 attempts in 1991 and 20 in 1992 demonstrate the lack of support he receives from the Rams' offense. Mike Lansford, whom Zendejas replaced in 1991, had averaged 26 attempts in his seven years with the team, and had never attempted fewer than 21 in a full season with the Rams. Get Zendejas up to that level, and his fantasy scoring should improve markedly. If you think the Rams' offense can get Zendejas up to 30 field goal attempts in 1993, he'll be a steal in the late rounds of the draft.

Fantasy Rankings: 1992—89 points (19th)
1991—85 points (24th)
1990—44 points (30th)
1989—130 points (3rd)

Past Performance Key: Zendejas missed only 1 field goal in the Rams' last 12 games in 1992. His lifetime NFL field goal percentage is 74.5%. He kicked 12 bonus boots in 1988–89, but has kicked only 6 since then. He had 37 field goal attempts with Houston in 1989; he's recorded 49 in the three years.

3. John Carney, San Diego Chargers   Like the Chargers overall, Carney came on with a huge rush in the last half of the 1992 regular season. After kicking only 10 field goals in the first 10 games of the 1993 season, Carney kicked 16 in the last six weeks, including 5 in Week Sixteen against the Raiders. He kicked 3 of his 5 bonus boots in the last four games of the regular season, and scored 74 of his career-high 128 fantasy points in the last six. Of course, he cooled off in a hurry in the rains of Miami, but you can't blame him for the Chargers' awful playoff performance. He was one of the principal players in their drive to the playoffs. With the capable Stan Humphries settled in at quarterback for the whole season in 1993, look for the Chargers' offense to give Carney plenty of opportunities to do his job and post excellent fantasy numbers in the upcoming season.

Fantasy Rankings: 1992—128 points (6th)
1991—97 points (20th)
1990—84 points (23rd)

Past Performance Key: Only two other NFL kickers improved their fantasy total from the 1991 season by as many points (31) as Carney did in 1992. (Del Greco improved 61 fantasy points, and Steve Christie 60.) Carney's field goals and number of attempts in 1992 were career highs. He kicked field goals in 13 of the Chargers' 16 games in 1992.

BIGGEST BUSTS

1. Jeff Jaeger, Los Angeles Raiders   Great things were expected of the Raiders' kicker in 1992 from his fantasy owners, after his great season in 1991, and Jaeger let everyone down with a thoroughly disappointing season. There is no doubt about Jaeger's ability to go deep; only two kickers in the NFL have more bonus boots than Jaeger over the past three seasons. But Jaeger's attempts dropped from 34 to 26 in 1992. More disturbing, he missed 11 of those 26 attempts, a lowly field goal percentage of 57.6%. Only two kickers missed more field goals than Jaeger in 1992. On the plus side, 33 percent of his kicks were bonus boots in 1992, the second-highest percentage in the league. Which Jaeger will show up in 1993? Everyone's entitled to an off year, and Jaeger had one in 1992. Look for a big improvement in the fantasy department from this quality kicker in 1993.

Fantasy Rankings: 1992—88 points (20th)
1991—134 points (3rd)
1990—100 points (16th)
1989—115 points (10th)

Past Performance Key: Of his field goals over the past three seasons, 27 percent are bonus boots. No NFL kicker with 20 or more field goal attempts in 1992 declined further in the number of successful field goals between the two seasons. (Jaeger kicked 14 fewer field goals in 1992 than he did in 1991.) He did not kick a field goal in the last four games of the 1992 season, and only 2 in the last six. Jaeger had made 81 percent of his field goals in 1990–1991. He kicked 15 field goals, with 5 bonus boots, in 1990.

2. Roger Ruzek, Philadelphia Eagles   The 1992 movie *Who Killed Roger Ruzek, Fantasy Football Style,* was a huge flop at the box office and among fantasy owners everywhere. Ruzek had a tremendous season in 1991, with a career-high 28 field goals in 33 attempts, as well as 6 bonus boots. His field goal percentage in 1991 was 85%, after three years of a combined 63%. Could 1991 have been the dreaded "career year"? Based on 1992's numbers, it sure looks like it. Ruzek made only 16 of 25 field goals, a percentage of just 64%, last season. His 4 bonus boots were fairly impressive, but his fantasy total of 100 points was a major disappointment. Ruzek will apparently have a great year every once in a while (he made 22 of 25 field goal attempts his rookie season in 1987 with the Dallas Cowboys). But he will have to be more consistent before he moves into the ranks of solid fantasy kickers.

Fantasy Rankings: 1992—100 points (14th)
1991—129 points (5th)
1990—114 points (8th)
1989—73 points (26th)

Past Performance Key: Ruzek has missed 9 PATs in the last three years; Nick Lowery has missed 4 in his 14-year career. Ruzek has kicked 12 bonus boots during the last three years. Only four kickers have more bonus boots during that time.

3. John Kasay, Seattle Seahawks   When you look up the definition of the dreaded and legendary "sophomore jinx" in the 1993 edition of the *Dictionary of Sports Expressions,* you will find this guy's picture illustrating the text. Kasay's poor performance in 1992 almost defies explanation, especially in light of his excellent rookie year. Kasay made 80.6 percent of his field goals in 1991, for a season total of 25, and kicked 4 bonus boots as well. His performance was the best by a rookie kicker in the NFL by a mile in 1991. But in 1992, Kasay only made 63.6 percent of his field goals, with no bonus boots. (His longest was 43 yards.) If you know why Kasay was so bad in 1992, and whether he'll be better in 1993, then go for him late in the draft. Otherwise, here's another dome kicker who goes to waste for fantasy owners in 1993.

Fantasy Rankings: 1992—56 points (27th)

1991—114 points (9th)

Past Performance Key: Kasay had 11 fewer field goals in 1992 than he did in 1991. Jeff Jaeger and Roger Ruzek were the only NFL kickers with 20 or more field goal attempts in 1992 who declined further in the number of successful field goals between the two seasons. Kasay and New England's Charlie Baumann were the only regular NFL kickers with no bonus boots in 1992. His 25 field goals in 1991 set the team record for the Seahawks.

4. Dean Biasucci, Indianapolis Colts   Biasucci's kicking skills have deteriorated along the same lines as golfers' skills diminish as they get older. Most top golfers, as they get older, are still great from tee to green. But once they get to the green, they have to putt with a polo mallet clutched against their chest, because the touch has gone completely. Biasucci still has the leg, but the finesse part of the kicking game, the accuracy, is going fast. His field goal percentage has declined in each of the last six years, from 89% in 1987 down to a rock-bottom 55% in 1992. Biasucci made only 16 of 29 field goals in 1992. Only one other kicker, Greg Davis of Phoenix, missed 13 field goals in 1992. It's a shame that his talent seems to have eroded so severely, since he does kick indoors. But if the yips have affected your golf game, then you might feel right at home with Biasucci on your fantasy squad this season.

Fantasy Rankings: 1991—71 points (25th)

1990—92 points (Tied for 18th)

1989—103 points (Tied for 16th)

Past Performance Key: Biasucci had 9 bonus boots during the 1991–92 seasons; only five kickers had more. He now has not scored 20 field goals in any of the last three seasons.

QUICK DRAFT TIPS: KICKERS

The following are some choice statistics designed to help you find the top kickers on Draft Day, 1993.

Bonus Kick Leaders
1992

Andersen	7
Johnson	7
Elliott	6
Biasucci	5
Christie	5
Carney	5
Jaeger	5
Jacke	5
Lohmiller	5
Ruzek	4
Reveiz	4
Stoyanovich	4

Bonus Kick Leaders
1991–92

Lohmiller	13
Andersen	12
Jaeger	11
Ruzek	10
Stoyanovich	10
Biasucci	9
Johnson	9
Davis	8
Anderson	6
Breech	6
Cofer	6
Elliott	6
Murray	6
Willis	6

Bonus Kick Leaders
1990–92

Andersen	18
Lohmiller	17
Jaeger	16
Stoyanovich	14
Biasucci	12
Johnson	10
Ruzek	12
Davis	12
Butler	11
Anderson	10
Cofer	10
Jacke	10
Christie	9

Field Goal Attempt Leaders
1991–92

Lohmiller	83
Stoyanovich	74
Anderson	69
Andersen	66
Carney	61
Jaeger	60
Treadwell	60
Ruzek	58
Breech	56
Davis	56
Biasucci	55
Butler	55
Cofer	55
Lowery	54
Jacke	53
Kasay	53
Stover	51
Bahr	50
Christie	50
Reveiz	49
Johnson	45
Del Greco	40

EIGHT

NFL DRAFT 1993

THE NFL DRAFT 1993 was in some respects the same as in past years. As usual, it was a media event of epic proportions, with live ESPN television coverage the entire afternoon and into the evening. The NFL draft was the main topic on all-sports radio stations across the country in the days leading up to it, and mock drafts were held to see who might end up where. The enormous attention paid to this event is a boon to the NFL, generating great publicity for the league in the lull between the end of the season and the beginning of preseason. It also has resulted in a booming cottage industry for so-called draft experts and their many publications touting player prospects prior to the draft. And of course, it's a great couple of days for talented college players who can't wait to cash the big NFL paycheck.

Despite all the hype, though, the NFL draft lacked a little of its usual suspense this year. I think you can blame this directly on the success of NFL free agency. So many name players had switched teams in the weeks leading up to the draft that it was hard to get pumped up for the potential contribution of that third-round selection from West Nowhere State. With real free agency in place, you saw fewer teams selecting the legendary "best player available" in the early rounds and more teams selecting players at a particular position to fill a specific void left, in many cases, by a free agency defection. And with only eight rounds, there are still plenty of talented, undrafted players to fill those last roster spots, probably very cheaply, at that.

While the draft may continue to diminish in importance as a method of stocking a team with talent, it was still interesting to watch the drama unfold, as NFL teams select players while the draftniks in the balcony of the Marriott Marquis Hotel ballroom let the teams know, rather vocally in some cases, what they thought of each selection. Sometimes a team's braintrust is right, sometimes the draftniks and the television commentators who talk about a selection being a "reach" are right. That's the beauty of the whole process and why it generates so much interest.

Despite all the uncertainty surrounding the draft, one thing you can count on is the fact that some NFL rookies will make significant contributions to their team's offense during the course of their first season in the league. As a general rule, rookie running backs are more likely than any other player category to make a contribution during their first season (kickers occupy their own special category, since they obviously are guaranteed to put fantasy points on the board if they win the kicking job in training camp, like Lin Elliott did with Dallas and Jason Hanson did with Detroit last year.) For example, Garrison Hearst, whom Phoenix coveted so zealously that they were willing to ship former Pro Bowler Johnny Johnson to the Jets to move up one slot in the draft, should move right into the starting lineup for the Cards, and score plenty of points for his fantasy owners in the upcoming season. On the other hand, it would be very surprising if either Drew Bledsoe or Rick Mirer posted solid fantasy numbers for either the Patriots or Seahawks in 1993, since it takes longer for quarterbacks to develop in the NFL.

When you are doing your homework for your fantasy draft, make a list of those rookies who have a chance to move into a team's offense right away and score points. You should also tailor your strategy with respect to drafting rookies to your league rules. For instance, some leagues *require* that you select at least one rookie for your fantasy roster. If that's the case, carefully measure the depth of the rookie talent pool, keep close tabs on the direction of your fantasy draft, and grab a good rookie before there are none left. If you are using my rules in your league play, you generally want to avoid selecting rookies for your roster until the first or second supplemental draft, unless your preseason research dictates picking a rookie as a third back or a fourth receiver. By the midpoint of the season, you should have a good idea of a rookie's fantasy value. However, if your league is using the expanded roster rules, then risking a selection on an unproven rookie becomes less of a gamble. In fact, under those circumstances the shrewd fantasy owner should stock up on a few rookies later in the draft just in case those players bust out in a big way during the season.

Here then is a team-by-team analysis of the NFL Draft 1993, designed to give you an edge in rounding out your fantasy rosters. This analysis lists those offensive rookies playing fantasy scoring positions by team and their order of selection in the draft by round and total position overall. Brief comments are provided for those rookies who appear to have the best chance to contribute offensively over the course of the upcoming season. Many fantasy owners dismiss rookies out of hand as they prepare their draft lists. However, if you do your homework during the preseason and follow rookie performances early in the season, you can find those rookie diamonds in the rough who will put points on the fantasy scoreboard for you. If history is any indicator, there are several gems out there waiting for the astute fantasy owner.

DRAFT ANALYSIS

The 1993 NFL Draft was not a fantasy owners' delight. For the second year in a row, the draft was generally loaded with talent and depth at every position except the skill positions of critical import to fantasy owners. Defense and beef were the objectives early on, with 14 defensive players selected in the first round as well as six offensive linemen. Fifteen defensive players were selected in the second round. On the other hand, only three running backs were selected in the first round, and only nine overall in the first three rounds. Two quarterbacks were selected with the first and second picks for the first time since 1971, when Jim Plunkett went to the Patriots and Archie Manning to the Saints. After the first two picks, only one more quarterback was selected in the first four rounds. As I mentioned above, rookie quarterbacks usually don't make a major impact statistically their first season in the league. So, after Garrison Hearst and Jerome Bettis, two running backs taken among the top 10 selections of the draft, pickings will be slim among NFL rookies for fantasy owners this season.

ATLANTA FALCONS

Mitch Lyons, TE, Michigan State	(6, 151)
Shannon Baker, WR, Florida State	(8, 205)

Atlanta filled needs on the offensive line by drafting huge offensive tackle Lincoln Kennedy with their first pick and filled other needs on defense as well. This doesn't leave much for fantasy owners here.

BUFFALO BILLS

Russell Copeland, WR, Memphis State	(4, 111)
Willie Harris, WR, Mississippi State	(7, 195)

Both Copeland and Harris have good size, combined with speed, for wide receivers. There might be some playing time available for one or both of them with James Lofton no longer on the depth chart in front of them.

CHICAGO BEARS

Curtis Conway, WR, Southern Cal	(1, 7)
Chris Gedney, TE, Syracuse	(3, 61)

Conway, rated by some as the best wide receiver in the draft, has the speed to be a game-breaker for the Bears, if Jim Harbaugh can get him the ball. Gedney is huge (6'5", 255), and should provide help at one of Da Bears' weaker positions.

CINCINNATI BENGALS

Tony McGee, TE, Michigan	(2, 37)
Doug Pelfrey, K, Kentucky	(8, 202)

McGee, one of the higher-rated tight ends in the draft, was selected to fill the void left by Rodney Holman, who signed with the Lions. Pelfrey will provide competition to Jim Breech in training camp. Otherwise, the Bengals, understandably, drafted defense and more defense.

CLEVELAND BROWNS

In a method that should become commonplace in the future, the Browns used free agency to fill needs in one area, signing Vinny Testaverde and Mark Carrier to bolster their passing game, while drafting to fill needs in other specific areas, defense and the offensive line. This strategy will improve the team on the NFL playing field, but doesn't leave any rookies for fantasy owners.

DALLAS COWBOYS

Kevin Williams, WR, Miami	(2, 46)
Derrick Lassic, RB, Alabama	(4, 94)

Dallas used their first pick to select a player Johnson recruited in his former coaching job at the University of Miami. Johnson was ecstatic, describing Williams as the fastest player at Miami, which means that he might be the fastest receiver in the draft as well as one of the best. Williams should be just the player Dallas needs to replace Kelvin Martin, especially since Coach Johnson immediately tabbed Williams, an excellent kick returner, as his punt-return man for the upcoming season.

DENVER BRONCOS

Glyn Milburn, RB, Stanford	(2, 43)
Jason Elam, K, Hawaii	(3, 70)
Kevin Williams, RB, UCLA	(5, 126)
Melvin Bonner, WR, Baylor	(6, 154)
Clarence Williams, TE, Washington State	(7, 169)
Antonio Kimbrough, WR, Jackson State	(7, 182)
Brian Stablein, WR, Ohio State	(8, 210)

Milburn might be the return man the Broncos have been missing for so many years. Elam, one of the highest-rated kickers in the draft, could put the heat on David Treadwell in preseason. Denver loaded up on wide receivers toward the end of the draft to fill the void left by Mark Jackson's departure to the Giants. One of these three amigos could move right into the lineup for the Broncos. Williams has great speed for a tight end (4.48 in the 40), and could contribute to the Broncos' passing game as well.

DETROIT LIONS

After obtaining All-Pro linebacker Pat Swilling from the Saints just before the draft commenced on Sunday, the Lions continued to emphasize defense in the draft. As a result, there aren't any rookies for fantasy owners here.

GREEN BAY PACKERS

Mark Brunell, QB, Washington	(5, 118)

Not satisfied with winning the Reggie White Sweepstakes prior to the draft, the Packers continued to beef up their defense in NFL Draft 1993. Six of the nine players drafted by the Packers were defensive players. Brunell will compete with Ken O'Brien for the backup job behind Brett Favre.

HOUSTON OILERS

Travis Hannah, WR, Southern Cal	(4, 102)
John Henry Mills, TE, Wake Forest	(5, 131)
Patrick Robinson, WR, Tennessee State	(7, 187)

Hannah is a small, quick receiver who could blend in nicely to the run-and-shoot offense for Houston. Mills has a great football name, but a name does not a valuable fantasy player make.

INDIANAPOLIS COLTS

Sean Dawkins, WR, California	(1, 16)
Roosevelt Potts, RB, NE Louisiana	(2, 49)
Carlos Etheredge, TE, Miami	(6, 157)
Lance Lewis, RB, Nebraska	(7, 184)

Dawkins is the type of big-sized, big-play receiver the Colts would have needed even if they hadn't lost Billy Brooks to Buffalo via free agency. Potts is a highly-rated fullback type (6', 245), who clocked out a touch faster then Jerome Bettis. Otherwise, there isn't much here of interest to fantasy owners.

KANSAS CITY CHIEFS

Darius Turner, RB, Washington	(6, 159)
Danan Hughes, WR, Iowa	(7, 186)

The trade for Joe Montana overshadowed all draft-day activity by the Chiefs. By the time they got around to drafting some offense, it was late in the draft. Turner could provide help at the big back position (5'11", 230), especially if the Chiefs trade Christian Okoye.

LOS ANGELES RAIDERS

Billy Joe Hobert, QB, Washington State	(3, 58)
Orlando Truitt, WR, Mississippi State	(5, 125)
Greg Robinson, RB, Northeast Louisiana	(8, 208)

Hobert has size and ability, but with the crowded situation at quarterback (Hostetler, Marinovich, and Evans, with free agent Schroeder not expected back), Hobert is a project for the Raiders' future. Truitt is an underclassman with size and speed who could help the Raiders at wide receiver. Robinson was one of the fastest backs in the draft (4.38 in the 40), but, like Hobert, he also must contend with a crowd at his position.

LOS ANGELES RAMS

Jerome Bettis, RB, Notre Dame	(1, 10)
Troy Drayton, TE, Penn State	(2, 39)
Russell White, RB, California	(3, 73)
Sean LaChapelle, WR, UCLA	(5, 122)

The Rams more than filled their need for a running back created by the departure of free agent Robert Delpino by selecting two running backs early in the draft. Bettis (5'11", 245) was generally rated the best fullback in the draft. He should get plenty of playing time in the upcoming season, and it would not be a surprise if he moves Cleveland Gary aside as the Rams' designated scorer at the goal line. Russell White was one of the highest-rated backs in the draft as well, and should contribute to the Rams' running game. Drayton is a highly rated tight end for those of you who need tight ends on your roster.

MIAMI DOLPHINS

O. J. McDuffie, WR, Penn State	(1, 25)
Terry Kirby, RB, Virginia	(3, 78)

The Dolphins filled a couple of needs with their offensive selections in the draft. McDuffie will help bolster the receiving corps, which is unsettled while the status of Mark Clayton remains unresolved. Kirby has the size to complement Mark Higgs in the Dolphins' backfield and should see lots of playing time, especially if Bobby Humphrey does not return to the Dolphins.

MINNESOTA VIKINGS

Robert Smith, RB, Ohio State	(1, 21)
Qadry Ismail, WR, Syracuse	(2, 52)
Gino Torretta, QB, Miami	(7, 192)

The Vikings had a solid draft from an offensive perspective. Robert Smith, an underclassman, is a great athlete with speed (4.44 in the 40) who will help if Roger Craig falters. Ismail, the Missile, is not as famous as his brother, the Rocket, but he's almost as talented. He will help the aging wide receiver corps in Minnesota. Torretta hopes to break with the past when it comes to the success, or lack of same, of former Heisman Trophy winners at the quarterback position in the NFL. (Since 1984, Doug Flutie, Vinny Testaverde, Andre Ware, and Ty Detmer have won the Heisman Trophy, and there isn't an NFL success in the bunch.) However, Toretta will most likely be no more than Jim McMahon's backup in 1993.

NEW ENGLAND PATRIOTS

Drew Bledsoe, QB, Washington State	(1, 1)
Vincent Brisby, WR, NE Louisiana	(2, 57)
Scott Sisson, K, Georgia Tech	(5, 113)
Richard Griffith, TE, Arizona	(5, 138)
Troy Brown, KR, Marshall	(8, 198)

Bledsoe is the big pick here. New head coach Bill Parcells says that they are not going to rush him into the starting lineup and that the Pats will play him when he's ready. On the other hand, they will not be disappointed if Bledsoe is ready on Opening Day. The strong-armed Bledsoe will play in 1993. How much, and how effectively, is another story.

NEW ORLEANS SAINTS

Irv Smith, TE, Notre Dame	(1, 20)
Lorenzo Neal, RB, Fresno State	(4, 89)
Derek Brown, RB, Nebraska	(4, 109)

The Saints filled a gaping need with Smith, who was generally regarded as the highest-rated tight end in the draft. The Saints continued to stockpile running backs by taking Neal and Brown with their fourth-round picks. They could help the Saints' running game, but probably not right away, with Hilliard, Dunbar, and Muster ahead of them.

NEW YORK GIANTS

Todd Peterson, K, Georgia	(7, 177)

Peterson will be thrown into the mix with Matt Bahr and Ken Willis in the preseason battle for the kicker's job. Otherwise, the Giants used free agency, not the draft, to bolster their offense.

NEW YORK JETS

Fred Baxter, TE, Auburn	(5, 115)
Adrian Murrell, RB, West Virginia	(5, 120)
Kenny Shedd, WR, Northern Iowa	(5, 129)
Richie Anderson, RB, Penn State	(6, 144)
Craig Hentrich, K, Notre Dame	(8, 200)

The Jets could have earned the title as the most improved team in football with all the free agent moves they made prior to the draft. But GM Dick Steinberg made some masterful moves on Draft Day 1993 that put the icing on the cake. Giving the league the impression that the Jets were interested in drafting Garrison Hearst by expressing interest in Cincinnati's Derrick Fenner and Seattle's Chris Warren, he enticed the Cardinals to give up Johnny Johnson in return for switching draft places with the Jets in the first round. This allowed the Cards to draft Hearst. On the other hand, the Jets eliminated their need to draft a running back while at the same time drafting the player they really wanted in the first place, Florida State's Marvin Jones, for their defense. The result of all this intrigue doesn't leave much here in the way of rookie talent for fantasy owners, although the availability of both Murrell and Shedd in the fifth round was a pleasant surprise.

PHILADELPHIA EAGLES

Victor Bailey, WR, Missouri	(2, 50)
Joey Mickey, TE, Oklahoma	(7, 190)

Bailey has nice size (6'2", 200) and speed (4.52 in the 40) for a wide receiver and could provide capable support for Fred Barnett and Calvin Williams.

PHOENIX CARDINALS

Garrison Hearst, RB, Georgia	(1, 3)
Ronald Moore, RB, Pittsburg State	(4, 87)
Steve Anderson, WR, Grambling	(8, 215)

The tremendously talented Hearst, generally considered the best running back in the draft even though an underclassman, could easily win fantasy rookie of the year honors. He should step into the Cardinals' lineup right away, and, behind the improved Cardinals' offensive line, impress from Week One. He'd be a steal as a third back on Draft Day 1993.

PITTSBURGH STEELERS

Andre Hastings, WR, Georgia	(3, 76)
Craig Keith, TE, Lenoir–Rhyne	(7, 189)
Alex Van Pelt, QB, Pittsburgh	(8, 216)

Hastings is another underclassman who could make an impression at wide receiver for the Steelers in 1993. Van Pelt is a local hero in Pittsburgh, but not for fantasy owners generally.

SAN DIEGO CHARGERS

Natrone Means, RB, North Carolina	(2, 41)
Walter Dunson, WR, Middle Tenn. State	(5, 134)
Trent Green, QB, Indiana	(8, 222)

The Means justified the ends here, as San Diego traded up to grab a back to replace Rod Bernstine in the Chargers' backfield. Means has the size (5'10", 230) and speed (4.55 in the 40) to help Marion Butts shoulder the load in the Chargers' rushing game. Green was two picks away from becoming Mr. Irrelevant (the last pick in the draft). He wins the award as far as fantasy owners are concerned for the upcoming season.

SAN FRANCISCO 49ERS

Elvis Grbac, QB, Michigan	(8, 219)

It seems like someone from a different area of the country spots Elvis at least once a week, depending upon which issue of the tabloids you read at the checkout counter. One thing's for sure though, there won't be too many sightings of the Wolverine Elvis lofting passes downfield for the 49ers in the upcoming season.

SEATTLE SEAHAWKS

Rick Mirer, QB, Notre Dame	(1, 2)
Terrence Warren, WR, Hampton	(5, 114)

Bitterly disappointed that the Patriots had drafted close-to-home-boy Bledsoe, the Seahawks went with what they hope is the next best thing in Rick Mirer. Barring unforeseen circumstance, Mirer should start right from the first game. Fantasy owners with a little riverboat gambler in their soul might grab Mirer as a backup quarterback if the draft hour is late and a roster spot is still open.

TAMPA BAY BUCCANEERS

Lamar Thomas, WR, Miami	(3, 60)
Rudy Harris, RB, Clemson	(4, 91)
Horace Copeland, WR, Miami	(4, 104)
Tyree Davis, WR, Central Arkansas	(7, 176)
Darrick Branch, WR, Hawaii	(8, 220)
Daron Alcorn, K, Akron	(8, 224)

It's pretty obvious what Tampa thought one of its weaknesses was going into the draft. The Bucs used free agency to shore up their defense, while drafting to fill offensive holes. Thomas is a potential star who holds the Miami school record for career receptions—144. Thomas's college teammate Copeland, who recorded a remarkable 43½ inch vertical leap for the NFL scouts prior to the draft, also has the ability to contribute to the Bucs' offense. Daron Alcorn was the real Mr. Irrelevant in the draft, the last player chosen in this, the first eight-round draft in the era of free agency. Alcorn may put some heat on Eddie Murray in preseason.

WASHINGTON REDSKINS

Reggie Brooks, RB, Notre Dame	(2, 45)
Frank Wycheck, TE, Maryland	(6, 160)

The Redskins got lucky with their second pick in the draft, as Brooks dropped down lower than expected. One of the highest-rated backs in the draft, Brooks combines the power of an inside runner with the speed of an outside runner (4.45 in the 40). He will push Ricky Ervins hard for a significant role in the Redskins' running game. With Joe Gibbs, who hated to play rookies, retired, Brooks might even get a fair chance to log some playing time.

NINE

THE FINAL WORD

SO, THERE YOU HAVE IT: more information about pro football than you ever thought reasonably necessary. I hope everything you have just read will help you as you take the plunge into the exciting world of fantasy football. And if you are hesitating about joining a league, let me encourage you once again. The game is exciting and fun, and will open up a whole new view of the world of NFL football to you.

Football fans, fantasy or otherwise, should look forward to the 1993 season with great anticipation. Cowboys fans, in seclusion during the 1980s, will root openly for America's Team as it begins its defense of the NFL championship. (With their victory in Super Bowl XXVII, the Cowboys join the Steelers, 49ers, Redskins, and Raiders as the only NFL franchises with at least three Super Bowl victories.) Cowboys fans will also root for their team to dominate the last decade of the twentieth century like it dominated the 1970s, during which it made five Super Bowl appearances. Football fans will watch to see if the AFC can produce a Super Bowl representative strong enough and talented enough to break the NFC's Super Bowl winning streak, which now stands at nine games. (Before football fans clamor for the abolition of the American Football Conference, remember that these things appear to go in cycles. Football fans weren't saying "Break up the NFC" when the AFC won 11 of the 13 Super Bowls from Super Bowl III to Super Bowl XV. Ironically, Dallas accounted for the only 2 NFC victories during that time.)

Many players will reach some significant personal milestones in the NFL in 1993. Jerry Rice, who passed Steve Largent's mark for most career touchdown receptions in Week Fourteen of the 1992 season, will try to catch the all-time touchdown leader, Jim Brown. Brown scored 126 career touchdowns, 1 more than Walter Payton. Rice has scored 108 touchdowns in his illustrious career.

Miami's Dan Marino, with a career total of 290 touchdown passes, needs 1 more to break his tie with Colts legend Johnny Unitas for second place on the all-time list, and 53 to pass Fran Tarkenton's record total of 342 touchdown passes. Marino has now thrown 4 touchdown passes in one game 17 times during his career, doing so in Week Seven of the 1992 season against New England, and needs just one more game with 4 touchdown passes to set the new NFL record in that category.

Continuing in the quarterback department, one of the game's great players, Joe Montana, needs 71 completions to join Fran Tarkenton, Dan Fouts, and Dan Marino as the only three players in NFL history with 3,000 completions.

Marcus Allen needs 2 touchdowns to reach a career total of 100, and Eric Dickerson needs just 4. Speaking of scoring, Chiefs kicker Nick Lowery ended the season with 1,367 career points, seventh on the NFL's career scoring list. He needs just 14 points to move past Jim Bakken, and 16 points to move past Mark Mosely into fifth place. Fourth place, in the person of Jim Turner (1,439 points), and third, a spot held by Pat Leahy (1,470 points), are also within his reach in 1993. Lowery has now scored 100 points in 10 separate seasons, adding to his NFL record, and has reached the century mark in five consecutive seasons and nine of the last 10. Morten Andersen is right on Lowery's tail, with seven 100-point seasons, tying NFL great Jan Stenerud for second place in this category.

Of course, new stars will emerge in 1993 to challenge the old ones, and questions in the inquiring minds of fantasy owners everywhere will be answered. Are new NFL stars like Barry Foster, Ricky Watters, Brett Favre, and Stan Humphries for real, or will they join the swollen ranks of fantasy flashes in the pan? Will an old star like Joe Montana find playing time with the 49ers, or will he move to a new team to polish up his final career stats and maybe add one more Super Bowl ring to his collection? Will Emmitt Smith become the first player since Earl Campbell (1978–80), and only the fourth player in NFL history, to win three consecutive rushing titles? Can Sterling Sharpe become the first player in NFL history with back-to-back 100-reception seasons? Which kicker will improve his number of field goal attempts by a substantial margin and jump to the top of the fantasy scoring list? Will Super Bowl XXVIII offer more suspense than Bud Bowl VI? And, finally, will your fantasy team, carefully crafted after studying all of the information in this book, dominate the opposition and charge to victory at the end of the season? I certainly hope so. Good luck to everyone in the upcoming fantasy season.

• A P P E N D I X   A •

SAMPLE FORMS
FOR
REPORTING WEEKLY RESULTS

INTEREST IN YOUR FANTASY LEAGUE will suffer without some kind of written summary distributed to its members. The commissioner of your fantasy league can use the following forms as a model to report your league's weekly action. If your league uses my basic rules of play, then you need only keep track of the points scored by each team. The first model form reports the cumulative league results under the basic version of my rules, while the second form reports the action in a league using the intermediate or expanded-roster rules. If your commissioner has any free time on his hands, and any creativity, he might even whip up a short commentary on the week's action. But make sure someone in your league puts something together to keep track of the standings during the season.

You should try to pick a team name that is creative, and maybe

Basic Version
"————" League Standings
Week Thirteen

Team Name	This Week's Scores	Total Points	High Points (Number of Times)
Markie de Sades	46	495	1
Tall Ar-Kays	32	471	1
Long Neck Buds	45	463	1
Coach's Road Holes	42	450	2
Valis Cowboys	41	426	2
The Duffers	28	413	2
Nit-Whits	27	409	0
Broadway Bill	34	357	0
High Schoolers	13	313	0
Darkman	23	299	0
Ten-Minute Ricers	33	298	0

Intermediate or Expanded-Roster Version
"————" League Standings
Week Thirteen

Team Name	Record	Total Points	Streak
Markie de Sades	10–3	561	W4
Tall Ar-Kays	9–4	541	W2
Home Rekkers	9–4	540	L1
Valis Cowboys	7–6	492	W2
Broadway Bill	6–7	491	L1
Nit-Whits	4–9	449	L2
Ten-Minute Ricers	4–9	390	W1
The Duffers	3–10	313	L4

High Points For Week Thirteen: Ricers with 52

even funny. You can do a play on words for your own name, or the name of some players on your team, once you've finished the draft. Anyone can be the New York Giants or the Green Bay Packers. But fantasy owners create their own teams, so why not try to have a little fun with your team name? Use your own name. Call your Team Ed's Packers, or the Chicago Smiths. If your wife's name is Alice, you can be the Alice Cowboys. Go ahead, it's your team; you can call it whatever you want. And if the name you come up with isn't as witty as you think it is, I'm sure your fellow owners will be the first to let you know.

SUGGESTED WEEKLY SCHEDULE FOR EIGHT TEAMS

WEEK ONE:	1 v. 2,	3 v. 4,	5 v. 6,	7 v. 8
WEEK TWO:	1 v. 3,	2 v. 4,	5 v. 7,	6 v. 8
WEEK THREE:	1 v. 4,	2 v. 3,	5 v. 8,	6 v. 7
WEEK FOUR:	1 v. 5,	2 v. 6,	3 v. 7,	4 v. 8
WEEK FIVE:	1 v. 6,	2 v. 5,	3 v. 8,	4 v. 7
WEEK SIX:	1 v. 7,	2 v. 8,	3 v. 5,	4 v. 6
WEEK SEVEN:	1 v. 8,	2 v. 7,	3 v. 6,	4 v. 5
WEEK EIGHT:	1 v. 2,	3 v. 4,	5 v. 6,	7 v. 8
WEEK NINE:	1 v. 3,	2 v. 4,	5 v. 7,	6 v. 8
WEEK TEN:	1 v. 4,	2 v. 3,	5 v. 8,	6 v. 7
WEEK ELEVEN:	1 v. 5,	2 v. 6,	3 v. 7,	4 v. 8
WEEK TWELVE:	1 v. 6,	2 v. 5,	3 v. 8,	4 v. 7
WEEK THIRTEEN:	1 v. 7,	2 v. 8,	3 v. 5,	4 v. 6
WEEK FOURTEEN:	1 v. 8,	2 v. 7,	3 v. 6,	4 v. 5
WEEK FIFTEEN:	1 v. 2,	3 v. 4,	5 v. 6,	7 v. 8
WEEK SIXTEEN:	1 v. 3,	2 v. 4,	5 v. 7,	6 v. 8
WEEK SEVENTEEN:	1 v. 4,	2 v. 3,	5 v. 8,	6 v. 7
WEEK EIGHTEEN:	1 v. 5,	2 v. 6,	3 v. 7,	4 v. 8

As a result of this schedule, the teams matched up in the first three weeks of the season will play each other three times. This imbalance is unavoidable due to the NFL's 18-week season in 1993.

• A P P E N D I X C •

DANNY SHERIDAN'S
OFFICIAL FANTASY STATISTICS
FOR THE 1992 SEASON

PLAYERS IN ALPHABETICAL ORDER

Running Backs/Receivers

Player	Standard Total	Bonus Points	Total Points	Player	Standard Total	Bonus Points	Total Points
Allen, Marcus (Raiders)	15		15	Broussard, Steve (Falcons)	9		9
Allen, Terry (Vikings)	84		84				
Anderson, Gary (Bucs)	6		6	Brown, Ivory Lee (Cardinals)	12		12
Anderson, Neal (Bears)	48		48				
Anderson, Willie (Rams)	21		21	Brown, Tim (Raiders)	21	6	27
Arbuckle, Charles (Colts)	3		3	Brown, Tony (Oilers)	6		6
				Bunch, Jarrod (Giants)	21		21
Armstrong, Tyji (Bucs)	3	3	6	Burkett, Chris (Jets)	3		3
Bailey, Johnny (Cardinals)	9		9	Butts, Marion (Chargers)	24		24
				Byars, Keith (Eagles)	12		12
Baker, Stephen (Giants)	6		6	Byner, Earnest (Redskins)	39	3¹	42
Ball, Eric (Bengals)	18		18	Calloway, Chris (Giants)	3		3
Banks, Fred (Dolphins)	9		9	Campbell, Jeff (Lions)	3	3	6
Barnett, Fred (Eagles)	18	3	21	Carrier, Mark (Bucs)	12		12
Barnett, Tim (Chiefs)	12	3	15	Carroll, Wesley (Saints)	9	3	12
Barrett, Reggie (Lions)	3		3	Carpenter, Rob (Jets)	3		3
Baty, Greg (Dolphins)	3		3	Carter, Anthony (Vikings)	6		6
Bavaro, Mark (Browns)	6		6	Carter, Cris (Vikings)	18		18
Baxter, Brad (Jets)	36		36	Carter, Dexter (49ers)	3		3
Beach, Pat (Eagles)	6		6				
Beach, Sanjay (Packers)	3		3	Carter, Pat (Rams)	9		9
				Cash, Keith (Chiefs)	6		6
Beebe, Don (Bills)	6	6	12	Cash, Kerry (Colts)	9		9
Bell, Nick (Raiders)	18	6	24	Centers, Larry (Cardinals)	6		6
Bernstine, Rod (Chargers)	24		24				
				Chadwick, Jeff (Rams)	9		9
Bieniemy, Eric (Chargers)	18		18	Chaffee, Pat (Jets)	6		6
				Clark, Gary (Redskins)	15		15
Birden, J. J. (Chiefs)	9	3	12	Clark, Louis (Seahawks)	3		3
Blades, Brian (Seahawks)	3		3	Clayton, Mark (Dolphins)	9		9
Brennan, Brian (Bengals/Chargers)	3		3	Coates, Ben (Patriots)	9		9
				Cobb, Reggie (Bucs)	54		54
Brooks, Bill (Colts)	3		3	Cook, Marv (Patriots)	6		6
Brooks, Robert (Packers)	3		3				

Running Backs/Receivers *(Continued)*

Player	Standard Total	Bonus Points	Total Points	Player	Standard Total	Bonus Points	Total Points
Cooper, Adrian (Steelers)	9		9	Green, Paul (Seahawks)	3		3
Craig, Roger (Vikings)	24		24	Green, Willie (Lions)	15	6	21
Cross, Howard (Giants)	6		6	Hall, Ron (Bucs)	12		12
Culver, Rodney (Colts)	48		48	Hampton, Rodney (Giants)	84	6	90
Davis, Kenneth (Bills)	36	6	42	Harmon, Ron (Chargers)	21		21
Davis, Wendell (Bears)	6		6	Harper, Alvin (Cowboys)	12		12
Davis, Willie (Chiefs)	9	6	15	Harris, Jackie (Packers)	6		6
Dawsey, Lawrence (Bucs)	3		3	Harris, Leonard (Oilers)	6		6
Delpino, Robert (Rams)	3		3	Hawkins, Courtney (Bucs)	6		6
Dickerson, Eric (Raiders)	15		15	Hayes, Jonathan (Chiefs)	6		6
Drewrey, Willie (Bucs)	6		6	Haynes, Michael (Falcons)	30	6	36
Dunbar, Vaughn (Saints)	18		18	Henderson, Keith (Vikings)	9		9
Duncan, Curtis (Oilers)	3		3	Hester, Jessie (Colts)	3		3
Duper, Mark (Dolphins)	21	3	24	Heyward, Craig (Saints)	18		18
Early, Quinn (Saints)	15	3	18	Higgs, Mark (Dolphins)	42		42
Edmunds, Ferrell (Dolphins)	3		3	Hill, Drew (Falcons)	9		9
Edwards, Anthony (Cardinals)	3		3	Hill, Randal (Cardinals)	9		9
Ellard, Henry (Rams)	9		9	Hilliard, Dalton (Saints)	30		30
Ervins, Ricky (Redskins)	12		12	Hoard, Leroy (Browns)	3		3
Fenner, Derrick (Bengals)	45		45	Hoge, Merril (Steelers)	3		3
Fina, John (Bills)	3		3	Holman, Rodney (Bengals)	6		6
Foster, Barry (Steelers)	66	6	72	Horton, Ethan (Raiders)	6		6
Frerotte, Mitch (Bills)	6		6	Howard, Desmond (Redskins)		6[3]	6
Fryar, Irving (Patriots)	12	3	15	Humphrey, Bobby (Dolphins)	9		9
Galbraith, Scott (Browns)	3		3	Ingram, Mark (Giants)	3		3
Gardner, Carwell (Bills)	12		12	Irvin, Michael (Cowboys)	21	3	24
Gary, Cleveland (Rams)	51		51	Jackson, John (Cardinals)	3		3
Gash, Sam (Patriots)	6		6	Jackson, Keith (Dolphins)	15		15
Gault, Willie (Raiders)	12		12	Jackson, Mark (Broncos)	24	3	27
Givins, Ernest (Oilers)	30		30	Jackson, Michael (Browns)	21	3	24
Glover, Andrew (Raiders)	3		3	Jefferson, Shawn (Chargers)	6		6
Graddy, Sam (Raiders)	3		3	Jeffires, Haywood (Oilers)	27		27
Graham, Jeff (Steelers)	3		3				
Gray, Mel (Lions)		12[2]	12				
Green, Eric (Steelers)	6		6				
Green, Gaston (Broncos)	12	6	18				
Green, Harold (Bengals)	12		12				
Green, Mark (Bears)	12		12				

Running Backs/Receivers *(Continued)*

Player	Standard Total	Bonus Points	Total Points	Player	Standard Total	Bonus Points	Total Points
Jennings, Keith (Bears)	3		3	McMurtry, Greg (Patriots)	3	3	6
Jennings, Stanford (Bucs)	3		3				
Johnson, Anthony (Colts)	9	3	12	McNair, Todd (Chiefs)	9		9
Johnson, Brad (Vikings)	3		3	Meggett, Dave (Giants)	6	6[8]	12
Johnson, Johnny (Cardinals)	36		36	Metcalf, Eric (Browns)	21	12[9]	33
				Metzelaars, Pete (Bills)	18	3	21
Johnson, Reggie (Broncos)	3		3	Miller, Anthony (Chargers)	21	9[10]	30
Johnson, Vance (Broncos)	6		6	Mills, Ernie (Steelers)	9		9
Johnston, Daryl (Cowboys)	6		6	Mitchell, Brian (Redskins)		6[11]	6
Jones, Brent (49ers)	12		12	Mitchell, Johnny (Jets)	3		3
Jones, Ernie (Cardinals)	12	3	15	Monk, Art (Redskins)	9		9
Jones, Hassan (Vikings)	12		12	Moore, Herman (Lions)	12	6	18
Jones, Tony (Browns)	3		3	Moore, Rob (Jets)	12		12
Jones, Tony (Falcons)	3		3	Morgan, Anthony (Bears)	6	3	9
Jordan, Steve (Vikings)	6	3	9	Muster, Brad (Bears)	24		24
Jorden, Tim (Steelers)	6		6	Novacek, Jay (Cowboys)	18		18
Junkin, Trey (Seahawks)	3		3	Okoye, Christian (Chiefs)	36		36
Kane, Tommy (Seahawks)	9		9	Orr, Terry (Redskins)	9		9
Kinchen, Todd (Rams)		12[4]	12	Paige, Tony (Dolphins)	9		9
Lang, David (Rams)	33	3	36	Perriman, Brett (Lions)	12		12
Langhorne, Reggie (Colts)	3		3	Phillips, Jason (Falcons)	3		3
				Pickens, Carl (Bengals)	3	6[12]	9
Lee, Amp (49ers)	18		18	Price, Jim (Rams)	6		6
Lewis, Darren (Bears)	24	6[5]	30	Pritchard, Mike (Falcons)	15		15
Lewis, Greg (Broncos)	24		24	Proehl, Ricky (Cardinals)	9	3	12
Lewis, Nate (Chargers)	12	3	15	Query, Jeff (Bengals)	9	3	12
Lofton, James (Bills)	18		18	Rathman, Tom (49ers)	42		42
Logan, Marc (49ers)	6		6	Reed, Andre (Bills)	9		9
Mack, Kevin (Browns)	36		36	Rice, Jerry (49ers)	36	3	39
Marshall, Arthur (Broncos)	6	6[6]	12	Richards, Curvin (Cowboys)	6		6
Martin, Eric (Saints)	15	3	18	Rison, Andre (Falcons)	33	3	36
Martin, Kelvin (Cowboys)	9	12[7]	21	Rivers, Reggie (Broncos)	21		21
Martin, Tony (Dolphins)	6	3	9	Russell, Leonard (Patriots)	12		12
Mathis, Terance (Jets)	15	3	18	Sanders, Barry (Lions)	57	6	63
McAfee, Fred (Saints)	6		6	Sanders, Deion (Falcons)	3	12[13]	15
McCaffrey, Ed (Giants)	15		15				
McDowell, Anthony (Bucs)	6	3	9	Sanders, Ricky (Redskins)	9	3	12
McGee, Tim (Bengals)	9		9	Schultz, William (Colts)	3		3

Running Backs/Receivers (Continued)

Player	Standard Total	Bonus Points	Total Points	Player	Standard Total	Bonus Points	Total Points
Sharpe, Shannon (Broncos)	6		6	Tillman, Cedric (Broncos)	3	3	6
Sharpe, Sterling (Packers)	39	6	45	Timpson, Michael (Patriots)	3		3
Sherman, Heath (Eagles)	33	3	36	Toon, Al (Jets)	6		6
Sherrard, Mike (49ers)		6[14]	6	Turner, Kevin (Patriots)	6		6
Sikahema, Vai (Eagles)		6[15]	6	Turner, Odessa (49ers)	6		6
Slaughter, Webster (Oilers)	12		12	Vaughn, Jon (Patriots)	6	6[16]	12
Small, Torrance (Saints)	9		9	Verdin, Clarence (Colts)		12[17]	12
Smith, Emmitt (Cowboys)	111	6	117	Waddle, Tom (Bears)	12	3	15
Smith, Steve (Raiders)	3		3	Walker, Derrick (Chargers)	6		6
Smith, Tony (Falcons)	12		12	Walker, Herschel (Eagles)	54		54
Stegall, Milt (Bengals)	3		3	Warren, Chris (Seahawks)	18		18
Stephens, John (Patriots)	12		12	Watters, Ricky (49ers)	60		60
Stone, Dwight (Steelers)	9		9	White, Lorenzo (Oilers)	45	3	48
Sydney, Harry (Packers)	15		15	Williams, Calvin (Eagles)	21		21
Taylor, John (49ers)	9	3	12	Williams, Harvey (Chiefs)	6		6
Taylor, Kitrick (Packers)	3		3	Williams, Jamie (49ers)	3		3
Thomas, Thurman (Bills)	63		63	Williams, John L. (Seahawks)	12		12
Thompson, Anthony (Cardinals)	6		6	Wolfley, Ron (Browns)	3		3
Thompson, Craig (Bengals)	6		6	Word, Barry (Chiefs)	24		24
Thompson, Darrell (Packers)	15		15	Workman, Vince (Packers)	12		12
Thompson, Leroy (Steelers)	6		6	Wright, Alexander (Cowboys/Raiders)	6		6
Tice, Mike (Vikings)	3		3				

[1]Byner threw a 41-yard touchdown pass in Week Fifteen.

[2]Gray returned a punt 58 yards for a touchdown in Week Two, and a kickoff 89 yards for a touchdown in Week Four.

[3]Howard returned a punt 55 yards for a touchdown in Week Two.

[4]Kinchen returned a punt 61 yards for a touchdown and another 35 yards for a touchdown, both in Week Seventeen.

[5]Lewis returned a kickoff 97 yards for a touchdown in Week Ten.

[6]Marshall threw an 81-yard touchdown pass in Week Fourteen.

[7]Martin returned a punt 79 yards for a touchdown in Week One, and another punt 74 yards for a touchdown in Week Eleven.

[8]Meggett returned a kickoff 92 yards for a touchdown in Week Twelve.

[9]Metcalf returned a punt 75 yards for a touchdown in Week Thirteen.

[10]Miller recovered a fumble in the end zone for a touchdown in Week Thirteen.

[11]Mitchell returned a punt 84 yards for a touchdown in Week Nine.

[12]Pickens returned a punt 95 yards for a touchdown in Week Three.

[13]Sanders returned a kickoff 99 yards for a touchdown in Week Two, and another kickoff 73 yards for a touchdown in Week Twelve.

[14]Sherrard returned a fumble 39 yards for a touchdown in Week Nine.

[15]Sikahema returned a punt 87 yards for a touchdown in Week Twelve.

[16]Vaughn returned a kickoff 100 yards for a touchdown in Week Sixteen.

[17]Verdin returned a punt 84 yards for a touchdown in Week Eight, and another punt 53 yards for a touchdown in Week Eleven.

Quarterbacks

Player	Passing TD Point Totals	Bonus Points (Includes Rushing Touchdowns)	Total Points	Player	Passing TD Point Totals	Bonus Points (Includes Rushing Touchdowns)	Total Points
Aikman, Troy (Cowboys)	69	9	78	Graham, Kent (Giants)	3		3
Bono, Steve (49ers)	6		6	Harbaugh, Jim (Bears)	39	9	48
Brister, Bubby (Steelers)	6		6	Hebert, Bobby (Saints)	57	9	66
Carlson, Cody (Oilers)	27	6	33	Herrmann, Mark (Colts)	3		3
Carlson, Jeff (Patriots)	3		3	Hodson, Tom (Patriots)	6	3	9
Chandler, Chris (Cardinals)	45	12	57	Hollas, Donald (Bengals)	6		6
Conklin, Cary (Redskins)	3		3	Hostetler, Jeff (Giants)	24	18	42
Cunningham, Randall (Eagles)	57	36	93	Humphries, Stan (Chargers)	48	30	78
DeBerg, Steve (Bucs)	9		9	Kelly, Jim (Bills)	69	15	84
Elway, John (Broncos)	30	18	48	Klingler, David (Bengals)	9	3	12
Esiason, Boomer (Bengals)	33		33	Kosar, Bernie (Browns)	24	3	27
Evans, Vince (Raiders)	12		12	Kramer, Erik (Lions)	12	6	18
Everett, Jim (Rams)	66	3	69	Krieg, Dave (Chiefs)	45	24	69
Favre, Brett (Packers)	54	12	66	Maddox, Tommy (Broncos)	15		15
Gannon, Rich (Vikings)	36	3	39	Majkowski, Don (Packers)	6		6
Gelbaugh, Stan (Seahawks)	18		18	Marino, Dan (Dolphins)	72	6	78
George, Jeff (Colts)	21	9	30	Marinovich, Todd (Raiders)	-15	6	21

Quarterbacks *(Continued)*

Player	Passing TD Point Totals	Bonus Points (Includes Rushing Touchdowns)	Total Points	Player	Passing TD Point Totals	Bonus Points (Includes Rushing Touchdowns)	Total Points
McMahon, Jim (Eagles)	3		3	Salisbury, Sean (Vikings)	15		15
Millen, Hugh (Patriots)	24		24	Schroeder, Jay (Raiders)	33		33
Miller, Chris (Falcons)	45	6	51	Simms, Phil (Giants)	15		15
Montana, Joe (49ers)	6		6	Stouffer, Kelly (Seahawks)	9		9
Moon, Warren (Oilers)	54	9	63	Testaverde, Vinny (Bucs)	42	18	60
Nagle, Browning (Jets)	21		21	Tolliver, Billy Joe (Falcons)	15		15
O'Brien, Ken (Jets)	15	3	18	Tomczak, Mike (Browns)	21		21
O'Donnell, Neil (Steelers)	39	6	45	Tupa, Tom (Colts)	3		3
Pagel, Mike (Rams)	3		3	Ware, Andre (Lions)	9		9
Peete, Rodney (Lions)	27	9	36	Willis, Peter Tom (Bears)	12	3	15
Philcox, Todd (Browns)	9	6	15	Wilson, Wade (Falcons)	39	3	42
Rypien, Mark (Redskins)	51	3	54	Young, Steve (49ers)	75	30	105
				Zolak, Scott (Patriots)	6	3	9

Kickers

Player	Standard Total (Field Goals + PATs)	Bonus Points	Total Points	Player	Standard Total (Field Goals + PATs)	Bonus Points	Total Points
Andersen, Morten (Saints)	120	21	141	Davis, Greg (Cardinals)	67	6	73
Anderson, Gary (Steelers)	113	6	119	Del Greco, Al (Oilers)	104	9	113
Bahr, Matt (Giants)	77	3	80	Elliott, Lin (Cowboys)	119	18	137
Baumann, Charlie (Patriots)	55		55	Hanson, Jason (Lions)	93	9	102
Biasucci, Dean (Colts)	72	15	87	Jacke, Chris (Packers)	96	15	111
Blanchard, Cary (Jets)	65	6	71	Jaeger, Jeff (Raiders)	73	15	88
Breech, Jim (Bengals)	88	3	91	Johnson, Norm (Falcons)	93	24	117
Butler, Kevin (Bears)	91	3	94	Kasay, John (Seahawks)	56		56
Carney, John (Chargers)	113	15	128	Lohmiller, Chip (Redskins)	120	12	132
Christie, Steve (Bills)	115	15	130	Lowery, Nick (Chiefs)	105	6	111
Cofer, Mike (49ers)	107	6	113	Murray, Ed (Chiefs/Bucs)	28	6	34

Kickers *(Continued)*

Player	Standard Total (Field Goals + PATs)	Bonus Points	Total Points	Player	Standard Total (Field Goals + PATs)	Bonus Points	Total Points
Reveiz, Fuad (Vikings)	102	12	114	Treadwell, David (Broncos)	88	6	94
Ruzek, Roger (Eagles)	88	12	100	Willis, Ken (Bucs/Giants)	57	3	60
Staurovsky, Jason (Jets)	15		15	Zendejas, Tony (Rams)	83	6	89
Stover, Matt (Browns)	92	3	95				
Stoyanovich, Pete (Dolphins)	124	12	136				

Defensive Teams

Team	Standard Total	Safeties	Total Points	Team	Standard Total	Safeties	Total Points
Atlanta	18		18	Miami	18		18
Buffalo	18	1	20	Minnesota	48	1	50
Chicago	12		12	New England	36		36
Cincinnati	24		24	New Orleans	36		36
Cleveland	30		30	NY Giants	12		12
Dallas	30	1	32	NY Jets	18	1	20
Denver	12		12	Philadelphia	32		32
Detroit	30		30	Phoenix	20		20
Green Bay	18		18	Pittsburgh	18		18
Houston	24	1	26	San Diego	6	3	12
Indianapolis	18		18	San Francisco	18		18
Kansas City	66		66	Seattle	6		6
LA Raiders	12	1	14	Tampa Bay	24		24
LA Rams	18	1	20	Washington	30		30

PLAYERS RANKED IN ORDER OF SCORING

Running Backs

Player	Points	Rank	Player	Points	Rank
Smith, Emmitt (Cowboys)	111	1	Culver, Rodney (Colts)	48	T11
Hampton, Rodney (Giants)	90	2	White, Lorenzo (Oilers)	48	T11
Allen, Terry (Vikings)	84	3	Fenner, Derrick (Bengals)	45	14
Foster, Barry (Steelers)	72	4	Byner, Earnest (Redskins)	42	T15
Sanders, Barry (Lions)	63	T5	Davis, Kenneth (Bills)	42	T15
Thomas, Thurman (Bills)	63	T5	Higgs, Mark (Dolphins)	42	T15
Watters, Ricky (49ers)	60	7	Rathman, Tom (49ers)	42	T15
Cobb, Reggie (Bucs)	54	T8	Baxter, Brad (Jets)	36	T19
Walker, Herschel (Eagles)	54	T8	Johnson, Johnny (Cardinals)	36	T19
Gary, Cleveland (Rams)	51	10	Lang, David (Rams)	36	T19
Anderson, Neal (Bears)	48	T11	Mack, Kevin (Browns)	36	T19

Running Backs *(Continued)*

Player	Points	Rank	Player	Points	Rank
Okoye, Christian (Chiefs)	36	T19	Johnson, Anthony (Colts)	12	T49
Sherman, Heath (Eagles)	36	T19	Meggett, Dave (Giants)	12	T49
Metcalf, Eric (Browns)	33	25	Russell, Leonard (Patriots)	12	T49
Hilliard, Dalton (Saints)	30	T26	Smith, Tony (Falcons)	12	T49
Lewis, Darren (Bears)	30	T26	Stephens, John (Patriots)	12	T49
Bell, Nick (Raiders)	24	T28	Vaughn, Jon (Patriots)	12	T49
Bernstine, Rod (Chargers)	24	T28	Williams, John L. (Seahawks)	12	T49
Butts, Marion (Chargers)	24	T28	Workman, Vince (Packers)	12	T49
Craig, Roger (Vikings)	24	T28	Bailey, Johnny (Cardinals)	9	T63
Lewis, Greg (Broncos)	24	T28	Broussard, Steve (Falcons)	9	T63
Muster, Brad (Bears)	24	T28	Henderson, Keith (Vikings)	9	T63
Word, Barry (Chiefs)	24	T28	Humphrey, Bobby (Dolphins)	9	T63
Bunch, Jarrod (Giants)	21	T35	McNair, Todd (Chiefs)	9	T63
Harmon, Ron (Chargers)	21	T35	Paige, Tony (Dolphins)	9	T63
Rivers, Reggie (Broncos)	21	T35	Anderson, Gary (Bucs)	6	T69
Ball, Eric (Bengals)	18	T38	Brown, Gary (Oilers)	6	T69
Bieniemy, Eric (Chargers)	18	T38	Chaffee, Pat (Jets)	6	T69
Dunbar, Vaughn (Saints)	18	T38	Gash, Sam (Patriots)	6	T69
Green, Gaston (Broncos)	18	T38	Johnston, Daryl (Cowboys)	6	T69
Heyward, Craig (Saints)	18	T38	Logan, Marc (49ers)	6	T69
Lee, Amp (49ers)	18	T38	McAfee, Fred (Saints)	6	T69
Warren, Chris (Seahawks)	18	T38	Mitchell, Brian (Redskins)	6	T69
Allen, Marcus (Raiders)	15	T45	Richards, Curvin (Cowboys)	6	T69
Dickerson, Eric (Raiders)	15	T45	Thompson, Anthony (Cardinals)	6	T69
Sydney, Harry (Packers)	15	T45	Thompson, Leroy (Steelers)	6	T69
Thompson, Darrell (Packers)	15	T45	Williams, Harvey (Chiefs)	6	T69
Brown, Ivory Lee (Cardinals)	12	T49	Carter, Dexter (49ers)	3	T81
Byars, Keith (Eagles)	12	T49	Delpino, Robert (Rams)	3	T81
Ervins, Ricky (Redskins)	12	T49	Hoard, Leroy (Browns)	3	T81
Gardner, Carwell (Bills)	12	T49	Hoge, Merril (Steelers)	3	T81
Green, Harold (Bengals)	12	T49	Smith, Steve (Raiders)	3	T81
Green, Mark (Bears)	12	T49			

Wide Receivers

Player	Points	Rank	Player	Points	Rank
Sharpe, Sterling (Packers)	45	1	Jackson, Michael (Browns)	24	T10
Rice, Jerry (49ers)	39	2	Anderson, Willie (Rams)	21	T13
Haynes, Michael (Falcons)	36	T3	Barnett, Fred (Eagles)	21	T13
Rison, Andre (Falcons)	36	T3	Green, Willie (Lions)	21	T13
Givins, Ernest (Oilers)	30	T5	Martin, Kelvin (Cowboys)	21	T13
Miller, Anthony (Chargers)	30	T5	Metzelaars, Pete (Bills)	21	T13
Brown, Tim (Raiders)	27	T7	Williams, Calvin (Eagles)	21	T13
Jackson, Mark (Broncos)	27	T7	Carter, Cris (Vikings)	18	T19
Jeffires, Haywood (Oilers)	27	T7	Early, Quinn (Saints)	18	T19
Duper, Mark (Dolphins)	24	T10	Lofton, James (Bills)	18	T19
Irvin, Michael (Cowboys)	24	T10	Martin, Eric (Saints)	18	T19

Wide Receivers *(Continued)*

Player	Points	Rank	Player	Points	Rank
Mathis, Terance (Jets)	18	T19	Mills, Ernie (Steelers)	9	T56
Moore, Herman (Lions)	18	T19	Monk, Art (Redskins)	9	T56
Novacek, Jay (Cowboys)	18	T19	Morgan, Anthony (Bears)	9	T56
Barnett, Tim (Chiefs)	15	T26	Orr, Terry (Redskins)	9	T56
Clark, Gary (Redskins)	15	T26	Pickens, Carl (Bengals)	9	T56
Davis, Willie (Chiefs)	15	T26	Reed, Andre (Bills)	9	T56
Fryar, Irving (Patriots)	15	T26	Small, Torrance (Saints)	9	T56
Jackson, Keith (Dolphins)	15	T26	Stone, Dwight (Steelers)	9	T56
Jones, Ernie (Cardinals)	15	T26	Armstrong, Tyji (Bucs)	6	T79
Lewis, Nate (Chargers)	15	T26	Baker, Stephen (Giants)	6	T79
McCaffrey, Ed (Giants)	15	T26	Bavaro, Mark (Browns)	6	T79
Pritchard, Mike (Falcons)	15	T26	Beach, Pat (Eagles)	6	T79
Sanders, Deion (Falcons)	15	T26	Campbell, Jeff (Lions)	6	T79
Waddle, Tom (Bears)	15	T26	Carter, Anthony (Vikings)	6	T79
Beebe, Don (Bills)	12	T37	Cash, Keith (Chiefs)	6	T79
Birden, J. J. (Chiefs)	12	T37	Centers, Larry (Cardinals)	6	T79
Carrier, Mark (Bucs)	12	T37	Cook, Marv (Patriots)	6	T79
Carroll, Wesley (Saints)	12	T37	Cross, Howard (Giants)	6	T79
Gault, Willie (Raiders)	12	T37	Davis, Wendell (Bears)	6	T79
Gray, Mel (Lions)	12	T37	Drewrey, Willie (Bucs)	6	T79
Hall, Ron (Bucs)	12	T37	Frerotte, Mitch (Bills)	6	T79
Harper, Alvin (Cowboys)	12	T37	Green, Eric (Steelers)	6	T79
Jones, Brent (49ers)	12	T37	Harris, Jackie (Packers)	6	T79
Jones, Hassan (Vikings)	12	T37	Harris, Leonard (Oilers)	6	T79
Kinchen, Todd (Rams)	12	T37	Hawkins, Courtney (Bucs)	6	T79
Moore, Rob (Jets)	12	T37	Hayes, Jonathan (Chiefs)	6	T79
Perriman, Brett (Lions)	12	T37	Holman, Rodney (Bengals)	6	T79
Proehl, Ricky (Cardinals)	12	T37	Horton, Ethan (Raiders)	6	T79
Query, Jeff (Bengals)	12	T37	Howard, Desmond (Redskins)	6	T79
Sanders, Ricky (Redskins)	12	T37	Jefferson, Shawn (Chargers)	6	T79
Slaughter, Webster (Oilers)	12	T37	Johnson, Vance (Broncos)	6	T79
Taylor, John (49ers)	12	T37	Jorden, Tim (Steelers)	6	T79
Verdin, Clarence (Colts)	12	T37	Marshall, Arthur (Broncos)	6	T79
Banks, Fred (Dolphins)	9	T56	McMurtry, Greg (Patriots)	6	T79
Carter, Pat (Rams)	9	T56	Price, Jim (Rams)	6	T79
Cash, Kerry (Colts)	9	T56	Sharpe, Shannon (Broncos)	6	T80
Chadwick, Jeff (Rams)	9	T56	Sherrard, Mike (49ers)	6	T80
Clayton, Mark (Dolphins)	9	T56	Sikahema, Vai (Eagles)	6	T80
Coates (Patriots)	9	T56	Thompson, Craig (Bengals)	6	T80
Cooper (Steelers)	9	T56	Tillman, Cedric (Broncos)	6	T80
Ellard, Henry (Rams)	9	T56	Toon, Al (Jets)	6	T80
Hill, Drew (Falcons)	9	T56	Turner, Kevin (Patriots)	6	T80
Hill, Randal (Cardinals)	9	T56	Turner, Odessa (49ers)	6	T80
Jordan, Steve (Vikings)	9	T56	Walker, Derrick (Chargers)	6	T80
Kane, Tommy (Seahawks)	9	T56	Wright, Alexander (Cowboys/Raiders)	6	T80
Martin, Tony (Dolphins)	9	T56	Arbuckle, Charles (Colts)	3	T116
McDowell, Anthony (Bucs)	9	T56	Barrett, Reggie (Lions)	3	T116
McGee, Tim (Bengals)	9	T56	Baty, Greg (Dolphins)	3	T116

Wide Receivers (Continued)

Player	Points	Rank	Player	Points	Rank
Beach, Sanjay (Packers)	3	T116	Ingram, Mark (Giants)	3	T116
Blades, Brian (Seahawks)	3	T116	Jackson, John (Cardinals)	3	T116
Brennan, Brian (Bengals/Chargers)	3	T116	Jennings, Keith (Bears)	3	T116
Brooks, Bill (Colts)	3	T116	Jennings, Stanford (Bucs)	3	T116
Brooks, Robert (Packers)	3	T116	Johnson, Brad (Vikings)	3	T116
Burkett, Chris (Jets)	3	T116	Johnson, Reggie (Broncos)	3	T116
Calloway, Chris (Giants)	3	T116	Jones, Tony (Browns)	3	T116
Carpenter, Rob (Jets)	3	T116	Jones, Tony (Falcons)	3	T116
Clark, Louis (Seahawks)	3	T116	Junkin, Trey (Seahawks)	3	T116
Dawsey, Lawrence (Bucs)	3	T116	Langhorne, Reggie (Colts)	3	T116
Duncan, Curtis (Oilers)	3	T116	Mitchell, Johnny (Jets)	3	T116
Edmunds, Ferrell (Dolphins)	3	T116	Phillips, Jason (Falcons)	3	T116
Edwards, Anthony (Cardinals)	3	T116	Schultz, William (Colts)	3	T116
Fina, John (Bills)	3	T116	Stegall, Milt (Bengals)	3	T116
Galbraith, Scott (Browns)	3	T116	Taylor, Kitrick (Packers)	3	T116
Glover, Andrew (Raiders)	3	T116	Tice, Mike (Vikings)	3	T116
Graddy, Sam (Raiders)	3	T116	Timpson, Michael (Patriots)	3	T116
Graham, Jeff (Steelers)	3	T116	Williams, Jamie (49ers)	3	T116
Green, Paul (Seahawks)	3	T116	Wolfley, Ron (Browns)	3	T116
Hester, Jessie (Colts)	3	T116			

Quarterbacks

Player	Points	Rank	Player	Points	Rank
Young, Steve (49ers)	105	1	Esiason, Boomer (Bengals)	33	T22
Cunningham, Randall (Eagles)	93	2	Schroeder, Jay (Raiders)	33	T22
Kelly, Jim (Bills)	84	3	George, Jeff (Colts)	30	25
Aikman, Troy (Cowboys)	78	T4	Kosar, Bernie (Browns)	27	26
Humphries, Stan (Chargers)	78	T4	Millen, Hugh (Patriots)	24	27
Marino, Dan (Dolphins)	78	T4	Marinovich, Todd (Raiders)	21	T28
Everett, Jim (Rams)	69	T7	Nagle, Browning (Jets)	21	T28
Krieg, Dave (Chiefs)	69	T7	Tomczak, Mike (Browns)	21	T28
Favre, Brett (Packers)	66	T9	Gelbaugh, Stan (Seahawks)	18	T31
Hebert, Bobby (Saints)	66	T9	Kramer, Erik (Lions)	18	T31
Moon, Warren (Oilers)	63	10	O'Brien, Ken (Jets)	18	T31
Testaverde, Vinny (Bucs)	60	11	Maddox, Tommy (Broncos)	15	T34
Chandler, Chris (Cardinals)	57	12	Philcox, Todd (Browns)	15	T34
Rypien, Mark (Redskins)	54	13	Salisbury, Sean (Vikings)	15	T34
Miller, Chris (Falcons)	51	14	Simms, Phil (Giants)	15	T34
Elway, John (Broncos)	48	T15	Tolliver, Billy Joe (Falcons)	15	T34
Harbaugh, Jim (Bears)	48	T15	Willis, Peter Tom (Bears)	15	T34
O'Donnell, Neil (Steelers)	45	17	Evans, Vince (Raiders)	12	T40
Hostetler, Jeff (Giants)	42	T18	Klingler, David (Bengals)	12	T40
Wilson, Wade (Falcons)	42	T18	DeBerg, Steve (Bucs)	9	T42
Gannon, Rich (Vikings)	39	20	Hodson, Tom (Patriots)	9	T42
Peete, Rodney (Lions)	36	21	Stouffer, Kelly (Seahawks)	9	T42
Carlson, Cody (Oilers)	33	T22	Ware, Andre (Lions)	9	T42

Quarterbacks *(Continued)*

Player	Points	Rank	Player	Points	Rank
Zolak, Scott (Patriots)	9	T42	Conklin, Cary (Redskins)	3	T52
Bono, Steve (49ers)	6	T47	Graham, Kent (Giants)	3	T52
Brister, Bubby (Steelers)	6	T47	Herrmann, Mark (Colts)	3	T52
Hollas, Donald (Bengals)	6	T47	McMahon, Jim (Eagles)	3	T52
Majkowski, Don (Packers)	6	T47	Pagel, Mike (Rams)	3	T52
Montana, Joe (49ers)	6	T47	Tupa, Tom (Colts)	3	T52
Carlson, Jeff (Patriots)	3	T52			

Kickers

Player	Points	Rank	Player	Points	Rank
Andersen, Morten (Saints)	141	1	Stover, Matt (Browns)	95	16
Elliot, Lin (Cowboys)	137	2	Butler, Kevin (Bears)	94	T17
Stoyanovich, Pete (Dolphins)	136	3	Treadwell, David (Broncos)	94	T17
Lohmiller, Chip (Redskins)	135	4	Breech, Jim (Bengals)	91	19
Christie, Steve (Bills)	130	5	Zendejas, Tony (Rams)	89	20
Carney, John (Chargers)	128	6	Jaeger, Jeff (Raiders)	88	21
Anderson, Gary (Steelers)	119	7	Biasucci, Dean (Colts)	87	22
Johnson, Norm (Falcons)	114	T8	Bahr, Matt (Giants)	80	23
Reveiz, Fuad (Vikings)	114	T8	Davis, Greg (Cardinals)	73	24
Cofer, Mike (49ers)	113	T10	Blanchard, Cary (Jets)	71	25
Del Greco, Al (Oilers)	113	T10	Willis, Ken (Bucs/Giants)	60	26
Jacke, Chris (Packers)	111	T12	Kasay, John (Seahawks)	56	27
Lowery, Nick (Chiefs)	111	T12	Baumann, Charlie (Patriots)	55	28
Hanson, Jason (Lions)	102	14	Murray, Eddie (Chiefs/Bucs)	34	29
Ruzek, Roger (Eagles)	100	15	Staurovsky, Jason (Jets)	15	30

Defensive Teams

Team	Points	Rank	Team	Points	Rank
Kansas City	66	1	NY Jets	20	T13
Minnesota	50	2	Phoenix	20	T13
New England	36	T3	Atlanta	18	T17
New Orleans	36	T3	Green Bay	18	T17
Dallas	32	T5	Indianapolis	18	T17
Philadelphia	32	T5	Miami	18	T17
Cleveland	30	T7	Pittsburgh	18	T17
Detroit	30	T7	San Francisco	18	T17
Washington	30	T7	LA Raiders	14	23
Houston	26	10	Chicago	12	T24
Cincinnati	24	T11	Denver	12	T24
Tampa Bay	24	T11	NY Giants	12	T24
Buffalo	20	T13	San Diego	12	T24
LA Rams	20	T13	Seattle	6	28

SAMPLE ROSTERS

As PROMISED IN CHAPTER FIVE, which discusses draft strategy, I have provided some more sample rosters for you in this appendix. These lineups should demonstrate how a fantasy owner, with preparation, could have put together a fantasy roster for the 1992 season that would have generated 38 fantasy points per week. As I discussed in Chapter Five, 38 points per week should have resulted in a winning season in 1992, and most certainly would guarantee success over an 18-week schedule in 1993. These lineups are not offered as proof that hindsight is 20-20, but to allow those of you who have never participated in a fantasy league to get a feel for lineups that work, or at least that worked last season.

As in the examples provided in Chapter Five, the rosters are provided by player position, not by order of draft. However, the players in each category are listed in the order of their probable selection. The points provided are the actual number of fantasy points scored by each player during the 1992 NFL season. Remember, a total of 646 points is the benchmark we are aiming for.

Here's the first sample roster:

D. Marino	78
J. Everett	69
Walker	54
T. Allen	84
Byner	42
A. Carter	6
Givins	30
Monk	9
W. Anderson	21
Andersen	141
Breech	91
Dallas	32
TOTAL	**657**

This roster is an example of the strength that a high-scoring kicker can lend to a fantasy team in the new era of low scoring in the NFL. Marino and Walker would probably would have been the first two picks by this owner. The third pick would have been Terry Allen, and the fourth pick Andersen. Andersen would have dropped down that far in most drafts because he had a very good, not spectacular, year in 1991, after a solid but not sensational season in 1990. Allen might have been a reach to some fantasy owners, but he was clearly going to be the Vikings' feature back in 1992, and he had demonstrated real ability in the second half of the 1991 season. Andersen and Allen's fantasy performances in 1992 transform what is an otherwise mediocre lineup into a potential winner.

Here's another roster that might have been put together by an owner drafting with the last pick in the first round.

Young	105
Hebert	66
N. Anderson	48
Cobb	54
Rathman	42
Rice	39
Duper	24
Brown	27
Novacek	18
Stoyanovich	136
Johnson	114
Philadelphia	32
TOTAL	**705**

Young and Rice would have been the double-down combo with the eighth and ninth picks. Neal Anderson would have been the pick in the third round, and then Stoyo would have been taken in the fourth. Stoyo would have fallen to the fourth round in most drafts because kickers are generally not drafted in the first three rounds. Owners generally load up on running backs and quarterbacks with their first three picks.

Finally, let's put together a dud lineup, a roster that would have seemed to be a can't-lose proposition at the conclusion of the 1992 fantasy draft:

Rypien	54
Elway	48
Baxter	36
Dickerson	15

Okoye	36
Clayton	9
A. Carter	6
Clark	15
Slaughter	12
Jaeger	88
Ruzek	100
49ers	18

TOTAL   437

This imaginary fantasy owner would have walked away from the draft fantasizing about crushing the opposition all season. Instead, this owner would be the crushee every week. Rypien, Jaeger, and Ruzek all fell from great performances in 1991 to dismal fantasy performances in 1992. Baxter was a major disappointment, as were Clayton and Carter. Dickerson suffered through his second sad fantasy season in a row, and Okoye was hampered by a slow start, not scoring his first touchdown until the 10th week of the season. Elway missed a significant number of games for the first time in his career, due to injury. The Rypien-Clark double-down combo was a bust. Overall, this bunch, rather than cruising to fantasy victory, would have been lucky to escape the cellar.

There you have it. The good, the bad, and, last but not least, the very ugly. Review these rosters and compare them with Player Scouting Reports in Chapter Seven. As I said earlier, you should also assemble a few rosters of your own before the draft, to get a feel for the action of Draft Day. With these sample rosters and all the other information found in this book, you should be well prepared for your fantasy draft in the upcoming season. Good luck with your Fantasy Team this year.

Danny Sheridan
Stinks